Triumph Cars

The Complete Story
New Third Edition

GRAHAM ROBSON
RICHARD M LANGWORTH

More books from Veloce...

1½-litre GP Racing 1961-1965 (Whitelock)
AC Two-litre Saloons & Buckland Sportscars (Archibald)
Alfa Romeo 155/156/147 Competition Touring Cars (Collins)
Alfa Romeo Giulia Coupé GT & GTA (Tipler)
Alfa Romeo Montreal – The dream car that came true (Taylor)
Alfa Romeo Montreal – The Essential Companion (Classic Reprint of 500 copies) (Taylor)
Alfa Tipo 33 (McDonough & Collins)
Alpine & Renault – The Development of the Revolutionary Turbo F1 Car 1968 to 1979 (Smith)
Alpine & Renault – The Sports Prototypes 1963 to 1969 (Smith)
Alpine & Renault – The Sports Prototypes 1973 to 1978 (Smith)
An Austin Anthology (Stringer)
An Incredible Journey (Falls & Reisch)
Anatomy of the Classic Mini (Huthert & Ely)
Anatomy of the Works Minis (Moylan)
Armstrong-Siddeley (Smith)
Art Deco and British Car Design (Down)
Austin Cars 1948 to 1990 – a pictorial history (Rowe)
Autodrome (Collins & Ireland)
Automotive A-Z, Lane's Dictionary of Automotive Terms (Lane)
Automotive Mascots (Kay & Springate)
Bahamas Speed Weeks, The (O'Neil)
Bentley Continental, Corniche and Azure (Bennett)
Bentley MkVI, Rolls-Royce Silver Wraith, Dawn & Cloud/ Bentley R & S-Series (Nutland)
Bluebird CN7 (Stevens)
BMC Competitions Department Secrets (Turner, Chambers & Browning)
BMW 5-Series (Cranswick)
BMW Z-Cars (Taylor)
BMW Classic 5 Series 1972 to 2003 (Cranswick)
BMW – The Power of M (Vivian)
British at Indianapolis, The (Wagstaff)
British Cars, The Complete Catalogue of, 1895-1975 (Culshaw & Horrobin)
BRM – A Mechanic's Tale (Salmon)
BRM V16 (Ludvigsen)
Bugatti – The 8-cylinder Touring Cars 1920-34 (Price & Arbey)
Bugatti Type 40 (Price)
Bugatti 46/50 Updated Edition (Price & Arbey)
Bugatti T44 & T49 (Price & Arbey)
Bugatti 57 2nd Edition (Price)
Bugatti Type 57 Grand Prix – A Celebration (Tomlinson)
Carrera Panamericana, La (Tipler)
Car-tastrophes – 80 automotive atrocities from the past 20 years (Honest John, Fowler)
Chrysler 300 – America's Most Powerful Car 2nd Edition (Ackerson)
Chrysler PT Cruiser (Ackerson)
Citroën DS (Bobbitt)
Classic British Car Electrical Systems (Astley)
Cobra – The Real Thing! (Legate)
Competition Car Aerodynamics 3rd Edition (McBeath)
Competition Car Composites A Practical Handbook (Revised 2nd Edition) (McBeath)
Concept Cars, How to illustrate and design – New 2nd Edition (Dewey)
Cortina – Ford's Bestseller (Robson)
Cosworth – The Search for Power (6th edition) (Robson)
Coventry Climax Racing Engines (Hammill)
Daily Mirror 1970 World Cup Rally 40, The (Robson)
Daimler SP250 New Edition (Long)
Datsun Fairlady Roadster to 280ZX – The Z-Car Story (Long)
Dino – The V6 Ferrari (Long)
Dodge Challenger & Plymouth Barracuda (Grist)
Dodge Charger – Enduring Thunder (Ackerson)
Dodge Dynamite! (Grist)
Draw & Paint Cars – How to (Gardiner)
Drive on the Wild Side, A – 20 Extreme Driving Adventures From Around the World (Weaver)
Dune Buggy, Building A – The Essential Manual (Shakespeare)
Dune Buggy Files (Hale)
Dune Buggy Handbook (Hale)
East German Motor Vehicles in Pictures (Suhr/Weinreich)
Essential Guide to Driving in Europe, The (Parish)
Fast Ladies – Female Racing Drivers 1888 to 1970 (Bouzanquet)
Fate of the Sleeping Beauties, The (op de Weegh/ Hottendorff/op de Weegh)
Ferrari 288 GTO, The Book of the (Sackey)
Ferrari 333 SP (O'Neil)
Fiat & Abarth 124 Spider & Coupé (Tipler)
Fiat & Abarth 500 & 600 – 2nd Edition (Bobbitt)
Fiats, Great Small (Ward)
Ford Cleveland 335-Series V8 engine 1970 to 1982 – The Essential Source Book (Hammill)
Ford F100/F150 Pick-up 1948-1996 (Ackerson)
Ford F150 Pick-up 1997-2005 (Ackerson)
Ford Focus WRC (Robson)
Ford GT – Then, and Now (Streather)
Ford GT40 (Legate)
Ford Midsize Muscle – Fairlane, Torino & Ranchero (Cranswick)
Ford Model Y (Roberts)
Ford Small Block V8 Racing Engines 1962-1970 – The Essential Source Book (Hammill)
Ford Thunderbird From 1954, The Book of the (Long)
Formula One – The Real Score? (Harvey)
Formula 5000 Motor Racing, Back then ... and back now (Lawson)
Forza Minardi! (Vigar)
France: the essential guide for car enthusiasts – 200 things for the car enthusiast to see and do (Parish)
The Good, the Mad and the Ugly ... not to mention Jeremy Clarkson (Dron)
Grand Prix Ferrari – The Years of Enzo Ferrari's Power, 1948-1980 (Pritchard)
Grand Prix Ford – DFV-powered Formula 1 Cars (Robson)
GT – The World's Best GT Cars 1953-73 (Dawson)
Hillclimbing & Sprinting – The Essential Manual (Short & Wilkinson)
Honda NSX (Long)
Immortal Austin Seven (Morgan)
India - The Shimmering Dream (Reisch/Falls (translator))
Inside the Rolls-Royce & Bentley Styling Department – 1971 to 2001 (Hull)
Intermeccanica – The Story of the Prancing Bull (McCredie & Reisner)
Jaguar from the shop floor (Martin)
Jaguar E-type Factory and Private Competition Cars (Griffiths)
Jaguar, The Rise of (Price)
Jaguar XJ 220 – The Inside Story (Moreton)
Jaguar XJ-S, The Book of the (Long)
Jeep CJ (Ackerson)
Jeep Wrangler (Ackerson)
The Jowett Jupiter – The car that leaped to fame (Nankivell)
Karmann-Ghia Coupé & Convertible (Bobbitt)
Kris Meeke – Intercontinental Rally Challenge Champion (McBride)
Lamborghini Miura Bible, The (Sackey)
Lamborghini Murciélago, The book of the (Pathmanathan)
Lamborghini Urraco, The Book of the (Landsem)
Lambretta Bible, The (Davies)
Lancia 037 (Collins)
Lancia Delta HF Integrale (Blaettel & Wagner)
Lancia Delta Integrale (Collins)
Land Rover Design - 70 years of success (Hull)
Land Rover Emergency Vehicles (Taylor & Fletcher)
Land Rover Series III Reborn (Porter)
Land Rover, The Half-ton Military (Cook)
Land Rovers in British Military Service – coil sprung models 1970 to 2007 (Taylor)
Laverda Twins & Triples Bible 1968-1986 (Falloon)
Lea-Francis Story, The (Price)
Le Mans Panoramic (Ireland)
Lexus Story, The (Long)
Little book of microcars, the (Quellin)
Little book of smart, the – New Edition (Jackson)
Lola – The Illustrated History (1957-1977) (Starkey)
Lola – All the Sports Racing & Single-seater Racing Cars 1978-1997 (Starkey)
Lola T70 – The Racing History & Individual Chassis Record – 4th Edition (Starkey)
Lotus 18 Colin Chapman's U-turn (Whitelock)
Lotus 49 (Oliver)
Making a Morgan (Hensing)
Marketingmobiles, The Wonderful Wacky World of (Hale)
Maserati 250F In Focus (Pritchard)
Mazda MX-5/Miata 1.6 Enthusiast's Workshop Manual (Grainger & Shoemark)
Mazda MX-5/Miata 1.8 Enthusiast's Workshop Manual (Grainger & Shoemark)
Mazda MX-5 Miata, The book of the – The 'Mk1' NA-series 1988 to 1997 (Long)
Mazda MX-5 Miata, The book of the – The 'Mk2' NB-series 1997 to 2004 (Long)
Mazda MX-5 Miata Roadster (Long)
Mazda Rotary-engined Cars (Cranswick)
Maximum Mini (Booij)
Meet the English (Bowie)
Mercedes-Benz SL – R230 series 2001 to 2011 (Long)
Mercedes-Benz SL – W113-series 1963-1971 (Long)
Mercedes-Benz SL & SLC – 107-series 1971-1989 (Long)
Mercedes-Benz SLK – R170 series 1996-2004 (Long)
Mercedes-Benz SLK – R171 series 2004-2011 (Long)
Mercedes-Benz W123-series – All models 1976 to 1986 (Long)
Mercedes G-Wagen (Long)
MG, Made in Abingdon (Frampton)
MGA (Price Williams)
MGB & MGB GT– Expert Guide (Auto-doc Series) (Williams)
MGB Electrical Systems Updated & Revised Edition (Astley)
MGB – The Illustrated History, Updated Fourth Edition (Wood & Burrell)
Micro Trucks (Mort)
Microcars at Large! (Quellin)
Mini Cooper – The Real Thing! (Tipler)
Mini Minor to Asia Minor (West)
Mitsubishi Lancer Evo, The Road Car & WRC Story (Long)
Montlhéry, The Story of the Paris Autodrome (Boddy)
MOPAR Muscle – Barracuda, Dart & Valiant 1960-1980 (Cranswick)
Morgan Maverick (Lawrence)
Morgan 3 Wheeler – back to the future!, The (Dron)
Morris Minor, 70 Years on the Road (Newell)
Motor Movies – The Posters! (Veysey)
Motor Racing – Reflections of a Lost Era (Carter)
Motor Racing – The Pursuit of Victory 1930-1962 (Carter)
Motor Racing – The Pursuit of Victory 1963-1972 (Wyatt/ Sears)
Motor Racing Heroes – The Stories of 100 Greats (Newman)
Motorhomes, The Illustrated History (Jenkinson)
Motorsport In colour, 1950s (Wainwright)
N.A.R.T. – A concise history of the North American Racing Team 1957 to 1983 (O'Neil)
Nissan 300ZX & 350Z – The Z-Car Story (Long)
Nissan GT-R Supercar: Born to race (Gorodji)
Northeast American Sports Car Races 1950-1959 (O'Neil)
Nothing Runs – Misadventures in the Classic, Collectable & Exotic Car Biz (Slutsky)
Pass the Theory and Practical Driving Tests (Gibson & Hoole)
Peking to Paris 2007 (Young)
Pontiac Firebird – New 3rd Edition (Cranswick)
Porsche 356 (2nd Edition) (Long)
Porsche 908 (Födisch, Neßhöver, Roßbach, Schwarz & Roßbach)
Porsche 911 Carrera – The Last of the Evolution (Corlett)
Porsche 911R, RS & RSR, 4th Edition (Starkey)
Porsche 911, The Book of the (Long)
Porsche 911 – The Definitive History 2004-2012 (Long)
Porsche – The Racing 914s (Smith)
Porsche 911SC 'Super Carrera' – The Essential Companion (Streather)
Porsche 914 & 914-6: The Definitive History of the Road & Competition Cars (Long)
Porsche 924 (Long)
The Porsche 924 Carreras – evolution to excellence (Smith)
Porsche 928 (Long)
Porsche 930 to 935: The Turbo Porsches (Starkey)
Porsche 944 (Long)
Porsche 964, 993 & 996 Data Plate Code Breaker (Streather)
Porsche 993 'King Of Porsche' – The Essential Companion (Streather)
Porsche 996 'Supreme Porsche' – The Essential Companion (Streather)
Porsche 997 2004-2012 – Porsche Excellence (Streather)
Porsche Boxster – The 986 series 1996-2004 (Long)
Porsche Boxster & Cayman – The 987 series (2004-2013) (Long)
Porsche Racing Cars – 1953 to 1975 (Long)
Porsche Racing Cars – 1976 to 2005 (Long)
Porsche – The Rally Story (Meredith)
Porsche: Three Generations of Genius (Meredith)
Powered by Porsche (Smith)
Preston Tucker & Others (Linde)
RAC Rally Action! (Gardiner)
Racing Colours – Motor Racing Compositions 1908-2009 (Newman)
Rallye Sport Fords: The Inside Story (Moreton)
Roads with a View – England's greatest views and how to find them by road (Corfield)
Rolls-Royce Silver Shadow/Bentley T Series Corniche & Camargue – Revised & Enlarged Edition (Bobbitt)
Rolls-Royce Silver Spirit, Silver Spur & Bentley Mulsanne 2nd Edition (Bobbitt)
Rootes Cars of the 50s, 60s & 70s – Hillman, Humber, Singer, Sunbeam & Talbot, A Pictorial History (Rowe)
Rover Cars 1945 to 2005, A Pictorial History
Rover P4 (Bobbitt)
Runways & Racers (O'Neil)
Russian Motor Vehicles – Soviet Limousines 1930-2003 (Kelly)
Russian Motor Vehicles – The Czarist Period 1784 to 1917 (Kelly)
RX-7 – Mazda's Rotary Engine Sportscar (Updated & Revised New Edition) (Long)
Schlumpf – The intrigue behind the most beautiful car collection in the world (Op de Weegh & Op de Weegh)
Singer Story: Cars, Commercial Vehicles, Bicycles & Motorcycle (Atkinson)
Sleeping Beauties USA – abandoned classic cars & trucks (Marek)
SM – Citroën's Maserati-engined Supercar (Long & Claverol)
Speedway – Auto racing's ghost tracks (Collins & Ireland)
Sprite Caravans, The Story of (Jenkinson)
Standard Motor Company, The Book of the (Robson)
Steve Hole's Kit Car Cornucopia – Cars, Companies, Stories, Facts & Figures: the UK's kit car scene since 1949 (Hole)
Subaru Impreza: The Road Car And WRC Story (Long)
Supercar, How to Build your own (Thompson)
Tales from the Toolbox (Oliver)
Tatra – The Legacy of Hans Ledwinka, Updated & Enlarged Collector's Edition of 1500 copies (Margolius & Henry)
Taxi! The Story of the 'London' Taxicab (Bobbitt)
This Day in Automotive History (Corey)
To Boldly Go – twenty six vehicle designs that dared to be different (Hull)
Toleman Story, The (Hilton)
Toyota Celica & Supra, The Book of Toyota's Sports Coupés (Long)
Toyota MR2 Coupés & Spyders (Long)
Triumph & Standard Cars 1945 to 1984 (Warrington)
Triumph Cars – The Complete Story (new 3rd edition) (Robson)
Triumph TR6 (Kimberley)
Two Summers – The Mercedes-Benz W196R Racing Car (Ackerson)
TWR Story, The – Group A (Hughes & Scott)
Unraced (Collins)
Volkswagen Bus Book, The (Bobbitt)
Volkswagen Bus or Van to Camper, How to Convert (Porter)
Volkswagens of the World (Glen)
VW Beetle Cabriolet – The full story of the convertible Beetle (Bobbitt)
VW Beetle – The Car of the 20th Century (Copping)
VW Bus – 40 Years of Splitties, Bays & Wedges (Copping)
VW Bus Book, The (Bobbitt)
VW Golf: Five Generations of Fun (Copping & Cservenka)
VW – The Air-cooled Era (Copping)
VW T5 Camper Conversion Manual (Porter)
VW Campers (Copping)
Volkswagen Type 3, The book of the – Concept, Design, International Production Models & Development (Glen)
Volvo Estate, The (Hollebone)
You & Your Jaguar XK8/XKR – Buying, Enjoying, Maintaining, Modifying – New Edition (Thorley)
Which Oil? – Choosing the right oils & greases for your antique, vintage, veteran, classic or collector car (Michell)
Wolseley Cars 1948 to 1975 (Rowe)
Works Minis, The Last (Purves & Brenchley)
Works Rally Mechanic (Moylan

www.veloce.co.uk

Also available ... Apps Download now from www.digital.veloce.co.uk

Also available ... eBook Download now from www.digital.veloce.co.uk

Kids Hubble & Hattie

Hubble & Hattie

EARTHWORLD EXPANDING HORIZONS

First published in September 2018 by Veloce Publishing Limited, Veloce House, Parkway Farm Business Park, Middle Farm Way, Poundbury, Dorchester DT1 3AR, England. Tel +44 (0)1305 260068 / Fax 01305 250479 / e-mail info@veloce.co.uk / web www.veloce.co.uk or www.velocebooks.com.
ISBN: 978-1-787112-89-6 UPC: 6-36847-01289-2.

© 2018 Graham Robson, Richard M Langworth and Veloce Publishing. All rights reserved. With the exception of quoting brief passages for the purpose of review, no part of this publication may be recorded, reproduced or transmitted by any means, including photocopying, without the written permission of Veloce Publishing Ltd. Throughout this book logos, model names and designations, etc, have been used for the purposes of identification, illustration and decoration. Such names are the property of the trademark holder as this is not an official publication. Readers with ideas for automotive books, or books on other transport or related hobby subjects, are invited to write to the editorial director of Veloce Publishing at the above address.

British Library Cataloguing in Publication Data – A catalogue record for this book is available from the British Library. Typesetting, design and page make-up all by Veloce Publishing Ltd on Apple Mac. Printed in India by Parksons Graphics.

Triumph Cars

The Complete Story

New Third Edition

GRAHAM ROBSON
RICHARD M LANGWORTH

VELOCE PUBLISHING
THE PUBLISHER OF FINE AUTOMOTIVE BOOKS

Contents

Foreword and acknowledgements..6

1 | The Quality Light Car...8

2 | The Last Word in the Smallest Class...19

3 | From Scorpion to Southern Cross..31

4 | The Smartest Cars in the Land..39

5 | The Big One that Got Away..56

6 | Dolomite and Demise..67

7 | War and Resurrection...81

8 | Roadster and Renown..92

9 | Mayflower: a Second American Invasion...108

10 | The Sports Car America Loved Best..117

11 | Hark the Herald Angle..135

12 | 'Bomb' and Beyond: The Spitfire Story..150

13	'Sabrina' and a New TR	159
14	Leyland Takes Over	174
15	Triumph Cars for the 1970s	192
16	TR7 and TR8	210
17	Acclaim and a Sad End	222
Appendix I	Triumph Derivations	225
Appendix II	Production Factories 1923 to 1984	233
Appendix III	Technical Specifications 1923 to 1984	235
Appendix IV	Triumph and Standard Body Sources 1945 to 1984	248
Appendix V	Triumph Production Totals 1923 to 1984	249
	Index	254

Foreword and acknowledgements

It was some time ago that we – Graham Robson in the UK and Richard Langworth in the USA – concluded that the Triumph marque deserved a full-scale history. At the time, both of us had already published part of it, Graham by writing *The Story of Triumph Sports Cars* and *The Triumph TRs: A Collector's Guide*, Richard by writing the booklet *Fifty Years of Triumph*, and editing the first three years' worth of a bimonthly United States club magazine, *The Vintage Triumph*.

In the process, hundreds of photographs, interviews, factory documents, letters and smatterings of data had come our way, none of which meant very much out of context, but all had considerable value to a work of this magnitude. Next, we began a round of meetings with publishers for, above all, we wanted to see a quality book, and we knew it needed much photographic material to complement the long and detailed text.

Although the archive resources had already been gathered over the years, we began writing the first edition in mid-1977, and finished by the summer of 1978. Jokingly, Richard suggested that he should tackle the prewar history, despite it being almost completely UK-centric as he'd just acquired a 1938 Dolomite and was enthusiastically delving into the car's prewar background. To his delight, Graham agreed, as his own considerable study of more recent events would therefore complement Richard's research perfectly; thus the massive study was eventually assembled.

Richard Langworth worked on the story up to the original company's financial collapse in 1939, the chapter on the Mayflower (another of his old loves), and produced the original appendix on derivations. Graham Robson then followed the history of the company and the name after its sale to Thos W Ward Ltd in 1939, all the way to the present day. Included in the latter, incidentally, are considerable references to Standard-Triumph directors' board minute books and other official company archives, which up to that point had never been available to historians.

The appalling industrial and financial problems that the marque suffered in the winter of 1977-78 were resolved in time for this story to be neatly concluded even if, at the time of writing, the latest developments in the TR7 saga were yet to be revealed – though it

needed little more than intelligent guesswork to deduce what these would be.

At this stage, a vast number of people were instrumental in assisting us, and it's important that they be credited. Without them there would have been no book – at least no book with the authoritative sources we needed. In the interwar period, we think of two former Triumph executives whose recollections were vital: Walter J Belgrove, the talented body designer, and Donald Healey, Triumph's great technical chief and competitions driver. Both also supplied photographs from their personal collections which, we think, hadn't been published before. Stanley Edge, the noted engineer who provided links between the Austin Seven and the Triumph Super Seven, provided fascinating detail about the company's 1920s operations.

Every word of the prewar manuscript was handed to two members of the Pre-1940 Triumph Owners' Club – whose knowledge we particularly respected – for checking: co-founder Glyn Lancaster Jones and former bulletin editor Chris Watson.

Without the careful original research of John R Davy, founder of the Standard Register, we wouldn't have known enough about the early relationship of Standard and Triumph. John Bath, historian of the Triumph Razor Edge Owners' Club, looked carefully at our Roadster/Renown chapter, and Alan Robinson, then the TR Register's historical guru, made sure that our sports car commentary had his seal of approval.

In the Mayflower chapter, our thanks are owed to Frank Callaby for his recollections, and for significant assistance in helping locate and identify many photographs for the postwar chapters in general. In the derivatives appendix, Tom Gratrix has our gratitude for recalling his Bond Equipe experiences, as does Peter Morgan regarding his company's relations with Standard-Triumph.

Research on the American side of the pond couldn't have been completed without the assistance of Henry Austin Clark, Jr, and his Long Island Automotive Museum Library; James J Bradley and the National Automotive History Collection, Detroit; and Mary Cattie and Lou Helverson of the Automotive History Collection, Free Library of Philadelphia. In the UK, our sincerest thanks to Michael

Ware and Nick Georgano at the National Motor Museum, Beaulieu; to Peter Mitchell and Michael Bullivant at the Coventry Museum; and the staff of the Coventry and Warwickshire Collection.

In the meantime, Graham set about seeking, finding and interviewing the most senior members of the postwar hierarchy, which included Lord Stokes, Alick Dick, George Turnbull, Harry Webster, Spen King, John Lloyd, Lyndon Mills, Harris Mann, Alan Edis, Peter Browning, and other helpful members of their staff. Race and rally reminiscences came from personalities as famous as Paddy Hopkirk, Keith Ballisat, Maurice Gatsonides, and 'Kas' Kastner, though for personal (and undisclosed) reasons, Ken Richardson refused to be associated with the book in any way.

The project would've been impossible without delving into the vast and detailed archive material held by The Autocar and Motor magazines, and their forbearance in allowing us to dig around in their records. In his own way, too, that doyen of historians, Michael Sedgwick kept encouraging us – just by being Michael. (Incidentally, after he saw the results of our labours, in his review Michael wrote: "I can't imagine that anyone who had not actually been there could write so authentic a story of those times," which made us very proud.)

We were originally and materially assisted in photo hunts and general USA research by British Leyland Inc in New Jersey, specifically by Michael L Cook and John Dugdale; the latter lent some photographs from his own collection and recalled his impressions of Triumph from his prewar career with The Autocar.

It would've also been impossible to do the job in Britain without the full co-operation of British Leyland, and the staff at the Triumph factories. In particular, we enjoyed complete access to the company's photographic records, and found some astonishing historical pictures which were cleared for us to use in these pages. Frank Callaby, and his successor Alan Luckett, allowed us to disturb the department for days on end, and couldn't have been more helpful.

Foreword and acknowledgements for the definitive edition

In 1978, what was then the title of The Complete Story should've perhaps included 'so far,' yet in a few years the Triumph marque was (temporarily, we hoped) retired in 1984. The machinations, problems and new opportunities caused by the continuing drama surrounding British Leyland (which became Austin Rover, then finally the Rover Group) and – as far as Triumph was concerned – by the arrival of Honda as a technical partner, all meant that the book needed an update; this duly came in the late 1980s.

From time to time (most particularly after BMW bought the Rover Group in 1994) the authors hoped that great things could still be brewing for the Triumph marque, and we had no doubt that this might be an ever-evolving history.

We'd been pleased to be able to take the story of Triumph cars to its conclusion in 1984, though later we were dismayed to have to accept that the Triumph marque seemed to have been laid to rest. With the exception of the V8-engined TR8 sports car finally put on sale in 1980, none of the 'great things' which were brewing in 1978 ever came to pass, and the Triumph name made its final appearance on, of all things, a Japanese-designed car assembled by Austin Rover. Still, the full story could then be told, and we were happy to offer this book as the complete record of one of Britain's proudest marques.

The technology in book publishing marched on, and we recently took the opportunity to revisit The Complete Story, not least to correct, extend and round off the continuing saga of a brand that refuses to fade away. Some new facts, figures and opinions were added as well as – most important to many Triumph enthusiasts – hundreds of colour images of the cars, including some of the models which started the Triumph car-making story more than 90 years ago, to make this an even more extensive record.

Both of the original authors – Richard in the USA and Graham in the UK – dug deep into their own ever-growing archives to find precious colour images, and many more have generously been made available to us by other stalwarts of the Triumph hobby.

This is where, therefore, we ought to thank: Simon Goldsworthy, the indefatigable editor of Triumph World; Mike Cook of the USA, a recognised Triumph expert, editor, archivist and commentator on all things transatlantic; John Clancy, not only a TR7 fanatic, but the maker of a series of excellent DVDs on a whole variety of Triumph subjects; Wayne Scott and Nicky Bate, of TR Action; Phil Homer, the mine of all knowledge at the Standard Motor Club; Graham Shipman, a truly remarkable source concerning all things Pre-1940 Triumphs; Peter Lockley, whose Swallow Doretti is an absolute paragon of its type; Chris Gunby of the TSSC, whose club knows all about the Herald/Spitfire/Vitesse/GT6 family; Kevin Warrington, a true expert on all things 2000 and the PI family; David Knowles, we wish we knew as much about Triumph sports cars as he does; Rob Marshall, the Toledo/1500TC/Dolomite expert; Lesley Philips, for Stag images; Jonathan Wood, for Triumph Dolomite straight-eight images; Martyn Goddard, for capturing the glorious 'Jabbeke' TR2 re-launch at the RAC Club; Simon Clay, for excellent TR images; and Bill Munro, for Carbodies production images. If there is anyone else who has not been mentioned above, our sincere apologies.

Richard Langworth
New Hampshire, USA

Graham Robson
Dorset, England

The Quality Light Car

Scores of manufacturers began producing motor cars in the early years of the 20th century, many having started as builders of bicycles, motorcycles, and even sewing machines. All three of those pursuits had engaged the early Triumph Company, and it took it an abnormally long time (38 years after its founding) to enter the auto market. By the advent of its first car in 1923, Triumph was well established as leading motorcycle constructors, with production and sales experience which augured well for its new venture.

To begin at the beginning, then, we must travel back through those 38 years and some more to November 1884, when a well-to-do German of 21 years came to London to seek his fortune. His name was Siegfried Bettmann.

Bettmann had been born to Jewish parents in Nuremberg in 1863. His father, Mayer, who managed an estate for a wealthy Bavarian landowner, educated his son well and schooled him for business. En route to London, Siegfried stopped off for a brief fling in Paris – he was conversant in French and English as well as his native German. On arrival in the British capital he began looking for a position where his linguistic skills might be useful. He soon applied to a publisher who needed a clerk fluent in German. We are fortunate to have access to his own unpublished memoirs in which he spoke of the subsequent events:

"I was engaged by Messrs. Kelly & Company at a weekly wage of 25 shillings," Bettmann wrote. Kelly published the London Directories and several commercial trade lists of foreign firms of interest to British businessmen. "My work was to compile out of Foreign Directories a suitable collection of such firms for its publications."

Multilingual he might be, but Bettmann was far too ambitious for this dull, plodding desk work.

"After six months I had the luck to be engaged as a Foreign Correspondent by the White Sewing Machine Company of Cleveland, Ohio, which had a branch in London in Queen Victoria Street, and here I may say began the history of the Triumph Company.

"After three or four months I induced the manager of the company, Mr George Sawyer, to employ me as his traveller in foreign countries. In this way I began to know most of the European countries and a large part of North Africa. I succeeded in gaining new customers for the company, and many of them in turn became my life-long friends. But after a year or so a quarrel arose between Mr. Sawyer and myself; this did not however break the ties of mutual friendship. I decided then to start in business on my own account by acquiring agencies of German firms, amongst whom was the firm of Biesolt & Lock, which was a sewing machine manufacturer at Meissen, in Saxony. With the exception of this firm, the agencies proved to be a failure, although to add importance to the firm I named it S Bettmann & Company."

Despite problems at the import end, the export position was excellent.

"It was about that time that the bicycle began its successful career – the penny-farthing, with the high wheel ..."

Bettmann soon decided to become an exporter of bicycles, and engaged the William Andrews company of Birmingham to manufacture the machines for him.

The bicycle, of course, needed a trade name. In bestowing one which would write history far beyond his dreams, Siegfried was typically modest and astute: "I gave it the name 'Triumph.' I chose this name for a single purpose. For a long time my customers, who were practically all on the Continent, called it the 'Bettmann.' Such a name could not be of permanent value. I therefore looked out for a name which could be understood in all European languages."

Already the export market was interested in Triumph – and vice versa! Little did Bettmann know that the name he chose would grow to become one of the most popular and respected British nameplates in the world, beloved as much abroad as it was at home. America, with Britain and the Continent, would learn to appreciate that name wherever, and usually on whatever, it appeared.

Fast to recognise a market, canny in naming his product, Bettmann was nevertheless not a seer of big horizons. It is likely he would have remained a small manufacturer had he not met the 'excellent and far-seeing man,' fellow German Mauritz Johann Schulte, who joined him as a partner in 1887. The partnership would last until 1919, and Schulte would become a key figure in the early expansion of the Triumph company.

Schulte soon pointed out that expansion was vital to Triumph's interests.

"In order to gain a real success we had to become manufacturers," Bettmann continued. "We therefore looked out for works in Coventry, which at that time was the metropolis of the Cycle Industry. Schulte preceded me and found suitable works in Earls Court, Much Park Street. The building belonged to Alderman A S Tomson, who was Mayor of Coventry."

Tomson, a pillar of the community, was earlier the founder of Coventry's ribbon industry and the city's technical institute; like Tomson, Bettmann, too, would serve as mayor – 'the first of 559 mayors to be "imported from abroad"' – in 1913.

"We worked hard, but under great difficulties," Bettmann wrote. "Our capital was small, it simply consisted of £500 given to me by my parents and £150 which Schulte obtained from his relations. In spite of this, however, we had a certain amount of success."

The sewing machine import business gradually waned as Triumph bicycles, at first strictly for export, gained acceptance and started to appear on the home market. The firm continued to be represented in London, where the office was entrusted to another Nuremberger Philip Schloss, who had invested his life savings of £100 in the small company.

"I was so pleased at getting his £100 that I offered him a directorship," Bettmann wrote of Schloss. "Schulte agreed, but at

Siegfried Bettman in his mayoral robes; the founder of the Triumph company was Mayor of Coventry in 1913 and 1914. He guided Triumph's development and destiny from 1887 to 1933.

the same time warned me not to be so lavish, in future, in scattering directorships around."

Bettmann heeded Schulte's advice. Just three directors were added when it was found necessary to raise Triumph's capital to £2000: the aforementioned A S Tomson; financier and former ribbon trader Alfred Friedlander; and George Sawyer, with whom Bettmann had maintained friendly ties despite their split. Sawyer was named board chairman, and £800 in shares was given to Schulte and Bettmann.

"A great deal of this £800 must have been represented by goodwill," Bettmann commented. The business was now registered as a limited liability corporation, with the title of Triumph Cycle Co Ltd. The timing was perfect: the 'cycle boom' was on!

Bettmann's memoirs provide an interesting glimpse at the size of some of his contemporaries when the penny-farthing hit its stride. For example, he noted that Singer & Company, floated for very little by promoter E Terah Hooley, was publicly organised with a capital of £800,000.

"As the actual assets of the company consisted of only about £150,000, the goodwill was, therefore, valued at the enormous sum of £650,000. Let me say that at that time the pound had real value and had not yet been depreciated as at present."

Triumph, though capitalised at a fraction of Singer, was soon humming with good sales and happy prospects for the immediate future, but still not a major factor in the industry. It took Harvey du Cros of Dunlop to alter the course once and for all.

The pneumatic tyre and the bicycle were greatly interdependent, of course, and the Dublin-based Dunlop firm was inevitably responsible for the success of both. Dunlop naturally kept track of the bicycle manufacturers, and in 1895 du Cros invited Bettmann to Dublin. He said he wished to invest 'a fair amount' of the surplus capital of Dunlop in Triumph. Bettmann couldn't have been more agreeable. Thus the firm was reorganised with a capital of £45,000, half preference shares and half ordinary, with Bettmann and Schulte as joint managing directors. The original Triumph Company's goodwill was established at £13,369.

Of ancillary benefit was a simultaneous increase in Triumph agencies: "My friend Mr John Griffiths was the Secretary of Dunlop," Bettmann noted. "Mr du Cros induced him to purchase the business of the most successful cycle dealers throughout the country, and ... I induced Mr Griffiths to take up the agency of the Triumph bicycle for some of his outlets, whilst in London we continued with the White Sewing Machine Company."

The bicycle boom continued, and Triumph shortly went public with a capitalisation of £170,000, including £90,000 in debentures and preference shares underwritten by Dunlop. The ordinary shares were "subscribed for more than ten times over; this of course was only done for the sake of speculation as most of the 'original shareholders' – amongst whom were some of my personal friends – sold them as soon as possible at any profit they could obtain," Bettmann said.

In 1907 the company moved to larger quarters in Priory Street, including buildings on both sides of the road. Today this location is partly occupied by the modern Coventry Cathedral – the Chapel of Industry actually stands over the place once occupied by the Triumph dispatch bay. The Much Park Street property was retained to house a sidecar shop, the subsidiary Gloria Cycle Company, and later the motorcycle service department. It is worth noting, incidentally, that this is probably the origin of the 'Gloria' name as applied to certain Triumph models in the 1930s. The Much Park buildings stood until 1970, serving last as headquarters for the Coventry Police Department.

In those days it was almost inevitable that a successful builder of bicycles would consider putting engines on them, and Triumph was no exception. The impetus here was, typically, forward-looking Mauritz Schulte. In 1897 Schulte proposed taking up British rights to the Hildebrand & Wolfmüller motorcycle, himself demonstrating a sample machine at Coventry Stadium and riding it about town. Nothing was done on the H&W, but the very next year Bettmann talked to Humber about his building the Beeston Humber motorcycle and tricycle. A prototype was built and a plan of action roughed out, but again nothing was done to bring it to fruition.

Perhaps it was the economic situation that caused Triumph to abandon immediate plans for motorcycles. A downturn had followed the boom years of the late 1890s and the bicycles were past their peak. By 1899 Triumph's balance sheet was in the red – though only to the tune of £1500 – and Bettmann's leadership was challenged.

"At the general meeting of the company a few shareholders kicked up a terrible row," he remembered, "and pretended to know that the loss was entirely due to bad management. I answered them, perhaps in somewhat vehement language, and Schulte tried to pull me down and told me to keep quiet."

Directors Friedlander and Tomson subsequently asked influential businessman John Rotherham to join the board. Rotherham declined, but did agree to review Triumph's affairs, and after a year begged leave to resign. According to Bettmann, "he had found by his interviews with me that the affairs of the company were in good and honourable hands."

With the Bettmann-Schulte leadership reconfirmed, Triumph proceeded to expand into motorcycles at last. In 1902 a Belgian Minerva 2¼hp engine with belt drive was bolted up to a modified pedal-cycle frame, reinforced to take the extra power, and the first Triumph motorcycle was under way. By 1905, after trying engines such as the JAP and Fafnir, Triumph had designed and built its own 3hp unit. Rapidly the motorcycle became the firm's dominant

business, though the business was still pitifully small – in 1906 only 533 units were produced.

Production increased rapidly, however, to 1000 cycles in 1907, 2000 in 1908, 3000 in 1909. Siegfried went on to political office, becoming a member of the City Council, then president of the Chamber of Commerce, before finally becoming mayor. Politically he was first a Liberal, but he became a Labour partisan with the rise of that party, and was subsequently a close friend of Labour leader Ramsay MacDonald. But he remained active in the business and, to the increasing ire of Schulte, in the bicycle department. Bettmann loved the product that had initially put him in business. During her Diamond Jubilee he had even presented a pair of silver-plated bicycles to Queen Victoria.

"There is no record," *The Autocar* noted wistfully, "of Her Majesty ever having ridden one."

1911 was a significant year for Bettmann, and could have been important for what we later knew as Standard-Triumph. The latter, it seems, might have been combined many years before 1945. In 1911 or 1912 Siegfried Bettmann became chairman of the Standard Motor Company!

Information on the Bettmann chairmanship is owed to research by Standard Register founder, John Davy, in period Coventry newspapers. A news article about Bettmann, dated September 10, 1913, mentions that he was chairman of directors at Standard. Prior to that, on Alexandra Day celebrations on June 28, he is reported exhibiting a Standard-based float.

Nothing more is heard of Bettmann's position after these articles. It is supposed that Bettmann provided some of the cash by which Standard managing director Reginald Maudslay purchased control of the business. If so, Bettmann would have joined Standard in late 1911 or early 1912 – retaining, of course, his Triumph relationship. Bettmann's tenure at Standard was probably short – but it is interesting to contemplate this early relationship between the two companies, some 34 years before they actually joined forces.

The advent of war ended Bettmann's tenure at Standard, but it did promise prosperity for the struggling Triumph Cycle Company. Triumph would make a lot of money – and friends – during World War I. Its profits would lead to its first car, and at the war's very outset, Bettmann met a young man who would figure prominently in Triumph's postwar history: Claude Vivian Holbrook, son of newspaper magnate Col Sir Arthur Holbrook, and then serving in the Army with the rank of Staff Captain.

Shortly after war had broken out, Bettmann remembered, he was phoned by the War Office. He was still mayor at the time – a unique position for a German.

"The man who addressed me was Holbrook; he asked me whether I could make arrangements to get 100 Triumph motorcycles packed to ship to France ... the motorcycles left at the requested time. I had occasion to see Capt (later Col) Holbrook frequently at the War Office, and from our interviews sprang a lasting friendship. I was so impressed by his capabilities that I later asked my co-directors to allow me to ask him to become the manager of the company." Holbrook acceded to that title in 1919; he was destined to direct production of the first Triumph motor car.

Known as 'Frisky Triumphs' by the public and 'Trusty Triumphs' by the military, its motorcycles were a boon to the company during the Great War. Some 30,000 belt-driven 550cc machines, with their Sturmey-Archer gearbox/clutch and chain-belt transmission, were supplied to British and allied forces between 1914 and 1918. After the war Sir Harry Ricardo, who would figure prominently in the Triumph car to come, produced the first four-overhead-valve air-cooled cycle engines, a startling technological development at the time, and during the Roaring Twenties the Triumph cycle went from strength to strength. In 1923 the company was producing 300 a week, 15,000 per year. By 1929, the peak year, those figures had doubled.

Exactly who decided to branch out into automobiles is not recorded, but it's likely that the project began, as usual, with Schulte. In this case it ended with Holbrook, for by Armistice Day the old Bettmann-Schulte relationship had gone awry. It was only natural that this should happen, Bettmann felt, "when two opposite characters have to work together for many years. My idea was that Schulte should retire, which he did on the payment of £15,000" – a nice pile, especially in 1919 pounds.

It was now that Col Holbrook was duly appointed manager of Triumph.

From Bettmann's memoirs it is apparent that Siegfried was the perennial conservative, and Schulte the adventuresome entrepreneur. Before the war Bettmann had remained enamoured of the dwindling bicycle operation, and afterwards it seems he resisted Schulte's notion that Triumph ought to build a motor car. Ironically, Holbrook was as much in favour of a four-wheeler as Schulte, and his appointment as manager guaranteed car production. Despite the profitable motorcycle business, Bettmann was later urged to abandon it, just as Schulte had urged the cessation of bicycle production.

Schulte had first explored beyond the two-wheeler in 1903, when he experimented with a tricar which was never produced. By 1919, the time was far more propitious. The war was over, the servicemen were home, and the nation's economy appeared stable after years of heavy defence production. There was no hint of the economic doldrums to follow in 1920. The situation was paralleled on the other side of the Atlantic; in 1920 the United States replaced Democrat Woodrow Wilson with Republican Warren G Harding, who promised undiluted prosperity and no further involvement in European politics. In America, as in England, the Roaring Twenties would seem somewhat muted to many smaller industries which recorded steady losses as the stock exchanges floated to higher and higher peaks. But in both countries, the opportunity for car makers seemed staggering. In Detroit and Coventry, plans were laid for bold assaults on the motor car marketplace. In 1920 the number of auto companies in the US and UK totalled over 250; a decade later they would be reduced by almost four-fifths.

The first Triumph car did not, however, immediately follow the appointment of Holbrook. There was Bettmann to be won over, for one thing, and there were motorcycles to build. Neither was there ready space at the works for anything as large as a car plant, though Triumph by this time had grown considerably – its Priory Street works was seven stories high. But plans were certainly in the works. A 2-litre side-valve saloon was run off experimentally in 1919, and, as early as 1921, *The Autocar* announced that it had "been known for some time past that the Triumph Cycle Co Ltd was interesting itself in the production of a light car. Triumph," the magazine announced, "have now purchased the shop and fittings of the Dawson Car Company, producer of the 12hp light car, on Clay Lane, Stoke–" (half a mile from Priory Street and then on the outskirts of the city) "–No announcement has yet been made as to the policy of the Triumph Cycle Co

It was motorcycles like this which originally made Triumph its fortune in Coventry before the First World War. During that conflict, thousands of such machines were supplied to the British Army for use in France.

This was Triumph's very first car, the 10/20: so simple and so typical of a British vintage car of the early 1920s.

Ltd in regard to the light car ... but its advent will be awaited with considerable interest, in view of the high quality of material and workmanship which have made the Triumph motorcycle famous." *The Autocar* also said that there were probably more Triumph cycles on the road than any other make.

Bettmann had earlier talked to Hillman, with a view to purchase the latter – Hillman's factory was next to Humber's, with whom Bettmann had communicated much earlier on the subject of a motorcycle. Hillman's plant manager had been the same A J Dawson who later tried and failed to put his own car into production, and it's likely that it was during these Hillman discussions, that the relationship between Bettmann and Dawson was established.

The Dawson car was produced between 1919 and 1921. Though outwardly resembling the forthcoming Triumph – spare, thin wings, artillery wheels, a large, Bentley-esque radiator – there was little resemblance under the skin. The Dawson engine was an overhead-valve, overhead-cam unit of 1795cc (69 x 120mm): an uncommon design for that period. Body styles included a two-seat and four-seat tourer and a cabriolet, all priced at £450, and production began in October 1919. Among Dawson backers was Malcolm Campbell, who acquired the London agency. But the enterprise was doomed to failure – possibly because the Dawson ended up costing almost twice as much as the targeted figure. Only 65 cars were produced through 1921, and none is known to have survived. It was obvious as soon as the first Triumph car appeared that Bettmann had acquired Dawson strictly as a property, intending to copy neither its high price nor its advanced specification.

Undoubtedly Bettmann was, as ever, determined to march to his own drummer. Through 1921, he had continued to view motor cars with mixed emotions. When William Morris' company ran into financial difficulties around that time, Bettmann had

been approached to buy it. In what would alter motoring history considerably, he steadfastly refused. With the Dawson works, he could at least build exactly what he wanted to, and that – announced to the public in April 1923 – was the Triumph 10/20.

Named for the combination of RAC horsepower (based on bore but not stroke) and actual bhp, the 10/20 was entirely Triumph's product, if not wholly Triumph's design. Its 1393cc (63.5 x 110mm) engine, for example, was the work of Harry Ricardo, and in some respects it was a rather interesting unit.

Variation from the norm was evident in its cylinder block and crankcase design. The detachable cylinder head was not extraordinary but the block casting was, since the lower ends of its cylinder barrels were enclosed within an upward extension of the aluminium crankcase. Instead of long studs from crank through block and head, studs were screwed into the cylinder casting. The obvious opening for locating valve stems and tappet heads within

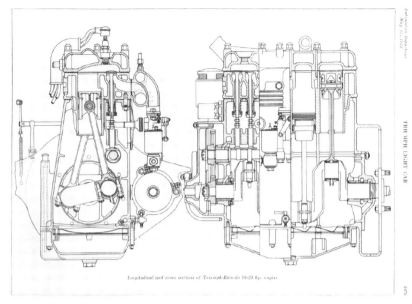

The right-hand side view of an installed 10/20 side-valve engine shows its neat and uncluttered lines. Note that there was no cooling fan.

Two sectional views of the original Triumph 10/20 engine, which was a very simple, easy-to-manufacture power unit, and had been prepared for Triumph by Ricardo.

the crankcase was passed up for a separate valve chamber at the side of the crankcase extension. Ricardo also used 'masked' inlet valves, their seats located below the combustion chambers, fitted with shallow parallel-sided pockets through which the valve head moved up before induction occurred, and vice versa.

"The effect of this sunken seat," noted *Automotive Industries,* "is to enable a cam profile to be used which gives a slow initial and final movement to the valve and yet provides a very rapid beginning and end to the induction stroke, the fit of the valve in its pocket being such as to give a slide-valve effect until one is clear of or enters the other."

The ultimate result, Triumph claimed, was higher efficiency with quieter valve operation.

The Ricardo design also employed 'slipper' pistons, a far-seeing innovation in which the piston dropped below the crankshaft counterweight level at the bottom of the stroke. The piston pins floated in un-bushed bosses and the bushed small-end of the connecting-rods, which reduced the weight of the rods by requiring a shorter rod length. The already unpopular government horsepower rating, encouraging 'stroker' engines, unfortunately did not allow the full potential of the slipper piston to be achieved. Sixteen years later, Cadillac engineer Byron Ellis used the slipper to develop Cadillac's short-stroke, over-square V8 which went into production in 1949 – hailed since as the progenitor of the modern V8 engine.

The 10/20 crankcase was a one-piece aluminium casting with four bearer arms and integral flywheel housing, and the camshaft ran in two bearings. The sump was a ribbed aluminium casting with a top plate held by screws, the four indentations forming

passages to allow excess oil to pass. The 10/20 was of splash-lubrication design, but unlike typical arrangements its oil pump was of the oscillating-plunger type. Triumph claimed that low wear, high lift and efficient discharge resulted from this type of pump, which needed no priming even if the suction pipe was airlocked, but some critics felt that the oil could drain completely out of the pump through its downward-slanted intake/delivery pipes. This was never, as far as one can tell, a typical 10/20 problem; neither did it adversely affect Ricardo's WWI tank engines, which had first seen the application.

Inlet and exhaust manifolds of the 10/20 were integral, the unit attached to the block by studs and nuts with the exhaust facing forward. Water circulation was by thermosyphon action, but, contrary to normal practice, the centre of the radiator was level with the centre of the water jacket, giving cold water as far to rise as hot water exiting the cylinder head into the top of the radiator.

The engine's cylinder-bore finish bears mentioning. Instead of being ground, in the usual fashion, the bores were rolled with a set of steel rollers 'assembled like a lantern pinion'. This allowed a hard, glass-smooth surface. In terms of power, the unit developed 9.62bhp at 1000rpm, 19.5 at 2000, and 23.4 at 3000.

General design and production of the new car was entrusted to draughtsman Arthur Alderson, engaged by Triumph in 1921. Alderson, who had earlier spent many years at Singer, had been hired in 1919 by R H Lea of Lea-Francis, and in fact he remained a Lea-Francis employee during the 10/20's design period. According to Barrie Price in *The Lea-Francis Story,* Triumph "paid Lea-Francis for the work on a contract design basis." Alderson was assisted by Alan Lea and Arthur A Sykes, the latter later becoming Triumph's chief designer.

The Alderson-designed 10/20 was fairly orthodox. The four-speed gearbox was mounted separately from the engine on a subframe. Hotchkiss drive was employed, with spiral-bevel gears and ball-bearing axle. Though Triumph would pioneer the four-wheel hydraulic brake system on its very next model, 10/20 brakes were conventional rear-wheel drums, with rod-operated mechanical linkage. The steering gear was worm-and-roller, and the steering wheel had four levels of adjustment. Rotating tubes ran along the steering column carrying magneto and throttle controls. Fuel feed to the updraught Zenith carburettor was by cowl-mounted Autovac tank with a three-position cock: full off; normal, enabling six of the eight gallons to be drawn; or reserve, giving access to the remaining two gallons. A polished aluminium dashboard carried controls for the Lucas electric lights and starters, the wiring being carried through a rubber tube to prevent chaffing.

The chassis was resolutely ordinary, a channel-section box frame with riveted crossmembers, semi-elliptic leaf springs at each corner and artillery road wheels. No shock absorbers are visible in cutaway drawings. The wheelbase measured 102in – Dawson's had been 105 – and the two-seater weighed 1900lb.

Triumph offered three standard bodies, all with alligator-type bonnets, hinged at the scuttle. There were two- and four-seat tourers, and a Weymann-type four-seat saloon, with prices ranging from £430 to £460 – the original Dawson target. The Regent Carriage Company of Fulham Road, London, was responsible for the bodies, which were held to reach a high standard of fit and finish.

At around £450 the 10/20 was by no means a low-priced car (the contemporary Morris Cowley 12hp sold for as little as £150)

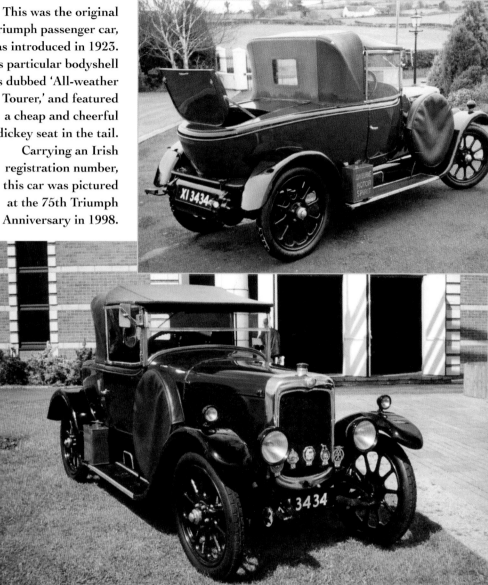

This was the original Triumph passenger car, as introduced in 1923. This particular bodyshell was dubbed 'All-weather Tourer,' and featured a cheap and cheerful dickey seat in the tail. Carrying an Irish registration number, this car was pictured at the 75th Triumph Anniversary in 1998.

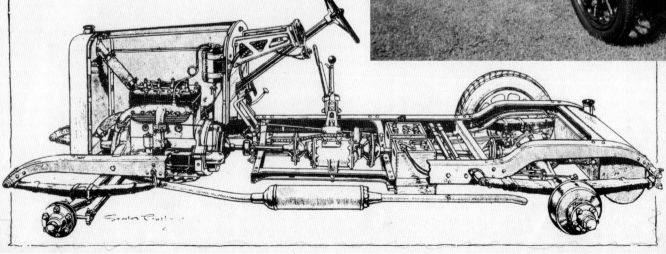

The 10/20 chassis laid bare, as drawn by *The Autocar*'s celebrated artist, Gordon Crosby. It shows that there was a separate gearbox, which was mounted on its own small sub-frame.

but Triumph hoped to sell it on the basis of quality, relying on its reputation for excellent workmanship. The 10/20 was thus well trimmed in quality cloth or leather; soft tops were black mohair twill. The facia contained cubbies left and right, and included both clock and speedometer. Attention to detail was evident in the half-section brake pedal, designed to enable speedy transfer of one's foot from the accelerator.

Testers praised the 10/20's handling and performance, achieving a 45mph cruise and 52mph flat-out at Brooklands. It was also easy to drive: a Birmingham owner noted that his wife "often flips the third in when about to descend steep hills to save the brakes, a thing she would never have attempted with an ordinary gearbox. No double-clutching is necessary. The gears are not unduly noisy,

and hill-climbing is good considering that the body is fairly heavy for such a small engine."

Another owner praised the Triumph's reliability, having achieved 25,000 miles without major failings, and finding its makers "very decent people to deal with." He had averaged 35 to 38mpg, which appeared to be the 10/20's general fuel consumption.

The Autocar's first road test stated succinctly the *raison d'être* of the first Triumph motor car: "a quality production of the kind which is well fitted, finished and equipped in the first place, and which will maintain its performance and smart appearance for year after year without frequent repairs. Extra high speeds for a capacity to climb hills very fast are not sought for in this design. The car is intended to run smoothly and quietly when travelling slowly in town or when touring at a reasonable average in the country ... Its running is refined, its appearance impressive, its finish exceedingly good, and its road performance all that could be wished for from a car of its size and type."

Triumph soon added a sporting two-seater (£425) to the 10/20 range – a pretty car with flowing wings and a duck-back body, running a 'fully turbulent' cylinder head with improved breathing. While the standard Regent bodies were of made steel panels over wood framing, the sports body was aluminium, and looked like an Alvis 12/50 duck-back. Its light body allowed it to weigh only 1568lb, which meant better fuel economy (over 40mpg) and a higher turn of speed (up to 55mph). Part of the specification was a revised set of gear ratios:

	Standard 10/20	Sports 10/20
1st	4.75	4.18
2nd	6.80	6.00
3rd	10.30	9.00
4th	15.80	14.00

Of this first Triumph, which we could conceivably view as 'sporting', *The Autocar* had kind words: "an intriguing car ... a neat specimen ... that burbled like a semi-Brooklands racer." The magazine again remarked upon "the magnificent materials and workmanship which have already characterised the make ... the high standard of finish, no matter at what part of the construction one may look. The tuned engine," they continued, "is naturally designed to rev at high speeds, and is timed accordingly. Thus finesse

Right from the beginning, Triumph was determined to keep the word 'sports' close to its image, and this was a 10/20 Sports model built in 1924.

Triumph's very first four-wheeler was the 10/20, seen here in open sports form on the Test Hill at Brooklands in 1923.

in engine behaviour, closely studied on the touring cars, is to some extent sacrificed ... while a high compression ratio will make its presence felt to the driver particularly at slow speeds."

Third, on the sports model, was now good for 45mph, and at Brooklands the car did 62mph along the Railway Straight – a remarkable performance for 1393cc in those days, all those years ago. On the Brooklands test hill, the 10/20 "sped quite comfortably over the 1-in-4 section on the low gear, confirming our road impression that no ordinary gradient would check its progress."

Despite the austere body style, *The Autocar* was impressed with this model's amenities. "Its seating accommodation is most natural, and provides far more back support than in the case of 75 per cent of such cars, small or large. There is ample legroom, the high sides affording protection and warmth ... Its controls are light, and the brakes ... are exceptionally smooth and progressive. It is as lively and responsive to the throttle as a good motorcycle – and that is saying much." Not so much, perhaps, for a product of the Triumph Cycle Company!

At this time in history, however, the 10/20 sports was as far as Triumph would go along the road to real performance. Still, the potential was there. As my co-author noted in *The Story of Triumph Sports Cars*, the failure to produce a real competitor at this time was due more to the absence of Triumph's own Cecil Kimber than to lack of potential in the 10/20, "both as attractive and potentially as rapid as the Morris Garages cars." Had that potential been exploited, Triumph might well have written as fair a competition history in the 1920s as it was to do a decade later.

The 10/20, Siegfried Bettmann concluded, "was a great success." That statement has to be viewed in context, for it didn't take many cars for Triumph to boast about this. Production figures are not available, but they couldn't have totalled more than a handful of cars a week. Apparently it was enough to convince management that further automotive developments were warranted. At least it convinced Claude Holbrook.

"For some reason which I could never fathom," wrote Bettmann, "Holbrook always wanted to change. A car which was successful had always to be replaced by something new and such experiments are very expensive." The first such expense was a companion to the 10/20, introduced at the 1924 Olympia Motor Show and billed as 'an Orthodox Type of Roomy Five-seater.' It was the Triumph 13/35, and it brought an important advance for the small firm – it was the first British car equipped from the start (later 10/20s had them too) with four-wheel Lockheed hydraulic brakes. The saloon version sold for £495 – a reasonable sum.

The 13/35 boasted a four-cylinder engine of

The 10/20's successor was the 13/35 of 1926, another very orthodox design in almost every detail. However, this was the very first British road car to be offered with hydraulic brakes.

1873cc (72 x 115mm), a three-speed gearbox, single dry-plate clutch, Hotchkiss drive and spiral-bevel geared rear axle. The chassis was conventional, with a 108-inch wheelbase. Bodies were less sparse-looking than the 10/20's, flush-sided, with fixed front seat, double-panel windscreen and full weather equipment on open models. The 13/35 weighed 2129lb, and would do between 50 and 55mph.

Following 10/20 design, the 13/35's four cylinders were cast en bloc with the crankcase and fitted with a detachable head. The crank ran in three bearings and aluminium pistons were fitted. Lubrication was force-fed, through a cam-driven gear pump mounted in the sump, feeding oil to the mains through holes in the crankshaft. Combustion chambers were fully machined, the exhaust and inlet manifolds separate and the carburettor an updraught Zenith. The Lockheed brakes used contracting bands instead of internal-expanding shoes, but were highly effective. Springing remained semi-elliptic at each corner, while the wide-ratio gearbox was supplied with either central or right-hand change.

Two years after its introduction, Triumph bored-out the 13/35 to 2169cc (77.5 x 115mm), increasing the UK tax rating to 14.9. The chassis was enlarged to a 112-inch wheelbase, the track slightly widened, and the kerb weight considerably increased, allowing little performance improvement. Body styles remained as before, the only refinement being provision of adjustable bucket-type front seats.

Despite its low rear axle ratio, the 15/50 (Light 15 from 1928) impressed as a good top-gear performer and a refined runner. On level roads it could accelerate from 10 to 30mph in top gear in 15¼ seconds, and in second gear in 11. Maximum speed remained in the neighbourhood of 55mph – which was hardly breathless for 2.2 litres – and 40mph could be reached in second. The high second gear and low top allowed the car to climb small hills rapidly under full load, while handling modest grades in top without downshifting or lugging. The Lockheed brakes could pull it up dead from 40mph in less than 100ft – a positive accomplishment indeed in an era when you mainly threw on all the locks and hoped for the best.

"The brake pedal requires only a slight pressure on it, even to make an emergency stop," reported one road tester, "and the brakes themselves go on with noticeable sweetness."

As was now a tradition, both 13/35 and 15 were luxuriously trimmed. On the 13/35 saloon, the driver's side had only a front door – and a very good idea it was, too – although a conventional four-door design was adopted with the 15. The six lights opened on spring balancers, and the rear light was wide, allowing good visibility. Both were comfortable cars and, if not rakish, styled with a degree of elegance, the waistline picked out by a body line in the manner of American coachbuilder Ray Dietrich, whose efforts graced much more expensive machinery. Equipment was as comprehensive as possible in the lexicon of the mid-twenties: spacious windscreen, pockets in all doors, curved rear corners with pockets above the back seat and a ramp-cum-toolbox behind the front seats. The three-way fuel tank cock was still a Triumph feature, and a beefy luggage rack was provided as standard.

"There will be many satisfied owners of the 15hp Triumph," concluded one road tester. "The workmanship is irreproachable."

The 15 should be noted for one other contribution before we leave it: it was the first of the marque to be exported seriously. Mainly, the markets were Australia and New Zealand. As early as 1926 bare chassis were being shipped to Sydney agents, where they were fitted with bodies of local manufacture. Triumph's long skein of export sales had begun!

While the 10/20 was phased-out of production in 1926 – this for reasons which will shortly become obvious – the Triumph 15, née 13/35, continued in production on a small scale through 1929 (some 1930 registered models do exist). It never sold as well as the 10/20, and the latter proved to Triumph that 'the quality light car' was the direction to follow. All Bettmann and Holbrook had to do was stay clear of the low-priced territory staked out by the Austin Seven. Otherwise, Triumph was ready for more production. A line of agencies had been established, Clay Lane had expanded rapidly, and motor cars definitely seemed destined to become the dominant transport of the common man.

Triumph was not the only company to look upon the success of the Austin Seven with a jealous eye. William Morris too, bouncing back from the doldrums, was planning to enter that tax rating with an up-market car of more luxurious specification. An almost concurrent analogy may be drawn across the Atlantic ocean, in Chevrolet's desire to sell a better and costlier car than Ford. By 1925, the Tin Lizzie's sales had peaked, and while Henry Ford was stubbornly insisting that it had reached perfection and could be built in its present form forever, GM's low-priced Chevys were eating into Ford sales with cars that were more attractive, better equipped, more luxurious, offered in more styles, and priced just a little higher than the leader. On either side of the pond, upstaging Number One – but not meeting him head-on – was the order of the day.

In 1925, therefore, the Triumph design office, on the seventh floor at Priory Street, began to look toward the future and a brand new 7hp car – cheaper than the 10/20, but just as nicely equipped, and more expensive than the Austin Seven. One of its early recruits, and a worthy one, was Stanley Edge, the brilliant draughtsman-designer who, along with Sir Herbert Austin, had conceived and drawn the original Seven in the billiards room of Herbert Austin's home.

Edge, who arrived at Priory Street in early 1927, provides a glimpse of the Triumph Drawing Office: "I found that the staff was larger than that of the Austin Motor Co. A A Sykes, chief draughtsman, had collected around him a man from practically every well-known motor car and motorcycle firm. I remember there was one from Siddeley, one from Rover, two from BSA and one from Humber, but no others from Austin ... Mr Sykes explained to me that they were well on the way to producing their prototype ... He said he would like me to check over all main assemblies and the details comprising them."

Even the most optimistic hands could not have known that the car they were about to spring would prove one of the most significant Triumphs of all time – the highest-selling model to that date, one destined to lay the foundation of Triumph's future reputation as a hardy, rugged, sporting automobile. In its lighter, open-bodied forms, it would be the first model one can legitimately term a sports car. As such, it would be viewed historically as a very notable development and, in its class, one of the best – the Super Seven.

By 1928 Triumph had begun to concentrate on producing quantities of the all-new Super Seven, so this 'coachbuilt' 15 of 1928 was one of the last of the individual pedigree to be produced. Simply engineered, rugged, and carrying the same sort of styling as most other British cars of the late 1920s, this is one of the very rare 15s to survive.

The Last Word in the Smallest Class

1927 was one of those years we have all wonderingly known – a period in which the western world brushed aside any doubts about its destiny in a climate of unbridled optimism. In Britain and America, long-established traditionalists commanded. Genial Stanley Baldwin was enjoying his second period as prime minister, with a two-to-one majority over the combined opposition. Calvin Coolidge presided stoically over an American government employing 100,000 people, with a budget of $3 billion and a surplus of $1 billion. At the end of the year, 'Silent Cal' announced that he would not run again in 1928. Perhaps he saw further ahead than most gave him credit for. Two years later the world would plunge from those days of plenty – and just as World War I swept away the Edwardian lifestyle, the Great Depression would banish all vestiges of the Roaring Twenties.

It was in such a climate that the Triumph Cycle Company, with perfect timing, launched its smallest and most economical car ever, the 81-inch wheelbase 832cc Super Seven.

"There are little cars and little cars," the firm said, "so before purchasing your new small car we advise you to consider ... the car of proved success manufactured by a firm of worldwide reputation ... Insist upon seeing the chassis naked and unadorned–" (like the 15, the Super Seven had four-wheel Lockheed hydraulic brakes, four-wheel dampers, sturdy ladder frame and semi-elliptic front leaf springs) "–compare the comfortable pneumatic upholstery and the soft and restful cushions with those usually fitted to small cars."

The Super Seven was priced well above the Austin Seven, of course, but it was beautifully built, fitted with an extensive list of standard equipment ('everything you can conceivably require'), so the price premium was obviously worth it.

Walter Belgrove, who became Triumph's distinguished chief body design engineer, arrived at Triumph around the same time as the Super Seven was being developed, and remembered it well. He also recalled what passed for a design department – a haphazard arrangement of draughtsmen and engineers.

"The company lacked a positive design section in those days," he said. "The models, like Topsy in *Uncle Tom's Cabin*, just 'growed.' This was not rectified until about 1931, I think, when Frank Warner joined the company (from Hillman) as chief body engineer, following a change of policy by that company."

Belgrove made no bones about the skills he was able to bring to this ad hoc department: "I was apprenticed to the craft of coachmaking with a polytechnic training," he says, "and in addition to practical ability, orthographic projection (draughtsmanship) etc, I had a fair grounding in aesthetics. I entered the design office at the request of Frank Warner, and some urging from Bert Harrison. They wanted me because, frankly and truthfully, I carried more experience than any other member of the drawing office. There was nobody there capable of seeing a project in the 'round,' or of picturing a working drawing in perspective, or building a scale plastic model – nobody carried this knowledge, and this included Frank Warner."

The aforementioned Stanley Edge, who was hired as a draughtsman at £4.75 a week, was given a desk in a large drawing office and was asked to check the main assemblies and details of the prototype: "I found very little to complain about, because Mr Sykes had collected a large team of good draughtsmen. Sykes did not have a private office – he sat at one end of the drawing office where he could see everyone and we could see him. There were, however, two adjacent rooms to the drawing office. In one of these, Sykes had installed a former Morris Motors draughtsman together with a stripped-down Austin Seven. What the Morris man did I never found out." From the description the reader may guess!

"The second separate room was occupied by Mr F Gordon Parnell. I learned that Mr Parnell had been the designer of previous Triumph cars. I never saw any drawings of these cars in the main drawing office, and it was certainly rumoured that Mr Parnell was merely working out his contract, ie doing nothing!"

In fact, Parnell was not working out his contract, as he stayed with Triumph until the end of 1930, completing seven years with the company. Parnell had a long-standing association with Lockheed. He had dealt with them when he was involved in the design of early Triumph cars (which led, of course, to the use of Lockheed hydraulic brakes on the 13/35), and eventually he would move on to Lockheed where, in due course, he took charge of

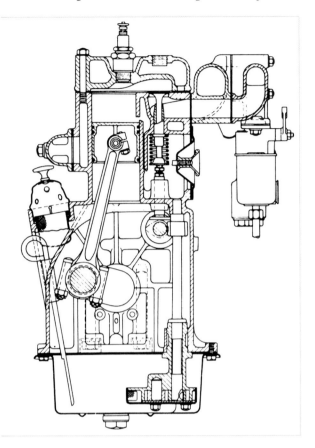

This was the original Super Seven engine of 1927/1928, which would feature (when further developed) in several different entry-level Triumphs of the next few years.

This cross-section view is of the 832cc engine, designed by Arthur A Sykes, which powered the Triumph Super Seven, and was a simple side-valve power unit.

brake design for heavy vehicles. At the beginning of 1931, however, Parnell moved across Coventry to join the new Rootes Group, where (as assistant to Capt J S Irving) he was much involved in the design of the first series of Hillman Minx models.

While checking the engine and gearbox assemblies for the forthcoming new model, Edge concluded that he had seen something similar before: "I found an article on the Triumph 15hp with sectional drawings of the power unit, and noted the similarity between the two – good orthodox designs of the 1920s, but no touches of inspiration."

Edge's view is a fair summation of the Super Seven – a quality light car, the old Bettmann slogan, without any ingenious features, cleverly priced just above, and out of direct competition with, the Austin Seven.

Arthur A Sykes is credited with engine design of the Super Seven, which did depart from the Ricardo head and masked inlet valves of its predecessors. Displacing only 832cc (56.5 x 83mm, only 50 cubic inches), it developed 21bhp at 4000rpm – a high-revver for those days. Initially the stroke was to have been 74.5mm for only 747cc, but this was never put into production. Despite its name, the car's RAC hp rating was 7.9, and in the UK it was taxed at £8.

Though conventional, the engine was robust. Both crankshaft and camshaft used three bearings, and the cylinder block and

crankcase were of cast iron. The aluminium pistons were straight-sided with three rings, two in the head and one in the skirt. Full pressure lubrication by gear pump and thermosyphon cooling with three-blade fan were featured. The carburettor was a vertical Zenith (Edge remembers B&B and Solex carbs also being used), with a twin-port induction manifold and four-port exhaust manifold. The timing-chain tensioner, Triumph-patented, eliminated the need for chain adjustments and maintained quietness of the timing gear. The tensioner was an idler sprocket with an eccentric mounting, a flat steel coil (clock type) spring, which kept the sprocket 'up to its work.'

Comparisons of the proposed 747cc and final 832cc Super Seven engines with the Austin Seven are interesting in that the original Triumph unit was within one cc of, and had nearly the same bore and stroke measurements as, the Austin. Reports of the former in *Automotive Industries* give the same bhp figures as finally realised with the 832cc unit – indicating either an editorial mistake or an optimistic dynamometer.

| | Triumph Super Seven | | Austin Seven |
	Proposed	Production	Production
displacement, cc	747.0	832.0	747.5
bore, mm	56.5	56.5	56.0
stroke, mm	74.5	83.0	76.0
bhp/rpm	21/4000	21/4000	10.4/2440
taxable hp	7.9	7.9	7.0

The Super Seven's engine, clutch and three-speed gearbox were mounted on the main frame with four-point support, the gearbox being enclosed in an aluminium casing. The propeller-shaft was somewhat unusual, being enclosed in a torque tube with a fabric disc, mounted up front. The shaft was supported through a ball-race at its front end, the fabric joint being relieved of the side loads passed through the shaft by a central spherical pilot bearing in the driving spider of the joint.

The Super Seven's ladder chassis was built of channel steel, and the fuel was fed by gravity from a dash-mounted four-gallon tank. The detachable wheels were pressed-steel hollow spoke types (wire wheels were fitted on some models), with 4.4 x 18in Dunlop low-pressure tyres. Beam axles were at both ends, with semi-elliptic leaf springs at the front and quarter-elliptics at the rear. Steering was by worm-and-worm wheel and the steering column was severely raked.

Parnell's favoured Lockheed hydraulic brakes were a major selling point, "an innovation in the small car," *The Light Car* remarked, "which constitutes, even today, a luxury amongst larger cars, and the three-bearing crankshaft is another refinement in such a small engine."

Super Sevens came in bare chassis form (£113) or in five standard bodies and one custom body, as follows:

1928 Super Seven	
Model (doors/passengers)	Price
Popular Tourer (2/4)	£149 10s
Tourer de Luxe (2/4)	£167 10s
Two-seater de Luxe (2/2)	£167 10s
Fabric Saloon (2/4)	£187 10s
Coachbuilt Saloon (2/4)	£192 10s
Gordon England Saloon (2/4)	£200

Because these were to be typical of Triumph construction for five or six years, we propose to describe them briefly here; readers familiar with this fairly typical style of late twenties construction may profitably skip ahead.

Popular Tourer: The line-leader, with seating for four (only the most optimistic factory men called it five), using front bucket seats 'nicely shaped to give adequate support to one's back and shoulders.' The driver's seat was adjustable for leg reach, the passenger's tilted to allow access to the rear. Rear floor wells augmented legroom. Like the other variants, the Tourer was a high-sided affair, but the low-built frame allowed it to come off reasonably well and afforded excellent weather protection. A 'one-man' hood and close-fitting side curtains were standard. The options included a clock, chromium plating of small exterior metal parts, 'Protecto' safety glass, hood envelope and spring gaiters. Finished in blue or maroon, the Tourer was held to be 'a smart looking little car with no suggestion of cheapness.'

This smart little Super Seven Tourer was very popular at the end of the 1920s.

Tourer de Luxe: Same layout as the Popular Tourer, some with rounded door corners instead of square corners. Waistline coach band fitted, plus clock, and hood envelope standard, and a choice of four duotone colours – brown and sand, green and grey, red and grey and duotone grey. The wings were domed, the upholstery in higher quality leatherette and door pockets and carpets were fitted front and rear. Wire wheels, a five-lamp set, shaded dash lamp and vacuum windscreen wiper completed the specification.

Two-seater de Luxe: Specification similar to the Tourer de Luxe, with duck-back two-seater body plus an occasional seat in the rear – a car for 'the man who motors for the sake of motoring.' Lightest model in the range, it was marginally quicker than its mates, Triumph somewhat optimistically describing it as "incredibly fast ... due to its low centre of gravity, it holds the road to perfection. High speeds are safe, all speeds are safe whatever the nature of the country." The same paint combinations as the Tourer de Luxe were offered, except that duotone grey was replaced by an attractive combination of black and primrose.

Coachbuilt Saloon: Truest example of 'the big car in perfect miniature': this model followed the styling of the larger 15 – gracefully rounded back, deep sides (*The Autocar* said, "high sides in closed coachwork are a sign of modern design") and a double belt line. This was a handsome car, available in maroon, blue, or any other colour to order. All accessories of the Tourer de Luxe were supplied, plus pneumatic upholstery and a roof light. The sidelights all opened by sliding, and a blind was fitted over the large backlight.

"In outward appearance the car is nicely balanced," offered the press, "and inside the body looks distinctly cosy."

Fabric Saloon: The Weymann type of fabric-covered body, light and airy in warm weather but providing complete cold-weather protection. All accoutrements of the Coachbuilt Saloon were offered – wire wheels, five-lamp set, roof lamp, shaded dash lamp, clock, vacuum windscreen wiper – and the body came in blue, red or brown. Upholstery was of moquette over pneumatic seats.

Gordon England Saloon: A more streamlined body design than the standard cars, at a premium price, with the patented Gordon England method of construction: "permanent body-silence at all speeds is ensured by the . . . system of three-point suspension, which insulates the body against all strain, even when passing over uneven roads." Gordon England bodies were rigid, not flexible, but mounted to the chassis with rubber blocks which absorbed most of the stress. The Gordon England saloon was upholstered in genuine leather, fitted with roof ventilator and above-screen vent, wide

doors and safety glass, plus a large exterior boot. It was available in silver with mottled black piping, black with red or green piping, and pale blue with fawn piping.

Other coachbuilders or dealers offered custom bodies almost from the beginning. Morgan Hastings of Berkeley Street, London, one of the largest Triumph dealers, entered an 'Arrow' two-seater for 1928, followed by no less than four special bodies in 1929: the 'Trophy' two-seater (£188) with V-screen and disappearing folding top, a boat-tail roadster; the 'Curzon' coupé, fabric-covered (£193) or coachbuilt (£199), with wide doors, single-pane screen and exceptional headroom; and the 'Berkeley' fabric saloon (£200) with winding windows. Another London dealer, Ratcliffe, ran off its own two-seater of more conventional design, with a long cowl and squared-off tail, lower steering wheel and seats adjustable for rake, selling it for £177 10s; Basil Roy sold a Tickford body with completely collapsible top; The New Avon Company had a two-door coupé with coachline from bonnet to boot and sliding windows; and Boyd Carpenter offered its own style of duck-back two-seater. But the Gordon England continued to hold the most popularity among the 'custom built' Sevens, and was usually seen in Triumph brochures.

Super Seven marketing plans, for which Bettmann may take the credit, were astute, for the Super Seven came in at about £15 more than the Austin Seven. If this seems negligible by today's standards, bear in mind that £5 per week was a very healthy salary in 1927 (more than Stanley Edge made, as we've noted), and three weeks' wages were not to be sniffed at. At around £150-200 the Super Seven was still a good buy, and the higher price assured a car superior

Neat, understated, but still definitely a four-seater, this was Triumph's own fabric saloon version of the Super Seven.

Fabric, as opposed to metal-skinned bodyshells were very popular at the end of the 'vintage' period, but cars such as this Super Seven did not usually endure to be appreciated by enthusiasts in the modern era.

the Super Seven's market position was predetermined, though fortunate.

While the two-seater Tourer de Luxe was certainly the quickest Super Seven, the first one tested by *The Autocar* was a Fabric Saloon. This model couldn't exceed 48mph. Its two outstanding characteristics appeared to be springing and brakes:

"Of all the problems which beset the designer of a small car with a short wheelbase ... that of securing springing which is comfortable either when the car is carrying one or four people and of stability

Nearly fifty years separate the manufacture of the Super Seven 2/4-seater, and this late 1970s TR7 Coupé.

in fitment as well as performance to the Austin Seven. In this approach, Triumph was alone with Singer among British makes, and it is instructive to look at the dimensions of both, alongside the popular Austin.

when travelling slow or fast over good or bad roads, is the most difficult–" (Lots of latitude for faults there!) "–The Triumph is really good, there is very little pitching, bad roads do not matter much, the roadholding is excellent and the stability leaves nothing to be desired on wet as well as dry roads ... the brakes are conspicuously good, as the stopping distances from 40mph (62ft) and 25mph (29ft) testify.

'Willing to a degree, and capable of withstanding any amount of hard driving, the engine runs smoothly enough to satisfy most people ... The carburettor is not quite as it might be, there is a

	Triumph 7	Singer 8	Austin 7
Price, Tourer	£149 10s	£140	£135
Dollar equivalent	$724	$678	$653
Displacement, cc	832	848	747.5
Wheelbase, in	81	90	75
Track, in	42	42	40
Length, in	118	139	119
Width, in	51	53	60c
Weight, lb	1064	1232	952
Seats	4	4	2-2
Fuel consumption	38	30	43
Max speed	57	55	52

The 1929 version of the Super Seven was a well-established and popular model.

One can see that the Super Seven's (and Singer Eight's) market placement was excellent. This did not necessarily imply canny foresight on Triumph's part, though that was undoubtedly a factor. Still, Triumph could not have competed directly with Austin because it lacked the production capacity and the dealers – although some, like Morgan Hastings, set a high standard. Finally, Triumph was, as usual, under-capitalised. To these extents disconcerting flat-spot when coming off the idling position, but on hills the performance is good."

The Autocar disliked the Seven's cramped interior, though it was not uncommon in light cars of the period. Shoulder-rubbing with four passengers aboard was de rigueur in such machinery for at least three decades. Only after the 1939-45 war did the British industry learn that people with £150 to spend were often as large as those with £1500. Nobody admitted it back in 1927, though Triumph would make some efforts to enlarge the Super Seven in later years.

The testers didn't care much for "an impression of slight rolling in the suspension" when climbing aboard either. Perhaps the dampers weren't up to the job. Things seemed fairly stable once in motion, though, and the Fabric Saloon scored 10-30mph in 12 seconds in second gear, which was good up to 36mph. It also recorded a commendable 42mpg, somewhat higher than the stated average. Later in the year the magazine received a favourable report from owner S Westcott of Devon: petrol consumption was an astounding 48mpg, accessibility of all parts excellent, and steering "simply splendid."

On a good surface the car will run over a hundred yards without a touch of the steering wheel. Westcott claimed 55mph for his four-seater Tourer de Luxe, and had recorded over 5000 miles with no appreciable problems. He praised the Triumph Company, which dealt "most courteously with all inquiries ... and gave exhaustive replies."

The 1929 Seven range, announced in September 1928, was basically identical to the 1928 range. Five-lamp lighting sets were now standard on all models, rear footwells modified for more legroom, cellulose finish adopted (blue and maroon, with other colours available). The Popular Tourer now had door flap pockets and a hinged seat back squab, to provide easier access to the side curtains. All other models had pneumatic upholstery, and the Tourer de Luxe was extended six inches in length. On saloons, a luggage box, polished instrument board, and roof and dash lights completed the specification. Saloons were also lower in price:

1929 Super Sevens	
Model (doors/passengers)	*Price*
Popular Tourer (2/4)	£149 10s
Tourer de Luxe (2/4)	£167 10s
Two-seater de Luxe (2/2)	£167 10s
Coachbuilt Saloon (2/4)	£172
Fabric Saloon (2/4)	£172
Gordon England Saloon (2/4)	£200
Special Sports (2/2)	£250

The Special Sports was an aluminium-bodied, duck-back two-seater introduced in mid-1929. An attractive car with good performance and sleek lines, it became the basis for whatever racing Triumph drivers did in those years, and (in company with Frazer Nash) it came equipped with a Cozette supercharger. René Cozette, whose blower came into some favour in the '20s, used the Roots principle – a simple pump that compresses air by delivering it to the engine faster than it can be used, creating a pressure increase between supercharger and intake valve. Cozette's design featured an outer sleeve, rotating in a slower lock step with a smaller inner rotor. This reduced rubbing velocities at the tips of the (usually six) vanes. In their home country, Cozette blowers found application on Amilcars, and were offered as bolt-on accessories for Citroëns and Renaults.

If the reader gathers that Triumph

For a short period, starting in 1929, the Super Seven Sports model appeared, complete with a Cozette-supercharged engine. Race-prepared examples appeared at Brooklands, and could lap at up to 90mph, which made the MG opposition sit up and take notice.

was principally concerned with showroom, rather than track performance, they are correct. Some enthusiasts raced Super Sevens, but Triumph never seemed to notice. The marque's most serious Brooklands exponent was Victor Horsman, who campaigned two Sevens, one supercharged, between 1929 and 1932. Horsman's monoposto bodies were well streamlined, and though they used the standard Seven drive-train, important modifications were made. According to William Boddy, in *The History of Brooklands Motor Course*, Horsman made a special camshaft by hand, a modified cylinder head gave the highest possible compression ratio of 7:1, lubrication to the main and big-end bearings was improved, and two Amal carburettors were fitted. It could lap at up to 90mph, partly because Horsman used a relatively high 4.5:1 axle ratio. On handicap, the Seven was impressive. Horsman won his first race outright, and was generally among the top finishers in his class. Culled from William Boddy's records, here are the most notable performances:

1929
1st (75.69mph), 75-mph Long Handicap, Easter (best lap 78.25)

1930
4th, Devon Junior Short Handicap, Whitsun (best lap 75.01)
3rd, Cornwall Junior Short, August (best lap 78.18)
1st (74.81 mph), Middlesex Junior Short, September (best lap 77.93)

1931
2nd, Lincoln Junior Short, March
2nd, Lincoln Junior Long, March (best lap 80.46)
4th, Warwick Junior Short, Easter
2nd, Somerset Junior Long, Whitsun

1932
3rd, Yorkshire Junior Short, September

Horsman's Cozette-blown Super Seven did less well, though for one thing its displacement had been reduced to 750cc for the Ulster Tourist Trophy, where it failed to finish.

"It was never a success," says Boddy, "either blowing the supercharger blade springs into the engine or blowing its cylinder head gasket."

Triumph had more luck with (and crowed more loudly over) rallies. In fact it's no exaggeration to say that the Super Seven's rally performance was the beginning of the marque's long reputation for ruggedness and durability. Examples of its prowess could be found all over the English-speaking world. In America, for example, G A Woods drove his Seven from New York to Vancouver by way of San Francisco, rarely taking his foot off the throttle. He had to stop once – to tend a puncture. Later, in a succeeding model Super Eight, he returned by the fearsome Pendleton-Cheyenne-Chicago-Toronto-Niagara route, covering 3538 miles in just eight and a half days – an unbelievable average of 458 miles a day! It was Triumph's first great North American performance. Many more would follow.

Back home, the Seven gained early laurels under the sure hand of Donald Healey, an enthusiastic Cornishman who would be heard from later, and at length, in the Triumph story. In 1929, Healey entered the always-formidable Monte Carlo Rally, his starting point was in frigid Riga, Latvia. Unable to get to the Baltic port because of wintry weather, he switched to Berlin, which wasn't enjoying much better conditions. Fighting his way through blizzards, and driving on ice most of the way, Healey arrived in Monte Carlo – two minutes outside his time limit. Donald resolved to fight again another year.

With the same car (registration WK 7546), Healey ran into similar weather in 1930. But this time the Super Seven was seventh overall, and the first British car to finish. It had averaged 30mph – with a top speed of only 47! For good measure Healey topped his class in the Brighton Rally with a 70mph Cozette-blown Seven, and in 1931 he won it outright with the same car. The factory still not reacting, Healey spent most of 1931 to 1933 in Invictas. When Triumph ultimately began to appreciate competitive performance, Donald Healey would join the company as experimental manager – but that would not be until 1933.

The only thing that seemed to excite Triumph's advertising at this time was the impressive showing of the Super Seven down under. With the Australian market a prime target, it was natural that the car's strength and reliability would be put to the test by local agents and enthusiasts. Late in 1929, a Super Seven won the Sydney Motor Club's reliability trial – 1150 arduous miles covered in three days, at a 32mph average, without a single point being lost. No road adjustments had been permitted; the Seven had run the entire distance with a sealed bonnet. Later, another car, driven by dealer W G Buckle, averaged 43.5mph for the 575-mile Sydney-Melbourne run, completing it in just 13¼ hours over the worst kind of back-country tracks. A third Super Seven set the Brisbane-Sydney light car record, running the 672 miles in 22 hours and 10 minutes. A New Zealand record fell to Triumph when another Seven ran 10,000 miles back and forth between New Plymouth and Auckland, 250 miles each way, crossing the main mountain range 40 times. That one took six drivers – but only one Super Seven.

In 1930, at the Australian RAC Trial, Triumph won the 1000cc class with a 1-2-4 finish. Later the marque recorded hill-climb, acceleration and flying-mile wins in the RAC Victoria Double 12-hour Trial, Triumph being the only car to gain 100 points in each event. By the end of the year, every Australian RAC contest in the up-to-1000cc class had been won by Triumph – a series of victories that has never been equalled. Included were seven categories for speed, hill-climbing and reliability; the total was seven firsts, six seconds and four thirds.

But the greatest performance of all had to be the epic crossing of the Australian continent by the intrepid P W Armstrong, a Perth dealer, the previous year. Driving across Australia in 1929 must have been like crossing the Sahara on a camel 100 years earlier, but Armstrong was a man who liked to drive, especially in Triumphs.

"Hearing the phrase, 'what a nice little town car,' in my showroom *ad nauseam* directed my thoughts," he wrote later. "If the Triumph could put up a good record over that big, rough journey, we should hear a little less of the 'nice little town car' and establish in one stroke the fact that the Triumph is a nice little car for any country."

Armstrong selected a Two-seater de Luxe from stock, and ran it in for 2000 miles. Spare parts were purchased, Mobil depots were pinpointed along the 3000-mile route – "a mishap might mean a 200-mile walk in the wilds for nearest help." With his brave companion, George Manley, Armstrong set out on September 30, determined to average 18mph (day and night) for the crossing.

Off they went, past the abandoned goldfields near Perth, across the Darling and Frasers Ranges and on to the granite-strewn plains.

"Travelling at a steady 30 over seemingly endless, featureless plains, with always the same unvarying section of illuminated track in front, has a hypnotic effect," yawned Armstrong. Gingerly, they descended frightful Madura Gorge, climbed upward again at Eucla and struck the Nanwarra Sandhills – "the Triumph fought her way up in second, lurching from rut to rut, 14 miles without one moment's relief or pause, and the radiator water was not even boiling."

In Nanwarra, Armstrong tried to hire a native guide, but the aborigine refused: "no mister, I'd like to go, but I'd lose my woman if I did." Women being scarce, even £2 wouldn't move

him. Very well then – alone! On they went, to Fowlers Bay, Penong, Ceduna, the Eyres Peninsula, then to 'Bullockies Playground' – a name which conjured a scene of bullock teams that stuck in the sand, whips cracking overhead, the air quivering to the howling of animals and blasphemy of drivers. But the Super Seven was no bullock, and it failed to get stuck.

Exhausted beyond belief, it was now that Armstrong and Manley lost their way, driving in circles. By chance, they found a signboard nailed to a tree, directing them to Port Augusta and Adelaide. They caught two hours of sleep while the car was serviced, then were off across the Murray River at Wellington, and on to Melbourne. Four more hours sleep and they tackled the last leg, across Mount Razorback and into Sydney. The statistics: 2954 miles in eight days and six hours – only a 14.9mph average including stops, but Armstrong was satisfied. Problems? The Super Seven had consumed one set of plugs and a fanbelt. "Beyond this we had not a single trouble with any part of the car, and it was showing more power at the end of the journey than when we started. To clinch the argument ... I drove it back to Perth, the driving-time average from Sydney being 290 miles a day."

Armstrong placed the little car in his showroom "with all the honourable dirt and stain of travel on her." So much for the 'nice little town car.' One may understand why rallyists liked the Super Seven.

With ten distinct models, the 1930 range was the peak of variety. The cars were immediately distinguished by their new radiator – "frankly of the latest American type" – a handsome thin-banded affair reminiscent of contemporary Chryslers, "which presents a more imposing front style," fitted to all models except the Special Sports two-seater. All the 1929 body styles were offered, plus three new ones:

This was how Triumph rather whimsically advertised its new models for sale in the early 1930s.

1930 Super Seven	
Model (doors/passengers)	Price
Popular Tourer (2/4)	£149 10s
Tourer de Luxe (2/4)	£167 10s
Two-seater de Luxe (2/2)	£167 10s
Fabric Saloon (2/4)	£179 10s
Gordon England Saloon (2/4)	£189 10s
Coachbuilt Saloon (2/4)	£197 10s
Special Sports (2/2)	£250
Two-seater Coupé (2/2)	£162 10s
Fabric de Luxe Saloon (2/4)	£192 10s
Saloon-Landaulet (2/2+2)	£197 10s

The Super Seven coachbuilt saloon of 1930 was a very
well-equipped and proportioned little car, complete with
two-tone colouring, and a built-out boot compartment.

Although Triumph set out to match the various MG Midgets, the
super-tuned Gnat was not a success.

Most novel was the new Saloon-Landaulet, "a departure in small car coachwork," which made extra room for the passengers by positioning the twin bucket seats further back and rendering the rear seat 'occasional.' (We should really say 'unusable'). The new Coupé was a commodious body style for two, with wire wheels and exterior boot. The Fabric de Luxe Saloon offered leather upholstery, pneumatic seats and safety glass all round as standard. The Two-seater de Luxe was fully redesigned, its new body fitted with a dickey, leather upholstery, extra chrome-plating, safety glass and spring gaiters included in the base price.

Generally, the 1930 models were more colourful, the Tourer de Luxe, for example, being available in crimson lake with grey trim, black with grey trim, and Mitcham brown with sand trim. The Gordon England Saloon came in maroon, blue, black or brown with red interior and wheels, and the Fabric de Luxe Saloon in black with red or blue roof/upholstery/wheels, or dark blue with stone-coloured roof/upholstery/wheels. This was, incidentally, the last year for the Triumph 15, which would be replaced by a new 11.9hp car in 1931.

The Olympia Motor Show of 1930, the last of the vintage era, saw further improvements in the Super Sevens. The luggage boot, which until then had ridden on the tail, tacked-on, became part of the body, which was more curving and streamlined; the spare wheel was carried inside the luggage compartment. The bottom-line Tourer had gone up in price, but the range was held at under £200.

A bevy of 1930 models had now been eliminated – the Gordon England and standard Fabric Saloons, the Coupé, the supercharged

Special Sports and Saloon-Landaulet. Two new models were an unblown two-seater jauntily named the 'Gnat,' and a Tickford Saloon built by Salmons and Sons of Newport Pagnell. Only one Fabric Saloon was left, fabric bodies having begun to fall out of favour. The new 2/4-seater was a modification of the previous two-seater with a dickey for two in the tail, fingertip controls on the steering wheel, and genuine leather upholstery. In addition to the usual maroon and blue, it was available in a bright red-and-cream duotone combination.

The Gnat, with its neat little aluminium-panelled body and high state of tune, was the most interesting of the 1931 range. Engine modifications included a larger carburettor, special inlet manifolding and combustion chambers, polished valve ports and tuned Vortex silencer. One of the most desirable and attractive Sevens ever built, it came in five duotone colour schemes; the wings and radiator painted in the contrasting colour. The windscreen pivoted, there was a sprung steering wheel and special dash with individual gauges: octagons (how dare they!) for the speedo and rev counter, hexagons for the minor instruments. A 10 per cent increase in power was claimed, which in the Super Seven meant all of 2.1hp – but the Gnat was obviously designed for the chap who enjoyed his motoring.

The sprightly Super Sevens, and their excellent rally record, were encouraging, but not good enough. Business had been in the doldrums since the American stock market crash of 1929, though Triumph couldn't have had a better model for hard times than the economical Seven. About 13,400 of them had been built between late 1927 and the end of 1931 – 100 units a week, approximately 2500 a year – but production had slowed as the Depression deepened. To bolster company morale and prestige in 1931, Siegfried Bettmann made two important moves: he invited local landowner and Coventry manufacturer Lord Leigh to be chairman of the company, and he promoted Lt Col Holbrook to assistant managing director.

Lord Leigh, 3rd Baron of Stoneleigh, was 75 years old at the time, but his participation was fortuitous. He had already run up a good record in connection with other motor car manufacturers including Armstrong-Siddeley (to whom he lent the name 'Stoneleigh' for one of its cars), and had been Lord Lieutenant of Warwickshire since 1921. Holbrook we have already met, but from this point on he would exert growing influence over the management of Triumph, succeeding Bettmann in 1933.

At the company's general meeting in December 1931, Lord Leigh regretted to recommend no dividend payment on ordinary shares for the first time in nearly 30 years.

"The whole year was overshadowed by a cloud of distress," he said, "financial, commercial, political and industrial, in every part of the globe."

Since Britain had left the gold standard, the monetary situation had become acute. Triumph's trading profit had fallen nearly 44 per cent to £50,641. "The motorcycle department ... was the greatest sufferer" – British cycle registrations had dropped 30 per cent in 1931.

As regards cars, Lord Leigh was more optimistic, reporting 'growing popularity' in all markets, and home sales increasing 30 per cent since the first quarter of 1931. Assets still outweighed liabilities by nearly £350,000, and Triumph was employing 3000 people – a far cry from the days when it had leased a little building in Much Park Street for £150 a year.

"I claim a future of continued progress and expansion," the chairman concluded, "built on ... honest work and fair dealing."

"The company," said shareholder A A Price, "has done everything it has been reasonably possible to do. It has been making good stuff, and if it goes on making good stuff it will retrieve the company's position and come out alright."

A dividend for preference shares was declared and the pension fund paid up. Triumph would carry on.

One obvious way to deal with falling profits was to increase volume by cutting prices. This is what Triumph did for 1932, offering seven Super Sevens well down in price from the year before. The Tickford Saloon hadn't done well and was dropped, while a 'standard' 2/4-seater was added to complement the de Luxe version, giving Triumph two cars selling at £140, the lowest price for a Super Seven in history.

1932 Super Seven	
Model (doors/passengers)	*Price*
Mark I	
Tourer (2/4)	£140
Tourer de Luxe (2/4)	£152 10s
2/4-seater (2/2+2)	£140
2/4-seater de Luxe (2/2+2)	£152 10s
Sports Two-seater (2/2)	£147 10s
Mark II	
Coachbuilt Saloon (2/4)	£150
Coachbuilt Saloon de Luxe (2/4)	£167 10s
Pillarless Saloon (4/4)	£157 10s
Pillarless Saloon de Luxe (4/4)	£169 10s

The 'Gnat' name was dropped from the Sports Two-seater, and its price was verily chopped, almost £40 from the previous year's with no change in specification except front-hinged rather than rear-hinged doors – transforming it from a high-priced sporty car to a very good buy indeed. But the most important change for 1932 was the introduction of new pillarless four-door saloons, part of the 'Mark II' Seven range.

Pillarless Triumphs first appeared in 1931 in the Scorpion range – the subject of the next chapter – though at least one 1931 Seven with this configuration is known, so the body style may have been a mid-1931 addition to the Seven line. A clever idea for such a small wheelbase, it provided maximum entry and egress from the tiny

The 1932 model Super Eight chassis and running gear was a lineal descendant of the original Super Seven, but established the front and rear semi-elliptic suspension layout which would be a feature of all Triumphs built up to 1939. Note the lever-arm dampers, and the worm-drive rear axle.

saloon body with no obstructions. That the rear doors were only 'occasional' is suggested by their lack of individual outside handles – they were also equipped with 'child locks' to prevent the kiddies from surprising dad at speed. Both standard and de Luxe models were finished in cellulose, and featured folding, adjustable bucket seats up front. The de Luxe, however, came with a four-speed gearbox, the first on a 7.9hp Triumph, along with genuine leather upholstery, electric wiper and safety glass throughout. Designer Walter Belgrove, it must be admitted, never thought much of the pillarless styles:

"On bad roads, either the doors came open or they jammed up, necessitating exit via the sliding roof!"

One of the oldest routines in the motor business is luxury down-grading, that peculiar process by which a manufacturer loads every possible goody on a long-standing model and simultaneously cuts the price. This accomplishes two things – it sparks sales, and helps use up shelf stock. Luxury down-grading was the fate of the Super Seven for model years 1933 and 1934, except that it was no longer known as a Super Seven. Triumph, finally accepting the rated horsepower it'd had from the start, called these cars the Super Eights:

1933/34 Super Eight	
Model (doors/passengers)	*Price*
1933	
Pillarless Saloon de Luxe (4/4)	£155
2/4-seater de Luxe (2/2+2)	£155
Tourer de Luxe (2/4)	£155
1934	
Pillarless Saloon de Luxe (4/4)	£175

Though the Super Seven engine was retained without change, these cars featured what Triumph called silent third gear: "the ratio selected makes it seldom necessary to change into second gear. The constant and close-ratio third-speed gears – of the double-helical type – are absolutely silent and the change between any gear is remarkably easy."

Super Eight bodies were much roomier than those of the Super Seven, particularly in the rear, where even a piece of headliner was scooped away for an added few inches of headroom. Triumph promoted them all as "coachbuilt – panelled in aluminium and produced under individual supervision." The chassis was also improved: semi-elliptic leaf springs were on all four corners (also a feature of Super Seven Mark IIs), and hydraulic dampers were mounted at the rear. Triumph loaded on every possible option as standard – leather upholstery, Leveroll adjustable front seats, winding/sliding sunroof on saloons, safety glass all round, spring gaiters, high-frequency horn, electric screen wiper,

The Southern Cross was Triumph's even more sporting replacement for the sporty Sevens, and was based on the Super Nine/Ten chassis and Coventry Climax engine, plus transmission.

chrome-plated bumpers and radiator stone guard, dipping-beam headlamps, fingertip steering controls, luggage grid, two-position (regular and reserve) petrol tap.

"The Super Eight," concluded *The Autocar,* "undoubtedly represents very high value for money."

The 1933 2/4-seater de Luxe was especially well styled, and looked like a much larger automobile. It had wider doors, a sloping tail capped by a spare wheel, adjustable metal-framed side curtains and wind wings. All three 1933 models came in either black with green trim or blue with grey trim; black wheels could be fitted in lieu of coloured ones.

1934 saw only the Pillarless saloon surviving, priced a bit higher but now featuring the four-speed gearbox and free-wheel. It had a longer bonnet, a more robust-looking body; its doors were arranged to close on a vertical axis for easier entry.

"For all its very comfortable body dimensions," said F J Camm of *The Practical Motorist,* "I found the little Triumph took to the road with a vivacity reminiscent of a sports model. Its acceleration was definitely above the average of its class, and it responded to urging with a suggestion of real eagerness ... the engine is one of the best arguments I have met with in favour of a good 'four' rather than an indifferent 'six' – there are many little details about the car's design and construction that make it exceptionally pleasant to drive. I should say the effect has been produced simply by absolute thoroughness of attention to the many minor details that go into the making of a good car, but whatever may be the secret of the Super Eight's charm, the result is an individual production, and an admirable one."

Camm found that his Super Eight would do better than the advertised maximum of 55mph, attaining 60 without labour in top, with third good for about 38mph. Petrol consumption was an impressive 43mpg, and oil consumption was nil. By now, the Super Eight was being billed as 'the car that is different,' and that it was. Indeed it was one of the most luxuriously equipped, solidly built light cars to come out of England to date. The little wonder had come a long way.

But now the way was narrowing. As heir apparent to Siegfried Bettmann, Col Holbrook commanded more and more authority over Triumph's affairs. He never particularly cared for the narrow-track, bolt-upright little Sevens and Eights, and by 1934 he had nearly eliminated them. Henceforth new models would be built, expressing Holbrook's own particular feelings about what a Triumph should be.

The Super Eights are thus the last of the line. Both model years account for perhaps 2200 of these luxurious little cats, certainly the rarest and most desirable types. But all of them were significant. Beyond their intrinsic appeal as light cars was the attitude they ushered in – that the makers of 'the quality light car' could also build machines competitive with the best of their class.

Triumph had thus far apparently weathered the Depression: though the motorcycle business was slow, the works had continued to produce upwards of 150 cars a week. Since Triumph's entry into the motor car business, 40 other companies had tried it and failed. Along with 11 other survivors – Alvis, Armstrong-Siddeley, BSA, Hillman, Humber, Lea-Francis, Riley, Rover, Singer, Standard and Swift – Triumph had continued to make a steady living in Coventry, a very logical place to build motor cars. With Holbrook pretty well running things, and the company pulling through, there was time for a breather – a new engine, several new models, and among them, Triumph's first true sports car.

This was arguably the most elegant of the neat little Super Eight range, complete with a two-door, four-seater bodyshell on a very compact wheelbase.

From Scorpion to Southern Cross

The Olympia Motor Show of 1930 saw a number of new trends in motor car design – caused, perhaps, by the deepening Depression and a need for economy, combined with an altogether understandable craving for cars that were easier to drive. Most motorists in those days tended to stick to top gear, refusing to change down, lugging up hills and overtaking with snail-like deliberation. Romance of the road aside, it was obvious that the typical driver didn't particularly enjoy changing gears. Manufacturers' approach to this problem was twofold. To encourage changing down, easy-change gearboxes of various kinds were invented; for those who still refused to change down despite all possible inducements, the industry began paying more attention to engines that pulled well in top.

By Olympia 1930 transmission design was improving rapidly, and stand after stand exhibited gearboxes that were simple to use. There was Daimler's fluid flywheel, 'with a box extraordinarily easy to handle'; the preselector gearbox, on such cars as the Armstrong-Siddeley; synchromesh, from American cars like Buick and Cadillac; freewheeling on Studebaker and Chrysler products; and 'silent third' on a number of European cars. At the same time, show-goers witnessed the surging popularity of the very small six. Wolseley's Hornet (1271cc) was the first of this breed, appearing earlier in the year; the new Triumph Scorpion (1203cc) was Priory Street's reply. Whether buyers of these suggestively named machines really 'got stung', as one Pre-1940 Triumph Owners' club stalwart earlier suggested, we will leave to the reader's conjecture. They seemed, indeed, like a good idea at the time.

Sixes had been replacing fours in the European motor industry for some years, much as eights had been replacing sixes in the United States – then a nation blessedly free from engine displacement taxes or high petrol prices. Almost every British manufacturer of note had introduced a new six of under 2-litre capacity by 1930, but Wolseley was the first to drop one to just 1.3 litres. The Hornet had sold well on introduction, and the idea of something of the same order must have appealed to Bettmann, who always championed 'the quality light car.'

The rationale of the Scorpion was simple – perhaps too simple.

There was no point, the reasoning went, in building larger-capacity fours. The 13/35 and the 15 had never sold well. With money getting tighter, people wanted economy, but it wasn't possible to make a big four run as smoothly as a small six. For one thing, rubber engine mounts had not come into general use. A six, furthermore, might provide an excellent power/weight ratio for decent performance, at a modest premium in road tax. And a good power/weight ratio would naturally minimise the need for that abominable necessity – changing gears. All this reasoning came together in the Scorpion. Though only slightly longer (5¾ inches more wheelbase) than the Super Seven, it was equipped with an engine 50 per cent larger, providing a lot more power for a little more petrol.

It's now necessary to dispense with two misconceptions about the Scorpion that are traceable to earlier works, one being this writer's. First, the small six was not, as the writer said in 1973, a device to take advantage of road tax loopholes: the RAC horsepower formula, which determined the tax, was based on total piston area (stroke length never counted, hence the long skein of British 'strokers' that continued through to the abolition of the hp tax after World War II). The Scorpion worked out to 11.85 RAC horsepower and was taxed at £12 ($60 at the time) – a healthy sum for a car its size. Second, it was not based on the Super Nine chassis and body, but rather the reverse – the Nine appeared after the Scorpion. We should study the latter as a prelude to the important Super Nine and the Ten, which followed at one-year intervals.

The Scorpion's side-valve engine, as might be expected, was derived from that of the Super Seven, using the same bore to keep the tax rating down and an 80mm stroke (5.5mm longer than the Super Seven, 3mm shorter than the Super Eight) for 1203cc. The engine was cast en bloc with the crankcase, the bottom of which was closed-off with a pressed-steel sump. Both crankshaft and camshaft ran in four bearings, the latter located at the side of the crankcase, driven by a roller chain which also powered the dynamo, adjustable for correct tension. Mushroom-end tappets were mounted in groups of four for ease of assembly, and the cylinder head was detachable. Conventional front-mounted fan and water pump were belt-driven. Heat control was provided by a thermostat concealed in the radiator header tank, which automatically opened and closed the radiator louvres. (It has been said that the connecting-rods were 'daylight-seeking' – how true we will not venture to say!)

Concerning the induction system, one reviewer noted that the ports ran "very straight, and have no tortuous passages. The inlets are so arranged that the delivery from the carburettor does not enter straight into the middle pair of cylinders, the spacing being evened out by 'siamesing' certain ports. The inlet and exhaust manifolds are of square cross-section, and the exhaust pipe drops downwards from the centre of its manifold, which provides a hot spot on the induction pipe opposite the delivery from the vertical Solex carburettor."

The rest of the specification offered no surprises and was in keeping with previous practice: six-volt coil ignition, full pressure lubrication via oil pump submerged in the sump, four Silentbloc mounts attaching engine to frame, engine and three-speed gearbox in unit and auxiliary transmission brake. A new single-dry-plate clutch was used 'to give light operation and an easy gear change.' Power was carried to the worm-drive rear axle by a two-piece propeller shaft, the latter half within a torque tube. Worm-and-wheel steering and hydraulic four-wheel brakes were, of course, de rigueur. The chassis, Super Seven-like, was a simple ladder unit of good strength with semi-elliptic springs front and rear.

Aside from its highly styled radiator grille, the Scorpion much resembled the Super Seven. A Sports Two-seater, and Coachbuilt Saloons with two and four (pillarless) doors were the initial offerings, all priced at £237 10s. The wire wheels (Dunlop Magna) were improved in appearance and strength from previous Triumph designs, with more spokes and larger-diameter hubs, the hub bolts concealed under a nave plate. The dashboard carried an interior illuminated instrument panel (speedometer, ammeter, ignition switch) and served as the mounting point for the petrol tank, carried scarily just ahead of the front passengers. Shortly added to the range was a two-door Coachbuilt Saloon de Luxe, with sliding sunroof and five duotone paint combinations. Scorpion two-door saloons featured extra-wide doors for ease of entry to the rear compartment, and all models were well trimmed throughout. The bodies were panelled in steel except for their fabric-covered roofs; setting a Triumph trend, Scorpion featured a faired-in boot instead of a tack-on afterthought, a commendable styling improvement. Safety glass and chromium plate were provided as standard.

The Scorpion was indeed a good-looking little car. As ever, the Triumph was praised for its smart finish, well above the norm for its class, and thoughtful inclusions evidencing Triumph's concern about detail – the dumb-irons, for example, were covered by a metal apron, an omission on much of the competition, and the top part of the radiator had raised ridges to harmonise with the vertical shutters underneath. The car would "undoubtedly come in for a great deal of attention," summarised one review, "because the underlying idea of it is somewhat of a new departure, whilst the appearance and general finish ... are unquestionably attractive and smart."

Triumph publicity naturally took things a bit further; in an exotic advert picturing its arachnid namesake the Scorpion was described as "silent, powerful and dignified. A full four-seater, yet compact, light and inexpensive to own and to run. If judged by road performance it stands unrivalled; if judged by appearance and outward line, it is inexpressibly beautiful ... the least expensive luxury six in existence today." Until that last line, they could have been talking about a close-coupled Darracq ...

Advertisements claimed 35mpg for the new model and, perhaps more important, 65mph by virtue of a power/weight ratio better than any previous Triumph. This made it Triumph's first 60+mph saloon car, despite a rear axle ratio (5.25:1) seemingly more useful for uprooting stumps! The configuration did, however, carry a penalty: the added engine weight upset the handling considerably, as one might imagine with a chassis weighing only 1100-odd pounds. After an initial spurt, the Scorpion did not sell well. It would last only through 1932.

Its second year did, however, see

The six-cylinder Scorpion was available with several different body styles, this being a four-door saloon of 1931.

considerable improvements, based on a design philosophy later carried to extremes across the Atlantic – it was longer, lower and wider:

Triumph Scorpion		
Model year	*1931*	*1932*
Wheelbase (in)	86 3⁄4	92¼
Length (in)	126	146
Width (in)	53	53½
Ground clearance (in)	10	8
Tyre size (in)	4x19	4.4x27
Track (in)	42	43
Price range (£)	230 to 237 10s	179 to 210

The Autocar provided this excellent 'ghosted' drawing of the six-cylinder Twelve-Six as revealed in the summer of 1932. This particular model had a permanent jacking system installed as standard.

The body design was now completely revised. There were three models: a 2/4-seater in standard and de Luxe trim and a four-door Coachbuilt Saloon. Open models similar to the 1931 Super Seven 2/4-seater, saloons forsaking pillarless construction for front-hinged doors, and the two-door saloons were abandoned. De Luxe models, at £17-19 extra, came with genuine leather upholstery (pneumatic on saloons), bow-type bumpers and, on saloons only, electric windscreen wiper. All de Luxe models were fitted with the four-speed gearbox, a somewhat dubious commentary on the pulling power of the car with the original three-speed. The facia now housed a clock, speedometer, ammeter, oil indicator and controls for choke, throttle, starting and lighting. There was a five-lamp set with dipping headlamps, finger-tip steering, electric horn, and hydraulic shock absorbers. Chassis modifications included a shift of the petrol tank (now holding 7¼ gallons) to the rear, and equipping it with an Autovac feed and two-way tap incorporating a reserve position. Scorpions were offered in an array of bright cellulose colours: black and maroon, duotone grey, black and green, blue and grey and – this suggesting all sorts of nasty comments – black and blue.

Accompanying the 1932 Scorpions was another new model, the roomy Twelve-Six, mounted on the Scorpion chassis and using the same engine. It was offered as a four-door (pillar-type) six-light saloon with winding side windows. Dimensionally almost identical to the Scorpion, the Twelve-Six offered more room in the rear by virtue of a seat set further back, and front-opening rear doors to allow easy access. To accommodate this seating change the body was built out more at the rear, the faired-in boot being eliminated and the spare tyre being mounted directly to the rear of the body. Standard (£198) and de Luxe (£214) Coachbuilt Saloons were offered, the latter with the same extras as its Scorpion counterpart. Each was only a fiver more expensive than the equivalent Scorpion, a reasonable price to pay if extra room was required.

By this time, unfortunately for the company, the small six boom was turning to bust. People were finding that the cars didn't really provide all the advantages they were thought to over

Although the Twelve-Six of 1933 was really a Scorpion by another name, it was offered with this smart coachbuilt six-light saloon car shell which, in modified form, would also find a home on Super Nine and Ten models too.

TRIUMPH "TWELVE SIX" COACHBUILT SALOON DE LUXE. 1933.

similar-displacement fours – they were thirstier and were taxed higher. Meanwhile, the widespread adoption of easy-change gearboxes eliminated the terrors of changing gears, and the advent of rubber engine mounts made the four-cylinder engine more pleasant to live with. Thus the craze ended.

It is interesting, though, that this little piece of Triumph history was to be re-enacted some 30 years later, when another small six appeared, to power the Vitesse range of saloons – and later, in 2-litre form, the successful GT6. There are more than a few instances like this in Triumph history, when a new model duplicates a much older concept with almost uncanny precision.

For the present, though, the small Triumph Six disappeared. Its last gasp was in 1933, when the Scorpion was dropped and the last sanction of Twelve-Sixes offered. Priced at £205, they were a four-door Coachbuilt Saloon, a Tourer and a 2/4-seater. In keeping with general 1933 improvements they were the most luxurious and comprehensively equipped in history – leather seats (buckets up front), sliding roof, door pockets, safety glass and single-pane windscreen, twin electric wipers, and the Saloon equipped with interior lights and carpets. At the price they were, a fair bargain, but few were built. More important by far were the new four-cylinder Triumphs, rapidly growing in performance and reputation. In 1932, the earlier Scorpion chassis was fitted with a brand-new engine, the first inlet-over-exhaust four on a Triumph, progenitor of the firm's first true sports cars. The result was the Super Nine.

If the impression has ever been given that the Super Nine was a revolutionary new model marking an entirely different approach by the company, that should be corrected right away. It was undoubtedly a product of Col Holbrook's drive for sportier machinery. Holbrook, by 1931, had set up Triumph's first serious body-design department under Frank Warner – who joined Triumph from Hillman the same year – bringing George Griffiths with him, and later attracting Bert Haddock from Rover. Walter Belgrove moved across to the design office from the experimental department about six months later, the two departments being cheek by jowl at the Briton Road end of the Clay Lane/Briton Road factory. Belgrove's special ability at that time was in preparing three-quarter perspective drawings and exploded pictorial representations – invaluable for showing top management what the styling staff had in mind.*

These stellar body engineers, joined by Bill Thornton in 1932,

This was the Super Nine chassis, complete with its Coventry Climax-designed engine, showing many design features which were shared with the Super Eight and the longer-wheelbase Scorpion/Twelve-Six chassis.

did not, however, affect Super Nine body design, which was at first much like the Super Sevens and Scorpions which preceded it. In its 2/4-seater and Coachbuilt Saloon form, the Nine was a lookalike to the Scorpion, the only obvious change being a somewhat shorter bonnet/cowl to accommodate its four-cylinder engine. It used the 1931-model Scorpion chassis with 86¾in wheelbase, giving it a length of about 12 inches less.

We can therefore dispense with a discussion of early Super Nine chassis and bodies, and move on to the most important feature: its 1018cc engine with a familiar bore/stroke measurement of 60 x 90mm, which was a Coventry Climax design. Located only a mile from the Triumph works, Climax was an obvious source of new engines, and Triumph – business being slow – could not afford to design them on its own. Neither, for that matter, did it have the appropriate staff with engine-design expertise at that stage in their development. Manufacturing them was going to be another problem, too, as Triumph didn't have much capacity there either – and that may be the reason the early units were built on a proprietary basis while Triumph itself kept producing the older side-valve fours and sixes through 1933. Ultimately, the transition would be made, with Triumph building nothing but IOE engines after 1933.

Climax was responsible for the IOE pattern – exhaust valves on the side, pushrod-operated inlet valves overhead, the crankshaft running in three main bearings. The cylinder head was detachable, the pushrod mechanism had its own detachable cover, and the

---

*Frank Warner left Triumph for Humber-Hillman in 1933, relieved by Bill Thornton, who departed in 1935, first to join Lea-Francis but very shortly to move on to SS. There he remained William Lyons' chief body engineer for more than 30 years. Walter Belgrove, who had been with Triumph since the Super Seven period, took over as chief body engineer early in 1935, answering to technical chief Donald Healey, whom Claude Holbrook had hired in September 1933.

sparking plugs were located over the exhaust valves and combustion chambers. As per Scorpion practice, the camshaft and dynamo were driven by the same chain, adjustable by dynamo position. But from the start the Super Nine had 12-volt coil ignition – the original Scorpion had only six volts but switched to twelve in 1932. The carburettor was a Solex 'self-starting' type, fed by a Petrolift electric pump from the rear-mounted 5½-gallon fuel tank, fitted with the usual reserve tap. The engine was bolted to an aluminium housing for the flywheel and single-dry-plate clutch, and then coupled to a proper four-speed gearbox – the first all-new model to appear with the four-speed. The low-ratio worm-drive rear axle was retained, driven by a split propeller shaft. Lockheed hydraulic brakes were fitted, together with Scorpion-style wire wheels.

Priced from £197 10s, these first Super Nines were rated at 8.9hp and capable of about 55mph. But they were soon joined by a sports car that would do about 15mph better than that, its name inspired from the heavenly constellation lighting Triumph's best export market: the Southern Cross.

It looked a little high-bodied for a sporting car, and it retained four seats (the rear seats, placed high above the axle, were often covered with a tonneau), but the Southern Cross was still a rakish proposition compared with what had gone before. The aluminium-panelled body is said to have been designed by Ratcliffe of London, Triumph agents at the time, though Patrick Motors of Birmingham has incorrectly claimed design authorship on the basis of a special coupé model it offered at the same time. (Triumph agencies, as we have noted, took considerable interest in the product, often fitting it with their own special bodies.) Southern Cross bodies were all built by Salmons and Sons in Newport Pagnell, who at the same time was applying its patented Tickford drophead style to Super Sevens. The initial price of £225 was quite reasonable, and included extensive standard equipment: flexible 18-inch four-spoke steering wheel, folding one-piece windscreen, dual electric wipers, carpeting, chromium-plated stoneguard and a thorough array of instruments including rev-counter. Duotone red and green were the first colours offered. Later in the 1932 model year an 1122cc version of the engine was made optional, an exceptionally squarish configuration for the time (63 x 90mm), rated at 10hp. Apparently the 10hp cars were not produced in great quantity for 1932, though the following year this was the only way a Southern Cross was equipped. (In 1934, the model changed finally to the 62 x 90mm engine.)

Motor Sport tested the 'New Sports Nine' in June 1932, praising its "robust chassis and excellent detail arrangement, in which nothing is skimped because the car is small ..." Their mean maximum speed was 64mph, which they considered low, the car not having been run-in. Acceleration was decidedly underwhelming, 0-40 coming up in no less than 18 seconds. "On second and third gear 30mph and 40mph can be reached, first gear not being normally required at all. The roadholding and cornering is very good, the suspension ... an effective compromise between comfort at low speeds and steadiness when travelling fast. The steering has avoided the modern tendency for ultra-low gearing, and gives very precise control as a result ... The whole car is a thoroughly high-classed production which should strongly appeal to the motorist who wants a car really economical both in running and in upkeep under the hardest condition."

Midway in the model year, early January 1933, Triumph produced another new range of standard passenger cars using the 10hp engine, simultaneously putting a halt to the unprofitable Twelve-Six. The Triumph Ten was a counter to typical practice in being a derivation of the sporting model, rather than vice versa. Initially, "solid support of the doors," one tester noted (referring surely to the flimsier pillarless saloons), "must help." As usual this Triumph was well appointed inside, with all the features already mentioned including leather upholstery, winding windows, sunroof and full instrumentation.

We have now fully described the new four-cylinder Triumphs for 1932 and 1933, but before delving into their road performance it is useful to summarise them here – if only because things were getting a bit confusing by this time. In 1932, remember, the range

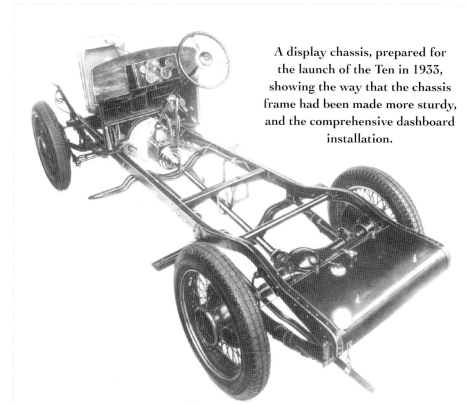

A display chassis, prepared for the launch of the Ten in 1933, showing the way that the chassis frame had been made more sturdy, and the comprehensive dashboard installation.

also included a variety of Super Sevens, Scorpions and the Twelve-Six; in 1933, it was Super Eights only of the old generation, except for the balance of Twelve-Sixes, which ended with the introduction of the Ten.

Model	Super Nine	Southern Cross 9	Southern Cross 10	Ten
Appeared	Aug '31	Aug '31	June '32	Jan '33
Model years	1932-33	1932	1932-33	1933
Capacity (cc)	1018	1018	1122	1122
B x S (mm)	60x90	60x90	63x90	63x90
Rated hp	8.9	8.9	9.8	9,8
Wheelbase (in)	87	87	87	96
Body styles	saloon, 2/4-seater	sports	sports	saloon, 2/4-seater

Documenting contemporary performance of the early Southern Cross has to be based partly on more modern experience, because no tests of that model appeared in 1932 or 1933. An approximation can be gleaned from Triumph's own technical data book for 1934, and from two tests of the Super Nine and Ten carried out by *The Autocar* within weeks of each other early in 1933. Surprisingly, Triumph's figures are considerably more pessimistic than *The Autocar*'s.

Testers found the Super Nine an excellent performer with miserly fuel consumption – 35mpg. "The machine does not feel over-bodied, the higher speeds being reached quite rapidly, and in normal driving ... the car is really lively ... The ordinary kind of hill is taken without effort; the car even accelerating up slopes on top gear." Tests showed 45mph to be a comfortable cruising

The Super Nine 2/4-seater Sports Tourer of 1933 had similar lines to the last of the Super Sevens.

speed (which it never was in the Super Seven or Super Eight!), and the gear change was rated 'extremely good.' The Nine would reach 50mph in third if pressed, though it was happier going to 40; it could pull away strongly in top, accelerating from 10 to 30 in 16 seconds, which wasn't bad for hardly more than a litre of displacement. Handling was considered light, brakes excellent and cornering steady. The ride was comfortable, except for "a certain tendency to fore-and-aft movement when a surface is not good."

The Ten, tested just a month later, naturally performed better, but its larger body did not follow that tendency of cars in its class to wallow and sway over winding roads under full load.

"The Triumph ... remains remarkably steady at all speeds, so that there is no need to watch the road surface and choose the easier ways ... At any speeds over 25 to 30mph it's as smooth as anyone could wish for ... If there is a periodic vibration it is so slight that its existence passes unnoticed. Response to the accelerator is immediate, and general flexibility is such that gear-changing is seldom necessary except for hill-climbing purposes. The engine ... will stand many laps of Brooklands track at full speed without signs of flagging."

Despite a high 5.75:1 compression ratio, the Ten did not pink when pressed hard on grades, and its maximum speed was high enough to permit cruising at over 50mph. Here are *The Autocar*'s performance figures, compared with Triumph's own data for the 1934 10hp Southern Cross:

1933 TRIUMPH NINE

This subtly shaded cutaway drawing of the 1933 Coventry Climax-engined Nine showed details of the first Triumph to use this advanced power unit.

	The Autocar		Triumph
Model	'33 Super Nine	'33 Ten	34 Southern Cross
Top speed	61.22mph	64.29mph	65mph
10 to 30 in 3rd	9.6 secs	9.6 secs	11.0 secs
10 to 30 in 4th	16.0 secs	14.0 secs	17.0 secs
20 to 40 in 3rd	11.6 secs	11.4 secs	13.0 secs
20 to 40 in 4th	17.6 secs	17.4 secs	19.0 secs
Hill test*	6.0 secs	4.4 secs	–
*Brooklands Test Hill, 15 yds, l-in-5, standing start.			

Why does the lighter Southern Cross compare so unfavourably? First, no two testers ever achieve the same results. Second, *The Autocar* doubtless sampled cars that were at least partly run-in; Triumph's figures may have been based on a car fresh off the line. One 1933 owner's experience, and modern-day driving of one, suggests that the Southern Cross could achieve 70mph when pressed, and this would mean clipping several seconds off the above acceleration times. If the Super Nine could be cruised at 45mph and the Ten at 50, it must have been possible to cruise at a mile-a-minute in the Southern Cross. But whatever figures one accepts, one must conclude that the new cars were excellent performers for their displacement, and that the Southern Cross was a true dual-purpose competition-pleasure automobile. The Triumph sports car had been born.

Testimonials to the achievement were not long in arriving. In June 1934, a reader of *The Autocar* wrote to praise his 1933 Southern Cross after 12,500 miles with no sign of wear. Petrol consumption was a pleasing 30mpg, oil consumption 1500mpg, the car kept its tune well and provided vivid acceleration.

Some performance figures were stated which might augment our conclusions above: "The maximum revs, advised according to the red mark on the rev counter, are 4600-4900rpm, and I have

The spaciousness of the six-light four-door saloon bodyshell of the Super Ten is evident in this view. Cars of this period tended to have much more generous rear seat space than those cars which followed in post-war years.

found the engine capable of climbing to this figure (70mph in top). The real charm of this car is undoubtedly its effortless performance, there being an almost entire lack of vibration and mechanical noise throughout the car's range, and it is a machine with which a really good average can be maintained."

The arrival of the Ten and Southern Cross marked an end to the old generation of cars that had its basis in the Super Seven and the Scorpion, though important evolutionary changes had occurred over the years. Both new models would last into model year 1934, though nearly eclipsed by the next series of motor cars that year. They were offered in a wider range of styles, including a price-leader, the Popular Saloon (£198), a Tourer (£215) and a closed Southern Cross (£225) – the only example of this unlikely configuration. Strangely – for it didn't change the annual tax at all – the 1934 models had their bore reduced to 62mm (1087cc, 9.5 rated hp), to reduce displacement enough to fall below the 1100cc limit, then an important racing-class boundary.

The Popular Saloon was based entirely on the standard 10hp saloon, with certain cost-cutting deletions – fixed roof instead of sunroof, centre gear change, smaller headlamps and no bumpers, gaiters or spare-wheel cover. The regular Ten saloon, the Tourer, and the 2/4-seater continued basically in 1933 form, with the addition of freewheel pre-selection by remote control (not offered on the Popular model), an automatic starting system and Biflex headlamps.

The 1934 Southern Cross Sports Saloon was designed by Bill Thornton – an attractive little two-door offered at the same price as the open version, though not selling heavily. There was a flush-fitting sliding sunroof, Protectoglass throughout, stainless-steel radiator shell, genuine leather upholstery, dual wipers, quick-wind windows, even a curved top windscreen. Basically the car was equipped like the larger Coachbuilt Saloon. Seemingly attractive? Perhaps, but it never caught on with the public. Maybe buyers could see no need for a close-coupled model when the basic Ten offered so much more room.

The Southern Cross Tourer for 1934 was generally unchanged in specification from 1933, except for the minute displacement decrease. Neither it nor its closed version provided freewheeling as standard, though this was part of the Ten saloon specification. The Southern Cross and Ten for 1933/34, incidentally, featured the Stevenson centralised jacking system, another example of Triumph's attention to detail. The mechanism was a simple affair – one inserted a jack handle at the side of the car, which linked to a ratchet lift that mounted centrally and lifted the entire car free of its wheels.

Triumph's financial condition by this time had worsened considerably. Though it had handily survived the initial depressed years of 1930 and 1931, the firm's fortunes nose-dived in 1932, and continued to plunge ever downward. The fiscal year ending August 1932 left Triumph with a sickening deficit of £145,856. This was also the last year dividends were paid to preference shareholders – ordinary shareholders had not had a dividend since 1930. The sale of the bicycle business to Coventry Bicycles in 1932 – against Bettmann's strong objections – had failed to improve anything. Motorcycles were still selling poorly, and Col Holbrook was in favour of dropping them as well – making or breaking the company with larger, sporty, more luxurious motor cars. Predictably, this didn't sit well at all with Bettmann, who favoured the light type of vehicle Triumph had built thus far. Apparently Holbrook had more directors on his side, and Bettmann turned the job over to him in 1933, retiring on April 18, his 70th birthday.

Beaten but hardly bowed, the founder of Triumph received lusty testimony from nearly everyone in the motor industry, who paid him homage at a Birmingham luncheon on May 1. Mayor Oliver M Flynn of Coventry presided, praising Bettmann's accomplishments and handing him an album autographed by nearly everyone of importance in the city. *The Autocar's* scribe wished him well, too, saying he found it hard to believe that Siegfried still looked so young, and quoting Emerson, "we do not count a man's years until he has nothing else to count."

Siegfried had a great deal to count besides his years: his long period at the helm, during which Triumph was generally successful; his standing in Coventry, where he was the first non-Briton to be elected mayor; the fact that he would continue to be involved with Triumph, as vice-chairman of the board. But underneath it all was the fact that he had been displaced, against his own wishes, and he didn't like it. It is fit to give him his due in this regard, by quoting from his memoirs.

Bettmann had no complaint with the money spent on expansion (Triumph had bought a factory in Briton Road, behind Clay Lane, in 1932 and its Coventry properties were six times their original size by the beginning of 1933), but he did feel his displacement had more to do with the general economic climate than any personal faults:

"After the boom follows the slump; the Triumph Company was struck by it. Although under the old management the company had large sums of money at its credit in the Bank and also large investments, it all disappeared and the company was obliged to obtain from the bank a considerable overdraft." (A debenture, favouring Lloyds Bank, London, taken out in 1933.) "I have a suspicion that Holbrook was of the opinion that I was in the way of success; without my knowledge he had arranged with the general manager of Lloyds Bank in London to send an accountant to investigate the firm's affairs." (This was Howe Graham.) "They all – the general manager of the Bank, the accountant and Holbrook – came to the conclusion that the man who prevented successful trading was I, with the result that I had to give up the managing directorship and become vice-chairman of the company. It was proposed that I should become chairman, but this I declined as I did not think it fair to ask Lord Leigh to resign, although I am sure that he would not have minded a bit doing so. The improvement imagined by my successors which would follow my retirement did not take place ..."

In this Bettmann was quite correct – but there's a great deal of irony in the events that followed. Beginning in 1934, Triumph would offer really brilliant motor cars, while the financial side would keep on sliding. In the golden age from 1934 to 1939, Triumphs would run up great achievements in rallies, and dismal records on the shares exchange. Exactly why this occurred will in due course become apparent. But, in a sense, Triumph was not unlike many other companies in the thirties. While building some of the finest cars in its history between 1934 and 1939, it was moving rapidly toward bankruptcy and oblivion.

Today it is those cars that are remembered and appreciated, not the balance sheets, and this is as it should be. The new generation which began with the Triumph Gloria was a memorable one indeed.

The Smartest Cars
in the Land

In January 1935, the locals said Umea, Sweden, was balmy. But a frigid wind whipped off the Gulf of Bothnia, chilling young Jack Ridley to the bone. Here in northern Sweden, just 200 miles from the Arctic Circle, was his starting point for the 1935 Monte Carlo Rally. With co-driver Roger Thacker, Ridley was to pilot a works Triumph in an attempt to better the firm's 1934 performance, which wasn't bad: the year before, Triumph had entered seven cars, and all seven finished. But they hadn't totally dominated the Light Car Class (up to 1500cc) against numerous competitors from Salmson, Peugeot, Lancia, Simca, Riley and Fiat. This time, Jack Ridley vowed things would be different.

Off they went, south-east along rugged but remarkably snow-free roads to Sundsvall, Stockholm and Helsingborg. Crossing the narrow Oresund to Copenhagen, Ridley's odometer showed 833 miles. A mere fraction of the route! Still, it had been easier than he'd expected, though many of the roads were narrow and hazardous, some of them mere tracks across barren wasteland.

The ferry ploughed through an ice field that closed solidly in its wake. More ferries, more icy waters, and they gained the Danish mainland. Now very deep snow was encountered.

"Once the wheels were off the beaten track," the factory later reported, "the cars sank in anything up to six feet of snow."

At swastika-bedecked Hamburg, the 1150-mile point, just short of half-way, Ridley and Thacker were on time and miraculously unscathed. In Hanover they checked the oil – down just half a quart after 1246 tortuous miles. Unbelievable! Ridley's expression "did justice to Eddie Cantor at his best." On to Brussels, then Paris. Jack fell asleep amidst the din of a French cafe, roused himself and embarked for Lyons. From there it was a relatively easy run to Avignon, Brignoles and finally Monte Carlo – in four days and five nights, Ridley and Thacker had crossed 2350 of the hardest miles in Europe.

At Avignon, where the other starting points eventually converged, Ridley uncorked his ace-in-the-hole for the driving tests at the finish: a centric supercharger. This helpful gadget was thought of late, and had no permanent fittings to allow installation at Umea, so Ridley had held back until the last minute to fit it. Jury-rigging the blower to an open chain drive from the crankshaft, he raced into Monte Carlo to take on Humfrey Symons' blown MG N-type and other assorted class rivals. Symons' steering jammed, but Jack merely chewed up a few gears. Result: a Light Car Class win for Triumph, and second place overall in The Riviera Cup was safe for the second year in succession. (Actually Jack could have taken all the marbles, had he only known he was but 0.6 seconds behind the big 5¼-litre Lahaye/Quatresous Renault.)

His teammates were also successful: Mlle Simone de Forest and Mme Odette Siko, two intrepid lady drivers, had arrived in Monte Carlo without losing a single mark, taking third in the Ladies Cup. But when Jack received his bauble from Col Lindsey Lloyd, in front of the Royal Palace of Monaco, everyone knew it had been his rally.

The 1935 Monte Carlo was the culmination of weeks, months and years of hard preparation by Triumph of Coventry – and probably the high point in the firm's prewar competition career. The cars responsible for the victory were ideally named. We speak, of course, of the Triumph Glorias – 'The smartest cars in the land'.

Its maker also called it 'Queen of Cars' and, allowing for typical hyperbole, it wasn't far wrong. The Gloria was indeed a queen among motor cars – lithe, low, fast, graceful in motion or standing still. It was not a masculine car, like a blower Bentley; its forte was grace and precision – and granitic strength. Years later, when the Classic Car Club of America added the Gloria Six to its distinguished list of greats*, the marque received a deserved tribute. Had it met CCCA's exacting criteria for base price, the Gloria Four might have made the list as well. In every sense of the word, Gloria was a thoroughbred.

To design this new breed of Triumph, Claude Holbrook had

---

*Some semantical variations: in America, the word 'classic' denotes 1925-48 cars recognised as such by CCCA, while 'vintage' is a generic term applied to any historic vehicle of high pedigree. In Britain 'classic' is the generic, while 'Vintage' applies only to cars built from 1919 through 1930. This book distinguishes the terms by capitalising the American 'Classic' and the British 'Vintage'.

rapidly built up his staff. Even in 1932, when Triumph had briefly held talks with Rover (who then built its cars in Coventry) about a merger, which failed because neither Bettmann, Holbrook, nor the Rover directors could agree on who should be the captain of the ship, it had also talked at length to Riley on the same subject. The industrial climate, we recall, was pretty grim at the time, and none of Coventry's independent concerns had finances in a very healthy state.

Col Claude Holbrook was one of Triumph's top bosses in the 1920s and 1930s.

Donald Healey reunited with a Triumph Southern Cross, in the 1980s.

The talks with Riley came to nothing (nor would they get much further in 1938 when Riley finally went broke), but at about this time there was an influx of staff from that concern. Captain Charles Ridley arrived to become works manager, and his son Charles Ridley Junior took over as foreman in the experimental chassis-testing shops. Jack Ridley and Lew Pearce also joined in 1933 – as testers and also as competition drivers – along with a balding young man, with a most vigorous outlook on life, called Donald Healey. Another ex-Riley man was Bill Thornton, who would become Triumph's chief body designer for a period after Frank Warner's departure, and who would later move to join William Lyons at SS Cars after a short tenure at Lea-Francis.

Donald M Healey didn't design the first Gloria – he'd signed on as experimental manager when it was about to appear – but he certainly had a lot to do with its early competition success and subsequent development. Born in 1898 and raised in Perranporth, Cornwall, he took an early interest in motors. Apprenticed to the Sopwith Aviation Company at Brooklands, young Healey had a first-hand look at Britain's splendid closed road circuit, which could only have increased his ardour. After a wartime stint in the Royal Flying Corps he returned home to Perranporth to open his own garage.

Healey began entering local competitions almost immediately, in a six-cylinder Buick and an air-cooled ABC – but his real rally career began in 1924, when he entered a 10hp Riley 'Redwing' in a London MCC trial. Here, he first became acquainted with disaster: on the journey to London the Riley caught fire and burned to a cinder. Healey shot back to Cornwall for his trusty ABC, reached the rally start in time, and took a gold medal. The same year he

and his father won the MCC Land's End Trial with an Ariel, a feat Donald repeated in 1925, in 1926 with a Fiat, and in 1927 with a Rover!

Donald Healey's first Triumph victory was on the 1930 Brighton Rally, in a supercharged Super Seven. He had seen Monte action in 1929, missing the time limit by two minutes but he came back to finish seventh in his Seven the following year. He drove Invictas for the next three Montes, winning outright in 1931. Late in 1933, he joined Riley, where he engaged in experimental work and made friends with Victor Leverett, who would later accompany him to Triumph and ultimately help apply Riley power to his Healey car. Donald arrived at the Triumph works in September 1933, where he fitted in immediately.

Walter Belgrove recalls, "Healey was a great enthusiast. He had the personality to get the best out of a very good engineering team. My direct association with him was a happy one and he needs no publicity from me – his record in the industry is sufficient."

Though Healey never met Siegfried Bettmann, he was fond of Col Holbrook, whom he calls "a fine gentleman, not an engineer but a good leader. I enjoyed working for him."

Another man Healey remembers with affection was Charles Ridley (Jack's father), Triumph's general manager: "Charles came from Riley and originated the Gloria range. He was responsible for my going from Riley to Triumph."

As for designer Belgrove, Healey shares mutual admiration: "I have a great opinion of Walter – he was probably the first real 'stylist'. We had always used engineers before to style the cars."

To my co-author, Graham Robson, in *The Story of Triumph*

Sports Cars, Healey revealed his reasons for coming to Triumph: "I was attracted by the Gloria project, which looked better than Riley's own Nine. I also had good friends at Triumph – particularly Gordon Parnell, who was then chief designer. After I talked to Charles … I had an interview with Col Holbrook and it was decided … My first job was cleaning up the Gloria range, which was just about ready for production. There was no technical director as such. I reported direct to Charles Ridley for a time, and after about a year became technical director myself."

Charles' son Jack, whose driving Healey respected, was made competitions manager. Holbrook now had a solid, enthusiastic team willing to pursue his sporting programme; moreover, people like Healey and the Ridleys brought a lot of expertise which Holbrook needed. The relationship was a good one all round, for Holbrook, Bettmann's reservations aside, was respected almost universally.

The Autocar's famed scribe typified the view of most of Holbrook's colleagues, describing him as "a pleasant business man with a strong strain of the sportsman in him. He has a merry twinkle in his eyes, and an enthusiasm which carries one along with him. He strikes me as a man who would accept his engineers' assurances that a design was right without forcing his own opinions upon them, but would hold them to it if trouble started. He seems very well liked by everyone in the Triumph organisation, and by all others with whom he comes in contact."

Holbrook introduced the new Gloria line in the autumn of 1933 with a declaration: "I believe that the combination of style, performance and price embodied in the Triumph Gloria results in the typical English car. Production is limited to the extent that every Triumph Gloria is a special car." The Gloria, he said, was "built to an idea … modern in conception, revealing lines of distinction that have never before been achieved."

The Gloria was distinctive. Only by standing alongside one, or viewing factory photographs where people are shown with the cars, can one realise how breathtakingly low and handsome the car really was. Frank Warner's styling was an abrupt departure from Triumph practice of the Bettmann years. Instead of strong but small machines known mainly for their complete equipment and sound engineering, Triumphs were now rakishly beautiful as well, comparing favourably with the best of their competition: Riley, SS, Alvis and others. At the same time, they relied on many proven components of outside manufacturers, including chassis frame, gearbox and axles. The engine, if Triumph-built, was Coventry Climax-designed, and Climax supplied the raw castings. Brakes were by Lockheed, the starting system by Lucas' Startix.

To this writer, the Gloria concept strongly suggests that of America's Jordan – another middle-priced 'assembled car' put together slowly with consummate skill, and sold on the basis of its individuality and exceptional performance. The Jordan had just gone into history by the time the first Gloria arrived – and 1933 was an inauspicious time to introduce any new car – but the idea was the same. Unfortunately, it would prove to be as unsuccessful for Triumph's balance sheets as it had been for Jordan's. But in the meantime the world was treated to an exceptional motor car.

By the time of its public launch, facilities at the Clay Lane works were being expanded considerably. The facade at the Briton Road end of the building had been built, and the important body drawing office had been removed to a new site below ground level, but – as it transpired – this would be a short stay due to the move to the new factory in Holbrooks Lane at the beginning of 1935.

At this time, completed rolling chassis were driven the short distance along Binley Road from the seven-storey Priory Street factory (near the city centre, and still mostly concentrating on

This is how Triumph advertised the arrival of the new range of Glorias, prior to the Olympia (London) Motor Show of 1933.

Detail of the unique and ingenious way in which Gloria Tourers were provided with the option of high-sided doors, or a sportingly cutaway type instead.

TRIUMPH "GLORIA" SPEED MODEL 4-SEATER
Remote Control Free-wheel Pre-selection (Optional).

Triumph 9.53 h.p. four cylinder engine 62 mm. bore by 90 mm. stroke, capacity 1087 c.c., specially tuned and with high compression cylinder head, inlet-over-exhaust valves, polished ports, three-point resilient engine mounting. Pressure feed lubrication, 3-bearing crankshaft. Lucas automatic starting system. Two "Easy Start" downdraught carburetters. Radiator of stainless steel. Four speed gear with Silent Third. Free-wheel pre-selection by remote control with automatic reverse gear connector. Frame outswept and underslung at rear providing level floor. Silent helical bevel drive. Hydraulic 4-wheel brakes. Semi-elliptic springs. Rear petrol tank. Dunlop Tyres 4.75—18 ins. (Five). Permanently fitted jacks to front and rear axles.

Coachbuilt Sports body panelled in aluminium, two wide doors, bucket seats in front and wide rear seat upholstered in finest quality leather. Enclosed luggage compartment at rear of body.

Complete equipment is provided. Finish : for colours see page 12. Track, 4 ft., wheelbase, 9 ft., ground clearance, 6¾ ins. Treasury rating 9.53 h.p. Tax £10. **Price** (at Works) **£285**

Triumph "Gloria" Dolomite Special Speed Model 2-Seater.

Similar specification to the above model. The engine is specially selected and is fitted with high compression cylinder head, high lift cams, larger valves, polished ports and the car is specially prepared throughout. This super-tuned speed model has phenomenal acceleration and is capable of maintaining exceptionally high average speeds over long distances. **Price** (at Works) **£500**

This original 1933 Gloria Speed Model advertisement is important, if only for the news of a then-mythical 'Dolomite' model, which was to have been sold for £500, but was in fact never put on the market. That particular project was de-tuned, redeveloped, and put on the market as the 1934 Southern Cross.

motorcycle production) to the Clay Lane/Briton Road plant, for partial completion, road test out to the east side of the city, and then for completion in the Clay Lane body shop.

Walter Belgrove recalls that at this stage Triumph never panelled its own bodies, though the ash frameworks were assembled at Clay Lane.

"Initially some were panelled in Chilvers Coton (not far from Nuneaton)," he told us, "but the main contractor was Henry Caton Ltd of Paynes Lane, Coventry. Production frames were dispatched to this concern where they were panelled in 16 SWG Birmabright aluminium alloy. The panels were usually wheeled, beaten and fitted first to steel-reinforced slave bodies."

It is also interesting to hear of the main suppliers of parts – which confirms what we have said about this generation of Triumphs really being assembled cars.

Chassis frames came from Rubery Owen in Darlaston, Staffs; front and rear wings, plus bonnets, came from Forward Radiator, Birmingham; radiators and shells usually came from Coventry Radiator & Presswork, Canley; engine castings came from Coventry Climax's own suppliers; and gearboxes and axles both came from ENV.

'Quality before everything else' was the slogan as Gloria premiered at Olympia in October 1933. The Super Eights and Tens were continued – for the time being – but the emphasis was naturally on 'the car that is different'. Fours and Sixes were offered, the former with the 9.5hp engine from the Super Nine and Ten: 1087cc, 40bhp at 4500rpm in standard form; 46bhp at 4600rpm

in 'Special' guise, with twin carburettors, high-compression cylinder head, high-lift cam, large valves and polished ports. The Six, displacing 1476cc, had the same 90mm stroke, while its bore was reduced to 59mm to undercut the Treasury rating of 13 RAC horsepower. Fours were mounted on a 108-inch wheelbase, Sixes on a 116, the difference being ahead of the cowl, making for a long and graceful bonnet on the latter. Though the six-cylinder engine shared the connecting-rods and valve gear of the Four, its crankshaft ran in four instead of three main bearings. It had lower compression, a larger sump and more horsepower and torque – 52bhp and 70lb/ft in the Special version.

The Gloria chassis was conventional – leaf springs at each corner, underslung at the rear, and cross-braced cruciform framework dipping under the floorboards and rear axle line to allow low-profile styling. My co-author has noted that the underslung characteristic remained a detail of Triumph styling right on through the postwar 1800/2000 Roadsters, being eliminated on later TRs by the criticism that it imposed too limited a movement on the rear wheels.

Glorias featured big, 12-inch hydraulic brakes, supplemented by a cable-linked handbrake operating on the rear wheels. Engine, single-dry-plate clutch and gearbox were carried in a unit on a flexible mounting. The ENV gearbox, featuring a free-wheel that automatically cut out if reverse was selected, was distinguished by an excellent remote change – Triumph's first.

One reviewer called it "one of the neatest things of its kind yet produced ... There are no unsightly gate notches or grease-covered hemispheres in view, and this appears to be as effective in practice as it is in appearance."

There was still no synchromesh, though the idea had by now spread to Britain – Triumph stressed instead its 'silent third', in which third and top gears were in constant-mesh, making changes relatively easy.

The drive was taken through an open propeller-shaft to a new banjo rear axle featuring spiral-bevel gears, Triumph having parted with its faithful friend, worm-drive. A 10.5-gallon petrol tank was slung on the rear, twin six-volt batteries were carried ahead of the rear axle and Burman-Douglas screw-and-nut steering was provided.

The styling of these cars was admirable and in many ways singular. A feature unique to Triumph was Frank Warner's clever combination of cut-down and conventional doors on tourers: a hinged section could be swung down on the inside of the door, or erected for weather protection. (This feature was patented, which explains why it was unique to Triumph.) Enthusiasts are divided on which configuration looks better today, but Triumph was certainly the only manufacturers to provide a choice at the time! There was little to fault in the comfort category on the luxurious

The star of the newly-launched Gloria range was the Speed Model Tourer, shown here in six-cylinder form with Miss Gloria, a well-known model of the day, at the wheel.

the size of a golf ball." Putting that on a radiator must have taken a brain the size of a golf ball, too. No matter ...

On the subject of nomenclature it is also worth noting that the name 'Dolomite' was first coined for a 1934 Gloria, and not, as many assume, for the straight-eight car which followed later. Derived from the rugged Italian mountains known to many a rally driver, the term was applied to a 'Gloria Dolomite Special Speed Model Tourer' in early 1934 catalogues. Priced at £500, this model was to be fitted with a super-tuned high-compression 1232cc engine and 'specially prepared throughout', offering 'phenomenal acceleration.' But it never appeared in production.

What is it like to drive a Triumph Gloria? It's a pleasant experience! Entering through wide, forward-opening doors, one drops into comfortable, leather, semi-bucket seats, set well down inside the body. There's a great sense of security, whether in motion or standing still. The remote-control gear change is easy to hand, an array of white on black instruments is spread across the facia, and one grabs a hefty, large-diameter wheel.

Next, one deals with the Startix: insert ignition key and turn toward 'auto'. If it's feeling good, the gadget will start the car. If you happen to be out of petrol, Startix is smart enough to stop trying, and emits a series of patient clicks to remind you of your stupidity. There are no pushbuttons, floor starter pedals, or other uncivilised contraptions; the whole unit works with simple solenoids. Startix, it seems, was mainly designed to eliminate the fear of sudden stalls in traffic.

The engine warms readily and moves the car off smartly, though the rate of progress varies with the individual car and driver. Here are some typical performance figures:

saloons. Against a nicely finished wooden dash was ranged a comprehensive set of instruments: petrol gauge, combination oil pressure/temperature gauge, speedometer and clock. A rev-counter was included on Specials. Gloria upholstery was in Vaumol leather over pneumatic seats. In the American sense, the cars were 'loaded' – there was safety glass throughout, Biflex headlamps, permanently fitted DWS jacks front and rear, a metal cover for the spare wheel, door locks, oil-filter elements, twin windscreen wipers, spring gaiters and a full set of tools. Saloons featured sliding sunroofs and rope pulls. The option list was small: Dunlop Fort tyres (£3 15s); extra spare wheel/tyre with cover (£8); and a Brooklands steering wheel by Ashby (£2 15s).

People have always been fascinated (without reason, as it turns out) over the origins of the Gloria name. In 1935, a dealer catalogue stated that "forty years ago the Triumph Company made a pedal cycle named the Gloria. Then followed the Triumph motorcycle which, with a Gloria sidecar, was regarded as a combination *par-excellence* by all knowledgeable motorcyclists. Today Triumph Gloria cars carry on the fine traditions ..."

But romantics liked to link the name with Selfridge's attractive model, Miss Gloria, who was conveniently photographed with the cars and presented with a Six Tourer. Some even suggested a liaison between this lovely girl and a Triumph director, which is hard to prove one way or the other. Miss Gloria's presence was probably just a lucky coincidence, of which Triumph took PR advantage. Historian Glyn Lancaster-Jones, who has thoroughly investigated the girl-car relationship, notes that "a mascot was made, which seems to have been an 'extra' as I have never heard of one on a surviving car. It was Gloria's head with flowing hair, and was about

	Gloria Four Standard Special		Gloria Six Standard Special	
	Saloon	Tourer	Saloon	Tourer
Top speed, mph	65	75	70-75	75
10 to 30 in 3rd, secs	11.0	8.5	9.0	8.5
10 to 30 in top, secs	17.0	15.0	15.0	14.0
20 to 40 in 3rd, secs	12.5	8.0	8.0	8.0
0 to 50, secs	26.4	-	19.8*	-
*From The Autocar. Other figures are Triumph's.				

You double-clutch, of course. With the free-wheel locked in, however, gear-changing becomes a matter of sloppy indifference. Big brakes pull the car down well and the steering is precise and untroubled by road shock. The Six takes much less changing than the Four, pulls well in nearly every gear and will ascend 1-in-10 hills in top. The car corners with stability and rides well, the springing a nice combination between firmness and comfort, with no side-sway or pitching. You will probably conclude, as most testers and this writer did, that Glorias were exceptionally roadable cars for their day. As a bonus you'll enjoy excellent fuel consumption: about 35mpg for the Four, up to 28mpg for the Six.

Counting the Donald Healey-designed Monte Carlo Tourer introduced in January 1934, there were seven Gloria models slotted into the highly competitive field from £285 to £340. The Four was up against rivals like the MG Magna (£285) and Riley Imp (£298), the Six against the 1.5-litre Singer (£285) and the Riley Lynx (£348). They probably cost a little more than Holbrook had intended, but nowhere was it suggested that they failed to provide value for money.

1934 Gloria		
Model (doors/passengers)	Wheelbase (in)	Price
Four, 9.5hp		
Standard 4-light Saloon (4/4)	108	£285
Special 4-light Saloon (4/4)	108	£300
Special Tourer (2/4)	108	£285
Four, 10.8hp		
Monte Carlo Tourer (2/4)	108	£325
Six, 12.9hp		
Standard 4-light Saloon (4/4)	116	340
Special 4-light Saloon (4/4)	116	£325
Speed Model Tourer (214)	116	£325

The Monte Carlo, introduced initially as the 'Sports Gloria', was the first evidence of Donald Healey's work as experimental manager. Resembling the Speed Tourer as far back as the passenger compartment, its stem quarters were revised to suit rally conditions. Twin spare tyres were mounted up against a huge 17-gallon petrol tank, and twin rear number plates 'for Continental touring' were fitted. The tyres were standard 18 x 4.75 inches, mounted on Dunlop knock-off wire wheels; there were permanently fitted Sessions jacks and Andre Telecontrol dampers. Service brakes were

Soon after he'd joined Triumph, Donald Healey (in the car, Jack Ridley outside it) posed with the newly-launched Gloria Speed Model.

unmodified, but Healey replaced the stock cable hand-brake with one operating on the transmission, which he felt was more reliable and positive.

The first Monte Carlo used the 9.5hp engine, but this was quickly discarded for a 10.8hp unit of 1232cc (66 x 90mm), aspirated by twin downdraught 30mm Zenith carburettors mounted on top and to each side of the rocker boxes. These were operated by a progressive linkage which kicked-in the second carburettor near half-throttle. Fuel feed was by an electric pump, with an auxiliary hand-pressure feed for emergencies. Freewheeling was omitted – one couldn't imagine a less essential feature for rallying – and the Speed Tourer's full set of instruments was fitted. Healey later bolted on aluminium wings for lightness. There was also a master electric switch which totally immobilised the car – useful for dealing with unexpected shorts as well as car thieves. (Some sources indicate that the 1087cc engine was offered as an option, but later research indicates this was not the case.)

Having thus 'cleaned up' the Gloria, as he put it, Donald Healey began to look forward to the 1934 Monte Carlo Rally. Col Holbrook himself had led a small squad of three Triumphs in the 1933 Alpine Trial, using 10hp Southern Crosses, and two cars had finished well – but Healey's 1934 Monte challenge, with no less than seven cars, was really the start of the serious Triumph effort.

There is only one way to describe the prewar Monte Carlo Rally – it was sheer hell. Getting there was half the fun, as Cunard used to say. Often it was more adventurous than the rally itself. One had to reach any of up to 12 starting points, some of them so far in the boondocks that well-equipped safari gear was helpful. The route from Athens, cradle of civilisation, was anything but civilised, a car-breaking cattle track mainly, across the Pindus and the Alps. It was so bad that extra marks were allowed for Athens starters only. A January scheduling insured bitter cold, rain, snow or all

The Gloria Monte Carlo's 1232cc engine was fitted with two downdraught Zenith carburettors and produced 48bhp. A 1087cc engine was also available for this model, but was very rare.

The original 1933 Gloria Speed Model, in four-cylinder form, on show in Maurice Newnham's London showrooms. Newnham himself is looking into the car, Lt Col Claude Holbrook glances at him and, as the original caption to this image told us, the lady "is not so real as she looks" – in fact she was a very elegant plaster model.

three, sometimes simultaneously. Usually snow was everywhere, mountains of the stuff, which often had to be shovelled out of the way by the barricaded driver. There were no organised sources of petrol – one got it where one could, sometimes from an open bucket, a gallon at a time.

You tackled the Monte with winches, chains, extra hoses, lamps, electrics, spares and prayers. One driver, caught sans petrol in the Alps, got his machine running on a bottle of something less volatile, destroyed the engine on the descent but managed to effect repairs and keep slogging. *The Autocar* mentioned a driver who cautioned the organisers not to use red rally plates anymore, because "on the Dragoman Pass that colour incensed a gigantic bull to such an extent that the quadruped went for the four-wheeler, a tale as delightful as any of those traditionally concerned with voracious wolves."

Mechanics, when taken along by the more artistocratic competitors, were expected to turn out to fix or patch under any conditions. One of them, finishing a job, found he couldn't get up – his jacket was frozen to the ground. And arrival in Monte Carlo wasn't the end of it. There, one faced the famed wiggle woggle and other flat-out driving tests. Arrivals were penalised for the slightest infractions: lamps out of action, no spare tyres, no inspection lamp, no starting motor. It was a genuine nightmare. Louis Chiron, the great French champion, once said he would prefer to drive ten Grands Prix than one Monte. He wasn't alone. At the same time, the event was important to manufacturers. Aside from the obvious opportunity for improving the breed, there was the chance to woo customers with feats of immortality. A potential customer often became a buyer when shown a car that was identical – well, almost – to one that had just won its class in the Monte. In Coventry, one of the great rally exponents in the early thirties was Riley, and cutting into its standing seemed, to Holbrook, a sensible project. He didn't have to press Donald Healey.

A fortnight before the 1934 start, Jack Ridley travelled to Greece to get the lay of the land. Of course it was rotten, but Ridley reported back that an Athens start was worth risking for the sake of the extra marks. Healey agreed.

The new Gloria Monte Carlo wasn't ready, but two of its tuned 1232cc engines were. They were installed in 10hp Southern Cross chassis with huge 16-inch wheels and bulbous wings, designed to deal with the snow and mud. Bearing number plates KV 6904 and KV 6905, they were assigned Ridley and R C Clement-Brooks, Healey and Tommy Wisdom, respectively. Just for insurance, five other Triumphs converged on Monaco from other starting points. From Tallinn, Estonia, came J Beck's Gloria saloon (he had to charter his own boat to get over there); from Umea, Sweden, Margaret Allan's saloon and Jack Hobbs' tourer set out (she blowing a gasket en route, he clanking into Monte Carlo after two disastrous shunts). From John O'Groats, Scotland, drove Maj. Montague-Johnston in a tourer (it was almost as much fun as the time he crossed the Sahara on a camel); and from Stavanger, Norway, came Edgar Kehoe in a saloon (after being held at gunpoint following an argument with a garage owner). Six cars arrived in time for the wiggle-woggle; Margaret Allan hadn't been heard from.

The first driving event, held on the quayside road used for the Grand Prix, consisted of a 110-metre acceleration-and-braking test. In the 1500cc class, Healey "surpassed himself with a beautiful clean run," besting Sangers' and Richardson's Rileys, though the determined Hobbs was fourth in his bedraggled tourer. (Margaret Allan still hadn't shown up.) No car in the 2-or 3-litre class could better Healey's time. Healey now tackled the high-speed wiggle-woggle. He was so fast that a protest was lodged, but his car proved legal and he had a clear win. The overall placement left Healey in third place (behind two heavies, a Hotchkiss and a Chenard-Walcker), with Ridley 6th, Beck 10th and the gallant Hobbs 12th. Beck put the cap on it all with a third-place win in the Concours d'Elegance, though Healey preferred "to perambulate proudly in the mud that formed his battle scars." Even Margaret Allan finally arrived. Every Triumph had finished! It was a spectacular victory.

"Congratulations to Donald Healey, and to the makers of the Triumph Gloria," bubbled the scribe. "It is a great achievement and a standing testimonial to British cars in general ... for a 10hp car (sic) loaded up with the things Healey had to take with him, to negotiate that tortuous route from Athens in winter, and then to score such a success in the final tests, is something very few people would have dared to prophesy ... I did not think he would get there in order to start, let alone make the journey. From being just a very good but quite ordinary motor car a year ago, the Triumph has leapt into the front rank of famous marques."

Holbrook must have loved that. Wasn't this just what he had been aiming for, these many years? And if there was any lingering doubt about his achievement, it was dispelled the following August in the French Alpine Trial.

This famous event awarded a confusing plethora of prizes:

Alpine Cups to teams of three drivers, Glacier Cups to individuals, and an assortment of lesser dust-collectors for minor achievements. Triumph fielded a fleet of six Southern Crosses and Gloria saloons. The Alpine Cup team consisted of Ridley, Vic Leverett (now Sales Manager) and Holbrook himself. Individual cars were driven by Healey, London distributor Maurice Newnham, and a ladies' team of Miss Joan Richmond and Mrs Gordon Simpson. The Southern Crosses used the 1087cc engine, bringing them within the 1100cc limit.

Holbrook, Leverett and Ridley poured across the route, scaled the Stelvio Pass (49 acute hairpins, 9000 feet of elevation), and zoomed through the treacherous Turracher Höhe in Austria on the 1800-mile trek from Nice to Yugoslavia. Their's was the only team not to lose a single mark – unquestioned winner of the Alpine Cup. Healey and Newnham won Glacier Cups for individual performances, and the saloon-mounted ladies might have, too, except that Miss Richmond was disqualified for righting a bent

Triumph's two star competition drivers, Jack Ridley (in the car) and Donald Healey, outside the Priory Street premises in Coventry at the time of the 1934 Monte Carlo Rally. KV 6906 was one of several works machines prepared for that event.

This never-seen-before image shows the back view of the rugged works car built for Donald Healey and Tommy Wisdom to drive in the 1934 Monte Carlo Rally, using an old-type Southern Cross chassis, and a much-modified Gloria Monte Carlo body. The crew were eventually rewarded with third place overall.

spring with a sledgehammer. It was another superb Triumph performance – the first year in which the same country, let alone the same make, had won both the Monte and the Alpine Cup. A year later, as we've related at the beginning of this chapter, Triumph did even better in the Monte Carlo Rally. The Alpine Trial was not run in 1936, or Triumph might well have repeated its double victory.

Victory was not Triumph's, however, on the financial side. The expense in tooling for the new Gloria models, and subsequent outlays on Triumph's new Val Page-designed vertical-twin motorcycle, saw 1933 losses at a record £168,705. Now the cash reserves were gone; the book had to carry forward a £78,316 deficit. Though Gloria sales had picked up a little in early 1934, thanks mainly to the Monte Carlo success, the company remained over £55,000 in the red for the fiscal year ending in August. Directors began to look upon motorcycles as an unnecessary distraction – particularly Maurice Newnham, who first sold, then rallied the cars, and finally ascended to the board.

Newnham and his son were already major dealers in London when they approached Bettman to take on Triumphs, around 1929. "The mistake I made," wrote Bettmann, "was that I not only listened to them but accepted their proposal. Mr Newnham's son, by his future conduct, did not gain my confidence, although in time he became a close friend of Col Holbrook." As a motor car man first and foremost, Newnham looked askance at the motorcycle business, especially after sales dropped off. Though it is not recorded, his vote must have been in favour of renaming the firm the Triumph Co Ltd in 1934, relegating the motorcycle business to a subsidiary. All signs pointed toward a coming estrangement between motor car and motorcycle.

By now, of course, Triumph had committed itself to the new range, and the most sensible thing to do was stop building Eights and Tens and concentrate on Glorias. This Triumph did for the 1935 model year, introducing the broadest range in its history.

1935 Gloria		
Model (doors/passengers)	*Wheelbase (in)*	*Price*
Four, 9.5hp		
Four-light Saloon (4/4)	108	£285
Southern Cross (2/2)	96	£275
Four, 10.8hp		
Four-light Saloon (4/4)	108	£298
Tourer (2/4)	108	£298
Six-light Saloon (4/4)	108	£298
Golfer's Coupé (2/2+2)*	108	£335
Foursome Coupé (2/4)*	108	£360
Short-chassis Coupé (2/4)	96	£288
Vitesse Four, 10.8hp		
Four-light Saloon (4/4)	108	£320
Tourer (2/4)	108	£320
Six-light Saloon (4/4)	108	£320
Golfer's Coupé (2/2+2)*	108	£345
Foursome Coupé (2/4)*	108	£382
Southern Cross (2/2)	96	£275
Monte Carlo Tourer (2/4)	108	£335
Short-chassis Coupé (2/4)	96	£310

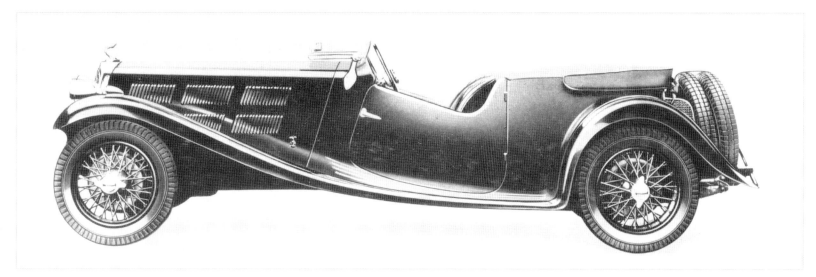

Factory artwork (slightly enhanced on the reality of the machine) showing one of the very rare six-cylinder Gloria Monte Carlo models, the long bonnet being the give-away.

1935 Gloria (cont.)		
Model (doors/passengers)	Wheelbase (in)	Price
Six, 15.7hp		
Four-light Saloon (4/4)	116	£350
Tourer (2/4)	116	£350
Golfer's Coupé (2/2+2)*	116	£385
Foursome Coupé (2/4)*	116	£410
Short-chassis Coupé (2/4)	104	£340
Vitesse Six, 15.7hp		
Four-light Saloon (4/4)	116	£385
Tourer (2/4)	116	£385
Golfer's Coupé (2/2+2)*	116	£425
Foursome Coupé (2/4)	116	£445
Flow-free Saloon (2/4)	116	£425
Southern Cross (2/2)	104	£335
Monte Carlo Tourer (2/4)	116	£398
Short-chassis Coupé (2/4)	104	£375
*Cross & Ellis bodies		

Though the 1087cc 9.5hp engine was retained for the price-leader, most Glorias ran the 1232cc 10.8hp unit, taking advantage of a decrease in the horsepower tax which saw this engine taxed at only £8 5s in 1935, compared to £11 the year before. The Six, meanwhile, was bored and stroked to 1991cc (coincidentally the same displacement as the latter-day TR2/3 would be, though the TR's was a Four, and a much squarer engine). Since there was a slight decrease in chassis weight (gearbox and freewheel housing was made of aluminium-alloy instead of cast iron) the 1935s had to be quicker than the 1934s. The track (except for the Monte Carlo) was also widened from 48 to 50 inches; the cruciform centre-frame bracing was lowered relative to the frame sides, allowing lower bodies without a loss of headroom. The rear crossmember was curved better to provide for the exterior spare wheels of sports models, and twin silencers were adopted. The engine fan ran on ball-bearings, new Hardy-Spicer needle-bearing U-joints were fitted to the propeller-shaft, the clutch was by Borg & Beck and minor changes were made to the four-cylinder engine mounts and manifolding. Rubber now covered pedal plates and arms and the top of the gearbox. The four-cylinder crankshaft was machined and balanced, while the Six's was provided with a torsional vibration damper.

Driver convenience was not forgotten. The steering wheel was four-way adjustable for reach and rake; its centre hub contained an ignition lever, a self-cancelling trafficator switch, and controls for horn and dipped beam. The freewheel dash control, displaced now

by the windscreen crank, was cleverly mounted just behind the gear change on a short bracket, where it could be reached easily. A new starting handle was fitted, in which the shank was permanently in place – "so that the handle is quite short and can be easily engaged" – and also used for the permanent jacking system. Triumph even provided a light spanner to fit the radiator cap. All 1935s had a new radiator, with black honeycomb replacing vertical slats, new badging, more slender headlamp brackets, front bumper and trafficators – all standard. Stone guards were fitted to Monte Carlos and Southern Crosses, and were optional on other models.

1935 marked the appearance of the lovely little Gloria radiator mascot – a small, single-winged female figure made by Walter Belgrove, an expert sculptor in addition to his other talents.

Glyn Jones speaks of an earlier mascot, also by Belgrove: "a figure of Mercury, which was never produced, though the original decorated 'Pixie Croft,' the Belgrove retirement home near Barnstaple in Devon. An illustration exists of the mascot mounted before the radiator on a badge bar on a very early Gloria saloon."

The main characteristic of the 1935 range was its diversity. It is best broken down into three groups: the fifteen models introduced in August 1934; the six additional types appearing in the weeks that followed; and the eight flavours of Cross & Ellis custom-bodied specials.

The basic saloon was not much altered – mainly the difference was at the rear, where the lines were more flowing and the boot larger. The flush-fitting windscreen opened through a winder fitted into the facia, and ventilators were added to both sides of the scuttle. The Monte Carlo Tourer was unchanged, even to its retention of the old 48-inch track. But a new six-cylinder Monte Carlo was listed (very few were sold) on the 116-inch wheelbase. Entirely new was the four- and six-cylinder Short-chassis Coupé, closed-coupled with extra-wide doors and a coachbuilt aluminium-panelled body. Its short wheelbase, Triumph said, provided a smaller-than-average turning circle, making the car particularly suitable for town work.

The new Gloria-Vitesse sub-series offered roughly the same models as the standard Gloria, sold for about £10-20 ($50-100) more, and was well worth it. The Vitesse designation referred to a higher-lift camshaft, larger valves, twin carbs with progressive linkage, polished ports, higher compression and horsepower and twin rev-counter and speedometer enclosing clock and trip odometer. Vitesse bodywork was identical to standard in Tourer and Coupé, but the Saloon was handsomely lowered and streamlined – a magnificent looking motor car. The 1935 (and 1936) six-cylinder Vitesse Saloons are among the most desirable prewar Triumphs, but unfortunately they are rare.

The next phase of the range included three Southern Crosses, two Six-light Saloons and the radical Flow-free Coupé, phased-in

This new Gloria Six is being handed over to the record-breaking British aviator Flt Lt Tommy Rose (centre) in 1936. Donald Healey is at the left of this group.

of its modest 1232cc engine and 8ft wheelbase, this is no small sports car but a comfortable, solid machine of generous size and strength." *Motorsport* found much to praise: an easy gear change, light steering, good engine flexibility, the Luvax adjustable shock absorbers. Cornering and roadholding were reported excellent, the car clinging gamely in spite of 'violent treatment'. The four speed gearbox with constant-mesh third/top allowed easy changes. The magazine concluded, "one could not ask for better value."

The Six-light Saloons, offered only in four-cylinder form for 1935, were designed to provide more space inside. They were not the prettiest Glorias, sacrificing purity of line for practicality, and there is not much to say about them other than that they seemed to solve a market problem. Yet they could not have carried much luggage, for unlike earlier Six-light Triumphs the spare was enclosed within the boot.

The Gloria Flow-free (six-cylinders only) was certainly the most exotic 1935 offering. Created by Walter Belgrove, it was a good example of streamlining as motor manufacturers saw it in the mid-thirties.

Walter said: "the manufacturers became conscious of aerodynamics and quite a few of them were showing their concepts. We were

The Autocar achieved 83mph in a 2-litre six-cylinder engined Southern Cross like this, which made it formidable competition for every other such open-topped British sports car of the period.

between August and the Olympia Show in October. The Southern Cross, mounted for the first time on a Gloria chassis, was one of Walter Belgrove's first body designs for production. Though resembling the Monte Carlo, it lacked a rear seat, and its cutaway doors did not have hinged panels. Included in the spec was a quick-release petrol cap, large, accurate instruments, a reversing lamp and twin Continental number plates. The 1232 and 1991cc cars were Vitesse-tuned (freewheel was optional), making them among the fastest Triumphs built to date. *The Autocar* managed 83.33mph in a 1991cc car at Brooklands with the weather protection off and aero-screens fitted, though a more likely top speed in touring trim was *Motorsport*'s 72-75mph. The latter found the Southern Cross "well sprung, comfortable and suitable for long-distance touring ... In spite

a long way from the wind-tunnel era, but we knew a little about the problem. The public, however, were in those days far more conservative than they are today, and it was a case of serving them a little at a time – one requires the time gap caused by a war to introduce a 'revolution' successfully.

"I designed this model, as my memory serves me, in or around 1933. The model was a two-door, four-light saloon and it carried a 'vee' screen with the vee continuing from front to rear on the roof longitudinal centre-line. The vee also carried on to the intersection at the 'tumble-home'; the roof and the sidesweep terminated at the tail. The roof was downswept in elevation and the rear wings carried twin filler caps ... Being about 58 inches high unladen, it was a good looker and ahead of its time. It was also a good deal

The Vitesse Six was ready for production in 1934/35, using a modified version of the Gloria running gear, but with a different and sleekly attractive four-door body style.

From 1933 onwards, all Gloria and Vitesse types used one or another version of this sturdy new chassis. This was the rolling chassis of the 1935 six-cylinder Gloria Vitesse, complete with the Coventry Climax 1991cc engine and the unsynchronised ENV gearbox.

Two views of the same (96-inch) short-wheelbase Triumph Gloria Southern Cross, which effectively was a shortened Monte Carlo model with only two seats. This was the four-cylinder model, which was on sale until 1937. There was also a rare, but technically exciting, 1991cc version on the original 104in wheelbase frame, but this type was dropped in 1936.

This brave line-up of three mid-1930s Southern Cross types – all of them with the four-cylinder engine – makes one wonder why they did not sell even better than they did.

quieter than its stablemates, with a noticeable absence of 'wind-roar.' It received a good press." (*The Autocar* called it "a modern conception ... graceful and quite individual.")

Sadly, the Flow-free Gloria didn't sell, and was withdrawn before the 1936 range appeared. Belgrove continued, "the public – God bless them – were not ready, as indeed they never are! Nevertheless I imagine that the best part of the initial sanction was produced, which in the Flow-free's case would have been 50 units. It is possible that the sanction was pruned, but the model was definitely sanctioned for production. I can remember the templates, patterns, spindle boxes, jigs and fixtures being made and the production models appearing."

The Pre-1940 Triumph Owners' club has records of four Flow-frees, none of which are located today. One duotone model recorded by Glyn Jones, but since scrapped, may have been the last survivor. One Flow-free body is mounted on a 1931 4¼-litre Bentley chassis, but that appears to be the lot.

Since the Flow-free arrived almost simultaneously with the Chrysler Airflow, this writer asked Mr Belgrove if one had influenced the other.

"I was not influenced by American design, or for that matter by European design," he said. "I remember the car as one of the few jobs to be designed on a modelling table first and on the drawing board afterwards. The names 'Airflow' and 'Flow-free' are almost incestuously related*, and as you say they debuted about the same

time. I like the Chrysler nomenclature, but I cannot say the same of Flow-free, which I always considered was more suitable for an advertisement for a salt dispenser. I did not christen the car, but it is not unlikely that Healey or Holbrook were perhaps influenced by the Chrysler name."

We come at last to the lovely Cross & Ellis variations on the 1935 Gloria chassis, available (theoretically) in eight separate versions: two models, a Golfer's Coupé and Foursome Coupé, to fit the standard or Vitesse, four or six-cylinder chassis. Both were dropheads with flush-folding hoods, coachbuilt with top-quality ash and aluminium panelling, fitted with Yale locks and landau bars. Painted in cellulose lacquer to standard Triumph colours, they were elegantly trimmed in hand-buffed leather and burr-walnut cabinetry. The pretty Golfer's Coupé had a small door ahead of the rear nearside wing, ostensibly to allow a bag of golf clubs to be inserted. (*Motor*: " ... an ideal car for the serious golfer to get about.") The Foursome was the same basic idea, except that it used the golf club space to house two additional passengers, who were guarded from prying eyes by an enormous hood. (There was a dickey for two in the Golfer's Coupé, but this accommodation must be viewed as strictly occasional.)

Glyn Lancaster-Jones, who was introduced to the marque through his mother's Golfer's Coupé, kindly provided us with considerable research and correspondence.

---

*Singer also marketed an 11 hp 'Airstream' model, and SS an 'Airline' in the same period.

Former Cross & Ellis designer Leslie Moore wrote to Glyn in 1966: "I well remember the pleasure I derived from executing these designs, because the design of the chassis, radiator shell and bonnet were so very suitable for the projects and well in advance

Walter Belgrove designed the original swept-tail Flow-free model in 1935, but very few were sold. This was the real thing, in black, a handsome but rare beast by any standards.

By any standards the Flow-free was a stylish machine, though it was only the rear-end of the bodyshell which was streamlined. Perhaps it was the 1935 price of £425 which helped to limit sales.

style-wise of most other cars. I mention this because I feel pretty certain that this was the work of my old friend Walter Belgrove. The front end was of course identical to the standard Gloria of that period, produced in fairly large quantities by Triumph themselves. Cross & Ellis produced a saloon also (Six-light, 1936) with a 'tucked in' rear end. Being the sole designer at Cross & Ellis, I was responsible for the style and the construction of this coupé and designed such things as the head-folding mechanism with the exterior over-centre locking irons ..."

Mr Jones also made contact with R A Ellis, managing director of C and E Motors Ltd, in 1966. Mr Ellis' father, A J Ellis was, in his son's words, 'a founder partner of the firm and managing director ... Messrs Cross & Ellis closed down in 1938 due to the competition of Pressed Steel, hence C & E Motors was started as a second string ... Regarding the bodies you mention, Mr A J Ellis and Mr H Cross would decide the style of body they required from inquiries they received and Mr Colin Cross (H Cross' nephew) made all necessary drawings.'

According to R A Ellis, only "five or six" Golfer's Coupé bodies were built, at least one of which was fitted to a Vauxhall 14. The firm built "a considerable number" of four-door Foursomes which, Ellis says, were "fitted mainly to Vauxhall and Wolseley chassis. But here once again it is possible that a Triumph was fitted with one ... Mr Newsome (not Newnham) of Triumph had several types of experimental bodies built."

As near as can be calculated (see Appendix V), Triumph built about 2000 cars for model year 1934, and less in 1935 – even with the huge variety that was offered. Despite the firm's suggestion to dealers that the average selling price of a Gloria (£325) would bring in "just the class of customer you would like to have," either the price wasn't high enough, or the volume inadequate, to put the company substantially into a profit situation. Even as the 1935s were being introduced it became obvious that further economies were going to be needed. The exuberance of Holbrook, Healey and Newnham to one side, the money had to come from somewhere.

After the loss report of August 1934, the company was reorganised. By the end of 1934 the board included Newnham, accountant T Dudley Cocke, and Lloyds Bank's Howe Graham. The last, obviously installed to protect Lloyd's interests, soon announced "a complete reorganisation of the company's affairs. Arrangements are being made to install an up-to-date costing system and other systems, and factories will be working under strict budgetary control." A slap at the old management?

Newnham, described as "full of enthusiasm,

unbounded energy and intimate knowledge of the car-buying public's requirements," was – as ever – pushing hard for more cars. But where would they be built? Not at Clay Lane, certainly. Yet production had to increase. If Triumph couldn't build enough cars, it couldn't generate enough cash flow to impress financial backers in the city, and without those backers it couldn't build enough cars. It was a circular treadmill leading nowhere but to receivership, and the company had to figure a way out. Between the Holbrook/Newnham automotive interests, and the Graham/Cocke financial interests, the answer seemed inevitable: sell off the motorcycle business and stake all on Gloria.

There are mixed feelings as to just how much the motorcycles contributed to the company after 1930. Before then, of course, they were the company's bulwark, selling at the rate of 4000 a month. According to Harry Louis and Bob Currie in *The Story of Triumph Motorcycles*, the two-wheelers continued to contribute: " ... the motorcycle side was doing its best to hold prices down (the ultimate was a 98cc Villiers-engined lightweight, at £16 16s the cheapest Triumph of all time, but offered, in 1933, under the Gloria label); the car people went to the opposite extreme."

If anything sealed the fate of the motorcycle department, it was Holbrook's purchase of a new factory, on the Foleshill side of Coventry, in April 1935, for the sole manufacture of cars. The new 'Gloria Works,' a large brick building next to Dunlop, was a former White & Poppe engine-manufacturing plant previously used for artillery shell-filling by the Government during the war. White & Poppe had been bought out by Dennis Brothers of Guildford in the early thirties, and in 1934 moved its operations there. The plant was on Holbrooks Lane (no relation to, actually a predecessor of, Col Holbrook) and close enough to William Lyons' SS Cars that the more curious could climb stacks and peer at each other. Motorcycle production was now isolated (and saleable) at Priory Street, while Clay Lane would be used only for the construction of bodies; all design, development and tooling work moved to Holbrooks Lane.

The purchase was announced to a party for distributors at London's Grosvenor House, where Holbrook, Newnham and Graham took turns with pep talks. They spoke confidently of the future, the trade press reported, "and they were supported by leading agents from Scotland and the North, who reported increasing sales for Triumph cars following recent notable competition successes." The new Gloria works "would provide ideal facilities for the manufacturing of chassis and the mounting of bodies for the car side of the business, so that the old factories could then concentrate entirely upon the other products." It sounded pretty dicey for the motorcycles.

A later Triumph press release continued: "On August 9 ... the factory was in full production, working with the most modern facilities. The shop had, in the meantime, been repainted from top to bottom, no less than 400 heavy machines had been transferred from the old works (or new ones purchased), new furnaces had been installed, stores erected and tracks laid down. During this period, production of the current season's models continued without any serious break and the new season's programme was being steadily advanced. During the three weeks ending August 31, output of the new season's (1936) models will have exceeded the number delivered during the first three months of the 1935 season, and supplies will continue regularly." Which says volumes about what 1935 production must have been like.

It is frustrating not to have any official record of Triumph motor car production, though the latest conclusions in that regard (see Appendix V) are the most accurate assembled thus far. They do indicate that the 1936 model year proved no better for production than 1935, and furthermore that it was a disappointment for Holbrook and company.

1936 Gloria		
Model (doors/passengers)	*Wheelbase (in)*	*Price*
Four, 9.5hp		
Southern Cross (2/2)	96	£295
Four, 10.8hp		
Four-light Saloon (4/4)	108	£315
Six-light Saloon (4/4)	108	£315
Foursome Coupé (2/4)*	108	£355
Vitesse Four, 10.8hp		
Four-light Saloon (4/4)	108	345
Tourer (2/4)	108	£325
Foursome Coupé (2/4)*	108	£365
Short-chassis Coupé (2/4)	96	£298
Southern Cross (2/2)	96	£295
Six, 15.7hp		
Six-light Saloon (4/4)	116	£395
Foursome Coupé (2/4)*	116	£415
Vitesse Six, 15.7hp		
Four-light Saloon (4/4)	116	£425
Tourer (2/4)	116	£390
Six-light Saloon (4/4)*	116	£425
Foursome Coupé (2/4)*	116	£445
*Cross & Ellis bodies		

The new range reflected woeful finances and the need to conserve capital. The theory now was to rationalise, to concentrate on the most popular models and forget peripheral types like the Flow-free. While some of the deletions made sense, others were astonishing. The Southern Cross, for example, was reduced to two four-cylinder models, and the Monte Carlo was axed altogether. Cross & Ellis offered the new Vitesse six-cylinder Six-light Saloon (the rear was modified from the Triumph design to accept more luggage), and retained the Foursome, but did not list any Golfer's Coupés. The latter, though, were built to special order through 1937.

Mechanical alterations were minor. Fours, save Southern Crosses, had larger 5.75 x 16-inch tyres; Sixes used 6 x 16-inch low-pressure tyres. Headlamps, except on Southern Crosses, were mounted on the wings, radiators readopted vertical slats, the front wings were lower in front to better hide the undercarriage and the front bumper acquired a central dip. In October, a synchronised Warren-patent gear control was offered as a £5 5s option – the device was apparently not often specified, since only one has been encountered in the field. It did make gear changing nearly foolproof, since it completely disengaged gearbox from engine when the clutch pedal was depressed. In November, another attempt was made to boost sales with a general price cut, bringing the four-cylinder Saloon down to £288 and the Six to £360. This was achieved by eliminating frills like chromium-plated radiator shutters and fitting non-low-pressure tyres.

A lot of breast-beating attended the 1936 premiere, though it was obviously an economic range of automobiles. At Grosvenor House 350 agents and press representatives were bought another lunch and treated to more speeches from Col Holbrook's ragtime band. Just 12 years ago, Newnham said, the British industry produced only 116,600 cars. Today it was producing better than twice that many, while the average retail price had fallen nearly 50 per cent. Just think of the opportunities that lay in store! Several agents shook their heads. They had heard it all before.

By the spring of 1936, it was still looking like production would hold up. In the first week of May Triumph built more cars than in any week since the Gloria range was introduced – but this was probably a misleading announcement. A works that could produce in weeks what the old plant took months to put out should have been setting a new record every week, and it wasn't. Money was still going out faster than it was coming in, and 1935 had ended with a loss of £16,891. Triumph's total losses now exceeded £90,000, its indebtedness reached nearly £250,000. Even with the new works, the company was existing strictly on the goodwill of its creditors – who possibly didn't pound the table because they knew it would do no good. The situation was very precarious. Cash was needed in a hurry. Again the subject of selling the motorcycle business arose.

Siegfried Bettmann observed all this from his innocuous roost

This neat 1935-model Foursome Drophead Coupé has the six-cylinder 2-litre engine, and a bodyshell by Cross & Ellis, the Coventry-based coachbuilder.

as vice chairman of the board, and his memoirs may be quoted again for the view of the loyal opposition.

"Mr Graham," Bettmann wrote, "had concluded a kind of firm friendship with Col Holbrook and Mr Newnham. His first idea was to give up the motorcycle trade and to restrict the resources of the company to the manufacture of motor cars.

"The rumours of such proceedings reached Mr Sangster (Birmingham builder of Ariel motorcycles) who went, as far as I know, immediately to Holbrook and asked him not to throw the motorcycle business away for nothing but to let him have it." This, Holbrook did. Sangster duly purchased the motorcycle subsidiary, the Triumph Engineering Company Ltd, its stock in trade and goodwill, on January 22, 1936. Holbrook leased a section of the old factory as a service and spares depot. Sangster appointed Ariel designer Edward Turner as managing director of Triumph Engineering – and Siegfried Bettmann as chairman!

Bettmann wrote, "I agreed to (take the chairmanship), but for some reason which it is not necessary to go into further but which was of the most friendly character, I retired from the chairmanship and this ended my active commercial life." Bettmann departed in 1939. One can't help wondering if his German background was again working against him, but he was by then over 75. He lived until 1951, however, and continued to contribute to his community,

founding a school for young business people, and serving as honorary chairman of several civic and industrial associations. Triumph's Depression fortunes aside, Siegfried's was a long and honourable career, and Triumph was fortunate to be guided by his sure hand in the early years.

The fate of the Triumph motorcycle under new management is well known: it was a stunning success, a virtual goldmine for its owners and shareholders. For this reason many have wondered how Holbrook could have possibly dispensed with "the most profitable share of the business". One expatriate Englishman, reviewing an earlier Triumph work, took the author to task for failing to satisfy him in explaining "this extraordinary manner of management."

We hope it is plain now that in 1936 there was nothing extraordinary about the split. Triumph, as constituted then, could no longer produce both cars and motorcycles in volumes sufficient enough to stay in business. There was some debate as to just how profitable the motorcycles were. But one side or the other had to go, and purchase of the Gloria works was only a temporary palliative.

Given the makeup and interests of Triumph's management, the choice was preordained, and it is patently ridiculous to hold any post-mortems about it. Those directors were not, after all, killing off a great English motorcycle. Neither, at the time, did they appear to be killing off a great English motor car. They appeared, indeed, to be saving it.

Body engineer Walter Belgrove had a sure eye for a line – the Gloria Vitesse of the mid-1930s being a more sporting, more rakish, restate of the Gloria theme which had appeared just a year earlier.

The Big One that Got Away

The first thing one may reasonably say of the supercharged straight-eight Triumph Dolomite is that it was the greatest Triumph ever built. That's also the second and the third thing. There is simply no way to refute this statement, unless by some miracle the brand is revived, is entered in Formula One, and wins the manufacturers' championship.

Introduced in October 1934, the Dolomite was totally unexpected, but from the day it appeared it was hailed as a supreme accomplishment – deservedly. That it was also ultimately a failure, with only two cars, three chassis and six engines built, is an irony worth pondering, but not for long. Given the atmosphere of the times, and Triumph's perilous financial state, the outcome was almost assured from the beginning. It's far better to dwell on its excellence as pure automobile, to praise its creator Donald Healey, and to be thankful that he had the chance to build it at all.

Fortunately, in modern times, a flurry of interest in the car has confirmed many details that were heretofore obscure. Research for this book added a few more, the most notable of which is that the Dolomite was potentially the progenitor of an entire line of big Triumphs – but we are getting ahead of the tale.

Britain's failings in international competition during the late twenties and early thirties were widely deplored by many patriotic sportsmen, who wrote saucy letters to *The Times* and *Motor*, begging the country to get hold of itself and face off the Continental opposition toe-to-toe. The problem was that the cc of the average British sports car was insufficient to figure in the large-capacity classes – the only serious exceptions being Lagonda and Bentley. The 4½-litre Bentley was a pretty ponderous machine by comparison with the MG Midget, and the sporting area between them was huge. The lack of middling-displacement sports cars and the emphasis on high-rpm buzz boxes was due to a combination of factors: the bizarre RAC tax rating that discouraged big engine bores while promoting long strokes; the satisfaction of manufacturers like Riley and MG with the small-displacement classes; the nature of the English landscape – narrow, rolling, challenging to little cars, but less fun for the biggies; and British roads, most of them former footpaths, unlike the string-straight roads of the Continent. This last characteristic remained part of the British scene for decades, not really being ameliorated until the commencement of the motorway programme in the late fifties.

Among those who deplored the situation was Sir Henry 'Tim' Birkin, who reviewed the stunted growth of English sports cars with a shudder.

"Sure there was Bentley," he wrote, "wiping its wheels with Brooklands and, of course, revenging itself on those sporting foreigners. But all the while the ground was slipping unobtrusively from Britain's feet, and the initiated saw the beginnings of a great cloud coming over the horizon ... Where was the money for an English car to compete with the ceaselessly improving foreign makes? Where were the means of correcting the ignorance and apathy of the public? ... There might be a miracle, a fairy godmother turning baby Austins into supercharged Napoleons. If there was no miracle, the motor industry might well coin a special 1930 model, and for Britannia on the reverse substitute Cinderella."

Donald Healey's eight-cylinder Dolomite was astonishingly attractive by 1930s (or any other decade, for that matter) standards – and was potentially one of the fastest cars in Europe at the time.

Birkin's friend Earl Howe, who shared his 1931 Le Mans victory in an 8C 2300 Alfa Romeo, suggested that the Alfa provided an ideal pattern for British manufacturers of competition cars. He even tried unsuccessfully to get William Morris to build one. Lord Howe has been accused of blind enthusiasm, of campaigning for questionable projects when Britain was on her back financially. But so was the rest of Europe, and Italy, France and Germany seemed to manage, the latter even before Hitler arrived to make motor racing a national priority. Birkin and Howe had an arguable case.

Donald Healey felt the same way, though it was some years before he was in a position to do anything about it. While it's not true to say that Healey came to Triumph solely to design the Dolomite straight-eight, it is probably in order to say it couldn't have occurred without him. The credit goes to Healey for not only conceiving the idea, but following it through to production. We are fortunate to be able to quote his own words on the car's development, which first appeared in the August 1972 *Motorsport*, following a rash of reader conjecture:

"After the great success of the Triumph cars in the Alpine Trial, Sir Claude Holbrook (actually he was not knighted until 1938), Tommy Wisdom and myself were deploring the lack of a good British sports car able to compete with the Continental cars of that date. Tommy ... suggested that we build a car similar to the then most-successful racing car, the 2.3-litre Alfa Romeo. Sir Claude agreed and I was given immediately a very tight budget to build such a car in the least possible time." Healey recalls that the figure was not more than £5000, or about $25,000 at current 1933 rates, which "would not have been enough to develop a scooter, today! To design and develop an engine of this type, with our limited knowledge of such a machine, would be a big undertaking ... I decided to get an Alfa Romeo and make a design-study of the engine, and to keep as close to its design as possible."

Note that Healey stresses keeping 'close to' the engine, not copying it exactly, which he didn't – though the end result was very Alfa-like from both styling and engineering standpoints. Healey mentioned that in the 1970s a concurrent British car (Rolls-Royce) had an engine influenced by an American (Chrysler) engine, in the same sense as the Dolomite borrowed from Italy. Alfa was interested, Donald Healey stated, "in our up-to-date range of motorcycles and considered the possibility of making one of them (the Val Page 650cc vertical twin) in Italy."

Even to this day there is controversy as to which Alfa Romeo was purchased as the reference model, for two cars seem to take the credit. In 1933, one was owned by Noel Rees and was being raced by the Hon Brian Lewis (later Lord Essendon), while another was owned and raced by Sir Henry Birkin. Both were contemporary 1933 models, but enjoyed a rather shadowy period at this part of their otherwise well-documented history, and our conclusion is that both must take some credit for the inspiration they provided to Donald Healey and his team.

"I also visited Italy and discussed our intentions with Alfa's chief engineer, the famous Signor Jano. Alfa Romeo was very pleased and honoured that a company as famous as Triumph had decided to follow its design – we even discussed the possibility of calling the car a Triumph-Alfa ... But we decided not to join up the names in any way.

"I was fortunate in that we had a first-class engine drawing office and probably the best tool room in Coventry. With much overtime working and a lot of enthusiasm we had an engine running in under six months. It was made completely by the 'knife and fork' method; even the Roots-type blower rotors were hand-contoured.

Although there is no concrete evidence (ie written proof in an archive which has survived), it seems certain that design work had started, in a private house situated some distance away from the main Triumph factory in Coventry, well before the end of 1933 – within three months of Healey's arrival on Triumph's payroll. As he later elaborated on the Alfa-study for Graham Robson, Healey said, "we stripped the engine right out, and I got a man called George Swetnam (my chief draughtsman) and his team to copy and draw up every last detail, down to the nuts and bolts. Our engine was a bit different, of course. I wanted a 2-litre, which meant that we used a smaller cylinder bore, and because we kept the supercharger like the Alfa, that automatically meant that our boost was higher. Our compression was higher, too." The Dolomite's bore was 60mm instead of 65mm; compression ratio was 6.5:1 versus 5.7/6.0:1 in the Alfa.

Many have wondered why Triumph stayed with the supercharger, since the RAC had decided to ban blowers from TT races, and supercharged cars might be subject to some penalties at Brooklands and elsewhere. The answer may lie in Donald Healey's preoccupation with rallying, where blowers were sometimes useful. (Note that he de-bored the engine to under 2-litres, certainly with the 2000cc limit in mind.) Further evidence that racing rules were incidental was Triumph's own announcement: it had "no intention of entering into a 1935 racing campaign." The Dolomite, Triumph said, was an "ultra-performance type, yet perfectly tractable ..."

Of the oft-rumoured Alfa lawsuit supposedly instituted for infringement of patents, there is no evidence whatsoever. "I can categorically deny this," Donald Healey wrote in *Motorsport*. Alfa "was extremely helpful, as I previously have mentioned." Added to that, research has turned up no legal records relating to the question; and Anthony Blight, who hinted of a suit in his book on the Roesch Talbots, later stated that he had no genuine evidence. Finally, there was the situation in Milan: the 2.3 engine itself was an old design by 1933, just barely still in production, and Jano was more interested in Grand Prix projects involving much larger engines.

The straight-eight Triumph engine was a very impressive design: 1990cc (60 x 88mm), rated at 17.85 RAC horsepower, developing 120 brake horsepower* at 5500 pm. It was built on a 104-inch wheelbase chassis, made light by virtue of using nickel-steel alloys wherever possible. It was a ladder type, with beam axles and semi-elliptic leaf springs front and rear, friction-type shock absorbers, spiral-bevel geared rear axle offering either 4.0:1 or 4.5:1 final-drive ratio.

The front springs were left free to move at each end, while the lightweight axle was located by horizontal radius-rods running from the spring mountings to a high point in the axle bed, for clearance purposes. This was criticised by *The Automobile Engineer* "in that the radius-rod, which has plain pin joints only, is subject to very heavy torsional stress when one wheel rises more than another ... Possibly the makers intend the bar to act as an anti-rolling device also, but the effect of this action on the bushes and the eye of the rod will not be very beneficial." This did not, however, prove to be a problem in practice. Says Donald Healey, "we used springs with an extra-large number of leaves to increase the natural damping, and these, coupled with Hartford dampers, gave an excellent hard ride, as we then thought desirable for a fast car. Later, I learnt, during four days and nights on the Monte Carlo Rally, how hard they really were."

The Dolomite brakes were splendid – huge 16-inch drums with Elektron steel liners, the centres pressed and riveted in, with aluminium-alloy Ferodo-lined shoes and Lockheed hydraulic actuation. The front-wheel cylinders were larger, to provide proper proportioning of braking effort, and the drum backplates contained air-ducts to assist in heat dissipation. Rally influence was apparent in the adjustment, which could be managed without jacking the car. A knurled adjusting nut was turned until the shoes contacted the drum, then backed off one click, ensuring a definite .025-inch clearance.

Donald Healey said, "Alfa Romeo was then using aluminium brake drums of very large diameter and very narrow shoes and, against the recommendation of Gordon Parnell (formerly of Triumph, then Lockheed), I had them made. Parnell had pointed out that the rubbing speed was far too high for the linings then available and they were never a success. Later on we changed to normal size brakes in cast iron drums, which proved as good as they could be got in those days." (The latter were 12-inch in diameter, but at least one of the Dolomites retained the 16-inch originals – and when magnificently restored, were unveiled in 2018 with both cars having 16-inch brakes.)

There was much less controversy about the straight-eight engine, a veritable gem. The intricate block and head castings were made of R.R. 50 Hiduminium alloy by High Duty Alloys, but aside from the twin-choke Zenith carburettor (later replaced by an SU to eliminate induction noise) the rest of the engine was Triumph-built. The cylinders, with Sheepbridge nitrogen-hardened cast iron dry-liners, were cast in two blocks of four, bolted together, and enclosed the gear-train drive to two overhead camshafts. The valves (inlets silichrome, exhausts

On the Dolomite Straight-eight, no attempt was ever made to provide a wind-cheating nose, however the chosen design looked both purposeful and attractive.

This motor show display example of the Dolomite's front suspension shows the original colossal size of the brake drums, which Donald Healey later intended to be reduced in diameter.

*Contemporary reports stated 140bhp, but Donald Healey told us it was nearer 120.

Although Donald Healey admitted that the Dolomite's 2.0-litre engine was very similar to that of Jano's Italian Alfa Romeo layout, it was entirely different in detail. This was the inlet side ... (Courtesy Jonathan Wood)

... and this was the exhaust side of the Triumph engine, of which only six were ever manufactured.
(Courtesy Jonathan Wood)

In this study, only the faired-in engine oil tank of the Dolomite Straight-eight is not functional, for initial testing showed that there were lubrication deficiencies in the engine. Henceforth the tank was empty, but for styling reasons it was left in place.

KE965 alloy) were inclined at 90 degrees to each other, two to a cylinder. Hemispherical combustion-chambers held centrally mounted sparking plugs. The cams bore directly on the valves and each cam was carried in six bearings.

The crankshaft was built in two sections, each carried in five bearings, connected by a spring coupling – this straight from the Alfa design manual. The crank was also fully balanced, with disc webs and a torsional vibration damper.

Donald Healey wrote, "I had a discussion with Mr Robotham, the chief engineer of Rolls-Royce, on the new bearing metal just discovered – lead-bronze. But unfortunately, our crankshaft was not hard enough and we badly scored and ruined the two halves of the crankshaft, probably representing 500 hours of skilled craftsman's work. So we changed back to white-metal-lined shells and had no further trouble – a retrograde step probably, as the crankshaft bearings were very narrow and theoretically overloaded; if we had

Fuel feed was via a duplex electric petrol pump. The manifolding was very clean and efficient, with one exhaust outlet for each cylinder and the inlets sweeping through by an unobstructed route. It was said to be "really the cleanest and most workmanlike on any British supercharged car."

The tight budget dictated a proprietary gearbox, one which could handle the torque, and Triumph had no suitable gear-cutting machinery anyway. Donald Healey chose a Wilson-designed preselector built by Armstrong-Siddeley – an enormous box, cased in Elektron steel, affording close and leggy internal ratios: 3.1, 1.85, 1.23 and 1.0:1.

"Siddeley had done a lot of work in developing a racing epicyclic preselector box for ERA," said Healey. "I decided to use this and never experienced any kind of trouble."

Though the gearbox was bulky, it was a fraction of the total weight, and careful application of light metals gave a chassis weight of just 1568lb. The complete car weighed just over 2100lb, the engine only 400lb.

These exotic mechanics were wrapped in a masterpiece of a body, often credited wrongly to Walter Belgrove.

"I had nothing to do with this model," Walter generously stated. "To (Frank) Warner should go the styling credit for all the original Gloria saloons, the Gloria tourers, and the Dolomite straight-eight."

Warner deserves at least several toasts for the latter, probably his last piece of work before leaving Triumph for Humber-Hillman. The Dolomite was breathtakingly beautiful. Announced by a rakish vee radiator grille, the lean and strong lines flowed smoothly from the long bonnet through cut-down doors, ending in the foreshortened, rounded tail, Alfa-accurate even to its central fin. It was surely no coincidence that there were resemblances to the Riley MPH, with which Donald Healey had also been briefly connected.

had time to further develop the crankshaft for lead-bronze bearings we could have raised the BMEP considerably. But we could not afford to be pioneers."

Balancing the nearside-mounted dynamo was the offside Roots-type supercharger, running at 1.5 times engine speed and providing a 10psi boost. It was driven from the central gear train.

As originally announced, as tested, and as run in the Monte Carlo Rally, the Dolomite wore cycle wings. But full-length flared wings were certainly intended as an option. They were illustrated in cutaway drawings (in which aero screens were fitted – the

As built in 1934, the Dolomite Straight-eight might seem to have a big ground clearance, but this is typical of cars of the 1930s.

So typical of the 1930s, this was the layout of the Dolomite's facia/instrument panel, complete with a sprung steering wheel, and with the speedometer ahead of the co-driver's eyes.
(Courtesy Jonathan Wood)

Monte car had a flat screen and aero screens) published upon announcement, and the only Dolomite catalogue published shows both configurations. More than one form of Dolomite was intended. In fact, as we mentioned at the beginning of this chapter, current research indicates these first straight-eights may have been the progenitors of a whole line of big Triumphs.

Consider the evidence. Triumph continually quoted two

Dolomite prices: £1225 for the finished roadster, and £1050 for the chassis. At the time the only other chassis in this class was the 3½-litre Bentley (£1380). Like the Bentley, the Triumph appears intended for a variety of bodies. Further evidence is a set of drawings by Charlesworth Bodies in the collection of Walter Belgrove, illustrating no fewer than four variations – a two-seater open roadster and a streamlined fixed-head coupé on 104- and 120-inch wheelbases. The latter are truly impressive, and one can only regret that they weren't built.

One other clue relating to this theory was a very sleek four-door, four-light saloon which was actually built. It was called the 'Continental'.

Walter Belgrove's collection of prewar records contained a number of renderings of long wheelbase Triumphs which, traditionally, were considered mere pipe-dreams. The wheelbases vary, as do the body styles:

Four-door Club Saloon	116in wheelbase
Coupé de Ville	132in wheelbase
Four-seat Tourer	132in wheelbase
Six-light Saloon	wheelbase unknown
Continental Saloon	wheelbase unknown

Until more recently all of the above were assumed to be fictional. Even Walter, who was responsible for most of them, held that they never reached full-scale model stage, let alone running form. Not so! Purely by accident the writer chanced across a classified advertisement in *The Autocar* of August 14, 1936, page D-56: "For Sale: 2-litre Triumph. Very special Continental sports saloon, 1936, only 8000 miles, cost over £400, Vitesse chassis underslung, free wheel, tyres hardly marked, telescope steering, showroom condition, written guarantee, licensed, beautiful car. £265." The ad had been placed by Taylor's Ltd, of Wheeler Street, Birmingham.

The car shown was the selfsame Continental Saloon from the Triumph photographic department, shown along with its mates in these pages. Is it a straight-eight? It seems not. But in line and stance it looks more like one than a standard six-cylinder Vitesse. Combined with the latter, there's some indication that a straight-eight range was considered. The car is no longer around to examine.

Of the two cars that were built (or about to be built at the end of 1934), much more is known, for both were displayed by Triumph, the latter as a chrome-plated show chassis, not all of it functional, the former as the completed article. Car 1 was to be prepared for the 1935 Monte Carlo Rally, and the team must have been burning the midnight oil, because its performance appears to have improved only gradually. The best contemporary report here is by Brian

Twist, who accompanied Healey from Coventry to Brooklands for testing, just before the Olympia Motor Show, and wrote about his experience in *The Autocar*.

Twist was happy for the opportunity, he said, because rumours had been circulating the Midlands about this car all summer. One even suggested that 120mph had been achieved in touring trim.

"As soon as we were clear of Coventry the car settled down to an easy cruising gait," he wrote. "I was immensely intrigued by a delicious whine, not from the supercharger gears, but caused by air rushing in through the twin choke tubes of the carburettor. As we dropped to third for a bend and then accelerated again, the tiny break in that thin whine when top snicked in seemed immensely satisfying. One must not talk about noise of any kind, however, and as a matter of fact it would be most unfair, since it is not audible outside the car."

Though most observers described the Dolomite ride as approximately equivalent to a sledge being dragged over a Somerset wheat field, Twist felt it wasn't bad with the shocks set for softness: "When I had been sitting in the passenger's side, even though we had several times reached about 85mph, I had rarely been bumped off the cushion." Most of his colleagues felt that he had to be kidding ...

One other observation was that "the brake bands in the Wilson preselector gearbox were inclined to slip, but the trouble was marked down for attention and cure. The taking of a full set of performance figures was impossible as the car at that time was only fitted with a rev counter, and that instrument was a chronometric one which registered at three-quarters of a second intervals. However, apart from the 102.47mph already mentioned (flying quarter-mile) a complete lap from a flying start was covered at 98.23mph, and from a standing start a quarter-mile was achieved in 17.8 seconds, the half-mile taking 28.6. The large drum brakes pulled the Dolomite up from 30mph in 24ft."

Brooklands testing was done by Donald Healey and Jack Ridley. The former has stated that 120mph was never attained, though 110 was. "Considering a rather wide touring body, we were quite pleased. One incident during testing – when doing something over 100mph on the London Road the car and I were spotted by a PC and reported to Coventry Police for dangerous driving. Fortunately my passenger was the Hon Cyril Siddeley, the then-Lord Lieutenant of Warwickshire, and his word refuted the dangerous driving charge."

Healey had high hopes when he entered Dolomite No 1, bearing the number-plate ADU 4, on the 1935 Monte Carlo Rally: "Having a car with such superior performance, I thought here was a chance to repeat my Monte Carlo Rally win of 1931. Starting from Umea in northern Sweden ... I demolished the front end of car No 1 in a collision with a train." What Donald didn't say was that he was lucky to escape with his life.

With four other competitors, Healey had chartered a special ferry to cut some mileage off the route and gain a little time. Travelling in thick fog after leaving the ferry in Denmark, the group encountered an unguarded railway crossing at an acute angle to the road. J W Whalley, just ahead of Donald in a Ford V8, saw an oncoming train headlight and dashed across in time, but Healey was unable to see the light. His car was caught at the bonnet and whipped around some 200 degrees, demolishing it as far back as the cowl and writing-off the painstakingly built engine. Jack Ridley redeemed Triumph fortunes by finishing second overall, while Healey retired with the remains of his Dolomite, eager to fight again another year.

In April 1935, following continued financial losses, Col Holbrook cancelled the Dolomite project. There was no relief in sight, and the decision was irrevocable. Healey continued to drive one of the cars around Coventry and gamely entered it in the 1936 Monte Carlo, its displacement now over 2.4-litres and its blower removed in the search for reliability. In this form, he says, it was greatly improved. Starting from Tallinn, he ran a fine rally, finishing without penalty marks and coming within five seconds of the winning Ford V8 in the driving tests – good for eighth place

This splendidly detailed study of the Dolomite Straight-eight of 1934 shows just how carefully Donald Healey's design team had 'packaged' the chassis of their new car around the bulky supercharged eight-cylinder engine. At the time, it was potentially the fastest road car then ready to be sold in the UK.

overall, the highest finish for a British driver. It was anti-climactic, of course, but it had proved the merit of the car. Donald Healey still feels the straight-eight could have been built – had only the money been available. At the time, though, it was the end of the road for a singular automobile.

Conjecture attends the fate of the remaining chassis and five engines, although their early history is known. In *The Autocar* of December 31, 1937, "the original Triumph Dolomite" was advertised, "together with all existing spare parts, more than sufficient to build a second complete car. This car holds the Leinster lap record at over 75mph and lapped the Donington circuit during the 1937 JCC 200-mile race in 2 minutes 16 seconds. Yet with present fully-equipped 2-seater body it makes a fast and very attractive car for everyday use. Sole reason for sale is that owner is buying ERA." A Chester box number was given, and the owner was young Tony Rolt, who had bought the lot from Triumph.

To my co-author, we are obliged for this first-hand comment from Major Rolt: "When Triumph decided to sell the Dolomites, Donald asked me, 'What about it?' I'd had one race, my first ever, in a Southern Cross at Spa, where we finished fourth in class –" (Rolt also competed in the Alpine Trial with a 2-litre Southern Cross) "– so I was quite happy about Triumphs, and I said 'How much for the whole package?' – which was two chassis, the original 2-litre engines, the bored-out 2.4s with the lowered blower pressure, the wheels, the huge brakes and the smaller production brakes (which actually worked a lot better) – I bought everything Triumph had, and I can't actually remember the price, but it was certainly ... less than a thousand. I think the price was £850!

"I put the whole bag of tricks into a back-yard garage at Chester, where a pal of mine, Jack Elliott, helped me prepare them. We did quite a lot of work ... we needed lower blower pressure to get the thing reliable. The rear suspension was impossible – Donald had counted the leaves in the springs of the Alfa and then he doubled

that figure – so it was very hard. The original very big brakes, with those lovely ribbed drums, never worked properly, because we could never get any 'bite' out of them. Maybe they were too big, and maybe they never got warmed-up properly ... but the ordinary cast iron Triumph production 12-inch brakes did a very good job. I think the car was over-braked in the first place. We sorted one out, ran it in a couple of speed trials, then I entered it for the Leinster Trophy."

Rolt might have won this July 1937 event if not for the handicap system (the actual winner was a Coventry Climax-engined Morgan), but he did set the fastest lap at 75.53mph. Contemporary reports quote his car as displacing 2482cc, indicating that it was bored out to 67mm – the same size as Healey's 1936 Monte Carlo engine. Despite his advertised time at Donington in August, this race was disappointing. "We were pretty slow, and had mechanical troubles." *The Autocar* noted that Rolt lacked the speed of his rivals (he was lapped after eight laps by the leading Maserati) and caused grief by spilling petrol from the filler cap. In his car's defence, this was really a race for monoposto racing cars – it was at a decided disadvantage against the likes of ERAs, Maseratis and R-type MGs. Rolt finished eighth, covering 72 laps against the winner's 77, behind three ERAs, two Maseratis, a Monza Alfa Romeo and a 2-litre Riley.

Major Rolt says he owned the Dolomites for around 12 to 18 months. Assuming he bought them in early 1937, he would not have owned them much beyond the spring of 1938. This ties

In standard as-built 1934 tune, the Dolomite was fast and exhilarating to drive.

Room for two – and only two – in the eight-cylinder Dolomite, with the steering wheel positioned close to the driver's chest.

in with a subsequent recorded mention, again in *The Autocar*'s classified section, during July and August 1938. Two cars, then one, were advertised, each time at £650 apiece, by the London firm of High Speed Motors.

After the JCC race, Rolt continues, "I decided to buy Remus from Chula." (He refers to the less-successful of two ERAs,

'Romulus' and 'Remus', driven by Prince Birabongse of Siam and managed by his cousin, Prince Chula.) "Having bought the ERA, and spent all my money, I decided to sell the Dolomites. I sold everything I had, mostly still in bits, but one complete car."

The Dolomites and pieces thereof were purchased by HSM's Giulio Ramponi (of Scott-Moncrieff Motors), who was soon

When the two Dolomites were revealed together at the RAC Club in 2018, they were seen to be in magnificent, better than original, condition. The two owners, Jonathan Turner and Tim Whitworth, posed proudly in front of the cars.

joined by Robert Arbuthnot. Eventually both were given new Corsica body-shells and 'HSM-Dolomite' badges on their Triumph radiators. After being advertised during July and August 1938, they vanished, only to reappear almost exactly a year later – in the same classified section at the same price. After 1939 the cars disappeared, not to be heard of until after the war, and very occasionally, in the 1950s, they surfaced once again.

Word of a surviving Dolomite broke in the early sixties, when one was discovered in a London suburb by Len Roxby, a stalwart in the Pre-1940 Triumph Owners' club. This car had been reported in the Nottingham area in 1947, and had taken part in some rallies around that time. When Roxby found it, the original engine was missing (Jaguar and Austin engines had provided interim power), but the owner had allegedly located the same straight-eight that had once powered this car – in a boat in Scotland! He was in the process of reinstalling it. The car bore the number-plate FYM 224 and the chassis number DMH-1 (Donald Mitchell Healey). It was fitted with the original 16-inch brakes and dry-sump lubrication system. Alas, Len Roxby passed away and, as he'd promised not to reveal the car's whereabouts, it then remained ephemeral for some time.

Many years later, however, one of the Corsica-bodied cars, whose lineage can be traced back to ADU 4, the original Triumph Dolomite prototype (it carried the legendary chassis number DMH-1 stamped on a chassis member), surfaced in the high-value classic car trade, and it was a real privilege for one of us (author Robson) to drive it once again.

This was a car which had flitted in and out of British sports car view in the 1950s and 1960s, but had lain dormant throughout the 1970s when a proposed restoration was stalled. Bodied as an 'HSM', this was the car which had, at one time, lost its engine to a proposed speed-boat project in Scotland, and had then been degraded for a time by the fitting of an Austin A135 Sheerline engine. This was eventually discarded in favour of a 3½-litre Jaguar SS100 power unit; then, after some years the speed boat engine was recovered from storage in the north, and re-united with the car. The red colour scheme, and a dreadfully non-standard facia panel were fitted at this time.

Sold by motor trader Dan Margulies, then re-sold and again re-sold, it was eventually bought by British-based Faud Majzub in 1986. After his untimely death, his daughter Claudia took it on, and during the 1990s a great deal of careful restoration took place on the running gear, though the body was left alone. When the engine was refreshed, the patched crankcase was noted, the engine was confirmed as 2482cc, and attempts to fit various Alfa Romeo pieces failed: it was, indeed, no direct copy! In the years which followed it was seen at important Triumph occasions.

During the 1980s, the other car also re-surfaced, was bought by an American, David Cohen, and completely rebuilt by British Alfa expert Tony Merrick. Difficult? Not by Tony's standards. This, after all, was a man who has rebuilt V16 BRM Grand Prix cars, Vanwall F1 cars, and even a couple of Mercedes-Benz 300SLRs as a commission by the Stuttgart factory. For a man who seemed to rebuild supercharged Alfa engines and Wilson gearboxes as a matter of routine, and who had himself raced ERAs, Vanwalls and other irreplaceable single-seaters, re-creating the Triumph held no horrors.

When we first saw this car in 1979, it carried two chassis numbers – DMH-2 and HSM 2003 – and was powered by engine number JCR 1. In 1979, it carried the registration number, GGT 925, which was issued in London in 1940. This machine, we believe, was re-constructed by HSM in 1939 (from the mass of spares), was based on the original Olympia Show chassis frame, and had never

In 1934 Donald Healey and his team had clearly not cut any corners in making these a pair of supreme prototypes.

previously been registered. Its HSM 2003 chassis number was an invention, for there were never more than two of these cars!

The result, as finished off in 1985, was a masterpiece. Better built in almost every way than the car which Donald Healey had inspired, it gleamed, and it worked well. There was no doubt that this was one of the finest historic Triumphs of all time.

In the restoration, Merrick re-created the original Dolomite, reversing what Robert Arbuthnot and Corsica had done in 1938. The original frame and all the running gear was kept, the bulkhead was moved back to its original location, and only a number of redundant mounting holes in the frame now told another story.

Preparing to drive these cars took time, for the cockpit is small, and there was much to learn. The steering wheel – big and rather springy, but absolutely 'right' for the period – was closer to the chest than would be ideal, nor was there much legroom, for Donald Healey was short, and the car had been designed around him.

We found that once it was on the move, this was a car with – say – Triumph TR3A performance, nothing extraordinary in the 2000s of course, but simply sensational when launched in the 1930s. Those were the days when a 3½-litre Bentley was happier at 80mph than a flat-out 95mph. Here, though, was a thoroughbred two-seater with a 100-105mph top speed – the fastest British car of its day. Not only that, but when mobile there was a delicious combination of sounds to add to the excitement – that urgent engine clamour, the whine of the supercharger, and the myriad mutterings from the epicyclic gearbox and the straight-tooth rear axle.

That was the sort of noise The Saint must have enjoyed when Leslie Charteris wrote of him in his original books, the sort of noise which makes schoolboys of all ages spin round, gape, and point.

The passengers had rather upright seating positions, and because the ride was rock hard – look at those short semi-elliptic leaf springs and the tightly-wound friction dampers, and you'll see why – this car made an immediate statement.

By modern standards, for sure, this was a car which needed real effort and real concentration to keep it on the road. The chassis flexed, the wheels lifted, the tyres chirruped and span, given half a chance, and somehow one knew that it was always going to be a challenge. But it was worth every minute. This, after all, was the most ambitious 1930s Triumph ever designed, with a unique character, and it was one of only two in the world. Remember, too, that Donald Healey sat here ...

Most importantly, of course, is that after that we knew that both the cars which re-appeared in 1979 had gone into good hands, and although both were sold on as time progressed, they continued to be well-loved.

In many ways, therefore, the Dolomite straight-eight was the prewar company's finest hour. Never again would there be a Triumph like it, and it's sad that it was prevented from being produced through no fault of its own. While its performance seems unimpressive today, we should remember that it was built over 80 years ago. And a 2-litre car that could do 100-110mph in 1935 stood a chance of being the fastest touring-sports car in England, faster than any contemporary Lagonda, faster than a Rolls-Bentley. It was a Triumph in the generic as well as the specific sense. Driving it, as few save Donald Healey were lucky to do at the time, was to experience the classic sports car in its most highly developed form. It was Donald Healey's masterpiece – the big one that got away.

Dolomite and Demise

Triumph in 1936 must have been a sad place to be. Rationalisation, management had learned, was not the panacea they'd hoped it would be. Despite the elimination of peripheral sellers, concentration on the 'popular' unsporting models, and cancellation of the straight-eight Dolomite, production still faltered. No official figures are available, and the production statistics in Appendix V are based on serial number examination, but Triumph couldn't have built more than 1000 cars in 1936. The financial situation was therefore terrible – worse, if possible, than at any time before. No longer were there motorcycles on which to fall back. There was no apparent source of ready cash; no ancient mariner like Bettmann to lend guidance. The plus side showed only a string of rally victories by Donald Healey and his colleagues, which everyone knew were not enough. Balance sheets for October 1936 showed a record loss of £212,104 for the past fiscal year, with total indebtedness over £450,000, although about £100,000 of this was written-off after certain undisclosed 'adjustments.' Many other companies had already gone into receivership with statements less chilling than this. But Howe Graham and Lloyds Bank gamely decided to keep plugging – why, no-one can imagine – and to that end another reorganisation was planned.

In a circular letter to shareholders dated December 21, 1936, Triumph announced discussions "with important financial interests for the complete reorganisation of the company's capital structure and the provision of additional capital, to enable the company to take advantage of the improved demand for its products." Lending Triumph money in 1936 must have been akin to buying that used car from Richard Nixon, but demand was improving after the '37s had been announced. Dispatches during November and December were double those of the same period a year previously. Newnham, ever the optimist, declared that everything would be fine if he could lay hands on that necessary cash.

One way to raise money is to issue more stock, and this Triumph announced at its 30th December Annual General Meeting. Ordinary shares worth £200,000 were to be offered – providing that the existing 400,000 ordinary shares were reduced from £1 par value to just 2s (10p in modern decimal currency ...), cutting the firm's ordinary share capital to just £40,000. Preference shares were not reduced, but their holders were asked to accept cancellation of arrears on their 6¼ per cent dividend (unpaid since 1932), in exchange for the right to buy the new ordinary issue. The resulting ordinary share capital following these manoeuvres would be £240,000.

The people supporting the new shares issue included a triumvirate of H A Reincke, T A W Allen and W P Meeson. Reincke, their leader, had a favourable background in the steel industry, and had served as chairman of William Beardmore and Co Ltd from 1930 to 1936. Lord Leigh, now ailing, had asked to resign and Holbrook had taken his place, but to make room for Reincke the Colonel was demoted to deputy chairman. Reincke took the chair, with Allen as his finance chief, and Bill Meeson took over as works director, to succeed Captain Charles Ridley, who had moved on to the prestigious-sounding British subsidiary of Delage. Maurice Newnham, he whom Siegfried Bettmann had come to distrust, took over as managing director and chief executive. Meeson, like several other good managers in the industry, had gained valuable experience at Humber, especially in the years when the Rootes family was busy rationalising it with Hillman. On March 1, 1937, 150,000 unissued ordinary shares at £1 were subdivided into 1.5 million at 2s, while corporate capital was increased to its former £600,000 by the creation of 3.6 million more ordinary shares at 2s. If this infusion of money couldn't do it, nothing could.

Donald Healey actually left Triumph for six months in 1937, between April and October. In early April he joined Joseph Lucas Ltd as racing and competitions manager, but by mid-October he was back at Triumph, and now a member of the board as well as technical director. Management had possibly decided they couldn't do without him!

Triumph's new backers and reconstituted board had some cause for optimism. The third generation of motor cars had now been released with body design by Walter Belgrove, and the first engines both designed and built by Triumph. Top-of-the-line was the new Dolomite (no relation to the straight-eight Dolomite), followed by the Vitesse and, later, the Gloria 1½-litre. In addition, there was a continued range of Climax-engined Gloria Fours. Overall the 1937 lineup represented the broadest effort yet to cater to the variable public whim, a do-or-die attempt to make the Triumph motor car commercially viable. Newnham had renounced his rationalisation theories, at least temporarily.

Even after new-generation engines were introduced in 1936, old-type Glorias with old-type Coventry Climax engines were produced for a final season in 1937. This was a commercially wise gamble, to make use of old-type engines already produced, and delivered in the previous sanction.

1937 Triumph Range		
Model (doors/passengers)	Wheelbase (in)	Price
Gloria, 1232cc		
4-light Saloon (4/4)	108	£268
6-light Saloon (4/4)	108	£268
Special 4-light Saloon (4/4)	108	£288
Special 6-light Saloon (4/4)	108	£288
Special Tourer (2/4)	108	£288
Special Foursome Coupé (2/4)*	108	£315
Special Short-chassis Coupé (2/4)	96	£278
Southern Cross (2/2)	96	£278
Gloria 1½-litre, 1496cc		
4-light Saloon (4/4)	108	£318
6-light Saloon (4/4)	108	£318
Vitesse 14/60, 1496cc		
4-light Saloon (4/4)	108	£318
6-light Saloon (4/4)	108	£318
Vitesse 2-litre, 1991cc		
4-light Saloon (4/4)	116	£348
Coachbuilt Saloon (4/4)	116	£368
Dolomite 14/60, 1496cc		
Saloon (4/5)	110	£338
Saloon de Luxe (4/5)	110	£338
Dolomite/Continental 2-litre, 1991cc		
Saloon (4/5)	116	£368
*Cross & Ellis body		

The vast number of Glorias was more accident than plan, since many were left over when Triumph moved their premiere to July in order to allow time to build up a supply of new OHV engines. Glorias for 1937 were very much second fiddle, and when the supply ran out in the winter they were speedily deleted from brochures, their place taken by the Gloria 1½-litre, coded 'CX12' by Triumph. Their departure, incidentally, meant the end for the attractive Southern Cross leaving Triumph without a sports car for the first time since the arrival of Donald Healey.

There is evidence that the Southern Cross was still present 'unofficially,' however. Three examples have been encountered, bearing factory identification plates and obviously factory-built: Southern Crosses powered by OHV Vitesse 14/60 engines. Genuine 1937-registered vehicles, these Vitesse Southern Cross models were never catalogued by Triumph and were probably produced to fill a need – as cars were at the works in those days. They carried their headlamps on their wings, used a Vitesse badged and styled radiator grille, had no starting handle or bracket and featured a pressed-steel apron between the dumb-irons. Serial numbers ranged between 0081 and 0084 and two known number-plates were CKV 560 and DOE 150. These numbers were issued in December and May 1937 respectively.

Gloria changes for 1937 were in detail only (or there were none at all, so states the salesman's manual), though prices were cut to help move them out. At £268 and £278 for Saloon and Southern Cross, the cars were indubitably bargains. It was sad to see the Gloria depart after just four years, but as fine a car as it had been, it had failed to provide the needed volume.

The new engines powering the rest of the range followed an industry trend in their all-OHV design, the work of Donald Healey's engineers. The old Climax side exhausts, he says, were hard to cool properly and tended to cause service problems from overheating and burning valves. On the new engines, the exhaust ports were on the opposite side from the inlets, with ample water passages surrounding both – a definite improvement. There was a close relation between the superseded Climax Six and its successor. The first Triumph Six used the same connecting-rods and

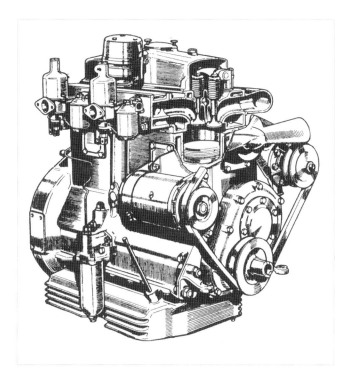

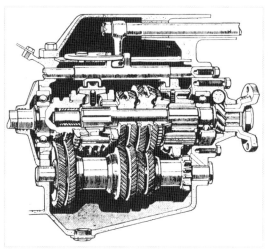

The technical analysis of the new Dolomite, published in *Motor* in July 1936, showed cutaway details of its all-new four-cylinder engine (left), and its synchromesh gearbox, which included gears supplied by Austin (above).

balanced. At 1496/1767cc, the Fours were larger and altogether different, but the Six was exactly the same size, down, even, to its 65 x 100mm bore and stroke.

It has been theorised that the new powerplants might have been capable of some enlargement – as much as 2650cc for the Six using 75mm pistons – but this would have been difficult without a major redesign of the block. While the Fours had been bored-out from the same-size block as the Climax, the Sixes retained the 65mm bore – for good reason. Gasket measurements suggest that 69mm pistons would have been barely possible, but 75mm pistons would have actually overlapped, since the cylinder centres are only 75mm (in pairs) apart. Larger Sixes could not have followed unless offset rods were used, which wasn't typical practice at the time. Finally, the Six block is narrow, and the valving arrangement in a larger-bore engine would be extremely cramped.

There were, of course, notable differences between the old and new engines. Aside from the all-overhead valve arrangement, the Triumph units used a 'crossflow' cylinder head. Unlike Climax Fours, Triumph Fours were not initially offered with single carburettors; all engines featuring twin SUs with air cleaners, fed by an electric pump. Crankshafts were extremely rigid, running in four large plain bearings in the Six, three in the Four.

The Vitesse chassis frames were essentially unchanged from those of the 1936 Glorias: as before, they were upswept at the front, underslung at the rear, with a cruciform centre member. The Dolomite had a similar, slightly wider frame to permit a roomier body with a three-passenger rear seat, and a slightly wider track. The most significant difference between it and the Vitesse lay in the rear-spring attachments, which were reversed. Among unaltered components were the brakes, shock absorbers and steering. Wheelbases remained the familiar 108/116 inches, while automatic chassis lubrication was dropped in favour of grouped nipples.

This magnificent show-finished example, shows the twin-SU installation of the new-generation six-cylinder engine fitted to Gloria/Vitesse types of the late 1930s.

pistons, and the dimensions of cylinder centres and main bearings were identical. The early Six also had the same chankshaft as its predecessor, though this was later redesigned, better shaped, and

The four-speed gearbox was new and much modified in design. Encased in light alloy, it featured synchromesh on second, third and top, enabling the company to drop freewheel. Triumph built the

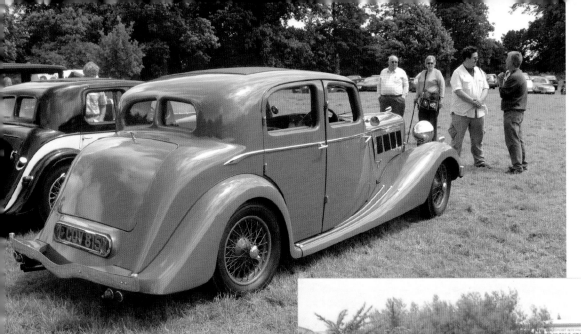

When Triumph announced a new range of cars in the summer of 1936, the top of the range model, with a new style, was badged Continental, and ran on a 116in wheelbase version of the familiar chassis, with the new in-house 2-litre six-cylinder engine, and was priced at £368. Stylist Walter Belgrove insisted that he had not been influenced by seeing the latest SS-Jaguar, but you must draw your own conclusions.

box, using gears purchased from Austin – it still lacked its own gearcutting machinery – and the unit was highly praised.

Mechanically, then, the new cars were evolutionary, not revolutionary. In body design they also represented gradual change, though the public didn't see it that way. And whenever a motorist accused Triumph of marching to a different drummer, he was usually referring to Walter Belgrove's new 'waterfall' grille on the Dolomite, the first die-cast grille on any British car.

Walter's frontispiece shocked conservatives and resulted in considerable flack – enough that poor Newnham took to writing impassioned defences of it, and even coughed-up the Vitesse grilled Continental. The reaction is an interesting case study in comparative attitudes on each side of the Atlantic. When Walter later asked the writer what was going on in America at this time, the answer was that die- or pressure-cast grilles were as popular as bathtub gin, that wonderful Prohibition brew! Following the leads of the Lincoln Zephyr and Chrysler Airflow, nearly every American manufacturer had adopted such decorations by 1937, and the public couldn't get enough.

Indeed, as many noticed, the Dolomite grille was a near twin to the Hudson Terraplane's. Obviously the Triumph would have been more uniformly accepted in Detroit!

Walter Belgrove encountered plenty of opposition to the idea, and his account provides an interesting glimpse at the typical British engineering department of the period.

"There were engine, body and chassis departments, each with their clearly defined spheres of operation and specification,"

The new range of Dolomites of 1936 onwards was always controversial because of this sweeping front grille. In later years, stylist Walter Belgrove accepted that it was visually like that of certain Mercedes-Benz and Hudson models of the period, but insisted that they never influenced his vision. Belgrove was always defensive about his themes.

Belgrove related. The aim and object was liaison and compromise, with strict lines of demarcation as to who designed what!

"A school of thought was emerging in Italy and America that this was a tradition-bound policy which hindered the primal object – that a motor car should be designed as a homogeneous whole, not as three separate concepts. This is a tradition-ruled country still, and in the prewar era it was an Empire-conscious, conservative stronghold of 'let well enough alone,' 'no change for change's sake,' 'hang the radicals,' etc. Anything new was automatically suspect and evoked feverish discussion from pulpit to Pall Mall, with the press baying like hound dogs after the fox. Radiator shells had always been traditional – rectangular forms housing the cooling block. They could be flat or vee, with honeycomb grille, vertical or horizontal slats; and they were the province of the chassis department, in conjunction with the radiator manufacturer.

"The desire to get away from this flat box, as I remember, came

from Maurice Newnham and Donald Healey, probably following their interest in the American pressure-cast fronts then in vogue. The traditional shell was perfectly suited to press-tool methods, but not to the two-dimensional swept forms envisaged by the American designers." (Triumph could not afford pressure-casting; the Dolomite grille was therefore die-cast, by R E Ormerod Ltd of Bromsgrove, the same company that provided its bonnet mascots.)

Continued Mr Belgrove: "It was felt that we should rethink a front-end, and get away from the strictly traditional. The exercise was taken away from the chassis department and given to me. The engineer who worked with me was Stanley Middleton. I was hard pressed at the time with a small department, plus a good deal of work on hand, and it was finally agreed that I would design the grille and carry out the full-scale work, leaving the chassis department to detail it for production. It would, however, still remain on the chassis specification.

When the revised Triumph range appeared in 1936, complete with its new-generation engines, the radically different 'waterfall' front grille caused a great deal of controversy. The factory was clever enough to arrange for this to be an absolute 'either-or fitment' on its bodyshells for customers who insisted ...

"I prepared several airbrush drawings of different schemes, and one was chosen for a mock-up following a full-size layout of the component parts. From these a grille was duly made from sheet steel, polished and chrome-plated, this same taking the place of a standard shell on the Dolomite car. It was accepted and the design frozen for production – I did not have to sell it. It was evidently what Newnham and Healey wanted and I cannot remember any reaction in the factory. But from the public it had a mixed reception, and as I remember, was both liked and loathed – no half-measures. Those who liked it thought it was a step in the right direction. The diehards, however, thought that it was a break with tradition, equivalent to walking bare-arsed into St. Paul's Cathedral during Lent ..."

The Autocar's contribution to the baying of hounds was a letter in their October 30, 1936 number, signed 'Real Radiator.' RR was quite horrified: "an achievement in mechanical construction is not necessarily an achievement of mechanical beauty," he spouted. "How often one hears nowadays, 'What a beautiful looking car,' and then, 'from the radiator backwards.'"

Maurice Newnham had a pat answer for such dissidents. First, he offered gripers the 2-litre Continental Saloon – identical in most respects to the 2-litre Dolomite, except for its Vitesse radiator and twin dipping headlamps. Second, he praised Triumph's pathfinding instincts. The grille was "an attempt to break away from the old shapes and conventions that have existed in British motor car design for over 20 years. In actual fact, the manufacture of this grille is a great achievement for British engineering. It is the first in the world to be produced by the gravity die-cast process, and American experts who were shown the design before the dies were completed asserted positively that it would not be commercially possible to make it." So the Americans were consulted! It would be fascinating to learn who – one doubts it was Hudson ...

There was, as Triumph's correspondence indicated, little controversy about the rest of the Dolomite. The lines were sleek and stylish, the Six especially well-balanced with its long bonnet and flowing wings, despite the interruption of an offside-mounted spare and large, high headlamps. Having owned a 1938 Dolomite 2-litre this writer can add that photographs rarely do the car justice. In real life, on the road especially, it has a rakish, hunkered-down look, as attractive now as it was in those distant years between Depression and World

With a body rather different from the earlier generation of Gloria/Vitesse types, this 1937 model 14/60 shows a smart update of what we might call the 'Belgrove theme,' still with a traditional type of radiator grille.

War. Dolomite and Continental bodywork was exceptional – of this there can be no question.

For some, the new cars were almost too attractive to have come from mere Triumph. A common rumour, which still circulates today among collectors, is that their styling was connected to that of SS-Jaguar. Like the SS, which appeared a year earlier, the Dolomite was a close-coupled saloon, and the doors, window line and curving structure around the rear light are very similar. Conjecture apparently stems from the fact that Bill Thornton, Triumph's chief body engineer, left – via Lea-Francis – to join SS Cars in early 1935. Since lead times were fairly short in those days of ash frames and aluminium panelling, it is possible that Thornton remembered advance sketches at Triumph when assisting William Lyons in the creation of the SS-Jaguars. While Lyons always made the final decision, he certainly listened to his engineers. An opposite theory is that Walter Belgrove was influenced by the SS. But Walter discounted any relationship either way.

"Nobody swiped anything," he told the writer. "The double swept-back on the later Glorias was a feature of Triumph before Jaguar used it. In the Dolomites I accentuated this feature by increasing the over-hang, lofting the waist at the elbow, and in general enlarging the boot capacity, which was the object of the exercise. We retained the split backlight." Sir Williams Lyons also feels that the resemblance was coincidental, telling this writer that the 1936 SS saloons were already well along in design when Bill Thornton arrived from Triumph.

The Vitesse series of four- and six-cylinder saloons was a different blend of the old and new: Triumph OHV engines powered saloon bodies from the previous Gloria-Vitesse. A 2-litre coachbuilt and 14/60 six-light saloon were also offered, and Vitesse chassis appear to have been sold for custom bodywork. At least

A characteristically excellent cutaway drawing of the 1938 Dolomite, with its 1767cc engine, by *The Autocar*'s John Ferguson.

one was shown with an attractive Swiss roadster body. Avon did not formally offer a coupé on Triumph chassis until 1938, but was apparently not unwilling to undertake special orders earlier.

Rounding out the 1937 line was a mid-year introduction, the 'new' Gloria – variously labelled the 1½-litre and Gloria Fourteen – with a 1496cc OHV engine. It replaced the vanished Climax-engined Glorias, on announcement in February 1937, and used the more upright body of the old Gloria. An additional body style offered in May 1937 was a six-light saloon, which was carried over unchanged into the 1938 season – the sole remaining Gloria that year.

Walter Belgrove's artistic talents as a sculptor became evident that year, with a most attractive lady bonnet mascot. Proudly undraped with flowing wings, she leaned forward from a Triumph 'world' disc, one knee bent, as graceful in her way as Rolls-Royce's 'Spirit of Ecstasy' – and less likely, as one enthusiast points out, to fall over the front end if the car stopped short. This mascot was fitted to the Gloria 1½-litre, the Vitesses and the Continental; Dolomites built through spring 1937 used an angular, stylised eagle instead, which didn't blend as well with their streamlined styling. Walter's lady continued through the 1938 models, and many hold her the prettiest ever to grace a Triumph bonnet.

Interiors of the new cars were up to typical Triumph standard, upholstered in leather and leather-cloth, with walnut facias/door fillets and soft carpeting underfoot. Saloons were fitted with sliding sunshine roofs and safety glass; instrumentation did not include a rev-counter, but was otherwise complete. Thoughtful extras included assist pulls, overhead magazine nets, and a steering-column adjustable for height and reach. Tyre changes were made easy with four jacking points and centre-lock wire wheels.

With larger-displacement four-cylinder engines, performance was enhanced. The Vitesse models, weighing as much as 250lb less than the Dolomites, seemed to be the quickest of the lot. *The Autocar*, testing four flavours of 1937 Triumph, provided these comparative figures:

	Gloria 1½	Vitesse 4	Dolomite 4	Vitesse 6
Top speed, mph	69.8	78.3	72.6	79.7
10-30, 3rd, secs	11.0	7.8	9.0	8.9
10-30, top, secs	17.0	11.3	12.9	12.0
20-40, 3rd, secs	11.6	8.7	9.5	10.0
20-40, top, secs	16.3	11.4	13.9	13.4
0-50mph, secs	22.9	15.9	19.8	17.8
0-60mph, secs	40.7	25.4	32.2	27.3

The Vitesse thus emerges as an underrated car at a time when the spotlight (and heaviest production) was given to the Dolomite. The 14/60, *Motor* said, was "smooth and flexible," able to reach a genuine 80mph, more than *The Autocar* had achieved: "Consequently the performance can rightly be termed comprehensive ... This capacity for fast and effortless travel makes the car particularly attractive when covering long distances, and it is combined with an adequate power reserve for climbing hills." Its rivals echoed its praise adding that Vitesse handling and ride comfort made for a perfect combination: "This car can be put round fast main road bends, and sharper turns as well, in an absolutely sure and certain manner, yet by no manner of means is the springing harsh in either front or back seats ... There is a taut feeling about the car, too, and the steering is very good indeed." The wheel position was excellent, the high-geared steering giving just 2¼ turns lock-to-lock. The Vitesse was termed "a splendid car ... one that ought to have a happy future." A little optimistic, in view of what was to come, but deserved praise nonetheless.

Similar approval marked the Dolomites' performance. *The Evening Standard*'s motoring correspondent went all-out, calling the 2-litre "the safest fast car of any British manufacturer I have yet driven costing anything like the price. During a four-day test this car glided through traffic, climbed steep hills, and sped along by-passes with silly ease." *The Sunday Observer*'s man, meanwhile, was enjoying the Dolomite 14/60: "You will have gathered that (it is) a fast car and a lively one, that it accelerates as you want it to, that it climbs. What I would like to make plain is that it does these and other things in a very unobtrusive manner." A lot of reviewers hedged on that controversial radiator design, though. *The Autocar*, whose editors rarely panned a car in those days, was being diffident indeed when they concluded that an 'orthodox' set of wings and bonnet just prevented the car from being 'freakish'. After a bit you'd get used to that grille, they said. It was 'very much a matter of opinion.' One could surmise what their opinion was!

One of the last additions to the range was the Dolomite de Luxe four-cylinder saloon at £348, introduced around the same time as the new 1½-litre Gloria. Reflecting Triumph's six months' experience with the initial run of Dolomites, it offered certain improvements: the grille was modified, its horizontal side sections made of pressed-

What a difference a decade made – this 1938 Dolomite being less then a decade younger than the tiny Seven/Eight/Nine-generation machine parked behind it.

steel instead of cast-alloy, and chrome-plated. Dolomite de Luxes also featured a foglamp, rear rope pulls, head cushions for rear seats, sun visor, and its own set of ten distinctive colour schemes. Early photos, incidentally, show it still wearing the stylised eagle mascot, suggesting that the flying lady was added very late to Dolomites.

All these new models suggested that the financial picture must improve, and indeed, by mid-1937, it did. The Climax-engined Glorias were finally out of the way, no major tooling was scheduled, and with Triumph concentrating on its own engine and new models there was actually a profit. For the nine-month period ending July 31, the company made £32,528. The Depression seemed to be easing, sales and production were high, and the Dolomites seemed popular, waterfall grille or not. (Triumph saw no need to continue the Continental for 1938.) The directors' report of July 31 noted that the business had "extended its manufacturing facilities and makes all the major components of its cars, including engines, gearboxes and the complete framing and paneling. Full provision has been made in the accounts for maintenance of plant and machinery, but with regard to the substantial rises which are taking place in the prices of machine tools, the greatly increased value of the company's designs, and the fact that an independent valuation of the fixed assets was carried out on October 31, 1936, no specific deduction has been made for depreciation." They recommended that a modest £5000 be placed aside for that area, while £3150 should be applied to expenses of the recent reorganisation.

The picture remained hopeful through most of 1937. In December, Triumph showed a nine-month profit of over £35,000. Looking to the future, Newnham began thinking about a partner who might help share the burden of further expansion and capital investment. Several discussions occurred, but the most promising was with Donald Healey's old firm, Riley, where Healey, now a Triumph director, still maintained personal connections.

Riley, as a Triumph partner, was a mixed bag. Its finances had been as variable as a sine curve for the past several years and, while it had a fine line of sporting saloons and a notable competition record, its products were more competitive than complementary. Whilst Triumph made money in 1937, Riley incurred considerable losses. From the Riley side, a merger must have looked enticing. Victor Riley had never considered partners in the past, but on February 19, 1938, his firm was placed in voluntary receivership; a partner, still making money and unaligned to the growing Rootes or Nuffield empires, was attractive.

About this time Riley issued a report by its directors: "Certain negotiations have been carried on in connection with a proposed merger [with Triumph] and the board are most hopeful that ... it will be possible to submit a reconstruction scheme, either by merger or otherwise." But nothing came of it, thanks to a better offer from one of the empire-builders: Riley was personally purchased in September 1938 by Lord Nuffield. He resold to the Nuffield Organisation, and under this command Riley's long history as a sporting marque reached the same abrupt end as MG's had under the same purchaser. Fourteen years later, Riley was swallowed up by BMC, and in due course by British Leyland – where it died an unhappy badge-engineered death in 1969. Victor Riley lasted only until the BMC merger, when he gladly quit.

"I can only continue in business as long as it holds some promise of romance," he'd said earlier. "Races, trials, round-the-world expeditions – this is the romantic side of the motor industry. When it's no more, I shall retire. I couldn't stand it if it were mere manufacturing, like sausage-making." He might have applied the same rationale to Triumph, whose 1938 range must have disappointed sporting motorists within and without the company. Eliminated forever was the Southern Cross, last vestige of the sporting past. Though the Vitesse and Dolomite were fine cars, they were heavy and luxurious conveyances, not the rally-dominating, bulldog-tough Glorias of years past. There was just one Gloria left now, a dowdy and upright six-light saloon. Aside from a pair of dropheads, the 1938 range was one of the blandest Triumph had ever produced. Fortunately the Dolomite Roadster Coupé hastened along in May 1938 to relieve matters.

1938 Triumph Range		
Model (doors/passengers)	*Wheelbase (in)*	*Price*
Gloria Fourteen, 1767cc		
6-light Saloon (4/4)	108	£288
Vitesse 14/60, 1767cc		
Saloon (4/4)	108	£298
Foursome coupé (2/4)*	108	£338
Vitesse 2-litre, 1991cc		
Saloon (4/4)	116	£388
Foursome coupé (2/4)*	116	£378
Dolomite 1½-litre, 1496/1767cc		
Saloon (4/5)	108	£328-335
Foursome coupé (2/4)*	108	£368
Dolomite 14/60, 1767cc		
Saloon (4/5)	110	£348
Foursome coupé (2/4)	110	£388
Dolomite 14/60, 1767cc		
Roadster Coupé (2/4)	110	£348
Dolomite 2-litre, 1991cc		
Saloon (4/5)	116	£388
Foursome coupé (2/4)	116	£428
*Avon bodies		

Triumph now attempted to offer as many combinations of body types and engines as was possible. The Gloria, with its higher-displacement Four, could be had with two-carburettor induction for £10 extra, for example. The Dolomite 1½-litre was available with both-size Fours – with the larger engine it constituted the 'Police package' at £7 extra, including foglamp and Lucas horn. Thus it filled a market gap between the 14/60 Vitesse and Dolomite.

An argument may be made that the Dolomite only looked its best on the longer wheelbases – the 2-litre cars seem better proportioned than the 1767s, which with a 110-inch wheelbase came off better than the Dolomite 1½-litre. But Triumph had to sell cars, and the drill was to try every permutation possible. It's worth noting that the Dolomite 1½ was not merely last year's 14/60 on the old wheelbase. It was actually an amalgam of designs. Door-hinge positions indicate that it did not have the standard Dolomite body and, while the frame was basically Dolomite, the springs were shackled differently. The body was more Vitesse than Dolomite, except for the waterfall grille.

No modifications were made to the Glorias or Vitesses, though the larger Dolomites had several improvements. The radiator shell now had cast, curved (instead of pressed, straight) side grilles, which improved its appearance, and its bonnet louvres were redesigned in a pointed motif. All Dolomites now adopted the boot-mounted spare wheel in lieu of the earlier side-mount, and one could get into the boot with the same Yale key that unlocked the ignition. Dolomites also switched to Luvax-Bijur automatic chassis lubrication and adopted a tandem master-cylinder, which made front and rear brakes independent of each other, while maintaining proper compensation between them. There were minor changes to ignition and carburation, and engines were modified for quieter running. The option list for all the 1938s included Ace wheel discs (£10 10s) and a Philco wireless (£18 10s); Dolomite 1¼s could be fitted with passing lamps and twin mellotone horns for about £10 extra. Eight colours were offered, none of them duotone, despite the occasional Dolomite seen with duotone colours today. A typical group for the period, they included dark, light and mistletoe green; amaranth or bright red; powder blue; ivory; and black.

The Avon dropheads listed officially that year were theoretically available on all Vitesse and Dolomite chassis. Not at all resembling the old Cross & Ellis designs, they were fundamentally different in three respects: the folding tops were of different pattern, there was an exterior-mounted leather trunk, and the paneling was steel instead of aluminium. In 1966, Reg Walton, managing director of Avon Bodies Ltd, recalled these models for Glyn Jones. The original design, he said, stemmed from either Alan Jensen (later co-proprietor of Jensen Cars), or A H Meredith (a director of the postwar Avon Company). Walton said the design was "primarily for Standard chassis, as they were our main products at that time ... the body appears rather wide for a Vitesse chassis." While he didn't know how many Triumph chassis were so fitted, he felt there were

"certainly more than ten." Whether any were fitted to Dolomites, per period catalogues, he did not know. According to Walton, the bodies were supplied on order to Triumph, so presumably they were assembled at the Gloria works.

The 14/60 Roadster Coupé introduced in April 1938 was the last sporty car of the prewar years, and more popular, as it turned out, than even Triumph expected. A lovely touring roadster, later with enhanced horsepower, it boasted comforts usually not found in this kind of motor car: roll-up windows with vent-wings, and a deck behind the main compartment which unfolded to accommodate two more passengers. Roadster Coupés were luxuriously trimmed in pigskin-grained leather, which was applied to the door panels and dashboard as well as the seats. There were two tool drawers mounted underneath the main seat, and a disappearing centre armrest was fitted. Buttoned-up, as it was obviously meant to be most of the time, it was a clean-lined model with a beautifully curved, swept-down rear deck. The dickey seat was really out of fashion by now, and not easy to reach in any case. The most graceful way to get in would have been to be lowered by a crane, though ostensibly one could clamber up on let-down steps built into the body sides – a dicey manoeuvre, especially if the climber wore skirts.

Walter Belgrove says, "the Roadster Coupé came from my drawing board and again much of the full-scale draft was mine.

A proud and ever-smiling Donald Healey standing alongside his Dolomite Roadster Coupé of 1938.

Just a handful of these smart Avon-bodied Vitesse Foursome coupés were built. They were very rare at the time, and it is thought that only one example – this one – survived into modern times.

With a design office always overstretched, this seemed the natural order of things in those days … It was, of course, a batch production vehicle as against being fully tooled and volume-produced – Birmabright panels on an ash frame. The decision by Maurice Newnham and Donald Healey to produce this type of vehicle proved right. It won consistently in all the Concours d'Elegance, in and out of its class, and it also took the Gold Medal in its class at Earls Court in 1938 – the last Motor Show before the war and the first at that exhibition hall … By the way, it has been inferred that I 'borrowed' the design of the Roadster Coupé from the 1936 Mercedes 170V sports-roadster, but as far as I was concerned I never saw it until the styling job was finished." (Walter also created a fixed-head coupé to be sold at £395, but only one pilot model was built before the project was abandoned.)

When the six-cylinder Roadster Coupé joined the Four in 1939, it too boasted a horsepower increase to 75bhp. Test results proved satisfactory: 0-50mph coming up in 15 seconds, 0-60 in 23, and with a top speed of over 80mph. On paper this made it about four seconds slower than the old Southern Cross, but the four-cylinder model was the one Triumph used in rally competition. A L Pearce, for example, won the 10-15hp class two years running in the RAC

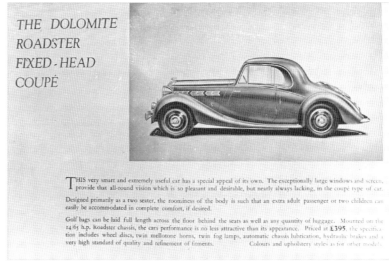

THE DOLOMITE ROADSTER FIXED-HEAD COUPÉ

THIS very smart and extremely useful car has a special appeal of its own. The exceptionally large windows and screen, provide that all-round vision which is so pleasant and desirable, but nearly always lacking, in the coupe type of car.

Designed primarily as a two seater, the roominess of the body is such that an extra adult passenger or two children can easily be accommodated in complete comfort, if desired.

Golf bags can be laid full length across the floor behind the seats as well as any quantity of luggage. Mounted on the 14/65 h.p. Roadster chassis, the car's performance is no less attractive than its appearance. Priced at £395, the specification includes wheel discs, twin mellotone horns, twin fog lamps, automatic chassis lubrication, hydraulic brakes and a very high standard of quality and refinement of fitments. Colours and upholstery styles as for other models.

Triumph showed this prototype hard-top version of the Roadster Coupé in 1938, but it never went into production.

Top: Was there a single angle from which the 1938/39 Roadster Coupé did not look elegant? We do not think so – even when the car had to have its soft-top erected.
Middle: The facia/instrument panel of the Roadster Coupé was as high a quality fitment as any other part of the car.
Bottom: Normally, an owner would use his Dolomite Roadster Coupé as a two/three-seater, but in that sleek tail is a concealed extra pair of seats – the 'dickey' option.

A 2-litre six-cylinder version of the Roadster Coupé was announced in July 1938, ready for the 1939 season. That is one of the buildings at the Brooklands race track.

Only one prototype fixed-head Roadster Coupé was ever built, which featured a sturdy steel roof. In this application the dickey seat provision was omitted, and the Triumph styling 'trademark' of a two-piece rear window returned.

Rally, although the six-cylinder did take more laurels than the four-cylinder in concours. In the RAC coachwork competition at Blackpool it gained first prize in the open-car class up to £350, and in the drophead coupé class was judged the finest open car regardless of price – the only model under £1000 to receive a premier award. Later, six-cylinder Roadster Coupés took first prizes in the Scottish, Welsh and Ramsgate concours, while a 14/65 won its class in the latter event. "It will thus be seen that the car has

received the highest commendation by expert judges both in its open and closed condition," said brochures.

Through these semi-new products and semi-competitive performances, Triumph maintained a stiff upper lip, but the proclaimed optimism turned out to be either ill-founded or purposely misleading. In April 1938, for example, the firm announced that production was up 56 per cent (compared with what, it didn't say) – yet the statement of accounts issued at the end of August showed only a 12.5 per cent gain in sales. Either sales dropped off radically after April 1938 – as Donald Healey believes – or the dealers were stuck with a lot of unwanted cars. Or both! It is certain that Triumph was not selling as many cars in 1938 as in 1937, and the new 1939 line reflected this, being reduced to Dolomites only, plus a mid-year introduction, the Triumph Twelve.

1939 Triumph Range		
Model (doors/passengers)	*Wheelbase (in)*	*Price*
Dolomite 1½-litre, 1496cc		
Saloon (4/5)	108	£332 18s
Dolomite 14/60, 1767cc		
Saloon (4/5)	110	£348
Royal Saloon (4/5)	110	£375
Foursome Coupé (2/4)*	110	£395
Dolomite 14/65, 1767cc		
Roadster Coupé (2/4)	110	£395
Dolomite 2-litre, 1991cc		
Royal Saloon (4/5)	116	£425
Foursome Coupé (2/4)*	116	£445
Roadster Coupé (2/4)	116	£450
Twelve, 1496cc		
Saloon (4/5)	108	£285
*Salmons bodies		

The price structure was left pretty much alone. Whether or not Triumph could make a profit at these prices, it really had no choice. There was tremendous competition in its field – never a big portion of the marketplace, anyway. Firms like SS were building saloons at least as good for less money, while the larger-engined SS dropheads were faster than the Roadster Coupé and undeniably attractive. Design changes were minimal: Walter Belgrove widened his Dolomite grille by adding more vertical bars, and invented a new bonnet lady lying on her stomach. (At first she wore transparent wings made of a material called 'Catalan', but these didn't hold up well and replacements with cast wings were supplied.) On the

The Dolomite Royal, sold only in 1938 and 1939, was the last, largest and most carefully detailed of all the Belgrove-Healey generation. It was always the most costly saloon in the range – £425 for the six-cylinder type – and because of the flush-fitting doors, and all-steel roof, more interior space and more headroom, it out-ranked the other Dolomites.

The 'entry level' Triumph 12, engineered hurriedly by Healey's team, and styled by Belgrove, was announced in March 1939, ready to sell at only £285. It used a much-modified version of the Dolomite 1½-litre body framework.

Dolomite 1½-litre, upholstery was reshaped to give more back support.

New for 1939 was the Dolomite Royal, the largest and most luxurious Triumph saloon in history. Its body was 2 inches wider and 1½ inches higher than standard, with a large extended luggage compartment. The fabric roof insert was done away with, in favour of all-steel construction, though the sliding sunshine feature was retained. Royal doors were countersunk to fit flush rather than overlap the centre pillar as on conventional Dolomites, presenting a cleaner appearance and cutting down on wind noise. There were glass louvres above the four side windows, new curved door handles, and shorter Lucas exterior-mounted horns. Inside, upholstery was rolled and pleated leather, and brown facia knobs replaced the standard white buttons.

Triumph dropheads were now built by Salmons & Sons, and had a new feature – self-tensioning rails to hold the fabric taut when erected. They were also considerably more expensive than their predecessors. The range offered three new colours – lavender, silver-grey and jade green. The Roadster-Coupé's novel pigskin grained upholstery was made available on the other body styles.

In March of 1939, Triumph made one more attempt to down-price its range with the £285 Twelve, using the 1496cc or 1767cc engines on Dolomite 1½-litre body framework. Belgrove carried out certain modifications: altered wings, a conventional squared-off radiator. Unlike the Dolomites, the luggage boot lid fully contained the spare tyre, but it was fitted completely into the lid and needed no cover on the outside. The boot lid was extended to be let down to carry extra luggage, for an auxiliary number-plate was mounted so as to be visible in this position. A creditable list of standard equipment was fitted – Luvax hydraulic shock-absorbers, polished walnut interior trim, clock, sun visors, sunshine roof, automatic chassis lubrication – but to economise there was a mechanical fuel pump and disc-type road wheels (wire wheels were optional). The Twelve was the last prewar Triumph to come from Walter Belgrove's drawing board. "I believe we made about 400 of them before the war stopped production," noted the designer. (Later research, in fact, indicates that only about 50 cars were built, of which just three are known to have survived.)

The Triumph company had now reached the end of a distinguished career. A small trading profit (£13,878) was realised at the end of 1938, but against this was an overall operating loss of £41,950, largely due to continuing demands for capital investment, and tooling expenses for the Twelve. Suddenly, Triumph declared the factory on Holbrooks Lane too large to build the few cars required – ironic indeed, since motorcycles had been abandoned to make room for cars only three years previously. A section of the works was turned over to aero-engine component manufacture for the 'shadow factories' operating in anticipation of war with Germany. On June 7, 1939, the inevitable became official; Howe Graham's Birmingham accounting firm of Gibson & Ashford was appointed receiver to safeguard the interests of the bank – to which Triumph now owed £160,000. In July, Gibson & Ashford offered factory and equipment "as a going concern with substantial orders booked" on the open market. A few weeks later, Donald Healey sold it on behalf of the receivers to Thomas Ward & Co of Sheffield.

Everyone we have interviewed, and many that we couldn't, had his own post mortems on the prewar company. Siegfried Bettmann felt it was mismanaged from the time he left: Holbrook, he said, wanted change for change's sake, and Newnham never should have been taken into the company, period.

Donald Healey says, "I am afraid through lack of production knowledge and the slump of 1938, differences between Newnham (and Howe Graham) resulted in the failure of the company."

Walter Belgrove said, "the products were never better in performance and looks than in the latter years of the decade. The company never built for stock – every vehicle was virtually sold off the line. The trouble was that we could never build enough of them, and the finance for extensive production reorganisation did not exist. I think that the company would have weathered the storm, but not the war as well.' Maurice Newnham said the bank's representatives knew nothing about merchandising motor cars, and were concerned only with the balance sheets. Howe Graham said the bank had gone just as far as anyone could realistically go. Had he been a seer, he might have quoted the later words of Sir Winston Churchill: 'Never give up – never, never, never, never – except to convictions of honour, or good sense.'"

Analysis of the company's failings may start with its consistent lack of capital, but must include several other factors, the presence of which contributed to its demise. In the blazing light of retrospect, we can see that selling-off the motorcycle business was a mistake. Another mistake was investing in the big plant on Holbrooks Lane, the Gloria works, while never acquiring the expertise to run it at maximum capacity. All these decisions must be laid at the foot of management, as they always are, for it is management and nothing else that spells the success or failure of a company. The product, at least after 1934, certainly had no serious flaws, and many virtues.

Still it must be admitted that the product after 1934 had too much competition, the sheer numbers of which made it nearly impossible to build up any volume. Once it had parted company with the Super Seven and its derivatives, Triumph had no 'volume' car. In its rarefied market segment, many other firms were in the same straits, and casualties were frequent. Lea-Francis, for example, was in and out of receivership in the 1930s. Riley, as we've seen, was always in trouble, finally going bankrupt in 1938 for the approximate reasons that Triumph failed a year later. Alvis survived – but mainly because of its aero-engine business, a diversification which Triumph attempted after it was too late. Wolseley was the happy exception in this field – but Wolseley was owned by Nuffield, directed by Miles Thomas, and produced real quantities of attractively priced, Morris-based, motor cars.

One could suggest, as the ultimate second-guess, that cars like the Eights, Nines and Tens would have written a more successful Triumph story in the 1930s, a decade when economy cars survived for their very raison d'être. But how dull Triumph's history would have been were that the case! The Gloria, from the bank's standpoint, was probably the wrong type of car; the motorcycles, from the bank's standpoint, should have remained in the fold. But many business failures have built great motor cars, and Triumph produced some of the finest in Britain during those bitter-sweet years, proving their merits on road and rally route, at home and abroad.

Thus ended the era of 'the smartest cars in the land.' And, notwithstanding the qualifications with which one must temper those words of Col Holbrook, in a very real sense they were. No-one should ever forget that.

War and Resurrection

If Adolf Hitler's troops had not marched into Poland on September 1, 1939, thus precipitating the Second World War, there might never have been any more Triumph cars. At the end of that hot and uneasy summer, prospects for a company revival were very uncertain. In a continuing peacetime situation, a solution to the company's problems might have evolved in a different way. But it was not the war, on its own, which ensured Triumph's rebirth. What was important was the six years of grace given to Britain's motor industry to rethink its future, the way its members progressed under the massive pressure of producing war materials, and a change in ownership.

By August 1939, Howe Graham was still looking for an equitable solution to Triumph's problems. At this time, production at the Gloria and Stoke works was down to a trickle. A few Triumph Twelves were being assembled, mainly from existing stocks of parts, but no serious plans existed for further new models to be developed. The entire Dolomite range, even the successful Roadster Coupés, had disappeared.

We must make it clear, right away, that Howe Graham was not merely a company doctor, not merely a soulless accountant, and certainly not the type of man who was merely looking for a way to recover the massive debts owed to Lloyds Bank and other creditors. He had, after all, been connected with another Coventry motor business – Rover – since 1932, was still on its board of directors, and would eventually become its chairman in 1954. It was Graham who, along with Spencer Wilks, masterminded a splendid financial recovery at Rover in the 1930s, to an almost identical brief from that company's bankers.

At Triumph his problem was rather different from that at Rover. The problem at Rover had been one of over-production and poor quality. At Triumph it was one of high quality but falling demand. There is no doubt that by the end of the 1930s, in spite of Claude Holbrook's and Maurice Newnham's rationalisations, the Gloria and Stoke works were under-utilised. Worse, with the future – if any – in mind, they were both under-capitalised and heavily in debt.

In Coventry, of course, there was nothing strange about a motor manufacturing concern getting into financial trouble. Marques had come and gone in the 1920s, Swift had been submerged in 1931, Lea-Francis disappeared for a time in the mid-1930s, and as recently as 1938, Riley had slipped ignominiously into the hands of Lord Nuffield.

But compared with the 1920s, times were changing rapidly. Since the Great Depression, Williams Lyons' SS concern was the only significant new marque to make its name in Coventry. Its cars were in direct competition to established names like Alvis, Riley and Triumph, and was stealing sales from them all. But the market for this type of middle-class car was not expanding, so the SS-Jaguar sales pushing through 3000 cars a year meant smaller shares for everyone else. We might, therefore, speculate what might have happened if Triumph's fate had not been settled by the onset of war.

The company as it stood had physical assets in the shape of the factories, design assets in the shape of a good range of engines, and personal assets like Donald Healey (already a famous technical chief) and Walter Belgrove, its noted stylist/body engineer. But nothing, as far as we know, was in the new-model pipeline. No important new developments had been planned since the launch of the overhead-valve Dolomites at the end of 1936. Everything that had happened in the years which followed had been a further development of the original Healey-inspired scheme.

Both the factories were relatively old, quite small, and only really suited to the manufacture of this type of car. Triumph bodies, in particular, were erected in the traditional manner, with metal paneling covering ash frames. Triumph sub-contracted most of its own standard coachwork, but it relied on other specialists in the area like Cross & Ellis for special bodywork.

In the brooding and rather depressed financial atmosphere of 1939, therefore, Howe Graham appeared to be faced with these options:

He could try to revive Triumph in its existing form, even though it would then be crippled with debt for many years to come. This possibility was not attractive – although the motoring press was always kind about the cars, there is evidence to show that demand was steadily falling at the same time as prices were edging up.

He could decide ruthlessly to close down the business. Certainly the factories and the company's goodwill were marketable, and would have cleared the decks. But this would throw many men out of work, and it would mean the end of the company's existing heritage;

He could try to sell the business as it stood, debts and all, to some syndicate or organisation big enough to start-up car production again, and willing to bear the losses for a time. This looked possible;

Finally, perhaps, he could try for a merger with another car manufacturer, and hope that the economies of scale would work in Triumph's favour. This, for a time, looked most promising.

Here in Britain we were getting familiar with the business of mergers. After all, if Rolls-Royce had acquired Bentley in 1931, then it must be a respectable business practice! In the 1930s, too, Rootes and Nuffield had blossomed by such tactics – they were the real experts. The evidence of what tended to happen after a merger was formalised was not, however, very encouraging to those who wanted Triumph's spirit to survive. Rootes, after all, bought up Sunbeam and Talbot in 1935, spent the next three years shaking all the individuality out of these concerns, then evolved Sunbeam-Talbots in 1938 which were no more and no less than fancy Hillmans and Humbers.

Lord Nuffield, for instance, had personally bought Riley in 1938, sold it off at no personal profit to his Nuffield Group, and authorised the new models of 1939 at a few weeks' notice. Even so, the 'new' cars produced so hastily had something in common with the engineering of his fast-selling Wolseleys. Rationalisation was very swift.

Howe Graham, with all the experience of his years at Rover to back his judgment, wanted Triumph to survive. He wanted to see the cars back in production, and he thought that the only way to ensure this was to get another industry name interested. But could it be Lord Austin or Lord Nuffield? William Rootes or William Lyons? Captain John Black of Standard, or Spencer Wilks of Rover?

None of these tycoons came forward, probably because they knew the extent of Triumph's problems, which became even more obvious after the receiver's public statements. Although Triumph's issued capital consisted of £50,000 in £1 preference shares and £250,000 in 2s (10p) ordinary shares, the stock market rated the company's worth at £54,000 before the receiver arrived, and a derisory £3100 immediately afterwards.

There had been no dividend for ordinary shareholders since 1930, and preference shareholders had seen one payout (in 1937) since 1932. The book value of the factories was £305,200 (a figure which Donald Healey stoutly insists was absurdly low compared with their true value), but the company was at least that much in debt.

It was also exactly the wrong time to try to get other motor manufacturers interested in expansion. The war clouds were so loomingly obvious, and the rearmament programme so demanding, that there was little time or incentive to think of major peacetime developments.

Most car makers were worrying about the alternatives which faced them when (no-one thought in terms of 'if' any longer) war was declared. Should they try to keep car manufacture going, should they convert their works ready to build war machines, or should they try to combine the two?

Even so, Howe Graham let it be known that Triumph was for sale as a going concern, with substantial forward orders (which can only be described as an optimistic statement!). In August, at last, he was approached by Ashley Ward, who was joint managing director of Thos W Ward Ltd, a respected engineering and steel-making group based in Sheffield, Yorkshire.

Ward must have liked what he saw (though we know now that he was interested in selling-off some of the assets as well as in getting car production going again) for he told his fellow directors at the next board meeting that he had "established contact with the receiver, and after certain preliminaries, an inspection had been made of the two works at Coventry, the Gloria works comprising 10¾ acres, the Stoke works comprising 3¼ acres, and after taking a full inventory and discussion of the matter with his chairman, it had been decided to make an offer for the concern ..."

The dates are significant. Ashley Ward had inspected the plant in August, made Howe Graham what was obviously an acceptable offer before the end of the month, and his company was able to tell the world that it had taken control of Triumph on September 1. That day, be it noted, was the one on which Hitler's panzer divisions struck deeply into Poland, and was effectively the day the war began.

Whatever Ward was planning for Triumph would have to be modified in view of the emergency, and Ward's company records make it quite clear that this was so. In September, however, public pronouncements were reassuring. Although the management team led by Maurice Newnham handed over executive responsibilities to Ward when the company was sold, Donald Healey was asked to stay on as Triumph's new general manager; he had, of course, been on its board of directors since returning from that short stay at Lucas in 1937. Ward made it clear that it wanted to continue car production as long as possible and "so long as supplies last." We now have no way of knowing how many cars were actually built, though it has been estimated that only about 35 12hp cars were assembled under new ownership, and that existing stocks of completed Dolomites were sold-off.

It seems to be clear, however, that Ward was never very interested in the long-term future of Triumph motor cars. This would be no Nuffield-style takeover and rescue, and indeed Ward intended to go in for a good deal of what we would now call 'asset-stripping.' During September (the first mention of Triumph in Ward's company records is dated September 4) various offers of work to fill the factory were considered, mainly connected with the production of military material. Ashley Ward spent some time negotiating with Armstrong-Siddeley, not with a view to combining Triumph with the other Coventry-based concern, but in order to take on production work of Armstrong-Siddeley aeroplane engines.

Donald Healey's main task, as the short-time general manager during the interregnum, was to find a buyer for the Gloria works, which was to be denuded of its motor car manufacturing capacity. Ward had decided to sell-off a major part of the Triumph assets, and would concentrate what Triumph car work remained in the Stoke works at Clay Lane/Briton Road.

Healey negotiated with several companies before getting seriously and successfully involved with H M Hobson (Aircraft and Motor) Components Ltd, who specialised in making carburettors. Hobson was very much involved in the drive to increase aero-engine carburettor production and needed all the capacity it could find. Apart from its own factories, Hobson's carburettors were about to be built in a shadow factory in the Standard Motor Company's grounds at Fletchamstead, facing out on to the new Coventry bypass (later it became Ferguson's Coventry HQ and – from 1959 – the Standard-Triumph Engineering centre), and it was also renting a portion of the Morgan works at Malvern Link. It was all very symbolic (if anyone had chosen to think about it that way), being the first time that Triumph, Morgan and John Black of Standard were brought together in a form of business relationship.

The sale was not entirely without its problems. Ward was under the impression that Hobson was buying the Gloria works on its own behalf, but by November it became clear that Hobson was actually operating on behalf of its principal clients, the Air Ministry! As Ward was still sticking out for the best price for the Gloria works (the sale was to include certain machine tools previously used for making Triumph engines), it was astonished to discover that its purchaser was actually the British Government, who could, and eventually did, compulsorily purchase the property.

As Donald Healey was offered an important job by Hobson, and because the sale of the Gloria works leaked out in Coventry, the motoring public had to be reassured. Ward said, in November 1939, that the Triumph motor car "would continue." It dismissed the sale of the Gloria factory, and stated that service of customers' cars, and the assembly of some new cars, would now take place at Clay Lane/Briton Road. Donald Healey was stated to be continuing a 'watching brief,' but would mainly be concerned with research into aircraft carburation, while Triumph would effectively be run by J H Owen (who was already company secretary), with support from Lew Pearce.

By then, in fact, the wheel of fortune had turned full-circle. Triumph was effectively back where it had been in 1921 when Siegfried Bettmann had taken over Clay Lane from the Dawson Motor Co. The Gloria works – an ex-Government shell-filling plant, and ex-White and Poppe engine-building factory – was now Government property once again. Interestingly enough, even though the Gloria factory was cheek-by-jowl with William Lyons' SS factory (the two premises shared a boundary wall), Lyons had never made an offer to buy it in 1939, and did not do so in 1945 when Hobson prepared to vacate it as the war effort ran down.

Donald Healey's 'watching brief' at Triumph was a very vague arrangement, as he joined Hobson to lay down and commission a very elaborate set of testing equipment for developing high-altitude aero-engine carburettors at ground level. Hobson's local chairman and managing director was none other than the elder Laurence Pomeroy, who had been the renowned technical chief at Daimler in Coventry in the 1920s and 30s.

In the meantime, Ward's intentions for the Clay Lane/Briton Road works were quickly changed by the intensification of the nation's war effort. No more manufacture of new cars could be authorised, as no new supplies of parts were coming in, and the machine tools which once made engine and transmission parts had been sold-off. Ward therefore had to search Coventry for a company which needed extra space, and eventually concluded a tenancy agreement with Sir W G Armstrong Whitworth Aircraft Ltd of Coventry. By the end of 1939, therefore, Clay Lane/Briton Road was being used to make sections of aircraft. The old Triumph business, effectively, had already been dissolved, though the company's name and what physical assets it still possessed were in the hands of Thos W Ward Ltd. The spare-part stocks for Dolomites, Glorias and even earlier models, were stored at Clay Lane/Briton Road.

Whatever plan Ward then had for Triumph was never made clear in its records, and was in any case never to go into effect. On the night of November 14, 1940, the massed German bomber fleet plastered Coventry in a murderous hail of firebombs and high explosives. The original seven-story motorcycle building in Priory Street (separate from the car-making business since 1936, of course) was completely destroyed, while the Clay Lane/Briton Road premises were badly damaged.

Although enough of the old factory was left standing for Walter Belgrove to be able to pay a visit to collect what drawing-office schemes and details remained, it was really the end of the Triumphs of the 1930s as enthusiasts knew them. No attempt was ever made to rescue and repair the spare parts, most of which were bulldozed into the ground or sold-off as scrap.

The prewar cars, therefore, were finally isolated from anything that could follow, and the skeleton staff dispersed to their wartime duties. Donald Healey stayed at Hobson until Laurence Pomeroy died, then moved on to the Rootes Group's Humber Road factory to get involved in the development of armoured cars. He will shortly re-enter our story. Walter Belgrove moved across to the Standard Motor Company in the autumn of 1939 to work in the production and process-planning areas. In doing this he ensured his place in history as the only staff man of any seniority who worked for both the prewar and postwar Triumph managements. He, too, will soon re-enter this story.

Maurice Newnham, that great salesman and controversial managing director of Triumph until the final crash of 1939, rejoined the Royal Air Force. Rising to the rank of Group Captain he became responsible for running the Parachute Training School at Manchester's Ringway Airport, winning something of a daredevil reputation for himself by insisting on testing all the new and experimental equipment personally before letting it loose on his pupils. In peacetime he returned to several years of active business life with the family motor car distributorship before seeing it taken over, whereupon he retired to Hampshire, and died as recently as 1976.

Sir Claude Holbrook, once managing director, and latterly vice-chairman to H A Reincke in the original Triumph company, rejoined the army at the outbreak of war in a staff post, became a full Colonel, but finally retired in 1943. He died in 1979.

From 1940 to 1944, the period after Stoke was blitzed and before it was sold-off, there is virtually no mention of Triumph in Ward's company records. Armstrong Whitworth renewed its lease from time to time, and the undamaged portion continued to help its aircraft-production efforts. Ward appeared to have planned no postwar developments for Triumph, and it seems clear that by mid-war it had really washed its hands of the marque, its assets and its future, except that it was interested in selling-off the trademarks and other company tit-bits as the final part of, to them, a successful company break-up operation.

For a time, however, Donald Healey sought to convince them otherwise. Although by this time he was merely an employee of the Rootes Group, he was absolutely determined to be an important personality in the motor industry when it got under way again after the war had been won. Although he was hoping that Triumph could be reborn, and that he would be in charge of its fortunes, his experiences with the new owners in 1939 did not give him complete confidence.

He also had a burgeoning desire to make cars carrying his own name, particularly as his technical and sporting reputation was high enough to support this; even in the depths of the war he had started thinking about a new 'Healey' car for the postwar era.

In theory there should have been no time for him to do this. Healey, like many of his colleagues, would have liked to be out

fighting, but as he was thought too old (which was ridiculous, for though he was bald and more than 40 years old, he was an enormously vigorous person) and technically too important to be released to become a mere fighting soldier. He had to make do with the design and development of war machines instead. Working six days a week (as everybody did in those exciting days) should have left him with no time or energy for spare-time activities; Donald Healey and his friends (including ex-Triumph colleagues with whom he had kept in touch) thought otherwise.

Work on the design of a new car (it didn't really have a name) began during the blitz, but it was not until 1943/1944 that it was ready for showing to prospective sponsors. Healey, incidentally, though a great leader and great motivator, was not a trained designer, and relied on others for his detailed engineering. His original collaborators were A C 'Sammy' Sampietro, an expatriate Italian chassis designer with experience at Alfa Romeo, Maserati, and then with Thomson and Taylor at Brooklands in the 1930s; Ben Bowden, a stylist and body engineer; and James Watt, who was a salesman. The first two were actually employed by Rootes at Humber, along with Healey, while Watt was in the RAF, but based nearby.

It was Ben Bowden who struck the first blow, and he did not let any existing traditions get in his way. First of all he schemed-out body lines on the wallpaper of his dining room in Coventry, and later took tracings from the originals! There were to be two proposed shapes – a fixed head four-seater with two doors, and a drophead equivalent. In the meantime, Sampietro, much impressed by Volkswagen and Auto-Union suspensions of the 1930s, schemed-out trailing-arm independent front suspension, while alongside him another Rootes employee called Ireland found time to sketch a new chassis frame for the new Triumph. All this mechanical innovation, need it be said, took place in normal weekday working hours, by Rootes employees on Rootes drawing-boards!

At this stage there were no fixed ideas as to the main mechanical components – engines, gearboxes and axles – though Healey expected that he would be using Triumph components which had, after all, been newly developed for the Dolomite range in 1936. But he must also have known that the machine shop, tools and fixtures for making the engines and gearboxes had been sold-off by Ward when it was getting rid of the Gloria works towards the end of 1939, and that there was serious bomb damage to the design office and company records at Clay Lane/Briton Road.

Even so, Healey pressed on with his intention to show his plans for a postwar Triumph to Ward. James Watt, quoted from his original interview about this period (in Peter Browning's book *Healeys and Austin-Healeys*, published by Foulis) had this to say:

"Donald and I began to feel that our little team was really

getting somewhere and we now thought we nearly had a good enough design to think about production and that the time had come for us to try and sell our ideas to Triumph. I had already made two fairly successful approaches to Triumph, and in February 1944 the opportunity arose for another meeting ... At first things seemed most encouraging and they (Ward, in Sheffield) genuinely thought that our scheme and ideas had merit. However, Triumph (ie Ward) had had a board meeting recently and I was tremendously downcast to learn that it had decided not to back Healey, mainly for the simple reason that we were not car manufacturers ... And so we put aside all thoughts of building our cars at Triumph ... We had begun to call the car 'the Triumph', but when we lost the Triumph deal we just called it 'the car.'"

It was all so sad, and it could have been so easily avoided. But since Ward had taken over Triumph in 1939 as a bankrupt but going concern, it had sold-off the corporate arms and legs, only later to discover that the body alone did not attract Ward after all. Therefore, Ward, too, was no longer interested in being in the motor car business, and was actually preparing to sell off the company.

In fact it was a specious insult, a lame excuse, to turn down Healey's plans on the grounds that he was not a car manufacturer. He had, after all, directed Triumph's technical fortunes from 1934 to 1939, and had not Ward itself made him its general manager for a time in 1939? But if we now look forward, and see what happened to that design, we can see how foolish these decisions look in retrospect.

The selfsame design was honed yet further, fitted with an engine

This was the Standard Flying Fourteen, first produced in the late 1930s, then revived in 1945 for post-war production. It was the engine, transmission and suspension assemblies of this car which would provide the vital running gear for the new Triumph 1800 Saloon and Roadster models.

and transmission by courtesy of Riley in Coventry, and Donald Healey began to manufacture the Healey motor car himself in 1946. The two body styles already mentioned became the original Healeys and very popular they were, too.

It is at this point that Donald Healey finally fades from our story. After a shaky beginning, his Healey operation in Warwick prospered, the cars were progressively refined, became famous, and eventually inspired the Healey 100 which Healey sold to Sir Leonard Lord for Austin to build at Longbridge. After that the Healey link with BMC lived on to 1970, and later Donald Healey became involved in the Jensen-Healey project (for a short time becoming the chairman of Jensen). Following the financial collapse of Jensen in 1975, Donald Healey retired from business life, celebrated his 80th birthday in 1978, and is revered by motoring enthusiasts all over the world.

Ward, in the meantime, was trying to sell-off its Triumph assets, but this was not brought to the attention of the directors until the autumn of 1944, when the chairman briefly told his colleagues that the company had been sold.

The sale was not, however, achieved as simply or as quickly as that. Although Ward let it be known around the Midlands that the rump of the firm was once again on the market, it was some time before a serious potential buyer appeared. The problem, of course, was that although the name and its traditions were intact, and very well respected, the physical assets (or remains, one might say) were almost non-existent. There was no rush to take over a bombed-out factory (almost everyone in the business had one of their own already!) and the rights to the company name and the trademarks would only be of interest to another firm in the motor industry.

Consider, now, Britain's car makers, as they lined-up in the 1940s. Who was expanding, and who was struggling? The 'Big Six' were firmly established at the top of the heap. Ford and Vauxhall (effectively General Motors) could immediately be discounted, as could Austin and the Nuffield Organisation, which were both so big that the last thing they needed was more complication, and yet another subject for rationalisation. This left only the Rootes Group – who was still in the throes of marque rationalisation with Humber, Hillman, Sunbeam and Talbot – or Standard.

Looked at in this way, Standard was always the most likely firm to come forward with an offer for Triumph, though its records make it plain that no interest was shown in 1939 when Triumph fell into its financial agonies. Even so, we must pause for a moment to consider the other Coventry independents before dismissing them altogether. But apart from William Lyons' SS-Jaguar concern, none was actively expanding. BSA-Daimler-Lanchester was quite large enough and diverse enough for its Birmingham-based masters to control, Alvis was finding it very profitable to make aero engines instead of more cars, Riley had fallen to Lord Nuffield, and

Armstrong-Siddeley cars were only the grace-and-favour offshoot of the aeronautical business.

In business terms, therefore, Standard was the obvious suitor, and a short survey of its immediate ancestry is appropriate. By the 1940s it had a dynamic, autocratic, but undeniably effective managing director in Sir John Black, more than enough space at its Canley/Fletchamstead site to consider yet more expansion, and it also had Sir John's burning ambition to succeed – to out-do other motor industry personalities with whom he did not coexist in friendship.

In those days there was still scope for companies to be controlled by real tycoons, and Sir John was certainly typical of that breed. Born in Kingston-upon-Thames in 1895, John Paul Black joined the RNVR early in the First World War, transferred to the Tank Corps in France, and was demobbed in 1919 with the rank of Captain, a 'handle' he was to use for the next 20 years.

In business, originally, he had been involved in a patent office (where, incidentally, he was involved in drawing-up specifications for H F S Morgan of the little Malvern Link company which was about to build three-wheeler cars) and after his military service he joined the Hillman Motor Company in Coventry. Soon afterwards, he wooed and won one of the productive Mr Hillman's six daughters – gaining Spencer Wilks as a brother-in-law; Wilks worked alongside Black at Hillman, had also married a Miss Hillman, and would go on to become the greatly respected chairman and managing director of Rover.

By 1928 John Black was known throughout Coventry's close-knit motor-industry circle as a talented organiser, with great drive, and a single-mindedness which really amounted to a streak of ruthlessness. It is significant that he moved out of Hillman as soon as the Rootes family moved in – there was no way that people with such startlingly similar characters could agree together, when one was expected to work for the other.

Black was invited to join Standard by R W Maudslay, who had set-up Standard as long ago as 1903. Maudslay was still struggling to convert it from a smallish concern to one of the industry's leaders. John Black was hired to do just that. Within a year he had been appointed a director (and general manager) and he set his sights firmly on the top.

John Black's ambitions, and the growth of Standard, now become firmly intermingled. How he, and his company, developed in the 1920s and 1930s explains precisely what was to happen at the end of the Second World War.

In the beginning, Standard had built cars in the centre of Coventry, but in 1916 Charles Band, a Coventry solicitor, helped Maudslay negotiate the purchase of a big tract of land on the western boundaries of the existing city. This huge triangle, at Canley and Fletchamstead, was that later occupied by the Standard-

Triumph factories of British Leyland, later the Rover Group, the difference being that in 1916 it was virgin farm land.

The original Canley buildings, placed in the south-east corner of the site, near Canley Halt railway station, included the historic Ivy Cottage administrative building, and were erected in order to allow the manufacture of fighter aircraft. After the war, Canley became the principal Standard assembly plant, and the Cash's Lane premises were relegated to machining and component assembly.

Rationalisation at Standard, and true quantity production, had begun to develop in the late 1920s, at a time when Triumph was still struggling to get established. John Black had big ideas for Standard – his first objective being to humble his ex-employer Hillman, on the other side of Coventry. He decided to achieve this by what we would now describe as the best product-planning methods. With a great deal of effort and careful planning from his designers and production staff, he unfolded a master plan which would concentrate all car machining and production in Canley. In due course this plan would allow two basic engine ranges and three gearboxes to power a whole range of Standards from 8hp to 20hp, as measured by the RAC formula.

But John Black was a very difficult man to like – or, rather, to like consistently. He was ruthless, a hard driver of men, and undeniably insisted on having his own way. In the early 1930s Maudslay's health began to deteriorate, and John Black was soon the effective ruler of the business. In September 1933 he became joint managing director with Maudslay, and outright managing director in September 1934. Maudslay died at the end of that year, when his company was poised for a great expansion.

In the next few years a succession of men became directors, suffered under Black's rule, and either retired and resigned. Only Ted Grinham, who had been the company's chief engineer since the beginning of 1931, seemed to co-exist in peace, and he became technical director in 1936.

Alick Dick, whose business career began with a Standard apprenticeship, and who was to climb the ladder rapidly as John Black's protégé, later recalled: "No-one hit it off with John Black really … you either hated or loved him. I was his assistant or deputy for years, and I alternated between the two fairly often!"

The single most important technical development,

Originally built in the late 1930s as a government-financed shadow factory, and facing the Coventry by-pass, this block was used by Standard to produce aircraft parts to feed to Banner Lane during the war, but later became Standard-Triumph's administrative HQ.

which shaped Standard's products for more than 20 years, was a new side-valve engine range – to be made in four-cylinder and six-cylinder form – introduced on the famous Standard Nine of 1927 as a 60 x 102mm, 1155cc four-cylinder unit. The six-cylinder derivative followed a year later. Until 1933 the range could be recognised by its characteristic 102mm stroke, but from September of that year the stroke was lengthened to 106mm. Versions of both engines, incidentally, were supplied to William Lyons' SS company once it began to market complete cars in 1931, and this very significant arrangement would be continued to 1948. The traditional use of a 106mm stroke, of course, persisted in Jaguar's XK engine design until the late 1980s.

The four-cylinder engine had several different cylinder bores – 60mm, 63.5mm, 69.5mm and finally (from September 1936) 73mm. All engines supplied to SS had aluminium cylinder heads, but this feature was not progressively phased in to Standard's own engines until 1935. An overhead-valve version of the largest (73 x 106mm, 1776cc) four-cylinder design (developed by Harry Weslake's little company in Sussex) was supplied to SS from the autumn of 1937, and would continue after the war. Synchromesh gearing was introduced in September 1933, at the same time as the engine stroke was increased to 106mm, and gearboxes with the same internals but with differing selector arrangements became standard on all medium-sized Standard cars. SS-Jaguar also took supplies of these boxes, the main difference being that while Jaguar used a short selector extension and a remote-control lever, Standard used direct selection and a long spindly gearlever.

We have detailed the ancestry of engines and gearboxes because it is all very important to the postwar story, and to the way Standard developed in the 1930s.

Built in 1939/40, Standard-Triumph's massive Banner Lane plant produced colossal numbers of Bristol Hercules aero engines until 1945, after which it was converted to be the major assembly plant for Ferguson tractors. From 1945 to 1959 this was also the administrative HQ of Triumph, and was where all the new models, up to and including the Herald, were conceived, styled, engineered and developed.

At first, Standard cars were completely conventional and rather undistinguished – that is, until the first of the Flying Standards made its debut in the autumn of 1935. The body style itself had been dreamed up by Pressed Steel, who was Standard's bulk supplier (there was no creative styling department at Standard in the 1930s); it was a unique fastback shape which did much to give the company a distinctive reputation in these conformist times. Flying 12s, 16s and 20s were first, but by October 1936 the entire range consisted of Flying cars – the smallest was a 9hp car and the largest was a sensational but unsuccessful 2.7-litre V8.

By the time war broke out in 1939 the Flying Standard range had been expanded and refined even further. A Flying Eight had been added to the bottom of the range in 1938, using the smallest of the Standard engines (not related to the 106mm family), with a separate chassis incorporating transverse-leaf independent front suspension, and with a body supplied from a brand-new Fisher and Ludlow factory in Tile Hill, Coventry, only a couple of miles from Canley.

In the same year some of the larger bodies had been restyled, with notchback instead of fastback shapes, and transverse-leaf suspension also became a feature on Tens and Twelves. All this, though unconnected with Triumph at the time, has a bearing on postwar events.

In the summer of 1936, too, Standard had been invited to join the new Air Ministry 'shadow factory' scheme. This policy was initiated to speed-up rearmament in the face of the Nazi menace, and was meant to provide a framework of new factories to build aero-engines and complete aeroplanes, in the 'shadow' of the established aeroplane manufacturers. The factories would be completely tooled-up and making war material at the British Government's expense, and would be managed on a fee-earning basis by chosen motor industry concerns. In the event of war looking imminent (this was still considered unthinkable in 1936) production would be stepped-up, manpower increased, and the theory was that motor car manufacturers would then have the expertise to manage these factories and to convert their own facilities to military production.

Standard, Rootes, Rover, Daimler and Austin were in the first such scheme, and in each case a new factory, paid for by the public purse, was to be provided. Unlike most of the other participants, Standard's shadow factory could actually be built in the ground of the Canley/Fletchamstead site, close to but not touching the Canley production lines. Captain Black was delighted about this, because as a very astute businessman he saw that the building could one day become available to him, and would be ideally positioned to aid Standard's expansion.

For those historians still somewhat confused by the complex layout of the Canley/Fletchamstead grounds, we should explain that this shadow factory later became known as Fletch South, was at the western extremity of the site, facing the Coventry bypass, started by building Bristol aero-engine components, eventually took on the manufacture of Rolls-Royce Avon military jet engines and – from the 1950s – Standard-Triumph transmission-production machinery.

But this had not been the end of Standard's expansion. At the end of 1935, John Black had decided to go ahead with the manufacture of a new spares-and-service block, which was duly erected at the north-west corner of the site, alongside Broad Lane, and facing the bypass. However, in the summer of 1938, Standard had received another approach from the Air Ministry, this time to accede to a request to have a further factory built in its grounds for the manufacture of Claudel-Hobson aero-engine carburettors, and so the new building was turned over to this task.

But the biggest and best development of all, as far as Standard was concerned, had come as recently as 1939, when the second phase of the Government's shadow-factory scheme was proposed. With even more capacity for aeroplane-engine construction being

No, of course, it was not a sports car, but what fun! This was one of the lightweight machines developed by Standard during the Second World War to be dropped by parachute. It was powered by what would become the Triumph Mayflower's four-cylinder engine.

By 1945, Standard's Canley factory had grown to this sprawling complex, close to the Coventry-Birmingham railway line (which runs across this image) and was where all the post-1946 Triumph road cars would eventually be assembled.

needed, Standard was asked to run a vast million-square-foot building at Banner Lane, Coventry, which was a few miles west of the existing Coventry built-up area, and stood in open countryside. Work started in late spring, and production began in 1940. This building, however, was so huge by even John Black's visionary standards, that he must have wondered if it could ever be useful to Standard after the war was over.

In a few years, therefore, from 1935 to 1940, Standard's expansion had been enormous – but so had John Black's ambitions. While he steered production of Standard cars from a low level to more than 50,000 a year in 1939, and while profits rocketed to £322,492 (after tax), he also became infected with the sporting instincts which Walter Maudslay never had.

The link with SS – Standard supplied engines, gearboxes, axles, and complete rolling chassis at first, though SS took over more and more of its own detail work later – started things off, and the supply of engines to Morgan (an overhead-valve version of the 1247cc Ten unit) encouraged it further. Captain Black also concluded a deal with Raymond Mays to supply chassis and redundant V8 engines to him for the Raymond Mays car (but he turned down an invitation to join the ERA board of directors), and it is not generally known that a few chassis were also supplied to AC for its cars at the end of the 1930s.

By 1944, therefore, when Standard was at its crescendo of wartime production (Mosquito fighter-bombers, Beaufighter fuselages, Oxford trainer aircraft, Hercules engines, light armoured cars, vans, fire pumps, carburettors, constant-speed units, bomb-release slips, and many thousands of other aero-engine components), the newly-knighted Sir John Black was looking again at Standard's car-making prospects.

He had, by then, developed a grudging respect for the way William Lyons had built-up SS from a tiny producer of rather flashy car bodies to a fast-growing manufacturer of fast sporting cars. The two firms continued to do business together, and Sir John had

Sir John Black was Standard's dynamic managing director in the 1930s and throughout the war years, and it was his vision which swept the moribund Triumph concern into Standard's orbit in 1944.

Standard's then-managing director, Sir John Black, was very proud of the original Vanguard, and posed with it on an early proving trip in 1947.

indulged himself just before the war with a 3½-litre SS100 sports car. More than this, in 1939 he had commissioned Mulliners of Birmingham to produce a splendid razor-edge body style for a 3½-litre SS-Jaguar chassis. But, Sir John being Sir John, he wanted to out-do William Lyons in the coming peace, and needed extra prestige and reputation to do it.

He wanted, in short, to give Standard a sporting image, and he wanted that image to be the best in town. He also wanted to come out ahead of SS-Jaguar. As so often with Sir John's motives, it is difficult to see quite why he should have developed this obsession. One reason certainly was that he thought Standard should have received, and should still be receiving, more credit for the way it provided the majority of SS-Jaguar's mechanical components in the 1930s. Another – dangerous where a man with Sir John's ego was concerned – was that William Lyons had abruptly refused a takeover offer from Standard when John Black had decided to go for a more sporting image at the end of the 1930s.

Alick Dick, then Sir John's personal assistant, in fact if not then in title, now sums up what happened when the Coventry 'grapevine' got to know that Ward was ready to sell off the remains of Triumph:

"Just before the end of the war, in 1944, Triumph itself was effectively still bust. John Black wanted another name alongside

Standard – just that. As far as I can remember, Sir John sent me out to the Stoke works with Charles Band, Standard's chairman. We looked at the place, which wasn't worth a farthing. But we went ahead and bought the place."

In that original interview, Alick Dick thought the price might have been £20,000, or even £10,000, but later research now shows it to have been much higher than that. Standard's board minutes from October 20, 1944 have this to say:

"Resolved that the action of the managing director in paying a deposit of £7500 for the purchase by the company of the freehold property known as the Triumph works, Briton Road, Coventry, subject to and with the benefit of the lease of a portion of such works to Armstrong-Whitworth Aircraft Ltd, together with all plant, stock, office furniture, fittings and effects, in and around such premises, including all finished and unfinished parts, together with the drawings and jigs and tools necessary for the manufacture of Triumph cars, including working drawings of engines, gearboxes and other parts, and together with the goodwill of the business, with the right to use the name Triumph in conjunction with any company to be registered by the Standard Motor Co Ltd, be approved ... It was further resolved that the aforementioned premises ... be purchased by the company at a cost of £75,000."

But Sir John was not interested in the bomb-damaged premises. As Alick Dick told me:

"We sold the factory to the B O Morris group for about the same amount, and all we got was the name – for nothing – plus, I suppose, an obligation to supply spares for Triumph cars. But as there were hardly any of them, we really didn't feel any obligation to the old customers."

So what was Sir John planning? Was he interested in the 1930s Healey-Belgrove designs?

"Not one tiny bit. We never even gave it a thought. But what you have to remember is that before the war Standard had been supplying parts to SS. Standard had special tooling for the six-cylinder engines, and for the overhead-valve version of the four-cylinder, of which Lyons took all supplies at the time. Bill Lyons wanted to buy the tooling – he wanted to make all of his Jaguars in the future – and John Black was willing to let him have that so that we could build a competitive car. We kept the four-cylinder tooling, but it just wasn't viable without a new chassis and a new name. So that's why we bought Triumph. Just because Bill Lyons made a sporting saloon, or a sports car. John Black was not going to let him get away with it!"

That new name incidentally, might not have been Triumph, but Lagonda. Lagonda had offered itself in March 1935 (before Alan Good came forward to rescue the Staines-based company, and before W O Bentley became Lagonda's technical director), and again during the war, this time dangling the bait of Bentley's genius, the magnificent V12 he had already conceived and the brand-new twin-cam 2.6-litre 'six' he was then working on.

Once started, the Standard-Triumph negotiations were finalised rapidly. The first approaches had been in October 1944, both boards were agreed on the deal within days, and the formal conveyance of Triumph to Standard's control is dated November 24, 1944. The final legal niceties were handled for Ward by Bernard Barnett, a chartered accountant from Nottingham. Under Standard's jurisdiction, the first board meeting of the Triumph Motor Company (1945) Ltd, was held on April 17, 1945, when Sir John Black was formally appointed chairman and managing director. (He was, at the time, only deputy chairman of Standard, having been so appointed in October 1944). Charles Band, chairman of Standard, was never involved in the new company, but this was of no significance, as the reborn Triumph company was a wholly-owned subsidiary of Standard, and its board meetings were always pure formalities.

The deal had been done for some little time before the public was informed. On November 9, 1944, Standard's publicists had this to say:

"The Standard Motor Co Ltd have purchased the Triumph Co Ltd. Sir John Black, managing director of the Standard Co, states that after the war the experience and technique gained in the production of aircraft will be applied to the production of Triumph cars of character and distinction."

For the time being, then, nothing more needed to be said. Private car production had not yet recommenced (although in the same week that Standard bought Triumph Sir John had gained permission from Hugh Dalton, President of the Board of Trade, to start planning for peacetime operations once again).

But now the stage was set. Sir John had captured his name. What did he plan to do with it?

Roadster and Renown

It would have made no sense for Standard to try to reintroduce existing Triumph designs from the 1930s, though many lovers of the marque wish it had. It simply wasn't possible – practically or economically. The old company had subsided into bankruptcy precisely because of the type of car it was building. Ward's action in selling-off most of the assets had effectively destroyed the company's ability to start-up again in the old way, and the German bombing had completed the job.

Sir John Black had not bought Triumph to keep old traditions alive, but to bring new and greater glory to Standard. Right from the start, in 1945, the Triumph and Standard programme was to be intermingled. Though Sir John was not planning to badge-engineer Triumph's pedigree into extinction, Rootes-fashion, he knew that the new cars would have to use Standard mechanical units while continuing to look distinctive.

He had no choice. Although the drawings for Triumph engines and transmissions of the 1930s still existed, the tools did not, and he already knew that Austin was not willing to supply gearbox internals to Standard, whom it viewed as a very definite rival. By modern postwar standards, too, Triumph's method of coachbuilding bodies was old-fashioned and expensive, while the cars had never boasted independent front suspension, something to which Standard had already become committed in the late 1930s.

But what Sir John might want to do with the Triumph name was enormously complicated by what he was going to have to do with the rest of his Standard empire, and let us make one thing quite clear – Sir John did, indeed, look upon it as his empire. He might not have been the controlling shareholder (Standard was a large enough public company to make that impossible) but he was the master of his board, and ran the company virtually without sensing or listening for dissenting voices. He was, in every sense of the word, a dictator, but as his methods produced good profits the shareholders loved him for it. His fellow directors saw to it that

he received regular helpings of lavish praise, a diet on which the dapper Sir John clearly thrived.

With victory in the West imminent, activity in the 'shadow' factories began to run down, and all over the Midlands firms were being asked if they would like to take up the leases for their own purposes. Sir John looked forward to converting the Fletchamstead South complex for Standard car production as soon as he had completed negotiations. During the war, too, he had taken over a nearly new building at Allesley, on the Coventry to Birmingham road, from a bankrupt Coventry business, and was planning to convert it into the company's service department.

The problem, at the beginning of 1945, was the vast Banner Lane factory; it was beginning to worry Sir John. Standard was the sitting tenant, as it were, but there was no immediate prospect of filling it with private car machinery (Canley-Fletchamstead could cope quite adequately with the forecast demand). Even so, the proffered lease was so attractive that Sir John was reluctant to let it go.

At this point, we must abandon the chronological sequence of

From 1945 to 1959, the vast Banner Lane factory was the home of Triumph's management and engineering activities. Sadly, it was emptied and demolished early in the 21st century.

This impressive façade was the new face of Triumph from 1945, this being Banner Lane, where the original Standard-Triumphs were designed and developed.

The Ferguson tractor deal, as sealed in 1945 and in production from 1946, was the cornerstone of Standard-Triumph expansion; it boosted cash flow, and was a prime user of the Standard Vanguard petrol engine that later made the Triumph TR2 so famous, too.

events slightly. Work on postwar Triumphs was already well-advanced by the time the fate of Banner Lane was settled, but the commercial implications of this transaction were so vital that it must be considered first.

Just at the time when it looked as though Banner Lane would have to be abandoned, the ebullient and controversial figure of Harry Ferguson arrived on the scene. Ferguson, of course, was the Irish-born maverick who had promoted a completely new concept in lightweight tractor design. The Ferguson tractor had been built in relatively small numbers by the David Brown organisation before the war, and by Ford in Detroit for a short time at the end of the 1930s.

In 1945, Ferguson set about getting established in Britain again, and as before, he was happy for another company to build his tractors if his own concern could have the selling rights. Trevor Knox, one of his directors, was installed in the Farmers Club in London, and began to send out feelers to his industrial contacts. In later years both Lord Nuffield and Sir Leonard Lord must have regretted turning down the Ferguson proposals. The approach to Standard evolved on the 'friend of a friend' principle. A director of the Distillers Company was living in the Farmers Club at the same time as Knox, knew of his brief, used to travel to and from London regularly by train, and just happened to know someone on the commuting train who handled Standard's publicity account! Thus it was that Sir John got to know about Ferguson's plans.

As a means to an end – filling Banner Lane, providing an outlet for new engines that Standard was developing, and spreading the financial load of operating overheads (something which Ferguson only realised when it was too late to renegotiate the deal) – it

looked ideal. Ferguson and Sir John speedily got together, aided and abetted by Sir Stafford Cripps, by then the President of the Board of Trade, who promised adequate supplies of sheet steel, which were severely rationed in postwar austerity Britain. The actual deal between Sir John and Harry Ferguson was reputedly cooked up on the back of a menu card over lunch at Claridge's Hotel in London.

It was an unlikely alliance. Colin Fraser, Harry Ferguson's biographer, summed it up well: "It did not take long for Sir John Black and Harry Ferguson to have their first serious differences of opinion. The fact that such arguments arose was as unavoidable as the crash between two express trains hurtling down the same length of track but in different directions. Both men were inflexible and aggressively certain that their opinions were infallibly right. Their basic attitudes were therefore incompatible unless they happened to agree entirely on a given topic."

In 1946, the arguments were such that Sir John would threaten to withdraw from the whole deal, even before Banner Lane was equipped to build the tractors. But there was also a point only a year later when Sir John was talking about shutting down private car production altogether in favour of 100 per cent tractor production!

Sir John and Harry Ferguson made what Standard's board minutes describe as a 'gentleman's agreement' on August 28, 1945, and Banner Lane produced its first tractor in July 1946. This act served to dictate the course of Standard's policy in the next decade, and therefore affected what Sir John had in mind for Triumph.

In the meantime, work had already started on the first generation of (if you will pardon the expression) Standard-Triumphs. Sir John's strategy was based on several factors: a deep desire to beat William Lyons at his own game, a dash to announce postwar cars as soon as possible, and the need to use as many of Standard's existing components, facilities, and expertise as possible. In particular there was the question of the overhead-valve 1776cc Standard engine, which until 1939 had been supplied exclusively to SS-Jaguar for its 1½-litre model. There were no plans to use this version of the engine on a postwar Standard, and the production lines in Canley were by no means working flat-out in 1939. In addition, Standard had a new asset in the expertise gained in fabricating aircraft structures during the war years. There were also certain special tools for shaping skin panels which might be useful for making car bodies.

In the autumn of 1944, when Sir John authorised the start of designing for postwar Standards and Triumphs, he was effectively his own technical director. Ted Grinham, appointed deputy managing director at the outbreak of war, had moved to De Havilland Aircraft in 1941, leaving an administrative vacuum behind him which Ray Turner, as chief designer, was not allowed to fill.

Logically enough, however, Sir John decided to use one basic new design, and evolve two body styles for it – a sporting tourer and a smart up-market saloon – both of which, he hoped, could be competitive and preferably harmful to SS-Jaguar. For reasons which will shortly become obvious, the tourer would be styled and built by Standard, while the saloon would be an outside job.

Although Standard had been modernising its chassis layouts in 1938 and 1939, there was really no suitable basis for a postwar Triumph already in existence. Engines and transmissions, however, were suitable, and would be used.

Ted Grinham was Standard's long-serving technical director, who would head-up the Triumph design and engineering team until the mid-1950s, after which Harry Webster took over.

Standard, in the meantime, sold-off the production tooling for the overhead-valve six-cylinder SS-Jaguar engines (it was not planning on making any six-cylinder Standards in the early postwar years), and retained the four-cylinder tooling, but not without complications, as Sir William Lyons, in his 1969 Lord Wakefield Gold Medal Paper, makes clear:

"Sir John Black told me that he would no longer be able to make our engine, and after some discussion offered to sell to us the special plant he had put down for its production ... I had a great admiration for John Black in many respects, but I quickly grasped the opportunity to obtain security. Therefore, within a few days, I sent transport to collect the plant and sent our cheque in payment for it. It turned out that I had been right to do so for it was not long before Black proposed that we should revert to the previous arrangement and return the plant to Standard. He pressed me very hard, even to the extent of suggesting that we should form a separate company together ..."

Sir John, by then, was not only interested in using the six-cylinder engine in his postwar Triumphs, but he had also been approached by other small car-making concerns for supplies of the unit – even though the basic design with the exception of block and crankshaft was now to the credit of SS-Jaguar.

For the new Triumphs, therefore, he decided to use the overhead-valve 1776cc engines (which would continue to be supplied to Jaguar for its 1½-litre). He would use the Standard/SS-Jaguar four-speed gearbox, though with a complex conversion unique to the Triumphs to allow for steering-column control, and he would use the existing design of Flying Standard back axle. Not only this, but the chassis would use Flying Standard independent front suspension, which combined upper wishbone links with a lower transverse leaf spring. Postwar Flying Standards, incidentally, would continue to use side-valve engines, and one interesting bit of rationalisation was that the little Standard Eight was also given the bigger gearbox, which meant that Standard-Triumph cars were completely common in that respect.

Sir John then set Ray Turner on designing a new chassis frame to suit all these well-known parts. It would be new so that it could accommodate alternative lengths of wheelbase, and so that Standard could assemble it itself at the Canley factory. It also had to take into consideration the fact that although casting steel and tubular steel looked to be in reasonable supply after the war, the Government had made it clear that sheet steel (for pressing) – and that included chassis frames – was going to be severely rationed. This was because sheet steel was going to be needed for postwar repair and rehabilitation of housing, and it was not until a new South Wales steel works at Margam was ready at the beginning of the 1950s that this situation would be transformed.

It is easy to see, therefore, that the chassis simply had

This tubular chassis formed the basis of both 1946 Triumph 1800 models, although the saloon had an 8-inch longer wheelbase.

to be tubular, with large-diameter side and crossmembers. Manufacturing and assembly methods perfected by Standard during the war (when multi-tubular structures were very fashionable for aircraft structures) would be used, and Standard had a good supply of skilled labour who were used to this way of working.

It meant that the front and back end of the chassis could be common, and a difference in wheelbase could easily be accommodated in the centre. Tooling and jigging was going to be rudimentary (Sir John did not consider either of the new Triumphs as a quantity-production machine), there was a large potential surplus of skilled labour due to the running-down of the war effort, and manpower was therefore more immediately available than expensive machinery. The cars, of course, could be priced accordingly. The minor complication of different wheelbases was shrugged off by the planners.

The basic design was very simple, with the main side members underslung of the back axle, as prewar Standards and Triumphs had been. Adequate axle rebound clearance was assured by flattening the tubes at the appropriate point, and local reinforcements served to restore the loss in beam stiffness inevitable at such an abrupt change of section.

The time had now come to commission the design of the two bodies. Sir John could not spare many of his people to work on the new Triumphs (there was also a postwar Standard car to be developed, and the war, after all, was still going on), so he decided that his own staff should tackle the tourer, while he would personally collaborate with Mr Louis Antweiller, managing director of Mulliners of Birmingham, over the styling of the saloon.

Mulliners, not to be confused with two other prestigious coachbuilding concerns, H J Mulliner of London and Arthur Mulliner of Northampton, had specialised in batch production of special bodies during the 1930s. It would supply bodies to

companies like Alvis, Daimler-Lanchester and the Rootes Group, always built in the traditional way – using ash body frames, with steel or light alloy cladding – in, for those days, considerable quantities.

At the same time, Standard told the world of its plans for Triumph. In a press release dated February 1945 it was promised that "with the object of getting back into its production stride as rapidly as possible after the cessation of hostilities, the Standard Motor Company Ltd has decided to concentrate on two up-to-date models, an Eight of 1000cc and a Twelve of 1600cc. It has also proposed to produce a 10hp Triumph of 1300cc and a 15hp model of 1800cc."

That 10hp Triumph, which would eventually become the Mayflower, did not appear in public until 1949, though the very first prototype (with an aircraft-style body construction in sandwiched ply-balsa-ply wood) was built on a Flying Standard chassis in 1945. Incidentally, whoever drafted that press release either could not work out the correct RAC rated horsepower figures, or genuinely wished to confuse the opposition, as Standard never had a 15hp 1800cc engine of any nature. The 1776cc unit was always rated at 13.2hp, and neither of the old 1930s Triumph engines fitted the bill either.

To have the saloon Triumph styled outside the firm was logical, for the simple reason that Standard still had absolutely no tradition of creative styling of its own. In the 1930s the layout and engineering of Flying Standards had not been done in Canley, but by designers from the body suppliers (Pressed Steel, Fisher and Ludlow, and occasionally Briggs), working to John Black's vaguely expressed requests. Although Black liked it to be thought that he personally styled the cars (here his attitude to William Lyons, who did style his cars, was surfacing again), his contribution was of the most general nature.

As far as the open touring Triumph was concerned, Standard's saviour was to be a young man called Frank Callaby, who had

The 1800 Roadster of 1946 was the very first 'Standard-Triumph' model to go on sale. Although much of the original engineering was lifted from the existing Standard Flying Fourteen saloon, the aluminium-panelled style was all new.

Like the 1938/39 Dolomite Roadster, the Triumph Roadster of 1946-1949 was equipped with a fold-away dickey seat in the tail, and was the last production car in the world to be so fitted. Access was by opening the panel (the lift handles can be seen), and climbing aboard was by way of rubber-faced steps on the corner of the rear bumper.

The style of the post-war Triumph Roadster was established very rapidly in the summer of 1945, ready for launch in March 1946, and was clearly influenced by the shape of the 1938/39 Dolomite Roadster.

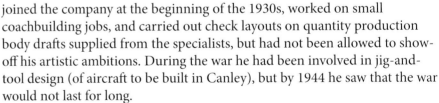

joined the company at the beginning of the 1930s, worked on small coachbuilding jobs, and carried out check layouts on quantity production body drafts supplied from the specialists, but had not been allowed to show-off his artistic ambitions. During the war he had been involved in jig-and-tool design (of aircraft to be built in Canley), but by 1944 he saw that the war would not last for long.

"Sir John was determined to be the first back into production, and he wanted a new sports car, a new Triumph. He gave Ray Turner a few ideas of what he wanted – Sir John had owned an SS100 sports car just before the war, and he wanted his car to look as exciting, and to be as low and sleek. I must have done dozens of small-scale sketches for him in about October 1944, and I must point out that it was Sir John who specified a dickey (rumble) seat, which was a throw-back to the prewar Triumph Dolomite Roadster.

"Both Arthur Ballard and I were senior draughtsmen at the time, and I

The Roadster of 1946-1949 used the same basic chassis and running gear as the razor-edge saloon, but ran on a shorter wheelbase, with an entirely different bodyshell.

had a bit of a flair for body shapes. Eventually I got approval for a particular shape on the basis of a one-eighth scale picture drawing for the new Roadster, which was to use an 8ft 4in wheelbase.

"Arthur and I already knew what the suspensions and the main mechanical components would be, so we could then get on with the detailed engineering."

The resulting style was, and still is, controversial. People with an axe to grind such as apologists of rival cars like the dreadfully old-fashioned MG TCs, thought it unattractive and said so. Cecil Kimber, sacked from his job as managing director of MG in 1941 by Miles Thomas, was actually asked by Sir John Black to be the nominal head of a revived Triumph concern, but he turned the opportunity down, not just because he disagreed with Frank Callaby's ideas on the style, but also because he could not see eye-to-eye with Sir John.

Detail styling then went ahead in an unconventional manner, as Callaby confirms: "once we had Sir John's approval, from this drawing Arthur Ballard and myself developed all the shapes and made the detail drawings. Arthur worked rearwards from the B-post, including the folding hood and the dickey seat, and I did everything forward of this, ie the front wings, radiator, bonnet and facia."

In body engineers' language, the B-post is the body pillar placed at the rear of the front door; on the Triumph Roadster the doors were hinged from this pillar.

Now, we've all heard of cars which were styled in more than one office, where a team doing the front were specifically asked not to talk to those doing the rear (like the Sprite/Midget face-lift of 1961, for instance), but the Roadster doesn't qualify as one of these. The overall style was done by one man – Frank Callaby – and the actual coachwork engineering, from that shape, by two men.

Walter Belgrove, shortly to become Standard-Triumph's noted chief body engineer, had nothing to do with this Roadster, as he was still involved in jig-and-tool design on aircraft at the time, and any philosophical similarity between this car and the prewar Dolomite Roadster is due to Sir John Black's liking for its layout.

The body was to be built in Canley, on a traditional ash frame (remember, though, that Standard saloon bodies of the late 1930s had all been of pressed-steel construction, and supplied complete from outside concerns), and the aluminium pressings were shaped on the rubber press which had been installed for the production of aircraft panels.

Development of the Roadster, therefore, was relatively simple

97

By any standards, the 1800/Renown Saloon was an elegant product, though its razor-edge style was already lagging behind the visual trends of the late 1940s.

The Roadster's facia/instrument panel, showing off the wooden veneer – and hiding the fact that the steering column gear change lever is hidden away to the right of the steering column.

Based on the running gear of the Standard Flying Fourteen, but with an overhead-valve version of the engine when announced in 1946, the 1800 was the very first Standard-Triumph saloon.

and straightforward, though it was always possible that it would induce howls of criticism from Triumph traditionalists – those who had loved the 1930s cars so much, but had failed to buy enough of them to keep the old company afloat! The shaping of the saloon was a more protracted and complicated story.

For its origins we have to go back to 1936, when the squared-off or 'razor-edge' style of specialist coachwork began to appear on the more expensive Rolls-Royces, Bentleys and Daimlers. Several coachbuilders, with Mulliners of Birmingham well to the fore, took up the vogue, and within a couple of years the razor-edge shape was very fashionable.

John Black himself obviously liked the idea, for he commissioned a special razor-edge limousine from Mulliners, to be mounted on a 3½-litre SS-Jaguar chassis. The shape, evolved by Black, Antweiller and the Mulliners draughtsmen, was uncannily like the Mark VI Bentley of 1946 – so much so that one has to ask the question: were they influenced, too? This car was ready in 1939, and used by Black throughout the war years. It was much heavier than a standard SS-Jaguar, and Harry Colley of the Standard-Triumph engineering department recalls that the rear springs were so stiff that they had to be clamped to a piece of angle-iron before they could be persuaded to fit their mounting pivots after a service!

Even before the end of the war, Sir John started talking to Antweiller about his thoughts for a new Triumph saloon. Through Ray Turner he asked Mulliners (Leslie Moore being its stylist, who later did the Mayflower, and even later worked at Standard-Triumph) to develop a razor-edge shape around the package of the existing Standard Flying Twelve/Fourteen.

This was rather a cramping brief, but Sir John was very proud of his Flying cars, and the seating and chassis package of the Twelve/Fourteen (which used the same basic engine and transmission as the new Triumph would have) appealed to him. Unlike the Roadster, his plan was that the saloon's shell would be pressed, assembled, painted and trimmed entirely at Bordesley Green, Birmingham, transported to Canley, and mated with its chassis on the same assembly line as the Roadster. Mechanically, apart from the difference in wheelbase, the two cars were nearly identical.

There was no question of a modification being done on the actual body of the Flying Standard (it was, after all, a quantity-production pressed-steel shell supplied by Pressed Steel from Cowley, near Oxford), but it was the actual packaging that Sir John wanted to use. Although he intended for Mulliners to produce a sumptuous coachbuilt body with light-alloy skin panels on ash framing, he wanted the car to use the same basic seating layout, the general size and layout of the interior, the same general proportions, and the same approximate outline of glass and skin shapes.

This Flying Standard, of course, was the largest Standard intended for immediate postwar production, but it dated from 1935, and had already undergone two metamorphoses. In the beginning, it was the very first Flying Standard, having a 108in wheelbase and the 1609cc side-valve engine. A year later it became the Fourteen with the 1776cc engine, and at the beginning of 1937, an alternative four-window notchback touring saloon shell was made available.

A big reshuffle of the model range in September 1938 gave the car an independent front-suspension chassis, a much-modified six-window notchback saloon style, and the 1609cc engine again; the wheelbase, incidentally, was down to 100in, all the cut being taken out of the front of the car. The 1945 model was given a widened version of this shell (the space across the shoulders inside the car was up by three inches), and a choice of 1609cc or 1776cc side-valve engines. The extra width, incidentally, was made possible because the rear track had been increased from 51in to 54.7in; this gave the car a reverse crab track, and Walter Belgrove insists to this day that it made his styling task almost impossible to do with elegance. "To achieve perfect proportions," he said, "all cars should be widest at or near the front wheels. With the postwar cars this was not possible, and I think it shows."

The dynamic Sir John, having made up his mind about the project, could not wait to get it started. Frank Callaby now takes up the story:

"One morning, before nine o'clock, Sir John marched straight into my office, straight from his car I should think, looked me in the eyes and said, 'We want a razor-edge saloon, and you can base it on the 12hp car. How long would it take for you to draw something up?' Well, even the quickest I could think of was two or three days, and I said so. 'That's no good. No good at all. I want to take something over to Mulliners to show to Antweiler after lunch.'

"Now, as you know, nobody argued with Sir John, so all I could do was dig out existing drawings of the Flying Twelve, fix tracing paper over one, and rough-out a razor-edge style around its basic contours! It only took two or three hours, and Sir John went off to Birmingham after lunch." Callaby then lost sight of the project, and was only reunited with it when the time came to start preparing detailed engineering drawings. Jim Wignall and Leslie Moore, at Mulliners, then took over, prepared a full-size mock-up, still on the stub-nosed 100in wheelbase, and submitted it for approval.

In the meantime, Walter Belgrove had been released from his war-time employment, and had taken up his job as the leader of the

Below left: The occasional, or dickey, seat of the 1946-1949 Triumph Roadster looked more useful than it actually was. Though the provision of the second windscreen was a nice touch. Consider the difficulties of getting into this seat by using the rubber-faced pads on the outer corners of the rear bumper – especially if one was a lady wearing high heels!
Below right: Taken from an unusual angle, this study shows off the potential for three-abreast front seating in the Roadster.

body-engineering department, something he had been promised by Sir John some time earlier. At this stage, in the spring of 1945, it was already too late to influence the shape of the Roadster (though by 1946 he had produced sleek and stylish proposals for a reskin which were never approved), and he did not know if he could even influence the saloon in time.

Even so, Belgrove worked-up a razor-edge scheme of his own. He was not at all convinced that Mulliners could do the best job, and as Sir John Black never stifled a bit of stimulating rivalry, he was encouraged to press on.

The Mulliners prototype duly arrived in Canley to be viewed – and was duly rejected. Although Sir John was no stylist, like most bosses he "knew what he liked." The Mulliners scheme was not it. As Belgrove told us: "Mulliners had carried-out its instructions from Standard, but the fact remained that the result was still recognisably a Standard Twelve."

This was obvious because the prototype kept the Standard Twelve front wings, the same short nose (on the 100in wheelbase) and almost the same side elevation. Sir John then suggested that Mulliners, Ray Turner and Belgrove should get together to combine the best of the two schemes, but he was astonished when Belgrove insisted that it was to be his scheme or nothing. Belgrove said that he was not willing to work for Turner, nor to rework his designs, but that he was willing to do a new razor-edge scheme on his own which would incorporate the best of everything.

Sir John, for once thwarted, and seeing no way out of the impasse (he admitted later that Belgrove's design was much more elegant), therefore decreed that Belgrove should work-up such a scheme, with the proviso that the Flying Standard's seating package should be retained, while the wheelbase should be increased to 108in as Belgrove's proposal had made clear. When it was all approved, the entire project would be handed over to Mulliners for tooling and manufacture.

Within weeks, Belgrove had crystalised his ideas, and his craftsmen produced a remarkably detailed one-eighth model, not more than 22 inches long and eight inches wide. This was built almost entirely from wood, but was decorated down to the last door handle and piece of trim. Not only was it beautifully made, but Belgrove obtained complete project approval from Sir John Black without even having to make a full-size mock-up.

This colour rendering, which dates from 1947, shows Standard's visual treatment of the original Standard Vanguard. This car, or a version of it, would bequeath developed types of its engine and transmission to the first of the TR2s.

In describing his work, Belgrove was scrupulously fair, and admitted that some features of the Turner-Mulliners scheme were kept: "I accepted the radiator shell, and scrapped the existing wings; the body lines in elevation and in plan view were retained."

It was the new wings which transformed the car's look. Originally, as borrowed from the Flying Twelve, they had no reverse curvature; all major curves, seen in side view, were struck using the road wheel centre as their origin. The Belgrove-shaped wings included a front wing nose punched well forward (he calls it a Hogarthian curve found in nature in the neck line of a swan), originally drawn freehand, followed by a graceful sweep down to the base of the doors. The same treatment was applied to the rear wings and a reverse curve was given to the tail. The boot, too, was much enlarged. There was a slight carry-over of ideas from Belgrove's 1939 Triumph 12 in the spare wheel/tools/boot lid arrangement, but nothing else of significance.

All this took Belgrove just a week – but he did admit that it would have taken much longer if the original glass lines had not already been settled.

The finalised model was so obviously razor-edge, and angular from most views, that a rather piqued Sir John Black, anxious as always to have the last word, enquired waspishly if Belgrove wanted to specify square pistons as well!

So, by the spring of 1945, Standard had evolved its basic postwar line-up of Triumphs. The cars would be launched in the spring of 1946, well before rival manufacturers were ready to show off their postwar ideas. (Cars like the RM-series Rileys and the Armstrong-Siddeleys which pre-dated the Triumphs had been designed in 1939/1940.) In retrospect, it was a good thing that the cars were designed in such a rush and in such a way, for by the

summer of 1945 Standard also had a vast new tractor project to contend with.

Ted Grinham rejoined the company as technical director in October 1945, after Sir John Black had made his historic deal with Harry Ferguson in August of that year. Harry Webster, who rejoined engineering from his production trouble-shooting job at this time, remembered that his first job was to go through the Ferguson drawings and patents with a fine tooth comb to see if there was any way that Standard could 'do its own thing' – even at this early stage of the agreement Sir John Black was looking for ways to get the better of Ferguson!

Work on the tractor, including making changes to suit it for Standard production, the re-equipping of the Banner Lane factory, and all the aggravation of shaking down a new product, took time, and it was not until 1946 (after the Triumphs had been announced) that work could go ahead seriously on the all-new Standard Vanguard project. This explains, incidentally, why there was no Vanguard engineering in the original Standard-Triumphs – in 1945, quite literally, the Vanguard only existed on paper. It was, incidentally, a Belgrove style based, as he admitted, on study of American cars which Sir John Black liked so much. The actual sketching was done from Belgrove's own car in London's Grosvenor Square, under the eyes of military patrols outside the American

Embassy – Belgrove becoming more and more convinced that he was going to be arrested as a spy!

Sir John, in fact, had decided very shortly after the end of the war that he was going to go along with the British Government's recommendation for factories to adopt a one-model policy. However, in this case, Sir John decided to interpret this as a 'one model range' policy, and he intended to commonise all existing cars around the expensively-tooled all-new Vanguard in due course.

In the meantime, at the beginning of March 1946, the two new Triumphs were unveiled, and were called the 1800 Roadster, and the 1800 Town and Country Saloon. Although they were shown together, only the Roadster was ready to be put, somewhat hesitantly, into production. Tooling for the saloon (costing only about £40,000) was not complete at Mulliners, and it was not until September that the first car was actually delivered. For a short time the Roadster was listed as being cheaper than the Saloon (in the UK, £625 compared with £650), but by the time both were actually available they carried the same price tag of £695 (with, in Britain, purchase tax of £194).

Production in that difficult first year (there seemed to be shortages of everything from steel to trim, electricity to coal, manpower to permits) could be measured in hundreds, not thousands, and people who blithely placed their orders were quoted

delivery delays in years. If you ordered your 1800 Town and Country Saloon in 1946 it would probably be delivered in 1950 or thereabouts – as a Renown at a vastly increased price. But this was not Standard's fault; it was a problem shared by the entire motor industry, which would experience the most phenomenal sellers' market for the next ten years, until the vast backlog of orders could be worked-off.

For two years, until

Once launched, and available on all world markets, the original Vanguard became a best-seller.

the summer of 1948, the Triumphs were the only modern motor cars being made by Standard at Coventry. The vast bulk of deliveries from Canley were of Standard Flying Eights (dating from 1938) and of Flying Twelve/Fourteens (dating, in essence, from 1935). Both the Triumphs were expensive by comparison with many other cars which were also haltingly in production, but in the buy-anything-that's-available attitudes of the day this made no difference. By definition the cars took very many man hours to build, and all this labour had to be costed. Unerringly, however, Sir John Black had allowed for postwar shortages when he commissioned the cars, and they did not suffer.

The implication was that progress would eventually catch up with them, and modern, completely engineered machines would begin to challenge on price and specification. The Vanguard was to change the face of Standard's look after this new era, and usher in the 'one model range' policy at the same time.

The Vanguard was announced in July 1947, with a flourish but with no showroom stocks. Standard boasted 50,000 cars (Eights and Twelves, with just a few Triumphs) being built since 1945, and stated that capacity for the new Vanguard engine was being installed for 1000 units a day to be assembled. Not that all these would be allocated to private cars – the Vanguard engine was also being adopted for use in the Ferguson tractor, now in production at Banner Lane.

It is interesting to recall that in July 1947 Sir John stated that 'the Triumph, itself a new postwar model, will be continued throughout 1948, after which there will be a new model.' The commonisation of the cars, it seems, was already being planned.

We must now talk, briefly, about the Vanguard, as its engineering had an enormous effect on other Standards and Triumphs built up to the 1960s. It had a conventional box-section steel chassis frame with coil-spring independent front suspension and semi-elliptic leaf springs at the rear (though coil springs were used on the first prototypes). Its wheelbase was short at 94in (Belgrove argued unavailingly against this, saying that it was impossible to provide enough passenger space, and that the style would look dumpy – he was right), and its styling was frankly transatlantic. It had a robust new three-speed all-synchromesh gearbox with a disgracefully vague steering-column gear change, and a new back axle with a 54in track. All this, however, was overshadowed by the new engine, a massively strong wet-liner unit which would later find legendary fame in the classic Triumph TRs of 1953 to 1967.

Too many people think the Vanguard engine was a copy of a Continental design, which is nonsense. The confusion is caused because the Ferguson tractor was built with Continental engines while the new Standard unit was still under development, but there is absolutely no other link between the two. Harry Webster once recalled, vividly, that the engine which influenced it most of all was the famous Citroën wet-liner traction avant design of the 1930s, and pointed out acidly that the only connection with Continental was that both units were eventually asked to tackle the same job on the tractor.

As a modern design, the Vanguard engine was no great shakes, but it was built with simplicity, long life and easy maintenance in mind. For this reason it was designed with slip-fit removable wet cylinder liners – a feature which made sure that every restorer and every out-back maintenance engineer in the world loved it. There was certainly never any intention to put in power-producing reserves: the fact that by the 1960s a much-

A sectioned view of the engine/gearbox assembly which was so important to Standard and Triumph immediately after the merger. This was the overhead-valve version of the Standard 1776cc unit, which had originally been developed for SS-Jaguar, and would soon provide power for the Triumph 1800 Roadster and Saloon, bridging the gap until the all-new 2-litre Vanguard engine was ready.

modified TR racing engine might revolve at 6000rpm and produce something like 70bhp/litre would have astonished the designers in 1945.

In its original form, as announced in 1947, the engine had a bore of 80mm and a capacity of 1850cc, but before production began a combination of the need for more power and torque, together with revisions in British motor taxation policy, led to the bore being changed to 85mm, and capacity to the well-known 2088cc.

The first complete Vanguard, with its bodyshell supplied from Fisher & Ludlow in Birmingham at a tooling cost of about £350,000, rolled off the production line in the summer of 1948, and Sir John's rationalisation plan began to evolve. On July 9 the last of 83,139 Standard Flying Eights (53,099 of them built since 1945) was made. By September, the 32,207th postwar Flying Twelve/Fourteen had been finished, and with it the prewar links were finally severed.

It was a signal for the same process to be applied to the Triumphs, and knowledgeable industry-watchers could see it coming. With the death of the Flying Standards, and Jaguar's decision to drop its 1½-litre from the summer of 1948, it was clear that these engines and transmissions could not continue to be supplied solely for the Triumphs. Sure enough, at the first postwar Earls Court Motor Show in London, the Roadster was shown with the Vanguard's engine, three-speed gearbox and back axle. There was a minor change in overall gearing (4.625 instead of 4.56:1), and the rear track came down slightly to 54in.

This was the later version of the razor edge saloon, the Renown, complete with a real-wood facia, and instruments lifted from the Standard Vanguard. The steering column gear change was on the left side of the column.

Whichever engine was fitted under the razor-edge's bonnet – the overhead-valve 1776cc power unit as originally supplied to Jaguar, or the later 2088cc Vanguard – it was a tight squeeze. This was the Renown power unit, and the brake servo on this car has been added by a subsequent owner.

At that time no parallel changes were announced for the saloon, but these duly materialised in February 1949. Now, at least as far as engines and transmissions were concerned, all Standards and Triumphs had been commonised, even down to identical axle ratios and power-output figures.

If the Roadster had been more of a sales success it might have been rationalised further still, but production ran out in October 1949. Just 2501 of the original 1800 Roadsters had been built in two-and-a-half years, while a round-figure sanction of 2000 of the Vanguard-engined '2000 Roadster' were built in the 1948/1949 season. However, even though cars were generally in short supply, the Roadster was neither fast enough nor stylish enough to sell well overseas, where cars like the MG TC were all the rage; of the 2000 cars built in that last year, only 184 were exported. In Britain's 'export or die' atmosphere, this was simply not good enough, so the Roadster was killed-off. Sir John, in any case, had other things in mind, but these were late appearing.

The saloon, however, had made its modest middle-class mark. Some 4000 of the original 1800 Town and Country Saloon (the name, incidentally, was soon shortened) were built up to the spring of 1949 and, with the adoption of the higher torque Vanguard engine, the car took on a new lease of life.

This half-modified 2000 saloon was built only from the spring to the autumn of 1949, and at Earls Court the car was further changed. Enthusiasts know these as the 'TDB' series cars, which were fitted with a 108in version of the Standard Vanguard's box-section pressed-steel chassis (the Vanguard, remember, had a 94in chassis), along with its coil-spring and wishbone front suspension and its steering gear. At the same time, the gear change lever, which had been on the right of right-hand-drive steering columns up until then, was switched to the left, and there were further minor but visually obvious trim changes.

This car was now the Renown – a name which became famous, and which was retrospectively (and quite wrongly) applied to all the razor-edge cars built by Triumph from 1946 to 1954. Sir John Black was then in his 'ship-appreciation period', which explains why the Vanguard (named after Britain's last battleship), the Mayflower (symbolic, this – it was hoped that it would help the car's sales in North America), and the Renown (a British battle-cruiser) all came along.

The only minor mystery is that the actual Renown name was not adopted at once – or if it was nobody bothered to tell the advertising agencies. At first the car was merely a '2-litre Triumph saloon', and the name 'Renown' was not mentioned until the end of November 1949. I discovered this when combing the adverts in *The Autocar* for that period of 1949. In the issue of November 18 the car was merely titled 'Triumph 2-litre saloon'. In the issue dated November 25, the same advert down to the last piece of artwork

and wording, calls it a 'Triumph 2-litre Renown'. Why? No-one can remember.

This, however, was the definitive razor-edge Triumph saloon, which in basic form was to continue in production until 1954, even though Standard-Triumph had a struggle to sell the last batch of cars. Indeed, by the beginning of 1953 there were 430 Renowns in stock in Canley, and production was down to a mere two cars a day. Sir John Black asked his planners to consider withdrawing the car from production at once, but eventually compromised with a big price reduction in June 1953 which was continued to the end of the car's life.

Between 1949 and 1951, however, the Renown was still a popular car, and by its own standards it sold well. Production of TDB series cars ran out at the beginning of 1952, with 6501 cars built. In the meantime, however, the car's attraction had been increased when Laycock overdrive had been made optional from June 1950. The feature cost £64, worked on top gear only, and was operated by pulling the gearlever, already in the top-gear slot, towards the driver. At the same time, the feature was made available on the Standard Vanguard.

We now come to what Sherlock Holmes would have called 'The Mysterious Case of the Three Inches.' This was the stretch in wheelbase given to the Renown in the autumn of 1951, ostensibly to make a limousine version more practical, and later (for commonisation reasons) given to the normal saloon-bodied Renowns as well.

The mystery is not in finding the extra three inches – it is there, for sure, as a side-by-side comparison of early and late Renowns confirms, and the bodies are substantially different – but that both Harry Webster and Walter Belgrove denied any knowledge of being involved in the change. Now this is really strange – Belgrove, after all, was Standard-Triumph's chief body engineer and stylist, while Harry Webster was in charge of chassis engineering (under Grinham) from 1949 onwards. Both, when tackled, could not believe that such a change had been made; both, when given proof, were astonished.

The extra three inches – a stretch in wheelbase from 108in to 111in – was needed to give that important bit of extra space in the Renown's passenger cabin. Sir John Black, who loved to be chauffeur-driven in his Renown, cooked up the idea of a middle-class limousine with Louis Antweiller and Colonel White of Mulliners. The car would have a division, like the very best of Rolls-Royces or Daimlers, and it would surely be a middle-class status symbol.

Belgrove assured me that the body changes were all done at Mulliners, without reference to him or his department at Standard-Triumph. To get the extra space for the back-seat-riding executive, or landed gentry, it would have been reasonable to put all the stretch in the back-seat foot-wells, and externally the extra length would have shown up in the rear door and windows; both Mercedes-Benz and Rolls-Royce carried out long-wheelbase conversions in this way. The long-wheelbase Renown, however, had an entirely different passenger box, with the extra length split between the front and the rear compartments. What could have been achieved with a relatively minor engineering change was actually accomplished with a great deal of time, expense and complication. Renown enthusiasts know that there is a world of difference between the important body panels of the short-wheelbase (TOA and TDB) and the long-wheelbase (TDC) Renowns, which extends to door, roof, floor panel, glass, trim panels and a host of other details.

In no way was this expensive and extensive re-engineering exercise ever worth the effort. The limousine, for instance, weighed in at 3024lb compared with about 2850lb for the short-wheelbase Renown, gave very little more effective lounging room, and cost £925 (basic) compared with £825 for the saloon.

Sir John, at least, did not confine this re-engineering to the limousine, as the TDC series of Renown saloons, with the 111in wheelbase and the bigger bodyshell, were phased unobtrusively into production at the beginning of 1952 (the limousine having been announced at the Earls Court show of 1951). He then made the fatal mistake of thinking that the cars were worth more, and could be priced higher, than before. The saloon rose in price to £925 by the end of 1952, after the limousine had been dropped, and it really is no wonder that demand plummeted accordingly.

The limousine, in fact, was a ghastly marketing error. Although Sir John himself liked the idea (it had, after all, been conceived to satisfy his own leanings in regard to the Renown), few other people did. The limousine was in production for just one year, and a mere 189 cars were sold –10 of these going to export territories. The TDC Renown, too, staggered from crisis to crisis. It was always too costly – at £925 in 1952, for instance, it had to compete with cars like the Rover 75 (£995), the Sunbeam-Talbot 90 (£865) or even the Mark VII Jaguar (£1140) – and in nearly every case the Renown was outclassed in style, in sporting cachet, or even in novelty appeal.

It was, in short, a car which the public had seen around for too long. By 1953, when sales were down to a trickle, it was in its eighth public year, and it was also becoming quite unsaleable in export markets. There was no volume demand for the traditional type of British styling (razor edge coachwork and genuine tree wood on the facia had a strictly limited appeal), and it showed up in the sales figures. Of the 6501 TDB Renowns only 814 were exported, and of the 2800 TDC Renowns built until October 1954 only 107 were sold outside Britain.

In 1950, although thought had been given to uprating the performance of the Renown (and the Vanguard) with a 90mm bore version of the wet-liner engine, which would have given 2341cc and much improved torque, the car was then virtually ignored by management and design staff while they buckled down to the Standard Eight, restyled Vanguards, and, of course, the TR2 sports car.

The price had to be slashed in June 1953 from £925 to £775 (basic), and by the middle of 1954 the directors were talking of producing a restyled Renown for the 1955 Motor Show, but this timetable was too optimistic, and Triumph enthusiasts will be glad that they did not completely pursue their resolve. A motor car did appear, in October 1956, with a lot of suspiciously Triumph-like touches, but fortunately for posterity it was badged as a Standard Vanguard Sportsman – and failed miserably!

Right up until the summer of 1956 the revised version of the Vanguard III (styled by an American consultant, Carl Otto) was called 'Triumph Renown', and anyone who has looked on that disastrously ugly machine, with its engine in TR2 tune, its pseudo-Triumph grille and the globe badges, must be glad that

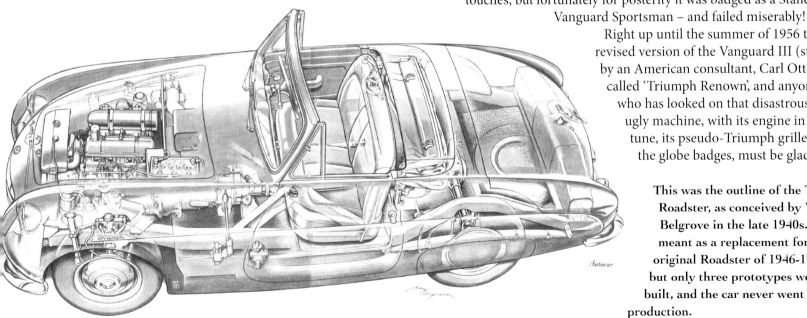

Autocar

This was the outline of the TRX Roadster, as conceived by Walter Belgrove in the late 1940s. It was meant as a replacement for the original Roadster of 1946-1949, but only three prototypes were built, and the car never went into production.

it was renamed. For all that, it was quite a quick car if you could bear to keep your eyes open when driving it; it had overdrive as standard, and it was little more expensive than a Renown at £820 basic. Only 901 were sold.

The Renown, then, died in dignity, and it would not be until 1959 that the Triumph name reappeared on a saloon car in Europe. The Roadster, too, had died without ceremony, and was to have been replaced with a new Roadster, if only the time had been ripe and the public keen enough to buy the car. The new Roadster, or the TRX as it was later known, was Walter Belgrove's creation, and appeared at the 1950 motor shows. By the spring of 1951, however, Standard had let it be known that "only a limited number of the Roadsters will be built in the immediate future ... in spite of the thousands of orders received ..." But why, and how?

The TRX belongs, in spirit, to only two men – Sir John Black and Walter Belgrove. Sir John conceived the idea of a full-width roadster, luxuriously trimmed and appointed, and left Walter Belgrove to get on with it. It was styled in 1947, and it should have been ready for showing at the 1949 motor shows.

Belgrove was given a completely free hand in the styling and body engineering, though he was directed to use a Vanguard rolling chassis (which meant a 94in wheelbase), and he was told that Ted Grinham would co-operate in providing mechanical and engine changes to give the car an appropriate image. This latter, in fact, was only given grudgingly, for Belgrove and Grinham were at daggers-drawn for years before the final spasm came in 1955, and Grinham in any case was jealous of the direct access Belgrove had to Sir John Black.

The 2088cc engine was equipped with twin carburettors, and boosted to 71bhp at 4200rpm, which was a miserable increase compared with the Vanguard's standard output of 68bhp. One series of mysterious factory pictures show an engine with an experimental crossflow cylinder head, in which the twin SU carburettors are on the left side of the car, but this head never appeared in public, and was never developed further for subsequent sporting Triumphs. Overdrive, never available on the Callaby-styled Roadster, was to be standard equipment, and built-in hydraulic jacks were a feature.

Belgrove spent many long and happy hours on his new creation, which he completed in early 1948. Although the full-width bodyshell had many double-skinned light-alloy panels and much double curvature, it could easily have been built in Standard-Triumph's own experimental workshops at Banner Lane. Sir John Black, however, decided to help out Helliwells (at Walsall, in Staffordshire), which was looking for such projects, and asked it to build him three prototypes in time for the 1949 show.

That was a mistake. Helliwells took ages to get the job done – Belgrove said that this was because it was applying aircraft-building standards to what was essentially a simple job – and fell so far

An intriguing view of a TRX prototype engine bay, showing the unique and experimental cross-flow cylinder headed version of the Vanguard engine, with its carburettors on the left side – an installation which was never seen again.

behind schedule that there was no hope of getting prototypes into the 1949 show. Belgrove nagged, complained and raged, and after Sir John threw one of his famous and fearsome-to-behold tantrums the partly-completed cars were hurriedly brought back to Banner Lane for completion.

TRX was so much of a Belgrove style that he was even allowed to include a 'B' badge on the wings just behind the front wheelarch, and this made Ted Grinham even more furious. However, not only had a complex body been specified, but electro-hydraulic operation of seats and headlamps had been included, and the fully tailored, padded and lined hood was also self-extracting and retracting.

It was a stimulatingly modern car which caused something of a sensation when first shown at the Paris show of 1950, and later at Earls Court. Even so, one has to say that it caused a great deal of controversy, and many of the comments received by the sales staff were not encouraging. The British motoring press, almost to a man, were kind to the car, and there was certainly enough genuine interest to consider putting the car into production, but there were still many nagging doubts. As with the existing Triumphs, TRX was going to be expensive (listed at £975, basic, it was the most expensive Triumph yet), and not everyone was at ease with the thought of all that electrical and hydraulic complication. Princess Margaret, no less, caused something of a stir at the show when she asked to see some of the gadgets work, whereupon they promptly burned out!

Standard's problem at the time was not that it wasn't completely sure of its model (though Belgrove was, and Sir John Black reputedly liked what he saw), but that it could not give the car any priority in its queue for tooling of bodywork. While it was beavering away to revise the Vanguard, there was already a proposal in the works to restyle the Mayflower, and Sir John had recently been talking to George Mason of the Nash Corporation with a view to Standard building the new NX1 car, which later emerged as the Austin-built Metropolitan.

The only possibility was that an outside contractor might be persuaded to take on the job of producing the body, and it was with this in mind that Walter Belgrove was sent off to talk to Carrozzeria Touring of Milan, even though the Triumph scheme envisaged building-up a shell from aluminium skin panels, while the Touring methods were well-known and entirely different! Much later, towards the end of 1951, Belgrove was again sent out to Italy to talk

to Pininfarina, and despite another promising set of negotiations this deal also fell through. It was at that point that Belgrove decided that the TRX would never actually go into production, and he was soon proved right. Within weeks, Sir John was on another tack.

Many were sorry that the TRX drifted off into obscurity and legend, though two of them were later acquired by the British car-collector John Ward, and (long after his death) to this day (though one is in awful condition) they still survive. What is a blessing is that the decision to cancel the car before it was tooled up really cleared the decks for a re-think. That re-think, carried out by the same team but to an entirely different brief, led to the 20TS and – as we now know it – the TR2. Could any sidelined prototype have a better successor than that?

Walter Belgrove's idea of what should replace the immediate post-war Roadster was the TRX, conceived in 1948 and launched in 1950. It was not a success, only three prototypes were ever made, but two of them survive to this day.

Mayflower: a Second American Invasion

Dylan Thomas once said of a fellow poet, "I still can't believe he could write such beautiful devotional poetry ... I once saw him fall downstairs wearing suspenders." Many must have felt something like Dylan on their first encounter with the Triumph Mayflower – that 'other Triumph' occupying the company's attentions while TRX was translated into TR2. Against the background of the prewar Triumphs, the elegant postwar razor-edge saloons and quixotic Roadsters, the Mayflower was a strange anomaly indeed. Nobody knew exactly what to make of it, though several tried. "I was standing (alongside it) on the Triumph stand at Earls Court, feeling particularly proud," Alick Dick said, "when some delightful society debutante type strolled up, dripping furs, hanging on to the arm of some rich playboy. Her only comment was, 'Oh, how perfectly bloody!' So much for two years'

work and, at that time I suppose, £1 million of capital – a singularly salutary experience!"

The Mayflower was singular – a car of great character, built by and for characters. Road tester Tom McCahill called it a slab-sided tobacco can, a geranium pot, a turnip. Those to whom it appealed nicknamed it the 'Watch Charm Rolls,' but others called it many worse things. Sir John Black, however, doted on the little dear, and at Standard-Triumph that was tantamount to automotive sainthood. Sir John got his come-uppance soon enough, when the Mayflower hit the American market: it sold by the half-dozen.

Many years later, the Mayflower appears a mere bagatelle, a strange beast with no apparent rationale, conceived without the benefit of a market survey and sold because, after all, in 1950 a British car company could sell anything. In reality it was a good product for its time, and had many fine points. Its name, taken from the ship that brought the Pilgrims to Massachusetts Bay in 1620, says a lot about its rationale – it was beamed directly at the American economy-car market.

In those days Great Britain commanded a towering 95 per cent of US import sales, and fed manufactured goods to a far-flung Empire and Commonwealth as well. If the latter areas were crying for tough, economical, roomy cars built in the mother country,

With a style whose theme was dictated to his engineers by Sir John Black, the slab-sided Mayflower was something of a throw-back to the late 1930s, but had a surprisingly roomy four-seater cabin, and an appealing character.

Posed in a typically British country house setting, the Mayflower went on sale in 1950.

the Americans might be, too. Prospects were particularly enticing since the dollar (we all mourn that long-lost age) was harder than any currency in the world except the Swiss franc, and the market for cars was bottomless. In 1941, 32 million American families owned about 30 million cars – a record figure. But by war's end the car population was down to 22 million, which was not too far from what *Fortune* called "the danger point (18 million) of a transportation breakdown." Of the cars on the road, half were over ten years old; many of those ready for the graveyard. Conservative estimates indicated that 20 million vehicles would be built before present demand was satiated. This might take three or four years, during which anything with wheels that could be built, floated to east-coast docks, unloaded and delivered could be sold.

Sir John Black, always a canny businessman, looked with envious eyes at the US inroads of MG and his old friend William Lyons of Jaguar. He duly decided that a piece of the pie belonged to Standard-Triumph. By courtesy of Sir Stafford Cripps and the postwar Labour Government, Standard was currently locked into a one-range policy, based on the Vanguard. But Triumph was hardly treading water with the trickle of saloons and Roadsters. Sir John had already earmarked Triumph as a sports car rival to MG: why not an economy saloon to go with it, covering the

Except for the two-tone colour scheme on this Mayflower, sold in 1950, which was added by its original customer, the car looks exactly as it did when Standard-Triumph built it in Canley.

two largest openings in the American market and hopefully driving MG, howling, to the wall? There was nothing wrong with the reasoning, but from a product-planning standpoint there was a lot wrong with the car.

Not that the Mayflower was badly conceived, but it was poorly suited to American conditions. It evidenced a peculiarly insular attitude toward North American sales which would later contribute to the undermining of the British car in that area: too often, cars designed for this huge market were created by people who had never set foot in Canada or the United States. Much later, when BMC launched its Issigonis 1100, the cars began wearing-out clutches in San Francisco and burning-up engines in Los Angeles. The LA dealers wanted higher axle ratios, the SF dealers lower, and BMC couldn't understand why two cities so apparently close on the map could require diametrically opposite specifications! The Mayflower's faults could not be remedied by different axle ratios – it just wasn't powerful enough for North American conditions. Even in 1950, people drove 600 miles a day over endless motorways, and the nature of the American motorist was to run a car hard 15,000 miles a year with only an occasional look at the dipstick, and a tune-up every six months. Try to tell this individual that good maintenance required a decoke every 25,000 miles and he'd walk away shaking his head.

It is not recorded that Sir John or his assistants spent much time visiting or analysing the US market. Americans liked Rolls-Royces, Rolls-Royces were razor-edged, therefore they would like a small saloon styled the same way. Louis Antweiller, managing director of Mulliners of Birmingham, made this very point. Sir John grabbed the ball and ran with it.

Concurrently with the introduction of the 1800 saloon and Roadster, S-T announced that Triumph would produce a 'Ten' by 1948 or 1949. Though the old RAC horsepower tax was shortly abandoned and the designation rendered meaningless, S-T was obviously referring to the Mayflower. Sources indicate that wooden mock-ups of the latter were extant about the same time as models of the 1800s, powered by a 10hp Morgan engine, ie a Standard engine. One Mayflower was even experimentally constructed on the ply-balsa-ply principles of the Mosquito aircraft – "a fascinating thought for a car," as Alick Dick says, "but not very good for Nader." Walter Belgrove, by then long-ensconced as chief of the body design office, recalled what happened next:

"I believe that the Mayflower was on the stocks in 1947 or 1948. This motor car was intended to be a short-wheelbase (84 inches) version of the razor-edge saloon, and also the first volume-produced Triumph. This was continuing 'knife edge' styling with a vengeance, and I believe the policy stemmed from Sir John Black's discussions with Louis Antweiller. I was responsible for its front-end and my department engineered it, and I also made

In the late 1940s, Triumph's most influential engineering personalities were (left to right) Harry Webster, Ted Grinham and Lewis Dawtrey.

The Mayflower's facia and control layout for a left-hand drive car. Note the steering wheel, which was later adopted for the TR2.

the quarter-scale model of the vehicle. But the Triumph Mayflower was really styled by Leslie Moore, chief body designer of Mulliners. Actual body production was carried out by Fisher & Ludlow, which also built Vanguard bodies and which would later build the Standard Eight/Ten bodies, since Mulliners was not equipped to build pressed-steel shells in very large numbers.

"It is not possible to reproduce the lines of the large razor-edge saloon on a 'shut-up' wheelbase, and inside the circumstances I do not think Leslie Moore's work could have been bettered. The side elevation was very good indeed, and although of contemporary 'slab-sided' style, the swept line from the headlamp boss to the tail endeavoured to retain some characteristic feature of the bigger model. It carried, however, a traditional front-end and was therefore a hybrid. As I had something to do with the front-end it could be said that I was a collaborator with Leslie in producing the amalgamation."

Lest we leave the impression that Sir John's Mayflower was naught but a whim, it should be recorded that its body design made

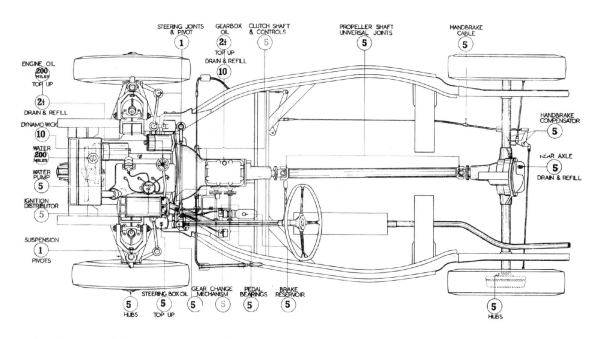

This diagram of the chassis layout of the Mayflower shows the positioning of the 1930s generation side-valve engine, as bolted to the Vanguard-derived three speed gearbox. The independent front suspension was all new, and would later be used on the side-screen TRs.

The 1247cc side-valve Mayflower engine was an evolution of the Standard Flying Ten unit from the 1930s. Although an overhead-valve version was supplied to Morgan, it was never fitted to the Mayflower.

a lot of sense. At a time when the products of most companies were dull and sometimes downright ugly, the Mayflower's upright radiator and 'formal' lines were arresting and unique. It was also extremely well built, with one of the first unit bodies – a deep box-section frame welded to a bonderized steel body forming a sturdy box of extreme rigidity without unnecessary weight. The razor-edge lines allowed spectacular space utilisation. A box, of course, is the optimum shape to enclose any given volume, so despite its small wheelbase the Mayflower held four big people with ease. Seat width was 48/38 inches front/rear, maximum interior body width was 53 inches. Against a total exterior body width of 61 inches, the Mayflower was using 86.8 per cent of its total width for interior space – an almost unbelievable figure. By comparison, the highest such percentage on a contemporary American car was Kaiser's 80 per cent, and even that was considered radical. Access to the roomy rear compartment was especially easy, since the doors were wide, and engineer Arthur Ballard had invented a novel front seat in which the cushion slid forward as the backrest was tilted. Several American makers adopted this idea years later, and called it a 'first'.

Moore used extremely thin 'A' and 'B' pillars, allowing an enormous glass area – the Mayflower must have led its field in this respect – giving the car a spacious feeling that was unique at the time. The square-shaped boot allowed lots of luggage to be carried. It was fitted with a let-down number-plate bracket and steel luggage loops so that bulky loads could be accommodated with the lid open. The spare tyre was cleverly concealed under the boot floor; it could be cranked down on its hinged platform by turning a depressed nut just above.

Flower power was also unique. Designed by E G Grinham's team, and descended from the prewar Standard Ten, the 1247cc 'four' (63 x 100 mm) was never used on another Standard-Triumph product. It combined a chromium-iron block with detachable aluminium-alloy cylinder head, and side valves operating from a four-bearing chain-driven camshaft. The crank was counter-weighted, hefty in size, with three main bearings; connecting rods were steel, with floating gudgeon pins and aluminium-alloy split-skirt pistons. Though the valving system was of obsolete design, it did allow the engine to operate quietly, developing 38bhp at 4000rpm and 58lb/ft of torque at 2000rpm. Triumph's performance figures quoted 0-50mph in 23 seconds and a maximum of 63mph, against fuel consumption of 35mpg. Inlet and exhaust manifolds were integral, leading to a flexibly-mounted (to cut noise) exhaust system. The carburettor was a single downdraught fitted with oil-bath air cleaner/silencer. Full pressure lubrication was supplied by a Hobourn-Eaton submerged pump feeding all main bearings. The clutch was a 7¼-inch Borg & Beck with balanced control linkage, preventing any clutch problems due to movement of the rubber-mounted engine.

The Mayflower's gearbox – the same as the Vanguard's with a different bellhousing – was an interesting unit, one of the earliest all-synchro three-speeds; synchro-first was of crucial importance to the low-torque engine, especially with only three forward gears. The change lever was always mounted on the inboard side, whether right-hand or left-hand drive, making it the same sort of Mickey Mouse unit as was in vogue in America at the time. Most engineers felt this sop to the export market was a mistake – the Mayflower engine was simply not flexible enough to get by with only three speeds, and the ratios were extremely wide. Harry Webster said he was nearly sacked for daring to argue with Sir John Black by suggesting four speeds. Chief engineer Grinham firmly believed in three speeds as a cost-saving item – later even pitching for a three-speed in the Standard Eight. As almost everyone agreed, Ted Grinham was not a driving enthusiast ...

The chassis was conventional, with independent front suspension by wishbones and coil springs, semi-elliptic leaf springs with live axle at the rear, and hydraulic, double-acting telescopic dampers all round. Brakes were hydraulic, with the handbrake operating on the rear wheels and controlled by a semi-flyoff type pistol grip. A single battery provided 12-volt electrics; tyre size was 5.00-15 inches for the home market and 5.50-15 for export. The gearbox led via a Hardy-Spicer propeller-shaft to the hypoid (Vanguard-type) rear axle, which offered a stump-pulling ratio of 5.125:1.

The Mayflower's list of standard equipment paid compliment to a car selling for only £520, or $1456 at the $2.80 pound. (The price, for New York, was $1685, in Canada $1595.) There was a locking bonnet (the cylinder was cleverly built into the mascot), locking petrol cap, and a full set of tools including non-slip jack and starting handle. Instrumentation included fuel/oil pressure/temperature gauges and a speedometer which until mid-1952 featured a trip odometer. US options included radio, heater and full leather upholstery, though cars shipped to Canada came with a leather front seat and a heater at no extra charge. Most export-market Mayflowers came with cut-pile carpeting, while the rest used a rubber floor mat. Basic colours were solids, but dealers would occasionally duotone a car by applying a contrasting shade to the panel below the belt line. There were trafficators, sun visors, wing vents, under-dash parcel shelves, even an auxiliary cowl vent for windows-up ventilation.

The Mayflower was introduced in Canley in the autumn of 1949, amidst great rejoicing. Sir John Black presided at a

This startlingly detailed sectioned Triumph Mayflower was originally prepared for display at the 1951 Festival of Britain.

This was the dramatic way in which Triumph linked the Mayflower's name to that of the original Mayflower ship – as shown in the centre of the dining room display prepared for the North American launch party.

round table encircling a huge model of the Pilgrim's Mayflower constructed by one of Standard's craftsmen. If Chrysler hadn't got to it first, he might well have called it 'Plymouth', after Plymouth Rock, the Mayflower's landing place. (Sir John liked Plymouths – during the Vanguard's design stage, it was actually Sir John who had sent Walter to the US Embassy for inspiration, as we previously mentioned. Walter diplomatically went, then forgot all about them as quickly as he could!

Mayflower publicity was traditionally imaginative. For the Festival of Britain in 1951, a car was laboriously sectioned to display literally every interior and mechanical detail, each metal part polished to a mirror finish. Brochures called the Mayflower "the light car of elegant British styling and unusually handsome appearance, designed for comfortable family motoring. It is well equipped, roomy, with wide doors ... the best in modern engineering, skill, design and performance." There were no historians at Standard-Triumph; had there been, the slogan might well have been Siegfried Bettmann's 'The Quality Light Car.'

Happily for Britons, Sir John announced that some of the initial run would go to the car-poor home market; the Vanguard, apparently, was tending to Labour's 'export or die' demand. Still the Mayflower's big goal was North America, followed by other export markets. In early 1950 Black announced that CKD parts for export would be available by August, and that the first complete Mayflowers were off the production lines, though this last statement was somewhat misleading.

The first Mayflowers had no sooner arrived in America when New York importer Joe Ferguson (brother of Harry Ferguson, Sir John's tractor customer) asked *Mechanix Illustrated* to test one. "Okay," said Tom McCahill, "but I want you to know I think it's a hell of a looking car and if it's half as bad as I think it looks I'm going to blast it wide open." In his report, Uncle Tom said the Mayflower had "more acute angles than you can find in the uplift ads, and is the only car in the world selling for less than ten grand that follows the knife-edge school of design–" (he forgot the Renown) "–To me it's a baby town car. It is a design most people either hate on sight or warm-up to gradually. It is about as sporty as shooting parrots in a cage and as streamlined as King Farouk doing a one-and-a-half off a ten-foot springboard." But McCahill was won over on his first corner. The Mayflower held the road "like a tar stain on a white shirt. The more I drove it the more I liked it. With myself and Joe (his Labrador retriever) and 500 pounds extra weight, it took my long 28 per cent grade hill-climb without the slightest sign of distress. Naturally this was done in low gear, but at the steepest point I stopped the car dead and then started off without a single buck. With one average-size driver alone in the car, the Mayflower would be a real treat on Switzerland's Matterhorn (really!). Considering its size and the fact that four people can go for a trip in this barge, the Mayflower is quite a mighty little atom."

From an economy standpoint, Americans felt the Mayflower measured up. One Richard Oblinger, writing in a 1953 issue of *Motor Trend*, said his first 8766 miles had cost him only $102.80, $76 of it for petrol: "We have averaged a little better than 31 (US) miles to the gallon of gas since we bought the Triumph. We have taken several trips around Florida, driving the Triumph rather than our full-sized car, which, incidentally, is a Lincoln. Needless to say, we are very happy with the 'Flower,' as we have nicknamed it, and would recommend one for a second car for someone who doesn't want to spend a small fortune on gas, etc."

People were already falling in love with the quaint-cute Watch Charm Rolls. Twenty years later an owners' club would blossom, to preserve a car of undoubted appeal.

At home the reactions were less overt, but even those who first looked askance often admitted that the Mayflower grew on them. *The Autocar*'s scribe, Michael Brown, said he had "looked at the Mayflower, read about the Mayflower, but said to myself that it was not my type of car. Now I am not so sure. The little but roomy square-cut saloon gets along the road in a very nice way, and provides the visibility and airiness for which the Renown is renowned ... I liked the Mayflower even better in the dark wet than I did in the light dry – a curious reaction which I have never before felt." His colleagues summarised: "actually this is a car of many attributes. It pleases the passengers for its comfort and visibility, and it pleases the driver for its dual personality, meaning that it cruises sweetly at 40mph as an aristocratic and quiet little carriage, and has a particularly smooth and flexible performance at the low end, which ensures that one can get away from a slow down without having to change gear (one wonders what kind of getaway that was!); or, it will swing up to a cruising speed of 55 to 60mph and hold it comfortably, giving a long-distance overall average of 40 miles in each hour on English roads, without any feeling of strain."

At Earls Court in 1950, a new Mayflower model appeared in the form of a dropheadcoupé. Frank Callaby, co-designer of the Roadster, recalls that "Sir John Black asked Mulliners to design it and build the conversions." With its enormous roof, blind rear quarters and landau bars, the Mayflower drophead was an ungainly looking car, but one which has remained highly sought-after by enthusiasts. As there has been some conjecture about how many dropheads were built, and where they went, it may be useful to list them here. The Standard Register provided the figures, from a copy of the postwar build records:

From 1950 to 1953, when it was supplanted by the all-new Standard Eight/Standard Ten model, the Mayflower was assembled at Canley in this space-saving manner.

Mayflower Dropheads			
Comm No	*Build Date*	*Engine No*	*Remarks*
TT 174 T4	29 Aug 50	23SE	Prototype; grey, grey leather
TT 215 LCP	4 Sep 50	264E	Grey, red leather; LH drive
TT 289LCP	12 Sep 50	419E*	Grey, red leather; LH drive
TT 359 CP	15 Sep 50	340E	Grey, red leather
TT 438 LCP	6 Oct 50	684E	Maroon, brown leather; LH drive
TT 441 CP	29 Nov 50	1928E	Grey, red leather
TT 442 CP	28 Nov 50	756E	Maroon, beige leather
TT 443 CP	28 Nov 50	677E	Grey, red leather
TT 444 CP	30 Nov 50	2000E	Grey, red leather
TT 3531 CP	19 Jan 51	3666E	Grey, red leather
*Originally 324E: engine changed			

Engine numbers indicate that the dropheads came fairly early in the Mayflower production run, which coincides with the fact that the car took abnormally long to get into volume production after its 1949 Earls Court debut. But by January the drophead was cancelled. We asked Frank Callaby about the reasons. "Tom Cox, who joined Standard-Triumph from Mulliners, thinks the high cost of converting the saloon body at Mulliners was the most likely reason that prevented it from going into limited production," Frank replied. The superstructure apparently had to be torched off and the body strengthened – the work involved must have been phenomenal.

Outside of North America, Mayflower sales were fair to moderate. "Ironically," notes Callaby, "the demand increased as the model was phasing-out." Exactly 34,000 were built between 1950 and 1953, with 17,605 for export and 16,395 for the home market. The cost of assembling its numerous sharply creased body panels – despite the TR technique of beaded two-piece wings – was considerable, and it made more sense to concentrate on the much higher volume small Standards then being developed.

Throughout the years of Mayflower production, various schemes were put forward for modifying the car, using its components in another car, giving it a more modern engine or otherwise keeping it in production. As early as April 1950, Sir John Black wrote to George Mason of Nash-Kelvinator in Kenosha,

Wisconsin, urging Mason to use Mayflower bits in his new NXI (Nash Experimental International), a tiny two-seat prototype which was to become the Metropolitan. Mason had begun exploring the idea of this very small car in 1948, the NXI being designed for him by freelancer Bill Flajole. Interestingly, NXI had the same 84-inch wheelbase and unitised body/chassis as the Mayflower, although the production Metropolitan wheelbase was 85 inches. Nothing came of the association. Sir John later told his board that petrol tax increases at home meant Standard would have to concentrate more on small cars, and could not commit any capacity to Nash. Mason ultimately went to Austin for his engine and running gear, and to Fisher & Ludlow – the Mayflower's builders – for bodies. Austin assembled the Metropolitan for ten years, 1953 to 1962. It may have been a bad decision by Standard-Triumph: close to 100,000 Metropolitans were built, always at a profit.

An overhead-valve Mayflower engine was being planned for phase-in 'as soon as possible' in August 1950, according to records of the Standard-Triumph executive directors. It never arrived, though the engine existed, having been supplied to Morgan for its 4/4 since 1939. A Mayflower restyle was asked for (from Fisher & Ludlow) at the meeting of September 19. But less than two months later Sir John gave the go-ahead for a new Vanguard, a project far more important, and plans for a restyled OHV Mayflower were shelved. This happened on November 8 – only a few weeks after the first dropheads had trickled out, inevitably to suffer the same cancellation order as the saloons.

The directors now began discussing a successor to the Mayflower instead of a restyle. This turned out to be the Standard Eight. (Board minutes, incidentally, suggest it might have been rear-engined, as the Renault 4CV was being studied for inspiration.) On August 22, 1951, Standard Eight styling proposals were made, using a Mayflower floorpan. The car was to have a three-speed non-synchro floor-change gearbox, certainly a backward step compared with the Mayflower, but no doubt cheaper. The first prototypes were promised (by the following April) on December 4, 1951, but the Mayflower floorpan scheme was dropped. Early 1952 minutes note that the Eight would use transfer tooling, and at first would be built (in 1953) with left-over Mayflower engine tooling. It is obvious from the foregoing that the Eight was the Mayflower's direct replacement, that there was never a possibility of the two being produced side-by-side.

What about Sir John's vaunted American market? Unfortunately, his timing turned out to be completely wrong. The Mayflower was too late for the great postwar seller's market, which levelled-off about the time the first Mayflowers arrived, and too early for the small-car boom of the late 1950s. By 1953, Kaiser-Frazer's Henry J small car had proved a failure, Nash's Rambler was barely surviving, while the Willys Aero (1952) and Hudson Jet

(1953) were both destined for short careers. Notably, well-managed companies like Ford and GM considered, but abandoned, plans to build their own small cars, and not until imports began edging towards 10 per cent of the American market did they respond with the 'compacts' of 1960.

Had it arrived in 1955 or 1956, the Mayflower might have written another story. It was attractive, and comprehensively equipped (which the Standard Eight and Ten weren't). Whether Americans would ever have accepted its thoroughly British styling in large numbers is, however, a question. Still, they seemed to like a Volkswagen designed in the early years of the Third Reich. Of course a VW sold for several hundred dollars less than a Mayflower and the model wasn't any more successful until about 1955. In 1952/1953 the Mayflower's price was equivalent to those of America's Big Three – Chevrolet, Ford and Plymouth – and nobody else, not even Studebaker, did well in their territory.

The VW comparison is, however, absorbing. Consider the relative specifications of a Mayflower against that of a Beetle built 20 years later:

	1953 Mayflower	1973 VW Beetle
Engine	L-head four	Flat-four
Displacement	1.2 litres	1.6 litres
Horsepower, gross	38 at 4200rpm	53 at 4000rpm
Compression ratio	6.8:1	7.5:1
Gearbox	3-speed synchro	4-speed synchro
Wheelbase – Length	84–154in	94½–160in
Width – Height	62–62in	61–59in
Passengers	4, comfortably	4, tightly
Kerb weight	2100lb	1825lb
0-60 acceleration	27-30 seconds	22-25 seconds
Top speed	63mph	82mph
Fuel economy (US)	40mpg	30mpg

All things considered, the Mayflower stacks up rather well.

In February 1953, Fergus Motors exhibited one of its last Mayflowers at the World Sports Show in Madison Square Garden, New York. It won first prize as 'The Light Car of Distinction.' Fergus' press release quotes Laurence Pomeroy (junior), whose remarks sum the Mayflower up well: "the bulk of my 1952 motoring has been in one of the best of small cars ... After 30,000 miles ... the steering and chassis parts appear as new, and the body structure sound and weatherproof ... Many would think that 30,000-odd miles with almost no trouble or loss of faculties is a matter of no great moment, whereas, those who have some detailed knowledge of the life led by a technical editor's car will consider such a feat a mid-century miracle. Certainly I can say that the Mayflower is indeed a trusty Triumph, with performance, visibility and size well suited to my annual 800 hours of London driving."

The departure of the Mayflower, and the Renown one year later, left Triumph without a saloon for the first time in its history – but not in the United States. By 1957, with the TR established and a dealer network in operation, Sir John Black's successors decided to go after the small-car market again – by now there was no doubt of its presence. Their method was to bring in the Standard Ten saloon and estate wagon, but in a wily piece of promotion they put a Triumph badge on it and sold it alongside the TR3 as the TR10. (Interestingly, the restyle for 1957 was originally to have been accompanied by a new model name – Triumph Mayflower.) As a Triumph, it was listed through 1960 (when the Herald was sold alongside it), always priced at $1699 (£607) and $1899 (£678). Sales brochures pictured the Ten next to a TR3, though there was no mechanical or physical resemblance, and claimed it had been inspired by S-T's successful sports car: "these cars have had over 50 years of driving experience in England and the Continent. They bring to American travel the years of experience developed from motoring over rough European roads, plus the stamina and power that TR3 race experience has developed ... there is no car made that can compare with the performance, economy and endurance of the Triumph."

Despite such heady talk, the Ten was really a Standard, and it properly belongs in a history of that marque. But since it was 'officially' a Triumph in the United States, a brief description is in order. With a unitised body, like the Mayflower, it rode the same 84-inch wheelbase (the body-frame design was completely unrelated, however) and measured 144 inches long. Suspension was by conventional coils and wishbones up front, and by semi-elliptic leaf springs and live axle at the rear. The engine was a modern OHV unit of 948cc, delivering 40bhp at 5000rpm and about 50 miles per (imperial) gallon, later further developed and used in the Heralds and Spitfires. Triumph claimed it would reach 78mph and accelerate from 0-50mph in 18 seconds. A four-speed gearbox with synchromesh on second, third and top was standard, as were tubeless tyres, twin sun visors and automatic turn indicators. Options included Lurex or genuine leather upholstery, whitewall tyres, heavy-duty heater, push-button clutch, chrome wheel rings, radio, and windscreen washer.

Clutchless 'Trimatic' (aka 'Standrive') transmission was a semi-automatic centrifugal clutch design to Newton Bennett patents, which promoters called 'fool-proof': "Put your thumb on the button in the top of the gearlever and shift – that's all there is to it. It works smoothly, efficiently and is amazingly simple." Trimatic appeared in 1956, and added to the car's sales appeal in automatic-acclimated America, giving S-T USA a vital slice of the economy-saloon market pending arrival of the Herald. The estate was quite popular, as it had little competition aside from the Hillman Husky. Though high and ungainly looking, it held a fairish amount of cargo. Most testers found the TR10 a strong, willing car, surprising in its highway performance and extremely stingy on fuel.

But throughout its four years on the American market, the little Ten remained strictly a secondary product, relying for sales on the reputation of the car that 'made' Triumph's reputation in North America. Whatever success the Ten did enjoy, it owed nearly all to another model, which literally saved the Triumph marque for posterity – the TR sports car.

The Sports Car America Loved Best

It's probably true to say that if the TR2 hadn't been an immediate success, there might never have been any more new Triumphs. Up until 1954, under Standard's control, the Triumph banner had not actually covered itself with glory. The Roadster, the Renown and the Mayflower had all been Sir John Black's personal projects, but they had done little for Standard's profits, and little for its reputation.

Yet from 1954 Triumph's reputation improved rapidly. Was it therefore no more than heavenly coincidence that Sir John Black's resignation, and the first TR2 magazine road test, both occurred in the same week at the beginning of 1954?

It was something of a miracle, in any case, that there was much time to think about new Triumph models at the beginning of the 1950s, especially with so little marque enthusiasm to urge things on. On all other fronts, Standard was enormously busy. Not only were sales of the Standard Vanguard booming, but Ted Grinham's engineers were developing a completely new small car for introduction in the autumn of 1953; not only was production of Ferguson tractors edging ever upwards, but the company had once again been invited to get involved in aero-engine manufacture; not only was it filling all its own factories with work, but it was actively looking around for new buildings to take up further expansion.

It was a frantic time for Sir John Black, but he had plenty of driving energy to cope with it all. Then, as in the 1930s and 1940s, he had to be the decision-maker for everything, and he certainly never encouraged his own executives to initiate, or to decide on, their own projects. The future of Triumph, and the cars connected with it, would merely have to take its place in Sir John's list of priorities.

After the relative failure of the Roadster and the Renown (and this was even before he knew how the public would greet the Mayflower), and after Jaguar's sensational launch of the XK120, Sir John knew that he could no longer hope to compete with Jaguar on either performance or prestige. But he still hankered after success with sporting cars, and we now know that he became jealous of the reputation enjoyed by Morgan and MG.

MG's postwar reputation had blossomed in exactly the way

Sir John would have wished for Triumph. But there was no way he could compete with, or influence, MG without actually building a rival car. He could not hope to take over the Abingdon concern as it was completely owned by the Nuffield Group.

On the other hand, he thought he could do something about Morgan, not just because it was a small firm, but because it had a long history of doing business with Standard. Sir John, in fact, had first met HFS Morgan in 1909/1910 when working for the patent agents who just happened to be preparing the original specifications for the independent front suspension of the three-wheeler.

Later, when already managing director of Standard, he had negotiated the supply of special overhead-valve versions of the 1247cc Standard Flying Ten engine to Morgan in 1939 for the 4/4 model. As recently as 1950, too, the Plus 4 had replaced the original car, and used the 2088cc Standard Vanguard engine.

But for Sir John this was not enough. With the idea of adding yet another marque to Standard's credit, he decided to take over control of Morgan. But this, needless to say, was before he contacted the Morgan family about it. It tells us much about Sir John's character that he firmly expected to succeed in this bid, but he reckoned without the independent and resourceful Morgans, father and son.

Standard's board records confirm that the approach was made in the autumn of 1950, so the then-managing director Peter Morgan's note to us is now seen as mildly inaccurate:

"During the 1951 Motor Show Sir John Black asked to see HFS and myself in his office at Earls Court. Sir John mentioned being impressed by the potential of the Plus 4 and asked my father if he would like to join forces with Standard-Triumph to make the car in larger quantities. Father was obviously flattered at this takeover suggestion, but said he would like to give the offer serious thought and would let Sir John know his answer at a later time. Sir John assured my father that whatever his answer might be, it would not affect the supply of engine units. He also said he had no wish to put my father or I 'out of a job.'

"Subsequent to the interview, I am sure my father and I wished to keep Morgan independent, and in two or three weeks' time, after a directors' meeting, a letter was sent to Sir John Black indicating that we did not wish to be absorbed by the Standard Motor Company."

Standard's board learned of this rebuff at the beginning of December 1950, by which time they had also absorbed the sales staff's feelings that the Belgrove-designed TRX Roadster was not the right car for that time. Although Sir John was as good as his word, and never restricted the supply of engines to Morgan, Alick Dick confirms that this episode made Sir John determined that one day he would 'get even' with Morgan. This was to be in the shape of a new sports car which would be a direct competitor in all respects to the Morgan and to the MG TD.

If he'd had plenty of staff to deploy on this project, this 'Morgan beater' might have been started at once, at the beginning of 1951, but Standard's engineering staff was too small to pick it up at the time. Work on the restyled Standard Vanguard (the Phase II car), project work on the new small car, and continuing work on behalf of Ferguson, all took precedence.

In the meantime, Sir John continued to talk to many people in the industry about this type of car, really to confirm his own convictions. Christopher Jennings (editor of *Motor*) takes some credit for this, for having recently completed a business trip to the United States he was sure that a yawning gap existed between the MG TD and the Jaguar XK120 which no other British car could adequately fill. Harry Ferguson's brother, who was running Fergus Motors in New York (it sold Triumphs *and* Morgans!), confirmed this opinion. He and others also convinced Sir John that a big luxurious car like the Triumph TRX was not the answer for export markets like North America, but that a light and fast two-seater would be ideal.

But throughout 1951 the new Standard small-car project was taking up most of Ted Grinham's and Harry Webster's time. Since the Standard Flying Eight had been dropped in 1948, the company's only small saloon had been the Mayflower, and on cost grounds this was by no means aimed at the burgeoning bottom-end of the market.

It had all started in the summer of 1950, first when an overhead-valve engine was proposed for the Mayflower (this would, in fact, have been the same as that engine just discarded by Morgan), and then when Fisher & Ludlow, as one of Standard's body suppliers, had been asked to consider a restyle of the original Mayflower, even though it had been on the market for less than a year.

A year later, by mid-1951, the Standard Eight was beginning to evolve. At first an all-new car with a rear-mounted engine had been proposed, and a Renault 4CV had been inspected closely for guidance. Next it was going to be based on the Mayflower's chassis, suspensions and floorpan, but with new styling and mechanicals which included a three-speed gearbox without synchromesh. By the end of that year, however, Ted Grinham had gained approval for a tiny saloon car with unit construction, a Belgrove-styled four-door shape, and – at first – a brand new side-valve engine. Fortunately for Standard-Triumph's future, however, that decision was changed before the first prototype was finished in May 1952, and every subsequent car had an overhead-valve 803cc engine.

A note in the company's records from March 14, 1952 is important, not because a new sports car is mentioned, but because it says that "all drawings for the small car have now been released." This meant that, at last, the engineering team could get their teeth into Sir John's obsession with a new sports car, and his pursuit of Morgan and MG.

John Lloyd, who was then a young man in the engineering department, later told the writer that Standard's first thoughts on chassis engineering included work on very crude and simple space frames, with angle-section members and pop-rivets holding things together at the joints, but these were soon discarded in favour of a conventional chassis. Styling work and body engineering began in earnest at the beginning of 1952, to a very restricting brief, as Sir John was not willing to commit much capital for new tools, or for a lengthy gestation period. The new car would have to use as many existing components as possible.

More than anything else, Sir John wanted the new car to be very simple. He had learned his lesson about complication with the TRX, and he was impressed by the way that Morgan and MG could build cars without using expensive body dies. At first, indeed, he was even willing to consider having the car built at a rate of no more than ten every week (which was about on a par with Morgan's capabilities, though even then MG TDs were being produced at the rate of 200 per week), with 'traditional' body construction methods – a wooden frame skeleton and simple skin panels – and he thought that traditional styling could still appeal to export customers.

Fortunately, Walter Belgrove, whom he briefed without even consulting Ted Grinham, would have none of this. Belgrove himself always complained that he was allocated an almost farcical sum for tooling costs on the new body:

"Sir John Black arrived in my office, unaccompanied, one morning, seated himself and delivered his opening gambit. 'Belgrove, the MG sports car is making a very big impression on the American market, and I think we should make an attempt to obtain our share. We need a light, high-performance sports car like the MG – in fact I don't care if you design a traditional MG. Output, let's say ten a week, 500 a year or thereabouts – cheap, no frills. You can have £16,000 for body tools.'

"Sir John's suggestion that traditional or MG-type styling might be adopted stuck in my gullet. It was just not going to be like that, and I did not intend to be tagged with plagiarism." Belgrove then summed it all up in this statement: "Thus the saga of the TR2 is the saga of under-tooling."

But before he could get to grips with a very simple body style, Belgrove had to get a decision about the chassis and the general mechanical layout. As with the TRX, he had a free hand, but only so far as the body was concerned. The chassis design was going to be a problem, for although engineers like Harry Webster were very interested in all types of high-performance motoring, Ted Grinham was not; he neither knew, nor really cared, much about such interesting little machines.

We ought to clear up the oft-quoted legend that the TR really evolved from a strictly one-off 'special' built by Ken Rawlings in 1950, and called 'Buttercup' because of its body colour. Rawlings worked for P J Evans Ltd in Birmingham, and built this rally/trials car out of surplus parts from the stores – which included a Standard Flying Eight chassis and a Vanguard engine/gearbox, along with bits and pieces from the Flying Twelves and Renowns. Harry Webster once stated very firmly that no other car influenced him in the general layout of the TR, and that he did not even know about Buttercup until his attention was drawn to it. Neither, for that matter, did Alick Dick or Sir John Black.

John Turnbull, brother of the even better-known George Turnbull, was given the job of laying-out a chassis design and was told to use as many existing 'off the shelf' parts and assemblies as he could. The kernel of the whole car was its chassis frame, and as at first the plan was only perhaps an 85mph car (with Sir John's original misguided thoughts of building ten cars a week) it could not be very special.

Both Webster and Turnbull confirm that at first (and this was early in 1952) they were surprised to hear that several hundred Standard Flying Nine frames were stored in the spares department stocks, and were now considered surplus to requirements. These, if suitable for conversion, would keep initial production going at least for the first year, after which there might be the chance to do something more suitable or more ambitious. John Turnbull said that he didn't think the frame was by any means ideal, but that in terms of possible tracks and wheelbase it looked right, and he could see straight away how an independent front suspension could be grafted on to it. (The Flying Nine and Ten wheelbases, respectively, were 85in and 90in – that of the new 20TS sports car was going to be 88in.)

The launch of the original Flying Nine dated from 1936, and the car had not been in production since the end of 1939, so

it was by no means technically advanced. Turnbull and Webster considered using the frame as it stood, but with independent front suspension grafted on. That wouldn't do, as many of the brackets, and particularly the position of the cruciform, were all wrong, and even by the time the first mock-up chassis was being built the original chassis parts which remained for use were down to the side-members and some reinforcements.

Money was not available for a new independent suspension design, and at the beginning of 1952 Standard-Triumph was building three different types. All had coil springs and wishbones, but the Vanguard system had lever-arm dampers and was not particularly modern, while the Standard Eight system was still at the design stage. That of the Mayflower, however, had been in production only since 1950, was originally to Webster's credit, and was at least that of a 'Triumph' already. To graft it to the 20TS frame, pressed steel towers were designed, and welded to the front of the chassis (which had previously accepted semi-elliptic leaf springs and a beam front axle), while a bolt-on crossmember, tubular in section, was run around the front of the engine bay to give much-needed lateral rigidity. At the rear of the car, and almost to keep it 'in the family', a narrow-track version (45in instead of 48in) of the Mayflower's axle was specified – this, of course, had a lot in common with that used in the Vanguard – sprung by semi-elliptic leaf springs, and with lever-arm dampers mounted above the frame, Flying Standard-style.

There was no question about the choice of engine. This would be a derivative of the wet-liner Vanguard unit, but with a developed version of the twin-SU installation first proposed for the TRX of

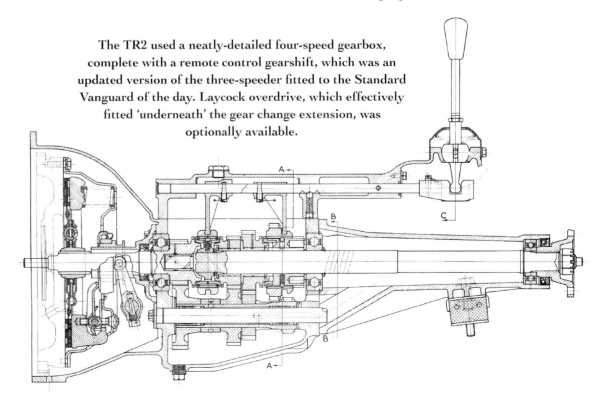

The TR2 used a neatly-detailed four-speed gearbox, complete with a remote control gearshift, which was an updated version of the three-speeder fitted to the Standard Vanguard of the day. Laycock overdrive, which effectively fitted 'underneath' the gear change extension, was optionally available.

1950. There was no sign (nor did it ever reappear) of the completely different cylinder head which had been fitted briefly to one of the TRX cars. To get the car within the necessary 2-litre competition class (Sir John hoped that his customers would use the car in races and rallies, even though Standard had no such plans to do so itself) new cylinder-liners and pistons with a bore of 83mm were installed; this brought the capacity neatly down to 1991cc. In its original form the engine produced 75bhp at 4300rpm.

The Vanguard's gearbox was to be used, but in a much modified form. Instead of a steering-column change with side-mounted casing selectors and three all synchromesh forward gears, it would have a central floor control and four forward speeds, first gear being without synchromesh.

Considering that this was to be a 'low budget' car the transmission change was a major operation, but Ted Grinham justified this with thoughts of how he could utilise the installation on later Vanguard and Triumph models. The very first prototype, coded the 20TS by the engineering department, took shape as a rolling chassis with a direct gear change lever angled well back towards the driver, but even before the car was first seen at Earls Court this was replaced by the later-familiar remote-control arrangement. The Laycock overdrive was to be optional, as on the Vanguard, but with a separate electrically-switched control. The brakes, of Lockheed manufacture, were nine-inch drums at front and rear.

Around this pragmatically-engineered chassis, Walter Belgrove now styled an open two-seater sports car shell. True to his resolve, he would not even consider a 'traditional' style, but this time there could be no elaborately double-skinned sections, nor any complex panels. Most internal panels were flat or very simply shaped, while he tried to keep double-curvature skin panels to an absolute minimum; with such a tight tooling budget, and with such small projected production numbers in mind, he could find no other way. The much-modified Flying Nine frame also circumscribed his freedom of movement, which partly explains why the original car had such a stubby tail.

Even so, by the middle of 1952, his proposed style had been accepted. There was no reverse-crab track (as on previous Standard-Triumphs) for him to overcome, but all the hinges (except those of the doors) were visible, and 'off-the-shelf' electrical fittings had to be specified. He chose a simple front style, with absolutely no radiator grille to decorate the ducting to the radiator itself, but at the rear he made some concessions to Sir John's liking for traditional styling by arranging for the spare wheel to be exposed; very cleverly, the fuel-tank filler-neck was positioned through the centre of the spare-wheel mounting.

The directors instructed Ted Grinham to have two of the new sports cars ready for the Earls Court show at their meeting on July 24. 1952. This meant that the department had less than three months to do the job, and there was in any case no way of starting actual construction before the middle of August due to staff holidays. In the end, effectively, it meant that Standard-Triumph had precisely eight weeks to build the first cars, something which it would barely achieve with one car only; the second car was never to be finished in its original form.

A more significant decision taken at the

The first TR prototype appeared at the 1952 London Motor Show, still totally undeveloped, and with original bob-tail styling.

same meeting was that Sir John's unrealistic target of ten cars a week was abandoned. The comment in the board minutes reads: "Mulliners are to be asked to undertake production of the bodies at ten per day at first." This was a bit more like it, though even at 50 cars a week the new 20TS car would not really have much effect on MG. It also brought the whole idea of using modified Standard Flying Nine chassis frames into doubt, and even before the first car was built a redesign was being considered.

Sir John's target for the car had been a basic price of £500, with a 90mph maximum speed, but by the time the first prototype was ready it was graced with a price tag of £555 basic (or £865 with British purchase tax). Even though this compared well with the opposition – £530 for an MG TD and £565 for a Morgan Plus 4 – there was a rather pretty prototype on show at Earls Court from Healey, which instantly became the Austin-Healey 100 and threatened to sell for £750 (basic).

The car's reception at the Motor Show was mixed. Most of the press liked the basic idea of the car, but were cautious about its prospects as it was known that it'd had virtually no development so far. There was also the memory of the stillborn TRX and the Roadsters to remind people that Standard really had no sports car tradition to support its ambitions. From the press, and from the sales inquiries made at the show, it was clear that the stub-tail style was not liked.

No matter. This time there were many clear indications that the new car could be a winner, if it could be got into production very soon. Sir John Black instructed his production engineers to start planning for twenty cars a day (100 cars a week), on the basis that chassis frames would initially be assembled in Canley, but later bought-in complete. He also began to think in terms of a 100mph maximum, and among other things he asked Mike Whitfield (his sales chief) if a supercharged engine would be an acceptable alternative to the normal unit.

Standard-Triumph had no testers with experience of such high speeds, so just before the car was first shown in public Ted Grinham made a phone call to a man called Ken Richardson at Bourne, in Lincolnshire; he was to have a good deal of influence on the car, its fortunes and its future developments.

Richardson had been involved in the ill-fated BRM Grand Prix car project from 1945, and was known to Standard already as it had been suppliers of machined engine parts of the complex V16 design. As the BRM project had just been sold to Sir Alfred Owen, Richardson was looking round for another job, and was both astonished and impressed when Grinham invited him to test-drive the car.

This drive took place immediately after Earls Court's doors closed, at the same time as a few privileged journalists were being given demonstrations. Richardson drove the car briefly up and

In the late 1940s, Standard had spent money and time supporting the BRM GP race car project, which was originally styled by Walter Belgrove. It was in this period that Standard-Triumph came to know Ken Richardson, who was BRM's chief mechanic, and part-time test driver.

down Banner Lane's service roads, around the factory grounds, then drew up in front of Ted Grinham and Sir John Black with a horrified look on his face. When asked for his first impressions, Richardson is reputed to have called the car "a bloody death trap!"

This surprised Grinham and Black because nobody else had yet driven the car for long, and certainly nobody in the factory would have had the courage to make such an outspoken comment. *Motor*, commenting at a later date, summed up the situation admirably:

"At this point the Standard company might well have thanked Richardson politely for his expert opinion, but pointed out that questions of production made it impossible to carry out any fundamental alterations to the design. And if it had done so, the TR would have died very soon after its birth."

As we now know, it was not too late to make fundamental alterations, so Richardson was invited to join the company as development engineer in charge of the project. In not more than three months, Harry Webster, John Turnbull and Richardson (as the intuitive seat-of-the-pants driver) were to work a real engineering miracle. The ugly duckling would be turned into a passable imitation of a swan. The born loser would be transformed into a machine which, given luck, stood a good chance of success.

The two big chances needed were a redesign of the styling

at the tail and a drastic improvement in the chassis stiffness and roadholding. Other matters like the development and improvement of the engine, and the detail connected with proving, durability and production tooling, could follow alongside.

With regard to the styling, Walter Belgrove and his team moved fast. They left the front alone (except that the side-lamps, previously free-standing on the crown of the wings, were moved down to be recessed in the front panel at each side of the air-intake hole) and concentrated on the tail. The exposed spare-wheel position was discarded, the fuel tank was moved from its position behind the axle to one above it, the spare wheel then slotted in behind the axle, and a neat squared-off tail was designed. In the process the length went up by 10 inches (from 141in to 151in) and a really useful boot was included. Belgrove also proposed an optional smooth hardtop in glass-fibre, but capital spending on this was deferred to 1954, until the company had an idea of how the car would be selling.

It was in regard to the chassis that Ken Richardson's contribution to the project was so important. He certainly did not redesign the chassis – Harry Webster and John Turnbull take that credit, along with their team – but he spent hour after tiring hour flogging the development car around MIRA, up and down the fast straight roads of Warwickshire, and up and down the hills of Wales. There was no time for any continental testing before the car went into production; its introduction to the French Alps was really when a works team started the Alpine Rally in 1954!

John Turnbull's new chassis was designed in October and November 1952, with the goal of vastly improving both beam and torsional stiffness. By the end of the year the entire chassis had been redesigned, and not one pressing of the old Flying Nine variety remained. The basic layout and shape of all the components and fittings was retained, but the definitive car was a much more rugged machine in all respects.

Thus it was that the 20TS project (retrospectively known as TR1 by some misguided Triumph enthusiasts – it was never badged as such, nor coded TR1 in factory records) evolved into the TR2, and by the beginning of 1953 endurance proving, as opposed to design, was under way. The directors were told at their December 10, 1952 meeting that the body design changes were complete, and that tooling of the revised version was under way. By February 1953 they were told that all body drawings had been released to Mulliners in Birmingham, and that delivery of 'off tools' bodies would begin on July 1.

The redesigned car was shown to the public at the Geneva Motor Show in March 1953, by which time bigger (10in diameter) front brakes had been adopted, and the engine had been boosted to 90bhp while retaining its reliability. This had not been easy.

This splendidly-detailed cutaway drawing shows the original TR2 engine in all its glory, an engine which produced a very durable 90bhp.

Large inlet passages, and twin SU carburettors were features of the TR2 engine. Note the 'wet-liner' feature.

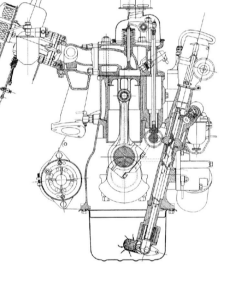

The heart and lungs of the TR2 was this immensely strong Vanguard-based 1991cc engine, notable for its slip-fit wet cylinder liners, and its very robust engineering.

First of all the compression ratio had been raised (to 8.6:1), which boosted the power from 75bhp to 80bhp. Next the valve lift was raised while retaining standard valve timing, and after that a camshaft with 30 degrees of overlap around TDC (instead of 20 degrees) was specified. That was worth 84bhp, and increasing inlet-valve sizes and port diameters helped produced another 3bhp. Further minor development work on carburettor and ignition settings helped tickle maximum power to 90bhp, which soon proved enough for the TR2 to achieve its new target of 100mph.

The power boost led to all manner of worrying development problems, including cylinder block cracking around the holding-down stud bosses, failure of white-metal big-end bearings, and a distressing tendency of the new camshaft to bend at high rpm. All these problems were sorted out with commendable speed and at minimum cost – the camshaft problem, incidentally, being solved by thickening-up just the front half of the shaft after experience had shown that doing all of it did not do the job.

In those days one of the regular sights at MIRA's high-speed track was of Ken Richardson belting a prototype round and round for hour after hour. Occasionally, something in the engine would break, but before long 100mph was routine for the car.

Slowly, and rather unbelievably, a new mood of optimism began to develop at Banner Lane. Perhaps the little TR2 could be a winner, and perhaps it could make its own way in the world? Perhaps this would not be another of the Black-inspired 'boulevard cars', and perhaps MG and Austin-Healey would have to look out. But with the Austin-Healey already haltingly in production (the first handful of cars were assembled at Warwick, and a mass flow would follow from Longbridge during the summer), and news of a revised MG (the TF) already filtering out of Abingdon, how could this new car be proved?

Either an endurance run or a high-speed demonstration was needed. It was Sir John Black who decided the matter. Stung by the fact that Rootes had announced a two-seater 100mph sports car (the Sunbeam Alpine), and that Sheila Van Damm had driven one at more than 120mph on the Jabbeke highway in Belgium (which is now a part of the Ostend-to-Brussels motorway), he

Famous car, notable occasion. MVC 575, the prototype TR2 which achieved nearly 125mph in Belgium in May 1953, was magnificently restored in the 2010s, and put on show in the RAC Club, London.

When prepared for its record attempts on the Jabbeke Road in Belgium, MVC 575 was kitted out with a neat metal tonneau cover, which made the driving position snug, to say the least!

To achieve nearly 125mph on the Jabbeke Road in Belgium, MVC 575 needed to be as wind-cheating as possible. This explains why the front end of the car looked as sleek as this.

rang up Ken Richardson one morning and demanded a similar performance from a prototype TR2. The Alpine's run had been quite remarkable considering its basic specification, and had only been made possible with a tuned-up engine and careful attention to streamlining; Richardson thought that similar attention to a TR2 could give equally gratifying results.

The result of this Belgian expedition is well known. On the morning of May 20, 1953, while the air was cold and thick, and before the wind got up, Richardson took a TR2 out for two-way timed runs over the flying-kilometre and flying-mile. In its original state the car (MVC 575, a left-hand-drive prototype) had a metal tonneau cover, no bumpers, a tiny aero-screen ahead of the driver, rear-wheel spats (skirts) and a full-length alloy under-shield. On its first run it stuttered through the traps at nearly 105mph, which was creditable enough, but not good enough. It might have gone better, Richardson suggested, if the fourth plug lead had not become disconnected!

On the next runs there was no mistake. More than 124mph was achieved for the flying-mile, and a best speed of 124.889mph was achieved over the flying-kilometre. That was startling enough, even though the car had achieved this speed due to the use of overdrive and nonstandard gearing. After breakfast, during which mechanics converted the car to something like standard specification again, MVC 575 achieved 114.89 mph for the flying-kilometre with its windscreen, hood and sidescreens in place, a figure reduced by only 5mph without the use of overdrive. Even though these last figures were achieved with the undershield in place (it was too complex a job to remove this item in the time available), it was still remarkable proof of the TR2's potential. With an engine 276cc smaller than that of the Alpine, the TR2 was several mph faster. Sir John was satisfied. All that now remained was for the car to be put into flow-line production as soon as possible.

To prove out the production tooling and get badly needed cars ready for motor shows in Canada and the Irish Republic, the engineering department undertook complete assembly of the first two 'off-tools' cars in Banner Lane – one with left-hand and one with right-hand drive; this was during July 1953 and marks the real start-up of production of the legendary TR sports car. Even though tremendous efforts had been made to urge the car on to the market (it was, in fact, only ten months after truly serious design for quantity production had got under way), short cuts still had to be taken. Sankeys, for example, would eventually be supplying the tough steel chassis frames complete, but Standard-Triumph would actually assemble the first 1400 frames itself. For a time, the building of TR2s was a very 'knife and fork' process, and only about 300 cars were finished before the end of the year, of which 250 were actually delivered; a mere

This is how good a TR engine bay could look if you had time to make it appear as it did on the day it was born.

50 of them allocated to British customers, mainly favoured dealers who kept the cars as demonstrators and possible competition cars.

Although the early TR2s were strongly in demand – it was still a seller's market in Britain, and the combination of low price, high-performance and potentially low running costs made the cars look attractive – they still had no sporting traditions on which to lean. The Jabbeke achievements were really not enough, and other sporting successes would be very welcome. In motor clubs up and down the land there were dozens of know-alls audibly ready to suggest that their MGs were real sports cars, and that they wouldn't trust a TR2 themselves. It didn't help either that the TR2 suffered its first substantial price increase in Britain (£555 to £595 in January 1954) at the same time as the first enthusiastic road test reports were being published. But the tests also showed that not only was the TR2 a genuine 100mph performer, it also became clear that the cars could be astonishingly economical. The rival from MG – the TF – was so much slower and so much more thirsty that Abingdon never let it out to be tested by reputable magazines.

After many years of serious neglect, TS1, the very first TR2 production car of 1953, was restored to super-standard condition.

Lord Tedder, perhaps better known as Marshal of the Royal Air Force and one of the most prominent personalities of the Allied operations in the Second World War, became Standard-Triumph's Chairman in 1954.

What an occasion. More than half a century after the first ever TR2 production cars – TS1 and TS2 – had been built, they were reunited on Harry Webster's front lawn in Warwickshire. Posing proudly with them was Harry Webster himself (right) and Joe Richards of Illinois, USA, who owned TS1 at the time.

Even at a very restricted rate of production (the TR2 would not be up to the planned rate of 100 cars a week until early spring of 1954), the new car was on its way. The first important options – overdrive and centre-lock wire wheels among them – were becoming available, and a hardtop would now follow in the autumn. A TR2 won its first motoring event, a club rally in North Wales, in January 1954, but the real breakthrough came in March when privately-entered TR2s dominated the RAC's International Rally, an event which demanded quick acceleration and consistent driving-test behaviour rather than ultimate ruggedness for day-after-day endurance motoring.

Standard, too, had new management, now that Alick Dick had become the company's managing director. Delighted with the TR2's reception (some of the directors had begun to think that no car they approved with a Triumph name would ever really succeed), it laid plans to make more of them, and part of the agreement with Mulliners in June 1954 was that 150 TR2 bodies a week should be supplied. This figure was rapidly achieved – 30 cars a day – and it made Sir John Black's predictions of ten cars a week, made at the beginning of 1952, look very sick.

By the autumn of 1954, however, everything was not sweetness and light for the TR2. On the one hand there were the important

Early TR2 models on the final assembly line at Canley in the 1954 period, with a parallel 'sideways' assembly line of Standard Eights and Tens in the background.

competition successes (Mille Miglia, Alpine Rally, Le Mans and the Tourist Trophy, plus the already-mentioned RAC Rally win) to celebrate, while on the other there were customer complaints of poor handling and a hard ride, problematical brakes, and, in some cases, an appalling racket from the exhaust system.

In view of the completely new start made by the TR2, export sales had gone well, but it is a fact that demand had already peaked

When the TR3 took over from the TR2 in 1955, the only styling change was the adoption of the 'egg crate' grille.

In the 1950s, Standard-Triumph found time to produce a limited number of Avon jet engines, for military use in Hunter and Canberra aircraft.

out by the end of the summer, and it looked as if no further increase in TR build would be justified.

Changes introduced in October (the optional hardtop, bigger and better brakes, a quieter exhaust system, and 'short doors,' which allowed the body to be stiffer and the high-kerb problem to be dismissed) all helped, but at the end of November the directors noted that "in view of the present stocks of TR2s it was decided to cut production to ten per day with immediate effect until the end of December 1954." They were no happier at the beginning of 1955: "293 home market and 588 export TR2s were in stock at the beginning of the year. No increase in 10-per-day production is planned until March 1955 at least."

The legend has grown over the years that the TR2 instantly took the United States by storm, and that after that it never looked back. It is a snare and a delusion, and it is incorrect. In 1955 exports dropped, so much so that more than 1700 cars were made available to the British sports car motorist, who avidly snapped them up and helped to give the impression that TR2s were everywhere. In 1955 only 1261 TR sports cars went to the United States and another 263 cars went to Canada. German sales (some to NATO-based American servicemen) totalled 325, and the South Africans took 253. The real bonanza was still four years away.

Perhaps the car was still a little too simple and basic, even though it was quick and frugal in its use of petrol. Whatever it was, the sales and engineering departments got to grips with the car, and continued to improve it rapidly. In the autumn of 1955 (the Commission Number TS8637 marks the change) the TR2 gave way to the TR3. The name change was almost as obvious as the styling improvements, which comprised an 'egg-box' grille for the radiator air intake. Under the skin, however, was a lustier engine (race-tested and found to be satisfactory at Le Mans that summer), with bigger SU carbs and 95bhp, while the 2nd-3rd-top overdrive provision had already been phased-in on later TR2s. An occasional rear seat was made optional, and became surprisingly popular, even though it was not very practical.

The introduction of the latest engine was not at all 'clean' in production terms, for there was at least one interim design of cylinder head and manifolds (called, internally, the 'Le Mans' head) on TR3s built up to mid-summer 1956, before the definitive 'high port' cylinder head, which helped the engine to develop a very sturdy 100bhp, was fitted. For months the two engines were each fitted to batches of TR3s, before the 'Le Mans' head was finally discontinued.

Trundling Along With Triumph

by Richard M. Langworth

Brockbank

This was how *Motor*'s celebrated cartoonist Brockbank saw how the open-mouth front grille of the TR2 could be used!

With the introduction of the TR3, sales bucked up considerably, and production rapidly got back to the 20-cars-per-day rate of 1954. Even though MG had introduced a face-to-face rival in the MGA, the recovery did not falter. At first the TR3 was priced at £650 (basic), which rose to £680 from May 1956. This compared with £595, rising to £610, for the MGA, but of course the TR was still a much faster car, and its many race and rally successes were beginning to weigh heavily in its favour. The real sensation, however, was still yet to come.

In 1955, a factory-prepared team of TR2s had competed at Le Mans, with full backing from the engineering departments. Although the cars were really no faster than the private TR2 entry of 1954, they had all been distinguished by the fitting of experimental disc brakes. One car had Dunlop disc brakes fitted all round, while the other two cars had Girling front-wheel disc brakes allied to 11in drum rears. It had been generally admitted that these differing installations were being assessed with a view to future production.

Nevertheless, it was a real surprise, creating a considerable stir, when at the 1956 Earls Court Motor Show the 1957 TR3 was revealed – the major change being that it would henceforth have Girling brakes as standard (instead of Lockheeds), and that the front brakes would be discs! After building just over 13,000 TRs with drum brakes, Triumph would be British disc-brake pioneers.

Incidentally, let there be no mistake about this: although a few sports racing cars like Jaguar's D-Type and the Lotus Eleven had been sold with disc brakes already, the TR3 was definitely the first British series-production car ever to boast this feature. It was not quite the first disc-braked car in the world, though, as the Chrysler Crown Imperial, in production from 1949 through 1954, held that honour, followed by the Chrysler Town and Country (1950),

the Crosley Hot-Shot (1950-1952), and the Citroën DS19 (1955 onwards). Jensen owners make much of the fact that the 541 was given four-wheel Dunlop discs at the same time – in fact, Triumph's announcement came weeks before that of Jensen, when the disc-braked TR3 was already in production, at a rate of at least 150 a week, while Jensen might hope to make two, or occasionally three, cars in a week.

In the midst of all this excitement one must not miss the TR3's adoption of a Vanguard III back axle, which was stronger and more robust. Nor must we forget that the factory had also decided to market a 'GT car kit', which would, by no means coincidentally, allow factory competition cars to compete in Grand Touring as opposed to sports car categories in the future. The kits had been devised for the 1956 Alpine Rally where the team cars were enormously successful.

Sales of the TR3 now really took off in a flourish. Even though British customers had to be satisfied with less than 500 cars in 1957, export sales doubled. Between January and August 1957, 6681 disc-braked TR3s went overseas. Production estimates were raised, and raised again. Before long Mulliners was struggling to build more than 200 cars a week, and it was having to plan ahead for 300, 400, or even more for the future. It was the start of Triumph's sports car bonanza, and the company was loving every minute of it. During those eight months 5379 TR3s were exported to the United States, almost as many as in the entire 1954-1956 period, and it now began to look as if the market, for the moment, was insatiable.

To its credit, Standard-Triumph refused to rest on its laurels. It would have been easy to continue churning out TR3s and not give a thought to the future of the model, but with the North American market particularly in mind it did not fall into that trap. Even in

Top: From 1958 to 1963, the TR3A, later to become the TR3B, was a huge success for Triumph in the USA, even though its style and basic mechanical layout had not changed significantly for some time.

Bottom: From 1953, right through the building of the last 'side-screen' TR in 1962, the rear end style stayed the same – simple, ruggedly built, and very versatile.

slightly recessed. Other minor improvements included exterior door handles (which the GT kit had pioneered), and lockable handles to the boot-lid. In June 1957 the directors noted that the TR3A (though they never actually called it that) would go into production on Monday, September 9, at a rate of 270 cars a week.

There was something about the TR3A which appealed to sporting motorists all over the world. Its looks, its capabilities, and – most important of all – its reputation from closely related TR3s and TR2s, all combined to make it a sure-fire success. Although just 22,000 TR2s and TR3s were built in four years, no fewer than 61,567 cars with the TR3A styling would be sold in the five years from autumn 1957 – of

1955 there had been thoughts on a new TR, and by the spring of 1956 a two-door four-seat car with winding windows and lots of plush was also proposed. But all this was discarded in favour of a mild face-lift on the TR3, designed in 1956, approved by the board in December, and scheduled for production at the end of the summer 'shut down' in 1957.

This was the TR3A, virtually unchanged in chassis engineering, but easily recognised by the restyled nose panel which included a full-width grille, and into which the headlamps were very

which about 58,000 left in the boom years before the autumn of 1960.

With hindsight, however, there is no doubt that Alick Dick and his directors became intoxicated and over-confident with the success of the TR3A, and effectively over-produced the car. Although the TR3A was to be price-listed until the autumn of 1961 (and would give rise to a short-lived successor, the TR3B, in 1962) it was really cut right back at the end of 1960, after which only a trickle of cars were made. Even by April in 1960 the sales department was beginning to trigger the alarm bells; this was after

This was the way that Triumph's publicity staff brought the TR3 to the enthusiast's attention at a mid-1950s London Motor Show. What a pity – no trace of that perspex-bodied TR3 still exists!

When Triumph challenged Giovanni Michelotti, who it did not then know, to produce a TR concept car in 1957, this 'dream car' was his first, flamboyant effort.

a frenetic year in 1959 when TR3As were sometimes being built at the rate of 2000 cars a month. All this, of course, occurred while an increasingly confused search for a replacement, the TR4, was going ahead. The story of this, and the fascinating special sports cars built at the time, belongs to a future chapter.

The TR4, when it was ready, would be able to trade on the 'classic' TR's reputation, and there is no doubt that this had been founded on the solid base of a splendid competitions reputation. Once enough of the first TR2s had been delivered, it was found that a TR2 could be a winner in rally or race, production car trial or economy run, driving test or long-distance marathon. Only the MGA, but certainly not the big Austin-Healey, was as versatile.

In the beginning, however, Standard had no competitions department, and no real interest in motorsport. It was only the fact that the customers were going to use their TR2s for this purpose (and because Ken Richardson was keen to get back into competition, preferably as a driver, as he had been with BRM in his last job) which caused it to change its mind. Johnny Wallwork's unexpected outright victory in the 1954 RAC Rally clinched the resolve.

Wallwork was a driving-test expert, and a tough-as-nails competitor from the north of England, so his win was by no means out of the blue. But the fact that he chose a TR2 for the job gave the car a remarkable international debut, and its overall worth was backed up by Peter Cooper's TR2 finishing second and Bill Bleakley's car finishing fifth.

The very first works TR2, prepared in the engineering department at Banner Lane, was entered for the 1954 Mille Miglia, with Richardson himself sharing the driving with the wily Dutchman, Maurice Gatsonides. Before this, Richardson had been relieved of his test and development job on the sports cars and told to set-up a professional little competitions department, which would share floor space with the engineering experimental workshops.

Richardson and Gatsonides took their solitary entry serenely through the 1000 miles of the Italian road race, averaged 73mph and finished 27th overall among a fleet of Ferraris, Lancias and Maseratis. Edgar Wadsworth and Bobbie Dickson then showed that a privately-entered TR2 was also suitable for long-distance circuit racing by averaging 74.7mph in atrocious weather in 24 Hours of Le Mans that June, and finished 15th overall. Just to rub in the message thoroughly, no fewer than six TR2s (entered as two teams of three cars each – one of them being the ex-Le Mans car of Dickson) started in the Tourist Trophy race, held on the Dundrod circuit in Northern Ireland. Not only did all six finish, but they took the team prize for the event in the most convincing fashion.

Richardson, in the meantime, was also setting up a rally team. Rallying was something about which he knew very little, though he decided that he would be good enough to drive a team car as well as

Third in the line of the legendary side-screen TRs, the wide-mouth TR3A was built in big numbers from late 1957 to 1961. The style, originated by Walter Belgrove in 1952/53, was, and remains, an all-time classic.

manage the operation. His long-term expertise came from Maurice Gatsonides (who had won the 1953 Monte Carlo Rally for Ford), while he also employed Jimmy Ray to drive a third car; Ray was one of the very best drivers on the British rallying scene, ironically enough having gained most of his successes in a Vanguard-engined Morgan Plus 4.

In high summer, three cars (Richardson actually using the Mille Miglia machine, as he was to do until the end of 1955) were entered by the factory for the gruelling and fast Alpine Rally. Several privately-owned TR2s, including that of Leslie Brooke (a car that was raced and rallied in its first year), joined them. Although one car (Ray's) was forced to retire, that of Gatsonides finished unpenalised, while the two surviving factory cars, plus the private TR2 of Kat and Tak, won the much-vaunted team prize. It was a splendid start to the TR's rallying career, particularly in the Alpine Rally, where it was to shine so brightly in the next few years.

Even though the TR2 was ideally suited for rallying, Ken Richardson still wanted to see the cars in truly international sports car racing. With the full support of his management, and especially after the fine first-time showing of a TR2 in the 1954 race, his department prepared a team of three TR2s to compete in the 1955

Not a line, panel joint, or curve out of place – this is how the famous TR style developed in the 1950s. This particular car is a left-hand drive USA-market TR3A, on which only the central 'bumper' (joining the two over-riders) was a dealer-applied option.

Author Richard Langworth posed two very different TRs outside his home in Hopewell, New Jersey, USA, in the early 1970s – his own TR3A, and a late-model TR6 (complete with the rubber bumper over-riders which had been made necessary by recent USA 'crash test' legislation).

OVC 276 was a famous TR2, built in 1954, and used almost exclusively as Ken Richardson's works competition car.

24-hour Le Mans race. Two entries were guaranteed a start from the outset, and one was on the reserve list (there was a limit of 60 cars which could start the event). All three cars actually came to the starting line as other machines either blew-up or did not even appear for scrutineering.

Outwardly and visually the cars looked standard, except for their lack of bumpers, their aero-screens and tonneau covers, and their individual paint jobs (for recognition purposes). The engines were mildly tuned (to the degree of about five brake horsepower) and had the Le Mans heads which would shortly go into production, but otherwise they looked akin to the sort of car which any serious private owner could prepare for himself. There was one exception to this – the brakes.

Triumph, like other quantity-production manufacturers, was experimenting with disc brakes for its road cars, but was rather embarrassed by choice. Dunlop, Girling and Lockheed were all anxious to break into this potentially vast business, and all had supplied prototype kits for test. As a final proving exercise, to confirm that a good disc brake was better, and at least as reliable, it was decided to enter the Le Mans TR2s as prototypes and to equip them with disc brakes.

Different installations were chosen for the two cars with guaranteed starting places. The Dickson/Sanderson car (No 28)

had four-wheel Dunlop discs, with servo-assistance, while the Richardson/Hadley car (No 29) had Girling front-wheel discs applied to oversize (11 x 2¼in.) Alfin rear drums, but without a servo. The third car, Morris-Goodall/Brooke (No 68), had a similar Girling installation.

The event itself, of course, was marred by the dreadful accident involving Levegh's Mercedes 300SLR, which ploughed into the crowd opposite the pits and killed more than 80 people. Even though many people agree that the event should have been abandoned immediately after that, it was allowed to continue. After 24 hours, all three cars finished strongly, and the disc brakes had proved themselves completely. Although the Morris-Goodall/Brooke car finished more than 230 miles behind the other two cars (which averaged 84.4mph), this was not because of a lack of performance or braking power but because the hard-driving Brooke had put the car into a sandbank at Arnage and spent more than an hour and a half digging his way back to the road again! Before the accident, in fact, he had been averaging more than 90mph. The cars finished 14th, 15th, and 19th overall.

This was enough to convince management that disc brakes had the durability production cars needed. Unfortunately, the Le Mans results did not give them any conclusive information about the rival discs' performance – those fitted with Dunlop and Girling installations, respectively, finished only one tenth of a mile apart after 24 hours and more than 2000 miles of racing. The decision, in the end, was governed by economics and by the need to provide a simple handbrake installation on production cars; on that score the Girlings took the business, and retained it on TRs in the years which followed.

Of these three cars, only one (PKV 376, No 28 at Le Mans) was ever used again by the factory. Dickson and Richardson raced it in the 1955 Tourist Trophy race at Dundrod in Northern Ireland, still as a 'prototype,' where it finished 22nd overall. One car stayed in France for a period, returning to Britain at a later date.

Later in 1955, Richardson and his co-driver Kit Heathcote took their TR2 (the same as Richardson had used in the Mille Miglia in 1954) to fifth place and a class win on the Liège-Rome-Liège rally. This provided the final piece of proof that a TR was versatile enough to compete seriously in any type of event – a long-distance race, a long-distance rally, a 'road racing' type of a rally, or a 'driving test' type. It was enough proof, if any more was needed, to convince private owners that a TR was most suitable for them.

For the next five years there was always a set of rallying TRs in the Richardson competition department, though the cars were not used on every event tackled by the factory team. Where

the regulations encouraged it, drivers might appear in Standard Ten saloons, often modified and quite fast. A team of Phase III Vanguards appeared in the 1956 Monte without success, and it was the ugly but effective Pennants which so nearly scooped the awards in the snow-hit 1958 RAC Rally.

From the 1956 season, in fact, the TR's rallying success story almost started to get boring – if only because it was so predictable. On the 1956 Alpine Rally, for instance, there were so many TRs in the entry (factory and private) that no fewer than five of them won Coupe des Alpes for unpenalised runs (the factory cars, of course, running as GT cars with the new-fangled optional kits which included the pressed steel hardtops).

In 1957, it was Bernard Consten's turn to excel in the Liège, when he finished third overall. That was the good news, as was John Waddington's class win in the Tulip Rally. The bad news was that the factory entered a car for Nancy Mitchell in the Mille Miglia, but she crashed it at Pescara after spinning at a railway level-crossing. Up to that moment, her car had averaged 86mph for the first 400 miles, but in the accident the radiator was punctured.

In the same year a race-prepared trio of 1956 rally team cars was sent to compete in the American 12-hour race at Sebring – their first 'official' entry – and this very astute move was rewarded by a class win and 21st overall, with that car principally driven by Mike Rothschild of New York.

There were several important innovations for 1958. Apart from the fact that Richardson took delivery of a quartet of smart apple-green TR3As, along with a fifth car for his new discovery, Annie Soisbault, to drive in Europe, there was the invention of the 86mm bore 2138cc engine in time for its use on the Alpine Rally. The bigger engine, little more powerful than the 1991cc unit but with much more mid-range torque, was useful when the rally classes peaked at 2500cc instead of 2000cc. On its debut, on this Alpine, it was good enough to let the team cars harry the 2.6-litre Austin-Healey 100/6s unmercifully, and good enough to give a class win to Keith Ballisat's TR3A, which also took fourth overall. In the same car Maurice Gatsonides took fifth place in the Liège later in the summer.

By 1959, Coventry's interest was turning back to Le Mans, but a new set of cars was obtained, and among other things Annie Soisbault used two cars to help her tie, on points, for the European Ladies' Rally Championship. The mixture, apart from this, was as before, with class wins almost everywhere a team car was entered, and team prizes when the entry was in bulk. The same cars were retained for 1960, when the steam had gone from Richardson's

Maurice Gatsonides, perhaps not as young as he once was, was nevertheless a king-pin of the Triumph works rally team in the 1950s.

interest in road events. The last major rally contested by the factory TRs was the Alpine of 1960, where new-recruit David Seigle-Morris won the 2-litre class. Three other team cars were eliminated either by accidents or by major mechanical breakdowns.

The writing had been on the wall for some time for the TRs as prepared by Richardson's mechanics. Although they were rugged and reliable, they were never any faster than the standard product. Fashions in motorsport do not stand still, and throughout the 1950s other manufacturers were developing faster and more special cars for their own use; rivals like the Austin-Healeys were improved almost beyond all recognition between 1957 and 1960, such that the still-standard TRs were in danger of being completely outpaced.

It was not that the cars were incapable of improvement – far from it. There came a time when privately-prepared cars were demonstrably quicker, as was proved by David Seigle-Morris when he took his personal TR3A to a good class-win in the 1960 Tulip Rally, ahead of the entire factory team. The problem was that there was an illogical bias against engine tuning inside the factory, based on the grounds of crankshaft breakage when engines were run persistently at about 5200rpm.

It was relatively simple to boost the TR's engine up to about 130bhp and to make it rev usefully to 6000rpm, and to keep up this behaviour for days on end, but the factory cars were never treated to such super-tuning. Two twin-choke Weber carburettors, a free flow exhaust manifold and a special camshaft grind was the key to such a transformation, but such parts were never homologated to make their use legal on the race tracks and the rally courses of the world. The fact of the matter is that such a TR3A, bravely driven, could have been a match for the best rally cars in Europe. The proof is in the performances set up by TR4s in 1963, which were properly modified. On representative sections where year-on-year times could be compared a TR4 was quicker than almost any car rallying up to 1961. The inference is obvious.

In the United States, however, where competition hang-on extras were banned in SCCA racing up to 1961, the TR3s and TR3As soon began to dominate the E-Production category. Later, with the TR4s, and with several worthwhile extras approved for racing after SCCA policy had changed, the Kastner-Tullius partnership became so effective that the cars were smartly moved up into the much tougher D-Production group.

Before the competition department began to concentrate completely on special twin-cam racing TRs, there was also time to go rallying in Triumph Herald coupés. Used for the first time in the summer of 1959 (when 'Tiny' Lewis took one to ninth place and won a Coupe des Alpes on the Alpine Rally), and for the last time in the spring of 1961, the 948cc cars were never really more than good class contenders.

The highlight of the Herald's rallying career, undoubtedly, was the Tulip Rally of 1961, and it was not a works-entered car which caused the sensation. In those days the Tulip, like other events in Europe, bent over backwards to give all cars a real chance of winning, by running their events with complicated handicapping systems linked to engine sizes and categories. On this particular event they instituted a class-improvement system whereby the winner would be that car which excelled in its class, for which an average performance would be computed at the finish. This was all well and good, except that the wiliest of factory drivers saw a way around the problem.

Everything was normal among the competitors until the last few minutes of the rally. Tiny Lewis, in the factory car, was being narrowly beaten by Geoff Mabbs in his own privately-entered Herald Coupé, and both were well clear of their opposition. It looked as if the young Bristolian could finish in the top five places.

But Lewis was an experienced campaigner. Arriving back at the finish in Holland, he drew up at the hotel, smilingly refused to hand in his time cards to the officials, and retired from the event. A bit of careful mathematics and a good deal of cunning had been worked out between the two Triumph drivers. Mabbs, who was in any case due to win his class, suddenly found himself with a whopping class advantage – and the Herald was pronounced the winner! Mabbs was delighted, and the Triumph factory astounded, for the previous year the same two drivers had finished in the opposite order, winning their class, but not being highly placed in general classification.

The result of all this, incidentally, was that class-improvement systems soon became even more complicated, but shortly began to fall out of favour altogether. By then, the smallest of rally cars could also be among the quickest, and Triumphs were not in that corner of the market. By then, too, the company was intimately concerned with a new sports car, where the competition was even more fierce.

Hark the Herald Angle

In the 1950s most Standard-Triumph enthusiasts tended to concentrate their attention on the Triumph TR2s and TR3s. Certainly these cornered most of the publicity at the time, even though sports car production was only a small part of the group's activities. Cars with 'Standard' badges dominated the scene in Canley in the 1950s (though there was the Triumph TR10 for the American market, as already mentioned in Chapter 9), and it was not until 1959 that a new Triumph saloon appeared. Before then, however, there were momentous corporate upheavals, which had a decisive effect on Standard-Triumph's future.

For nearly 20 years, of course, Standard's fortunes had been dictated by John Black, and no other executive got a look in. To anyone who never worked at Standard this might sound sweeping and over-assertive, but the fact is that Sir John was very much the master of all he surveyed. His board of directors were all, to a man, subservient to his wishes, and he had absolute power to promote – or sack – anyone in the company.

It was established fact that Sir John was apt to come back from a holiday or from a prolonged business trip and decide that Standard was over-staffed; sackings would inevitably follow. In the bad old days of the 1930s and 1940s wrongful dismissal existed, but the sufferers could do nothing about it.

As long as the company's fortunes were on the up and up, most of the directors and all the shareholders could put up with this. Indeed, to keep Sir John sweet, he was regularly and lavishly praised at company meetings. His salary (and commission) was reputedly higher than anyone else in the industry apart from William Lyons (and knowing Black's thoughts about Mr Lyons this must have rankled him), and indeed he was thought to be so invaluable to the company that the other directors voted in 1949 to make him a present of 100,000 Standard shares (valued at about £25,000) in exchange for an assurance that he would never go and work for a rival concern. The British Government of the day found out about this, introduced vicious and retrospective legislation, and taxed the gift out of existence.

By 1950 he had agreed to sit for a portrait in oils to hang in the boardroom, and in late 1953, when Charles Band decided to retire, he was immediately invited to become the company's chairman, while retaining his position as chief executive.

Under him, Sir John had one 'iron man' and one 'young lion'. The iron man was Ted Grinham, chief engineer of Standard since 1931, technical director since 1936, and deputy managing director (with a war-time break) since 1939. Grinham was a hard man, some say a sour and embittered man, with an imposing presence and no apparent sense of humour. He could not see any fun in working and, according to one of his colleagues, "I don't think he had much of a home life," and he didn't see why any of his subordinates should have one either. By the beginning of the 1950s Grinham was spending less and less time on engineering (he left that to Harry Webster and Lewis Dawtrey), and more and more on management; his ambitions were aimed directly at Sir John Black's chair in due course.

The young lion was Alick Dick, an ex-Standard apprentice who had been in charge of purchasing in the 'shadow' factories during the war, and continued a meteoric career by becoming personal assistant to Sir John Black in 1945, joining the board as assistant managing director in 1947. By 1951 he had become deputy managing director (alongside Ted Grinham, who did not like that move one bit) at the tender age of 34 years old.

Sir John, of course, regularly had to do business with Harry Ferguson over the tractors that Standard was building in huge numbers for Ferguson to sell. Ferguson, like Black, was used to getting his own way, and the relationship between the two soon deteriorated to an icy formality. Even though Standard's tractor production was carrying the major proportion of the company's administrative overheads – which, by implication, meant trouble for private-car financing if ever they were hived off – Sir John was deeply unhappy about the deal with Ferguson, and often talked about dissolving the partnership.

When the board heard that Ferguson was proposing to merge with Massey-Harris of Canada they were adamant that Standard should get out of its agreement, which still had a few years to run, as soon as possible. They must have been amazed and shocked when, in October 1953, Sir John blithely announced that he had signed a new long-term agreement (for 12 years, until 1965) with

Ferguson, and that much more investment and a new larger diesel-engined tractor was to be introduced.

That was bad enough, but within days Sir John was badly knocked about in a car crash, and the company drifted for weeks while he recovered. It was actually a prototype Swallow Doretti sports car, with Ken Richardson driving, in which Sir John was hurt, and the accident, which involved another car, took place right outside the main gate at the Banner Lane factory.

By early November Sir John was recovering his biting wit, if not his physical health, and a note he sent to Walter Belgrove on November 11 confirms this:

"It won't be long before I come in and have a look at you, you old devil, and see what you are up to, and see if you have got rid of that Belsen line, and the Otto line, and as far as I am concerned anyone can have the Doretti line!"

The Belsen line referred to the very spartan furnishing of the new Standard Eight, just getting into production, the Otto line to the Phase III Vanguard style produced by Carl Otto, who was a consultant stylist, and the inference to his crash is obvious.

If Sir John had been difficult before this, he was positively schizophrenic after it. No decision was now taken other than by mood, and many management staff were terrified of what their managing director might decide to do next. They did not have to wait long.

As was his habit, Sir John turned up at the firm's Christmas party, and decided as usual that the company had too many staff. This time, it was the turn of Ted Grinham!

There was absolutely no rhyme nor reason behind this move (unless it was taken to remove a rival for the still-ailing Sir John's job), and it was the last straw – one of many, in fact – for the rest of the board. At a meeting hastily convened by Alick Dick ('I felt awful

about this – Sir John, after all, was a relative of mine as well as a business colleague'), a letter was drafted, the entire board descended on his home at Bubbenhall (a village near Coventry) and demanded his resignation.

The game was up. Sir John realised that if he had to face a public meeting, with his entire board, and as many of the staff who could bring themselves to speak against him, his fate would be sealed. On January 4, 1954, he signed the hastily-drafted letter, which gracefully and quite wrongly hid the truth:

"As a result of consultations with my doctor today, I have been advised that I am not considered fit enough to return to the enormous responsibilities as managing director of our very important company, and I am recommended to go away for an extended period to overcome the effects of the very serious accident which I recently received ..."

The result was that Sir John resigned with immediate effect. He had been managing director from September 1934, without a break, during which Standard's profits had shot up from nearly nothing to £644,330 (after tax) in 1953. There was a loss of face, balanced somewhat by a retirement present of £30,000, a Bentley, a Mayflower, and the use of the company's bungalow near the Welsh coast. That was one sensation, but another – known only to a few – followed immediately.

The unfortunate Grinham, saved from unjustified dismissal by his fellow directors, now found that they preferred Alick Dick to himself, and he had to resign himself to the deputy's job for the rest of his working life. So it was that Alick Dick, at the age of 37, became managing director of Standard-Triumph, with awesome responsibilities and a mass of corporate problems to be faced. He always liked to describe himself as '*primus inter pares*,' which to a certain extent was correct, and there is no doubt that the company's management instantly became a more open and logical business. It can be summed-up easily by referring to the directors' minutes. Until the resignation of Sir John Black, the meetings had been short and the note-taking terse; afterwards the meetings were more fruitful, and much more was discussed and noted for the record. In the absence of a full-time chairman, incidentally, Charles Band returned on a meeting-by-meeting basis, and it was not until June 1954 that Marshal of the Royal Air Force, Lord Tedder, was invited to take the chair. It was, in any event, a happy transition. It was an end to dictatorship and the beginning of democracy.

Alick Dick, who had been in the shadow of John Black for

One of the last official pictures taken of Sir John Black, with a new model (in this case the original Standard SC/8hp of 1953). The SC would be the first car to use the now legendary four-cylinder engine and its associated four-speed gearbox, which would be used on so many future Triumphs of the 1950s, 1960s, and 1970s.

some years, knew instinctively what his policy should be. He had to come to terms with the fact this his company's reliance on tractor manufacturing as a sheet anchor for employment and profits could not be continued indefinitely. Harry Ferguson, after all, had sold out to Massey-Harris of Canada in the autumn of 1953, and since M-H was already a tractor manufacturer it would eventually want to become directly involved in the making of its British products instead of letting an agent do the job.

The complex Ferguson-Banner Lane-Massey-Harris deal, inevitably, would one day have to be unscrambled. Alick Dick realised that even with a multi-million-pound bag of gold this deal would liberate, Standard-Triumph would become the smallest and the most vulnerable of the motor industry's 'Big Five.' At a time when the age of mergers was beginning to evolve, and when 'bigger' was becoming synonymous with 'safer,' Dick realised that Standard-Triumph could not indefinitely continue to be alone. His fears were intensified when Austin (as part of BMC) made a successful takeover bid for Fisher & Ludlow in 1953, which meant that the future of Standard's mass-production body supplies was also thrown into doubt.

"From the very beginning," Alick Dick told us, "my mission at Standard-Triumph was to look around for a partner, a partner to secure our future. In the next few years I had flirtations with almost every other independent concern except Chrysler. I never talked to them."

There was also the medium-term question of modernising and expanding the company's range of private cars. Apart from the brand-new TR2, which was still struggling to get established at the beginning of 1954, it was a pretty stodgy line-up. While tractor production looked after a goodly proportion of the profits and shouldered much of the financial burden, all at Banner Lane, car production at Canley was dominated by two ranges: the bulbous but popular Standard Vanguard, and the spartan but fast-improving Standard 8/10 range. The Renown was still around, but only just. Engines for the 8/10 cars were still not being built on the proper transfer-line tools, as they had not yet arrived and would not be completely commissioned until March 1955. Sir John had tried to make a deal with Willys for Jeeps to be built in Britain, but this had come to nothing.

To replace the Vanguard Phase II, a new monocoque car had been designed, not, as one would expect, by Walter Belgrove's department, but as a consultancy job by an American, Carl Otto. This would have its body-shells produced by Pressed Steel at Cowley, and would go on sale in the autumn of 1955.

Standard-Triumph was terrified that BMC's new ownership of Fisher & Ludlow would soon lead to having to find a new source for the Standard 8/10 saloon shell. In 1954, if one forgot the new commercial circumstances, the set-up was ideal, with the little

Standard shells being pressed and assembled at Tile Hill and being delivered the two or three miles to Canley by road. But if BMC, headed by the bluff and unfeeling Sir Leonard Lord, should decide to throw its customers out, what then?

With this in mind, Alick Dick began to look for ways to secure his company's future body supplies. Straight away, during 1954, he concluded a highly satisfactory deal with Mulliners of Birmingham. This much-modernised coachbuilding company had been building more and more of Standard's bodies in recent years – apart from making the Renowns, and now pushing ahead with the TR2s, it had also been responsible for the Vanguard estates, vans, and pickups, and would shortly go into production with similar versions of the Standard 8/10 cars.

In addition it was also building bodies for people like Alvis (the 3-litre saloon), Daimler-Lanchester (the 14-Leda), Rootes (the Alpine two-seater) and Aston-Martin (the DB2/4 coupé). It was, in effect, the largest of the small bodybuilding concerns.

Alick Dick then pulled off a very astute coup. From June of 1954, he secured an agreement from Mulliners that it would clear its commitments to existing customers to put the whole of its production capacity at Standard-Triumph's disposal for the next ten years. Even in 1954, before the TR2 took-off in the popularity stakes, this meant that it would be supplying up to 600 body-shells every week.

This was brilliant. Without spending a penny of his company's capital, or raising any new money to finance the deal, Dick had secured one good and experienced supplier of bodies. It was not enough, but it was a start. Pressed Steel would be able to look after the Vanguard for as long as necessary, and Dick hoped it would be able to take on a successor to the Standard 8/10 when this became necessary.

We would like to dismiss the little 8s and 10s (TR10 in America, from 1957-60) from the story as quickly as possible, but purely because of their engineering ancestry this is not possible. The entire power train, after all – engine, gearbox and rear axle – was going to have a bearing on Standards and Triumphs of the future.

Standard's first postwar small car had been the Flying Eight, of 1930s ancestry, which was dropped in the summer of 1948. The Mayflower was John Black's idea of what the company's next small car should be like, but almost from the day it went on sale in the summer of 1950 it became clear that not everybody agreed with him. A restyled Mayflower was being discussed at board level by the summer of 1950, and the Mayflower's successor by the end of that year. By July 1951, Ted Grinham was ready to submit his first thoughts on a new small car, which might once have been rear-engined (the company borrowed a Renault 4CV for study of its layout), and might eventually have been based on the Mayflower's existing floorpan and suspensions.

By the end of 1951, the SC (as the 'small car' had been coded) was evolving as an all-new project in its own right. There would be no carry-over from existing models, and at that stage of the discussions the stark little four-door machine was to have had a side-valve 800cc engine and a three speed gearbox without synchromesh! This was something which Walter Belgrove never personally boasted about, though his department was responsible for it. Cutting product costs to the bone was as fashionable then as it became at the end of the 1960s. There were, thank goodness, limits to how far management would let the car sink. Even though they committed it to production without an opening boot-lid, and with boot access via individually folding rear seats, they made sure that every engine except the first prototype had overhead valves, and that every gearbox had synchromesh and four forward speeds.

Fisher & Ludlow at Tile Hill were to make the bodies, engines would temporarily come from redundant Mayflower machine tools, and the first off-tools machine would be ready for the road in May 1953. At first, incidentally, they might have been called 'Beavers,' but this proposal was dropped after some discussion.

The little car was launched in September 1953, and got a very good reception, except that it became immediately obvious that more trim, more luxury, and more performance would all be needed to stake out a long-term future, even if this did mean having to sell the cars for more than the competing Austin A30s and Morris Minors. The car soon found a big market, distinguished itself from other cars in factory shots by coming down the final assembly line, closely packed-up to its neighbour, but completely sideways, and even attracted some sporting customers after Stirling Moss won races in one, and Jimmy Ray's works-prepared 10 won the RAC Rally outright in 1955.

It was restyled in 1957 (as the Standard Pennant – a car which

might have been called the Triumph Mayflower if original plans had been carried through), and exported to many countries, often with Triumph badges to give it a bit of spurious glamour. Well over 200,000 examples had been sold before the last one was built in 1959.

It is the planning of the successor to the 8s and 10s which really begins to concern us here. The directors first began to consider a new small Standard-Triumph car in the spring of 1956, and certainly at a meeting in April of that year there were discussions about 'a completely new 8/10hp range, for tooling-up during 1957, for introduction at the 1958 Earls Court Motor Show.'

At this stage there were two problems of overriding importance. One was that of deciding on an acceptable style and basic engineering for the car, and the other was finding some suitable organisation prepared to build the bodies in sufficiently large quantities. Arriving at the right style was most urgent, and this caused all manner of headaches. The reason for this, quite simply and understandably, was that the company had recently lost its chief stylist, Walter Belgrove, after an intense, blazing and abrupt row.

For some years Belgrove and Ted Grinham had cordially hated each other, and matters were not helped in the early 1950s when a disagreement arose over the nature and philosophy of the 8/10 car, and later because an outside consultant's style for the Vanguard III was chosen when Belgrove's own sleek European-style proposal had been spurned.

The final bust-up occurred at Earls Court in 1955, over what now looks like a triviality, and Belgrove walked out. It was the end of nearly 30 years of involvement with Triumph cars, and it was also the end of Triumph's dependence on British stylists until the TR7 of the 1970s.

At Coventry there was an uneasy interregnum. Attempt after attempt was made in the Banner Lane studios to arrive at the right sort of modern shape for the new car. Harry Webster told us that at about this time he had asked his administrators to draw up a series of project codes, all with four letters and all beginning with the letter 'Z,' "so that none of our competitors would understand what we were planning." He also explained what the new car's code – Zobo – actually meant; "in the dictionary a Zobo is described as a Tibetan pack animal of indeterminate sex, half-way between a bull and a cow. Believe me, somehow or other that is what the damned thing looked like at first!"

The need for the car had originated from Alick Dick and Martin Tustin (general manager since mid-1955), who wanted something that would be relatively cheap to tool-up, and which could easily be

This display exhibit shows a twin-SU carburettor version of the 948cc SC engine, used in the original Triumph Herald of 1959.

assembled in under-developed countries. Standard had factories in India, Australia and South Africa, and was looking with interest, if not with a lot of financial backing to support them, at other territories. It wanted a car which could be built with different basic styles – saloon, coupé, estate, van and convertible – without disturbing the general engineering of the vehicle.

Standard-Triumph's difficulties in finding a supplier to build the Zobo body are now well known, but we must make it clear right away that this was not the reason Harry Webster chose to have a separate chassis for the car. Harry insists: "we had to provide a good foundation for assembling all those different bits and pieces … and if we sent 'knocked down' cars for assembly in other countries we could use the chassis as a jig if necessary." But if Standard could have had a monocoque built by one of the largest British firms, in time for a 1958/59 launch, would Harry have opted for such modern construction? "No, I wouldn't have done so, unless we didn't have to consider the overseas assembly possibilities."

So even before the car's style had been settled, and certainly before the method of building the body-shells had been decided, the separate chassis frame had been agreed. The problem, still, was to get a proper style.

It was Harry Webster, along with Martin Tustin, who first met the little Torinese stylist Giovanni Michelotti, through a chance encounter with a businessman called Raymond Flower (who approached Standard for mechanical supplies in order to build and sell a new design of car – the Frisky– in Egypt). It was Flower who told them that he could get bodies styled and built "in two to three months," something which would have been impossible in Britain at the time, and it was Flower who introduced this quick-working miracle man to Standard-Triumph.

Michelotti's first job for Standard-Triumph was the black-and-white finned TR3 dream car which was first shown at the Geneva motor show in 1957. He was then put on a loose and informal retainer to Standard-Triumph, with the Italian coachbuilder Vignale as the craftsman who could build the prototype bodies in such a remarkably short time.

Harry Webster told us more of the story.

"We had tried and tried with all these styles in Coventry and what we finished up with was a mechanical bathtub on wheels. I can't describe it as anything else. It looked dreadful! Dear old Giovanni came along at our invitation, and for weeks and weeks

he tried to make sense out of it, but by the summer of 1957 we were getting nowhere.

"I then went off on holiday to Italy, and on the way I called in on Michelotti in Turin. There was still nothing doing, but I decided to call in on my way back from Sorrento in September.

"I will never forget that occasion. I parked in the street outside – it would have been about 2.30pm – and went upstairs, leaving my wife and daughter in the car. It was still the same hopeless scene, nothing at all promising with the bathtub body we were trying to improve.

"Then I said something like: 'We are wasting our bloody time. Look, suppose you could start from scratch here in Italy, based only on this chassis, what would you propose?' Well, to Michelotti that was like a red rag to a bull. Within three or four minutes he had sketched-up the Herald as we now know it, and we instantly started transferring this to a full-scale draft on the wall.

"It was so exciting that both of us completely lost track of time, and by the time I surfaced it was after midnight, my wife and daughter were fast asleep in the car, and I had forgotten all about them! But that was the breakthrough. I cabled Alick Dick, saying hold everything, and the following day started driving back to Coventry with a sheaf of drawings – eighth-scale, front, rear, side elevation and sections, Michelotti was that quick when he got inspired – and more importantly, I made a promise that I could have the first prototype shell before the end of 1957."

Alick Dick later confirmed that he was tremendously aroused

When pictured with the original Herald Coupé prototype, Martin Tustin (left) and Harry Webster were clearly proud of what had already been achieved.

by the new style. "The body arrived on a lorry, as promised, actually on Christmas Eve. We put it straight into the styling studio, on the turntable, and we were all so thrilled with that coupé body style that we all downed tools and went out for a pint!"

It was a fabulous bargain. The formal contract, signed after work had begun at Vignale on this first car, called for three shells – coupé, saloon and estate – all for the tiny sum of £10,000. The work, more than anything else, sealed Michelotti's relationship with Standard-Triumph, and subsequently British Leyland, for well over a decade.

The problem of how the bodies should be made remained. Standard's management wanted it to be tooled and ready in record time (the delay in settling the right style had already ensured that it would not be ready until 1959), and they were looking for large-quantity production of more than 2,000 bodies every week.

Although Alick Dick had the gravest forebodings, he hoped that Fisher & Ludlow (now owned by BMC, which was a deadly rival, particularly with this sort of car) would take on the job. "But when I went to see Len Lord, he turned me down flat. He said something like, 'I'm not going to use the Austin Motor Company's money for the benefit of the Standard company; you can push off and look somewhere else.' Even though he was cutting off his nose to spite his face – the Tile Hill factory was no good at all to F & L if it wasn't making bodies for us – he wouldn't take on the job."

Things began to look desperate. "I negotiated with Pressed Steel," Alick Dick said, "but it hadn't the tooling capacity at the time. Joe Edwards would have loved to have the business, but we couldn't wait, the other models were dying, and we had to have it by 1959. That was when it became clear that we had to have our own pressing and body-assembly division, and for the next few years all our policy was directed to this."

It was a development of Dick's conviction that Standard-Triumph either had to get bigger, or it had to find a partner. Negotiations with other firms, in fact, had been going on ever since Sir John Black was ousted, and though they are all peripheral to this story, they all had a bearing on the company's later history.

The rest of the industry, to be frank, had never fancied being linked with a Standard company controlled by Sir John Black, but as soon as Alick Dick took charge the atmosphere changed. On the one hand Dick considered it inevitable that he would have to sell-off his tractor interests to Massey-Harris, though in the early years the atmosphere between the companies was cordial and businesslike. Nevertheless, Massey-Harris soon developed an unshakable conviction that Standard's cost control was not all it might have been, and that it (Massey-Harris) was having to pay too much for the completed tractors. It soon decided that it ought to take a more direct interest in Standard-Triumph, and – through nominee holdings – began to buy substantial numbers of the company's shares.

By March 1954, Standard was talking mergers with Rover, another sizable independent concern, by then relocated in Solihull, and famous both for its rugged Land Rovers and its carefully-built middle-class saloon cars. Rover's chairman, Spencer Wilks, was John Black's brother-in-law (but never talked to him if he could help it), and also related to Alick Dick (whose uncle had married one of William Hillman's daughters, as had Spencer Wilks and John Black). These talks came to nothing for several reasons, the most important of which was that Rover did not want to get entangled with the Massey-Harris-Ferguson deal, even if the agricultural link between tractors and Land Rovers made some sense.

Next along was the Rootes Group, also with its industrial base in Coventry, and controlled rigidly by the Rootes family. At first these discussions centred around a joint overseas marketing agreement, but they later developed into full-scale merger talks. By the spring of 1957 there was talk of a new company – R & S Holdings Ltd – with directors from both sets of management. Somehow, too, this was never going to work, for there was constant bickering and jockeying for position. Rootes insisted that Sir William Rootes should be chairman, and the best that Alick Dick could achieve for himself was joint managing director alongside Geoffrey Rootes.

Not even extended talks (including a visit to Nassau where Sir William Rootes happened to be making a visit) could resolve the vivid personality differences, and the negotiations were abandoned.

At this point Dick turned to Massey-Harris-Ferguson, and within days the tractor giant had agreed to mount a takeover bid for Standard, though the companies would continue to have their own separate existences. By that time, in any case, Massey-Harris already held 20 per cent of Standard's share capital, and it was on discovering this (the holding had been built in considerable secrecy) that Dick and his directors began to suspect that they might not be selling-out to an altogether friendly associate.

Soon, however, the fortunes of the British and Canadian stock markets came to the rescue of this ill-starred deal. The takeover was to have been on the basis of share swaps. M-H-F shares then dropped, Standard shares rose, and when M-H-F refused to make a better offer to give Standard shareholders the same effective deal the whole programme collapsed.

From this point on Dick was completely convinced that he would have to shake-off the ties with Massey-Harris-Ferguson. No matter what was proposed, or for how long their manufacturing agreement persisted, he could never see a friendly relationship returning. He had already begun to build-up Standard's industrial base, and this impasse made him more determined to do so.

His first acquisition had been Beans Industries of Tipton. Beans had committed itself to major expansion in connection with castings for the new big Ferguson tractor which Standard would begin making in 1956, was financially overstretched, and was happy to be taken over in the spring of 1956. To do this Standard issued no fewer than 12 million new 5/- (25p) ordinary shares.

A year later, Standard took over the lease of part of Daimler's original (late 1930s) shadow factory at Radford, in North Coventry, and began to concentrate its axle machining and some gearbox work there. Radford, like Banner Lane, and the Fletchamstead part of Standard's main production complex, was owned by the British Government, and was therefore rented to Standard-Triumph on a long-term basis.

A year later, Alick Dick moved again, and it was this deal which finally triggered the final break with Massey-Harris-Ferguson. For some time it had been clear that to all intents and purposes Mulliners in Birmingham, was entirely beholden to Standard-Triumph for its future. In its own way it was a very profitable concern, so in May 1958 an agreed offer was made by Standard for the whole of the Mulliners share capital.

This was made on the same basis as the Beans Industries deal – in Standard shares – and it caused the Massey management to see red. Such a move would increase Standard's overall capital, and it would therefore dilute Massey's percentage holding. Therefore, in July 1958, and without even informing the Standard board of its intentions, Massey offered to buy every one of the new shares from the bemused Mulliners shareholders. It was an astonishing slap in the face to Standard's corporate dignity, and even though as a business ploy it did not succeed, it made Alick Dick quite determined to unscramble his links with the Canadian concern. It also made him adopt a future policy of company acquisition only in terms of cash, and not in shares – this decision being the most vital in terms of the happenings of 1960/1961, and one which contributed to Standard's financial downfall.

Mulliners was a great capture, formalised in July 1958. Not only was Mulliners itself a sizeable builder of bodies and body sections (it would play a vital part in the Herald jigsaw), but it also had a controlling interest in the Forward Radiator Company (who made radiators and steel pressings). Standard was therefore well on its way to self-sufficiency.

Tooling for the new car, however, was well advanced. Codenamed Zobo, and originally to have been called the Triumph Torch, it was soon renamed Herald after Alick Dick's boat. Harry Webster's

From 1959 to 1971, Triumph was wedded to the idea of using swing axle independent rear suspension like this – this in fact being a layout which persisted on the Spitfire until 1980.

separate-chassis layout had been agreed without dissension, and although the car was always to have four-wheel independent suspension, an original scheme for transverse-leaf springs at front and rear never progressed beyond the talking stage. "We were always under tremendous pressure from the sales people," Harry Webster said, "to keep the costs right down. This explains why we never went for a pivoting rear leaf-spring right from the start (though we always knew this would be better than the simple swing axle layout), and it explains why the first prototypes were built without even a front anti-roll bar! The handling on those was *very* exciting …"

Even as early as August 1957, when the directors gave the formal go-ahead for the Herald project, they were talking about "minimum modifications necessary for production of a small sports car for the USA market" – which would eventually mature as the Spitfire, and later evolve, too, into the GT6.

At this time it was still hoped that Job 1 (which is the production engineers' slang for the start-up of series production) would be in October 1958, but it was also noted that the "body supply source was still to be decided." All this, of course, took place before Webster and Michelotti had their memorable meeting in Turin to scheme-out an entirely fresh style.

To get round the body-supply problem, Webster's engineers then took the major decision of having the bodies manufactured in sections. For the first time since the prewar days of batch production and individual coachbuilding, the bodies would take

This was the very first prototype Triumph Herald Saloon, as viewed in the styling studio at Banner Lane in 1958.

shape in several different locations, and would only come together at Canley. Even more important was that when they did meet up, they would be bolted, not welded, together. This, though unorthodox, meant that all the different variations could be planned without vast expenditure on assembly jigs and welding fixtures. Right from the start there would be two-door saloons and coupés, with convertibles, estate cars, and even light vans to follow. But there was no doubt that quality control, and very careful sealing and matching of the separate sections, was going to be critical.

Panels and subsections came from far and wide. Pressed Steel, unable to take on the complete job, supplied some sections; Mulliners and Forward Radiator supplied others, and the bonnets came from Liverpool. The Liverpool factory, however, comes into our story just a little later.

In the rush for growth, Alick Dick was trying to negotiate his way out of the manufacturing agreement with Massey-Harris-Ferguson, and at the same time approving major renovations at Canley. Fisher & Ludlow's involvement would fall into disuse when it had supplied the last Standard Pennants in 1959, so Standard agreed to buy the factory for itself, for the integration and assembly of the Herald bodies before arrival at Canley. In the heady days of 1958/1959, when expansion was being planned, the company was talking of selling

Michelotti's neat and simple style for the Herald first appeared in 1959, and was then built as a 948cc, 1147cc and 1296cc saloon for the next twelve years. Commercially, it was a great success.

Not only did the Herald give rise to a succession of smart estate car derivatives, but there was even a commercial van type, badged 'Courier,' on the market at the same time.

As was traditional with small-engined Standards and Triumphs, the new Herald was mounted sideways to progress down the final assembly line. This was a very early production line shot in 1959, for supplies of saloon bodies had not yet begun to filter through the system.

Soon after Standard-Triumph had sold out its interests in making tractors for Ferguson, it invested heavily in a massive new assembly hall at Canley, which was completed in 1961, and was immediately nicknamed 'the Rocket range.'

At Canley, too, it was obvious that the existing assembly halls, basically unchanged since the end of the First World War, could not take the strain for much longer. Dick's balancing act, therefore, was that the money he would liberate from the tractor business sale could be used to finance a vast and up-to-date assembly hall, which would plug the gap between the Canley and Fletchamstead buildings. Work on this building began in the spring of 1958, and the facility was planned to be ready by the end of 1960.

It took time, a great deal of time, and much niggly negotiation, before Standard-Triumph was free of its financially-rewarding but unhappy commitment to build tractors. The urge to sell had become even more intense after the shock and embarrassment of the Mulliners intrigue, when (in August) Massey took over Perkins, which was a large-scale supplier of proprietary diesel and petrol engines.

Even while the Herald was being launched, and while the vast new assembly hall took shape, the two boards were working their way out of a legal and financial maze, but by August the deal was done. Standard benefited to the tune of £12.5 million in cash, and shareholders received a tax-free share-out of 2/6 (12.5p) for every share they held. As part of the deal, Standard would move its offices and the design/development departments from Banner Lane to Canley/Fletchamstead, while Massey would vacate the old carburettor-building 'shadow factory' block at Fletchamstead North (this, very conveniently, would become the newly-located Triumph engineering block, a function it carried out until the 1980s). As part

more than 260,000 cars by 1961 (it had no idea of the country's coming recession which would blow it well off-course), and at one time it proposed building a covered conveyor (for which planning permission was granted) parallel to the main-line railway from Tile Hill to Canley.

of the deal, Massey passed over nearly eight million Standard shares, and henceforth would have no influence on the company's fortunes.

To protect its own interests, Massey insisted that Standard agreed to not start selling a competitive tractor for at least two years. Even so, the Standard 'Zero' tractor project was started-up at once, and as Alick Dick reminded us, "until the day before it signed the agreement Massey didn't realise that it hadn't arranged to buy all the spares for the original Ferguson TE20 tractor. We were well aware of this, and we could have gone ahead with production of that tractor as soon as we were allowed. Incidentally the loss of our engine contract because of its Perkins deal meant that we went back and screwed a lot more cash out of them, and we finished up with a much better price than I think we deserved. But that's business, and I think I did a very good job there!"

In the meantime, the Herald was finally launched in April 1959. It was the first of a new wave of technically-interesting small British cars (the Mini was to follow it in a matter of months), and at first it was available in single-carburettor 948cc two-door saloon form, and twin-carburettor coupé guise. There was no mention of further variants yet to come, but the more trustworthy of the motoring press were let into the secret even at this stage.

There was much outraged comment about the separate chassis (and Standard was not forthcoming as to its reasons for adopting this method of construction), much praise for the splendid steering lock (with a 25ft turning circle it was the smallest of almost any car then in

production in the world, and in the UK was rivalled only by the London taxicabs), many generous comments about the excellent engine compartment accessibility (the entire bonnet and front wings hinged forward, pivoted from the front of the chassis frame), but much doubt about the swing axle rear suspension. Even by 1959 standards the roll-oversteer, caused by the jacking-up of the rear wheels and crossply tyres, was excessive if the cars were driven hard. Curiously enough, a coupé with its rear suspension set low could be driven like a veritable sports car, as early rally and trials results showed. In the 1959 RAC Rally, for instance, a team of Herald coupés prepared by Ken Richardson's department finished second in the team prize contest – beaten, need we add, by the works team of TR3As!

Sales, however, took off at a goodly rate. Coupés were available at once, and saloons a few weeks later (this was a consequence of

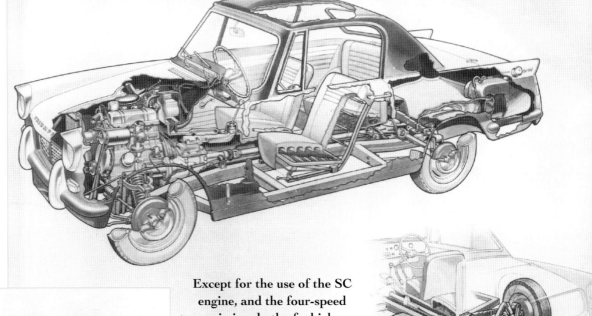

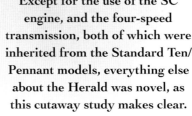

Except for the use of the SC engine, and the four-speed transmission, both of which were inherited from the Standard Ten/Pennant models, everything else about the Herald was novel, as this cutaway study makes clear.

Originally built as a 'shadow factory' by Standard in the late 1930s, Fletchamstead North became Ferguson's HQ after the Second World War, and was then occupied by Standard-Triumph's design, styling, and development departments from 1959 onwards.

the way the styles had been approved and tooled-up. Michelotti's first sensational prototype had, of course, been a coupé). The saloon, priced at £495 (coupé £515), had to compete with Ford's old-fashioned Anglia at £400, Austin's A40 de Luxe at £458, and Morris' Minor 1000 de Luxe at £436. The price gap was significant, but all the competition was stodgy and conventional. For the time being the public was prepared to pay a premium for advanced engineering, and the Canley production lines were kept very busy. By November, Herald production was up to 1,400 a week, with 2,000 and even 3,000 a week being talked about for the future. When the tractor cash became available in September, the company mentioned major expansion in facilities, and noted that it would be able to make 180,000 cars a year as soon as the new assembly hall was running to capacity.

The problem, at first, was one of quality. Although the Herald was well equipped (indeed, it had some fittings like swiveling oddment trays under the facia which the sales department soon found superfluous, and were deleted), the quality-control staff had problems in getting the separately-sourced body sections to match together completely and correctly, and one persistent early problem was of water leaks. Road filth found its way into the engine compartment (metal curtains from radiator to bulkhead solved that one), nylon bushes, extensively tested in prototype form, proved unsatisfactory in quantity production (rubber bushes and grease points were substituted), and rather creaky bodies had to be stiffened-up with additional gussets and brackets at strategic points. More obviously, even on the best of Heralds, the 948cc engine was really not sturdy enough for its job – more power in the shape of the twin-carb engine helped, but this was accompanied by a loss of torque. Future Heralds would have to have the only known cure – more cubic inches, or (in British terms) a larger engine.

Meanwhile, Standard-Triumph's acquisition of supplier companies continued. Right from the start it had placed its order for pressing and assembly of Herald bonnet panels (which included the front wings and the entire nose) with a Liverpool company, Hall Engineering (Holdings) Ltd, and at the end of 1959 it announced that it was making a takeover bid (another already-agreed bid) for the company. The purchase price was about £2 million and, in Alick Dick's words: "we paid cash for Hall, which was really a mistake. We should have been more liquid in 1960 when the financial tide turned against us if only we'd paid Hall in shares and a small dollop of cash, but I didn't want to let a company like Massey embarrass us again by bidding for the new shares. We'd had quite enough of that in 1958 over the Mulliners business.

"I think perhaps we over-estimated the possibility of the same tactics being applied against us again, and I think it was an error, but we really had gone through a lot with Massey, and I wasn't prepared to suffer that sort of thing again."

No matter. The purchase of Hall, that just happened to have a controlling interest in a fine little Dunstable company called Auto Body Dies Ltd, was very prudent, and its established business in making office furniture was soon swept aside. Frank Dixon, managing director of Hall, kept his position and joined the board of directors at Standard-Triumph.

Almost at the same time, Standard-Triumph bid for, and succeeded in acquiring, the Alford and Alder Ltd business based at Hemel Hempstead. It was a respected supplier of front suspension and steering components to several British car-makers (its principal business being with Standard-Triumph), and once again this was a very prudent purchase on the assumption that Standard's production and sales were to continue to rise in the future.

The biggest scheme of all, involving the commitment in due course of more than £11 million, was the company deciding to set-up a new major factory to build bodies and eventually complete cars. It wanted to finish this expansion in Coventry, but Government policy would not permit it to do this, and it was forced to look at a 'development' area. South Wales, Scotland, or Merseyside were all offered, and in view of its links with Hall Engineering, Standard opted for the Liverpool area. Despite the fact that Pressed Steel then approached Standard, asking to take over Herald body production, a large site was acquired near the Hall factory, and potentially was capable of looking after the future of the company for at least the next 20 years. This, of course, was the ill-fated Liverpool No. 2 plant, which closed down in 1978.

Alick Dick cut the first sod of this 104-acre plot of land, which could – financial considerations permitting – have been ready by 1964 or 1965. It was the first move likely to shift the company's entire centre of gravity. All previous acquisitions had been made with the view of feeding components to Canley. This new factory would stand up on its own account, and the implications of two-way, or even multiple-way traffic between Coventry, Liverpool and the satellite concerns was enormous.

While all this was going on, a further series of talks with Rover at Solihull (the first session having been abandoned in July 1954) took place in 1959. Rover had become interested in the spring of 1959 as soon as it became known that Standard would soon be free of its ties with Massey-Harris-Ferguson, but while talks continued for some months it seemed no more likely to succeed than those of 1954.

It was not merely that there were personal differences (on who should work for whom, which personality should head-up the combined company, and what it all should be called), but Rover was not really very impressed by Standard-Triumph's profits record (especially when the tractor profits were lost), even though the 1958 after-tax figure was more than £1 million and 1959's record looked as if it would break through the £2 million barrier.

Before talks broke down (it was really a case of an irresistible force meeting an immovable object, with the unhappy merchant bankers trying to introduce some flexibility between the two parties), both engineering groups were astonished to realise that they were proposing to build the same sort of 'executive' 2-litre saloon car in the foreseeable future. Rover had already settled on the bare bones of the P6 Rover 2000 project, while Standard-Triumph was still trying to settle the prototype version of an advanced six-cylinder car coded Zebu.

By 1960, therefore, Standard-Triumph still stood alone, and was still very much the smallest of the British industry's Big Five concerns; the others were BMC, Ford, Rootes and Vauxhall. It had an ambitious expansion programme coming inexorably to fruition – the new Canley assembly hall being at the centre of all this activity – and a projected line-up of new products including a TR4, a tiny sports car, and the large Zebu saloon all under consideration by Harry Webster's engineers. This was all well and good, and might have provided Standard with an exhilarating ride in the 1960s if Britain's economic weather had stayed fine. The fates, however, were unkind to Alick Dick and his company. Just at a time when Standard-Triumph was least able to deal with adverse business conditions, and when much of its liquid cash had been spent on purchases of component suppliers, the nation's economy turned down. Where as recently as September 1969 the sales department had been talking airily of 185,000 sales for 1960/61, within a year that estimate was cut by nearly 50 per cent. The company's cash-flow situation deteriorated rapidly, thousands of production-line workers were put on short time (a three-day week was introduced in the winter of 1960/61), and the future looked grim.

As in all good stories, however, a fairy godmother, in the shape of Leyland Motors Ltd of Lancashire, was shortly to appear. How and why it happened, and what the consequences were, is a story which belongs to a later chapter. The Herald and its derivatives, however, must still be considered here.

The Herald Coupé was the first of the entire family to go into series production, early in 1959. More than 20,000 would be built before it gave way, gracefully, to the Spitfire sports car which followed.

Even in 1959, and with the Herald barely known to the public, Harry Webster knew that it would need a larger engine before long. It was not a question of changing his mind in haste. The 948cc engine, after all, had been in production since the launch of the Standard 10 in March 1954. The question of an even larger version of the small-car engine (which had never consciously been laid-out in the first place with any stretch beyond 948cc) was also complicated by the company's desire to make a smooth 'six' in due course, to succeed the lusty old wet-liner Vanguard engine. Even amateur historians will know that the six-cylinder engine duly appeared in the Vanguard Luxury Six of 1960, but they probably do not know that Ted Grinham was first asked to consider such a design as early as July 1952.

Harry Webster continues the story: "We were all looking desperately at how to get the capacity of that 948cc engine up, and we weren't getting anywhere. One night, at home, I woke up after some sort of bad dream (Oh, yes, we had those, and my wife will confirm that it happened!), and couldn't get back to sleep, so I went off to my study and it was then that I suddenly had this idea of moving the cylinder axes across, putting in a bit of desaxe so that we could clear the studs, and (bingo!) we could have the extra cylinder bore we needed.

"In fact, I realised that with a stroke increase as well, we could eventually get up to 1500cc, but Alick Dick thought we should keep

that up our sleeve for a time, and stick to the 1147cc size at first. In detail, of course, there was much more to the stretch than that, but in essence the desaxe was the clincher.

"At about the same time as this we decided that the right way to produce a 'six' was really to stick two cylinders on to the end of the small 'four', which is in effect what we did. There was nothing new in this approach – Standard had done it in the 1930s, like most other firms in the business.

"I told Jim Parkinson, who was looking after the job for me, to leave a bit of room for expansion, because I would like to have 2-litres one day. For this engine we really did think about stretch. The very first one was only 1422cc (with the same bore and stroke as the 948cc 'four'), but by the time we went into production it was already out to 2-litres. At first, as you know, we intended the engine for the Zebu, which we wanted to replace the Vanguard III, but it eventually found its way into the Vanguard first, and of course the last of all was only made in the summer of 1977."

The 1147cc Herald engine, with a bigger cylinder-bore and quite a lot more muscle, was a reliable unit right from the start, and with it the idea of single-carburettor or twin-carburettor versions was dropped for the time being. The 948cc Herald range, indeed, had been quite complicated, with twin-carb engines standard on the coupé and the convertible, single-carb engines standard on the saloon, but with a twin-carb option. Just before the 948cc range was

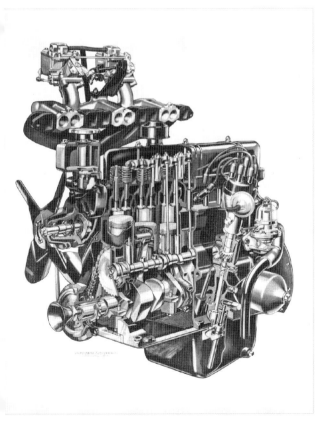

To replace the valiant old wet-liner engine in the 1960s, Standard-Triumph evolved an all-new six-cylinder power unit, originally in 2-litre form (as shown here) for use in the Vanguard Six, and later in a variety of Standard and Triumph models. Developed versions, for instance, would eventually power models as different as the GT6 and the 2000, the Vitesse, TR6 and 2.5 PI.

revised, too, a cheap Herald S was also introduced, priced at £468, to combat the too-keen competition from Ford's notchback Anglia and the astonishingly successful Minis.

The convertible Herald had arrived in 1960, in 948cc form, and the first of the estate cars was a 1200, announced a few weeks later than the other 1200 cars. The cars' basic specification was unchanged, but the accent was on better quality of production, fewer but more luxurious fittings and trim items, and a great effort to convince the world that the Herald was in production as a long-term prospect. This was important. With the company's financial troubles widely discussed during the winter of 1960/61, and the new owners – Leyland Motors – making no attempt to disguise its opinion that Standard-Triumph was in need of a good shake-up from director level to shop floor, a boost to the sales department's morale was essential.

The effects were gratifying, for public acceptance of the much-improved Herald 1200 range was immediate. For the next ten years, in one form or another, and in spite of the launch of front-wheel drive Triumphs, which had originally been meant to replace the Herald, the car was a persistent high-volume seller. Its peak year was in 1963/64, when Triumph's fortunes were burgeoning under Leyland ownership, and more than 52,000 vehicles were sold. This was not as many as in the 'dash for growth' year of 1959/60, but the Herald 1200 family sold with a much better reputation, and in competition with much more modern competing models from the rest of the Big Five.

In the ten years from 1961 to 1971 – the last of all, a Herald 13/60, was built in September of that year – there were few significant engineering changes, and virtually nothing was done to the styling. The idea of transferring bodyshell production from its scattered sources to the Pressed Steel company was abandoned during the cash-flow crisis of 1960, and the only obvious style change was to the bonnet for the 13/60 models in 1967. A four-door saloon Herald was built in overseas territories, but never produced in Britain.

The Herald coupé was dropped in 1964, as demand fell away. Originally it had been an attractive alternative to the saloons, but once both the Spitfire and the six-cylinder Vitesse had arrived it was clearly only living on borrowed time. The light van (the 'Courier,' originally to have been called the 'Carrier') was also dropped in 1964, because it did not sell well against the cheaper Fords, Austins and Morris commercials.

Front-wheel disc brakes were made optional in the autumn of 1961, then standardised on the 12/50 and 13/60 models. The estate car and van had wider-rim wheels, which were later homologated for the Spitfire competition cars and found to be very valuable.

As an addition to the 1200s, the 12/50 was announced in 1963. This had the disc brakes, a sunroof as part of the normal

The four-cylinder engine Herald received its one and only face-lift in 1967, with the launch of the 13/60 model (to replace the 12/50), which prolonged that family's life to 1971.

specification (at a time when these were very rare indeed), and an 1147cc engine boosted from 39bhp to 51bhp.

At one stage, Leyland was so concerned that people would assume that the Herald was a dying car, that in 1964 it made it clear that there "would be Heralds in production for at least the next five years." Even so, it was not until 1967 that the third and final important change was made to the line-up.

To get the move into context, we must point out that the front-wheel drive 1300 had already been on the market for nearly two years, but the cheaper down-market versions of it were not even partly developed. In just one move, all the existing and very successful Herald 1200s and 12/50s (except for the basic 1200 saloon) were swept away, to be replaced by the 13/60 range. In effect this was the mixture as before, but with the 1300's single-carb 1296cc engine (a simple over-bore from the desaxe 1147cc unit), a new facia, a single-headlamp version of the Vitesse's bonnet, and rather more rear-seat passenger space in the saloon version only. Sadly, the sunroof was demoted to an option, though a good proportion of customers bought their 13/60s with one fitted.

The Herald was now in the autumn of its career. The best 13/60 sales figures were 24,000 plus (in 1967/68, along with more than 8000 1200 saloons), but demand thereafter dropped off. When the conventional Toledo saloon arrived in 1970 it spelt the imminent end to the separate-chassis Herald's life. The 1200 and 13/60 saloons disappeared at the end of the year, the estate cars and convertibles dying in September 1971.

In 1962, of course, the Herald spawned the Vitesse (the 'Sports Six' in America), a slim but good example of the 'big engine into a small car'

philosophy. Although this transplant had not been planned originally, Triumph's engineers found that it was just possible (by squeezing the radiator matrix into the nose of an attractively restyled bonnet) to get the six-cylinder version of the Herald's engine into the engine bay. Under-bored (and with a new cylinder block casting to take advantage of this) to 1596cc and with a close-ratio gearbox, the Vitesse sold in saloon and convertible form – there never was an estate in production, though one or two 'hand-built' cars were made – and was fairly fast, if possessed of rather strong understeer until the swing axle rear suspension took over.

Although never sold in the UK, there was also a four-door saloon version, which finally went into production in Leyland's Indian factory, and was further developed for that market alone.

Work going ahead in the works competitions department before the 1963 Monte Carlo Rally, with Vitesses and the TR4 '5VC' in this study. Author Graham Robson is 'working' on the fog lamp installation of one of the Vitesses.

Not only did the Vitesse always have this smart four-headlamp nose, but it was driven by a silky-smooth six-cylinder engine, the smallest-capacity such unit on sale in the UK at this time.

If only the engine had been more tunable in its original narrow-cylinder head form, the Vitesse could have been a useful rally car, but after one or two abortive outings by the factory that project was cancelled. A very special 2-litre Vitesse prototype, complete with TR4 gearbox, was used by Vic Elford on the 1963 Liège, but was burnt out after a carburettor fire in deepest Yugoslavia when challenging for the lead.

Like the 13/60, there would be Vitesses until the end of 1971, though the car's subsequent development was closely tied-up with the evolution of the sports car line. But considering that the

Standard sales department had first signalled its need of a car of this engine size in 1955, it made little of the Vitesse. Perhaps its accommodation was not in line with its engine size, and certainly after the arrival of the Triumph 2000 it was a bit of an orphan, but it was an engaging little car that deserved to sell more strongly than it did – just over 8000 were built in its first year, 1962/63.

It was also overshadowed by the sports cars spawned by the Herald's philosophy. Already being considered by Michelotti and Harry Webster in 1957, these did as much for Triumph's name in the United States as the Midget had done for MG in the 1940s.

'Bomb' and Beyond: The Spitfire Story

Triumph enthusiasts probably know that the Spitfire project came within a hair's breadth of being cancelled. The car – one prototype – existed when Leyland Motors took control of Standard-Triumph at the beginning of 1961, and had stood forlorn and undeveloped under a dust-sheet in the engineering department for some months. If Leyland had decided to cut back drastically on Triumph's activities there would never have been a Spitfire at all. As it happened, it decided to push ahead with expansion, and the Spitfire was the first major new project to see the light of day in the autumn of 1962.

Right from the start of the Zobo project, Alick Dick had wanted to see a sports car version of the new family car. Michelotti's rendering of the Herald coupé was so elegant that for a time it was thought that a sports car might not be necessary. Indeed, even when the company was financially healthy, there was the question of whether it could afford the time and effort to carry it through, as all kinds of exciting things were planned for the TR range.

The irrepressible little Italian, however, had already decided about the small sporting car and had shaped a sleek and graceful little body around a shortened (83in wheelbase) Herald chassis

frame. As Alick Dick recalled: "Michelotti was always reeling off new designs; you just couldn't stop him. If you took him out to dinner he'd get practically every menu card in the place, design cars and leave them as souvenirs for the waiters! He could design a car in four or five minutes, and the nice thing was that he would do it to our ideas, not just his own."

But the new sports car was Michelotti's own, and by comparison with the ugly little 'frog-eye' Austin-Healey Sprite it was a stunner. The Standard directors liked it from the moment they first saw the sketches, though in April 1960, when it was first formally proposed to them, there was indecision over the body construction – it could have been either in pressed steel, or in glass-fibre. Approval to build the first prototype followed in September, though by then Michelotti was already well on the way to building a car himself!

Once resurrected by Leyland Motors, the sports car project, coded 'Bomb' by Harry Webster's whimsical planners, got under way very quickly. The only styling changes made between prototype and production were that the top line of the doors was raised slightly (to suit complete retraction of the winding windows – the Sprite/Midget would not have such an important feature until 1964) and a new facia was designed which was suitable for left-hand or right-hand drive cars.

As Forward Radiator was to do the tooling for the car, and the body would therefore be in pressed steel, it was apparent that a lot of beam and torsional strength could be built into the sills, so the short-wheelbase chassis frame was redesigned into what was effectively a backbone structure, but it continued to use the familiar but slightly modified Herald/Vitesse front and rear suspensions. The rear suspension radius arms, however, now pivoted from the bodyshell itself, as there were no chassis crossmembers in this Spitfire application.

The name came along late in the day, and caused controversy only among the do-gooders, who thought that

Launched in 1962, the Spitfire was a pretty little car which soon began to outsell the Sprite/Midget competition from BMC.

This show exhibit of 1962 demonstrates the neat backbone chassis of the Spitfire, which would be used, in further developed form, for the next eighteen years.

The original Michelotti style for the two-seater Spitfire of 1962-1967 was a pretty little creation, which went on to found an ultra-successful dynasty.

such a name would encourage furious driving among the new car's owners. Spitfire, in any case, evoked memories of RAF fighter aircraft in Britain, and high-spirited young ladies in North America.

With its spacious two-seater passenger compartment, its splendid styling, and equipment superior to that of other competing small cars like the Sprite and Midget, the Spitfire was an immediate success. As with other cars announced later by Leyland Motors, the sales department soon revised its estimate of its potential – upwards! With its 63bhp (net) twin-carb version of the Herald's 1147cc engine, the little car was capable of 90mph, quite enough to make it exhilarating to drive, and though the swing axle rear suspension could still cause problems, the car's general response and agility were well-received. Before long an overdrive, wire-spoke wheels, and a steel hardtop all became available as options, and there was really a Spitfire for all occasions. The one-piece bodyshell, still with a separate front-hinged bonnet, was surprisingly rigid, and it is not generally realised that the windscreen was shared with the TR4.

With the Spitfire in such huge demand, in Britain and everywhere else in the civilised world of motoring, there was no need to thrash around looking for dramatic improvements. It is not surprising, therefore, that the same basic Spitfire sports car was in production from December 1962 to November 1970, and that even after a major restyle the same basic chassis and suspension layout (with the substitution of a pivoting rear leaf-spring) was still being made in large numbers at the end of the 1970s.

More than 45,000 of the original Mark 1 Spitfires were

made, then in March 1965 the Mark 2 arrived, with a little more horsepower (67bhp instead of 63bhp), a diaphragm-spring clutch and more luxurious fittings and seats.

That lasted until the spring of 1967, when the Mark 3 car, distinguished by its 'bone-in-teeth' front bumper position, took over. Still very similar to the original design, the Mark 3 had the new 1296cc engine, complete with eight-port cylinder head, and produced a very lusty 75bhp at 6000rpm. There was also an improved fold-away hood, and there was no doubt that the Mark 3 was a very desirable little car. In favourable conditions a 100mph maximum speed was possible. The 100,000th Spitfire of all types was built with a publicity flourish towards the end of 1967.

In the meantime, the twin pressures of United States legislation and changing fashions were beginning to affect the Spitfire's prospects. North American legislation meant that more and more attention would have to be paid to features like the contents of the engine exhaust gases and to the variously-defined crash-resistance of the bodywork. Although this was not yet seriously damaging to existing designs, the implications were most dispiriting.

The question of developments in fashion was easier to discern. Spitfires had now been on sale for more than five years, and drivers who had already bought their third or even their fourth Spitfire were beginning to wonder if next time they should try something which looked different. In any case, as Forward Radiator's quickly-constructed 'temporary tooling' was beginning to fray at the edges, it was decided to look seriously at a restyle.

Michelotti was asked for his ideas in 1968, based around the retention of the existing scuttle, centre-section and doors.

By the end of the year he had evolved a new shape, essentially unchanged in outline, but with a sharply cut-off tail (this was to be his Triumph trade-mark on other models like the 'Stag' and the restyled 'Innsbruck' 2000/2.5 cars) and with a bonnet incorporating concealed pop-up headlamps.

It was an attractive proposal, but the pop-up headlamp was hurriedly killed-off when it began to look as if future American legislation would outlaw such features. Spen King, Harry Webster's successor, was very disappointed as he had also wanted to see such a scheme on the Stag, then also in its prototype stages. The tragedy of this, of course, was that the threatened restrictions never materialised, and pop-up headlamps then came back in the styling picture with a vengeance and were seen at Triumph on the TR7/TR8 sports cars.

The finalised Mark 4 Spitfire, therefore, had an extensively reworked bodyshell with many new skin panels and different assembly arrangements, even though at a casual glance it looked much the same as before. The swing-up bonnet was merely a smoothed-out and retooled version of the original. There was a new and rather angular optional hardtop, and the tail was tastefully reshaped with a flat rear deck and the sharp cutoff, graced by new taillights and details. A feature of the newly retouched interior was the facia and instrument panel, with its dials in front of the driver.

The most important engineering changes, major in their effect if not in how obvious they looked, were to the transmission and the rear suspension. After years of obstinacy in the face of mounting criticism of the car's handling, Triumph adopted a new development of the swing axle system, where the transverse leaf spring was allowed to pivot on top of the differential casing. This effectively eliminated the rear roll stiffness, and it also reduced wheel-camber changes to an absolute minimum. This change, one thought up by Triumph as early as 1959, was a great improvement, and transformed the car's behaviour – even if we recall that Spen King managed to turn over a development car while exploring the its roadholding limits!

The other improvement was to the gearbox, where the Mark 4 car inherited the all synchromesh installation from the Toledo (which would soon be commonised with that of the new Morris Marina). Overdrive was still optional and 4½in wheel rims were standardised.

Surprisingly, in view of the occasion's importance, the Mark 4 was not launched until immediately after the Earls Court Motor Show of 1970; Triumph, presumably, was more interested in the car as a 1971 model in North America than in its impact in Britain.

The problem for the Mark 4 was that with each succeeding year its engine was becoming more and more strangled (and less economical) to meet American exhaust-emission legislation. Although Spitfires for the rest of the world suffered very little in this process, the sad fact was that the cars were gradually getting slower. Inevitably, too, future plans for the Spitfire became closely linked with what British Leyland had in mind for all its other sports cars, and these are described in a later chapter.

Once the Spitfire had been announced in 1962, the deadly rivals from Abingdon – MG and Austin-Healey – made quite sure that the world knew about their competition's heritage and breeding, while inferring that the opposition had none. It was an attitude that soon had to change, for the factory was quite determined to prove that the Spitfire was not only pretty, but effective as well. The competitions department, which had been running TR4s on a tiny budget for a couple of years, were given a great deal more money to plan for 1964 and beyond, and they put it to great effect.

Starting before the end of 1963, and with two distinctly different events in mind for June 1964, a total of nine very special Spitfires were laid down. Not only would four factory-entered and one semi-detached rally cars be built, but four cars were also to be prepared for the Le Mans 24-hour race.

This was not merely for publicity purposes. The whole operation revolved around the fact that an eight-port cylinder head, with much-improved breathing, had already been proved effective by

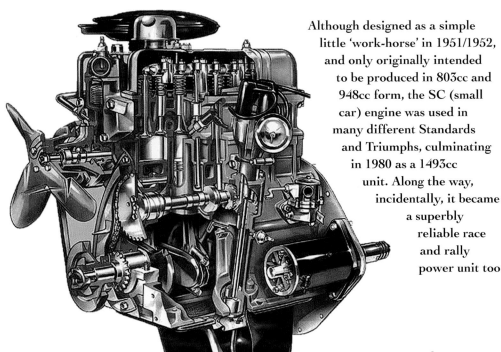

Although designed as a simple little 'work-horse' in 1951/1952, and only originally intended to be produced in 803cc and 948cc form, the SC (small car) engine was used in many different Standards and Triumphs, culminating in 1980 as a 1493cc unit. Along the way, incidentally, it became a superbly reliable race and rally power unit too.

the engineers, and this – cast both in iron and in aluminium – was developed for motorsport with twin dual-choke Weber carburettors, a free-flow exhaust system and a really 'wild' camshaft. The '70X' engine, as it was always known inside the engineering department, took time to become reliable (pistons and crankshaft bearings being the principal problems), but it wasn't long before the 1147cc engine was persuaded to give about 100bhp (87bhp/litre) in a tune which could be raced for 24 hours or rallied for several days. Although the engines were real pigs to start from cold (there was no choke and the tiny 10mm spark plugs didn't help) and the torque curve was very peaky (the engines peaked-out at about 7000rpm and maximum torque was developed at more than 5000rpm) they were remarkably lusty and extremely effective.

In fact cast iron heads were chosen for Le Mans in 1964, and for sale to customers, while the rally cars had aluminium heads with even higher compression ratios, and it was these engines which proved to be the most powerful. With a camshaft overlap of 104 degrees that was only a start, and a year later the Le Mans engines were boasting 109bhp at 7300rpm (compared with 98bhp for a cast iron engine and 102bhp for an alloy engine in 1964) with reliability. For the Alpine Rally of 1965, in which prototype cars could be entered, 1296cc engines were used, and these pushed out a mighty 117bhp at 7000rpm, with much improved torque and flexibility.

Three different gearboxes were used in the three years the works cars were active.

The 1964 Le Mans cars used the very strong all-synchromesh TR4 box, because the strength of even the Vitesse item was in doubt. The rally cars had to use production boxes, so the Vitesse close-ratio cluster was homologated as an option, where it proved to be quite strong enough, even where repeated pass-storming was involved. However, this box lacked a synchronised first gear, which the drivers considered essential, so Harry Webster's enthusiastic development engineers produced a batch

This high three-quarter rear view of a works Spitfire rally car shows how the fastback coupé style was skilfully grafted on to the basic Spitfire body shape.

of prototype GT6 all-synchromesh boxes which were used ever afterwards – in spite of the fact that for homologation purposes they were strictly 'illegal.' For 1965, in fact, the Le Mans cars adopted the GT6 box, as it saved a great deal of weight compared with that of the TR4.

Entirely reworked differentials were also built, using prototype GT6 parts and incorporating limited-slip differentials. These, incidentally, did more for the car's high-speed handling than any amount of development of spring and damper settings. Work on the suspension was no chore where the Le Mans cars were concerned, as this circuit's surface was good and smooth, and the rear suspension could be tied well down. For the rally cars, which in any case were somewhat heavier, more work was needed, as the cars would sometimes have to cope with rough roads. Even so, and in spite of the fact that an 18-gallon fuel tank was to be used in some events (when fitted it took up all the space of the existing tank and most of the fresh air behind the seats), the rest of the chassis was almost entirely standard, apart from bigger brakes, though for 1965 the Le Mans cars had standard-looking but much-lightened frames.

The sensational differences were all in the bodywork, where the two sets of cars had to run to two sets of regulations. The rally cars, being production cars, had to use the normal steel bodyshell, but with aluminium skin panels (bonnet assembly, doors, wings and tail), while the race cars were constructed with every pressed panel being of light-alloy or glass-fibre. These light-alloy panels, incidentally, were pressed on production-line tools, usually at the

Left: The rear ends of the works Spitfire rally cars were carefully detailed, to allow the spare wheel to be loaded into the tail.

Below: In 1964 and 1965, the works competitions department built and ran two different sets of Spitfires – the green ones being for Le Mans racing; the blue ones for international rallying.

Not only did the 1965 works racing Spitfire look purposeful with its sleek fastback body style, it could reach up to 140mph on a long straight.

end of a normal batch being run-off, and consequently the panel sets took several weeks to be collected together.

For their first event only the rally cars used conventional hardtops. The race cars, however, were given full-length fastback tops, which eliminated the normal boot altogether. These tops, made in glass-fibre (there was no effective roll cage, as such things were not considered essential in the 1960s), were actually moulded from the prototype Spitfire GT's shell, which Michelotti had built in 1962/63. That car, of course, evolved into the GT6, which is described below, and it is not correct, therefore, to infer that the GT6 shape was developed from that of the Le Mans Spitfires – the reverse is true.

Left: ADU 7B, the most successful works Spitfire, won its class in the 1964 Tour de France, beating all the works Alpine-Renaults.

Below: By 1965 the works Spitfires – ADU5B, 6B, and 7B – had been honed into formidable little class-competitive rally cars.

For their second event, the rally Spitfires were converted to fastbacks, and they always appeared in this form afterwards (the conversion was expensive and extensive, and returning the cars to standard would have been quite impractical). Only on that second event – the 1964 Tour de France, where the only surviving Spitfire trounced what remained of the formidable Alpine-Renault works team to win its class in the ten-day 4000-mile event, to confound Alpine and delight Triumph's French importers – did the rally cars sport faired-nose bonnets, which they borrowed from the Le Mans cars for the occasion. This, incidentally, should convince the sceptics who think that the Le Mans cars were used on this lengthy race-cum-rally.

The Le Mans and the rally cars were always operated separately. Initially this was because Le Mans and the Alpine Rally were scheduled to clash in 1964, but it was always thought that the razor-edge tuned Le Mans cars should be in the care of the experimental department's engineers; this is where they were built, rebuilt and prepared in 1964 and 1965. The rally cars lived alongside the TR4s and Triumph 2000s in the normal competitions shop, and were just that little bit less specialised.

Three Spitfires started at Le Mans in 1964, two crashed and the third car finished 21st at 94.7mph, notching a radar-checked top speed of 133mph along the Mulsanne straight; it beat the works-entered Austin-Healey Sprite by no less than 125 miles. One car then won its class in the 1000km sports car race at Montlhéry that autumn, and of three cars which raced at Sebring in the 1965 12-hour race, two took second and third places in their class.

These were prepared to lightweight 1965 specification (GT6 boxes, thin-gauge frames and other details), and all four started at Le Mans in 1965. This time two cars finished in 13th and 14th places, at almost the same speeds as in 1964, but with a straight-line speed up to a remarkable 137mph. The rally cars failed to win honours in their first event, the 1964 Alpine Rally, by one minute, which was the margin by which Terry Hunter's machine missed a penalty-free Coupe des Alpes. In the Tour de France, as already mentioned, Hunter and Rob Slotemaker won their class

Right: The works Spitfire race cars were developed with top speed in mind, which explains why the front bumpers were removed, and why the size of the radiator cooling aperture was reduced.

Below: On the works Spitfire race cars, built-in brackets were added to the chassis, so that quick-lift jacks could be used to speed up the pit stops.

outlawed. At one time it was thought that the Le Mans cars might be converted to an altogether more exciting specification, which involved the use of highly-tuned six-cylinder engines and strut-type independent rear suspension. By the beginning of 1966 work on the first car was well advanced, with a team entry at Le Mans in prospect, but in the face of big cost estimates the project was then cancelled and the car was never completed. In the meantime, Bill Bradley carried out a works-supported sports car racing programme with one of the cars. This was subsequently written-off in a racing accident, and there was a quick substitution for one of the others which was gathering dust. In the end, however, the remainder were either 'used up' (Ray Henderson's words) or sold to private owners. As far as is known, only one or two cars still exist in anything like their original form.

triumphantly, and a few weeks later Hunter took a splendid second place overall in the Geneva Rally, with Thuner's sister car fifth. For 1965 one new car, in left-hand drive form, was built for the Finnish star Simo Lampinen to drive and this, like its 1964 sister cars, now had a revised bonnet with auxiliary and quartz-halogen headlamps mounted neatly on the nose.

In 1965 Slotemaker's car took a class second on the Monte, but in the Alpine Rally, where four 1296cc cars started, two finished first and second overall in the prototype category, after the more favoured Porsches and Alfas had dropped out with mechanical failures. Lampinen and Thuner were the drivers and they, too, had shared the fastest Le Mans car at the Sarthe circuit a few weeks earlier.

At the end of 1965, however, the rules of motorsport changed considerably, which effectively banned these cars, as items like light alloy bodies and alternative engine specifications were to be

One might ask what all the fuss was about. The answer, quite simply, is that this handful of Spitfires – there were precisely eleven in all if you count the car prepared and maintained for Valerie Pirie of the Stirling Moss Automobile Racing Team – were very highly developed, very effective and, for their engine size, quite incredibly fast. They proved once and for all that the swing axle rear suspension could be made to work really well if a soft ride was not considered essential, and they also proved that a car did not need a huge engine to be of interest to motorsport enthusiasts. They were cars which surprised their competition and they made many friends inside and outside the factory.

While all this competitions activity was in progress, the engineers were busy developing another major variant of the

Spitfire, though as often happens in large organisations, what appeared ready for sale to the public was not what was intended in the first place. By 1963, with the Spitfire in production and in great demand on both sides of the Atlantic, thoughts were turning towards making a GT version. This, as originally conceived by Michelotti and Harry Webster, would basically have been a Spitfire with much more luxurious trim, and with a permanent hardtop.

One prototype was completed by the end of 1963, which sported a very attractive and shapely fastback in pressed-steel, complete with a large upward-opening rear hatch. The directors thought that this car could be introduced at the 1964 motor shows, called simply the Spitfire GT, but by the spring of 1964 their attitudes were changing. The sales force did not think a four-cylinder car with such an unavoidable price premium could be sold in sufficient quantities, and they asked if a six-cylinder car could be built instead.

Although the Spitfire had originally been badged as a 'Spitfire 4,' which immediately led to the know-alls saying 'When will we be seeing the Spitfire 6?', there had not, at first, been any plans for such a version. However, the fact that the Vitesse had evolved so easily and smoothly from the Herald meant that a similar conversion could also be considered on the Spitfire.

In the meantime, Triumph learned that MG would be announcing a fastback MGB – the MGB GT – at the end of 1965, and this was the final factor in the decision to make a six-cylinder car. The one and only Spitfire GT, after a quick trip to Le Mans in the spring of 1964 (but not to race) was speedily converted to a six-cylinder 2-litre specification, and by May the board was being asked to approve the production tooling. The engine, incidentally, was never considered in 1596cc form, because thoughts of a 2-litre Vitesse were already being ventilated around the place.

The new car, soon named GT6 without dissension, matured rapidly, but unhappily for its reputation, Triumph was looking for refinement and a soft ride at the expense of roadholding and response. This was because its North American reception was considered most vital to its sales prospects. The suspension, therefore, was little altered from that of the Spitfire, and the damper settings were even softer. The engine, even though it was a snug fit under the bonnet (which needed only a sleek Jaguar-type bulge), was a long way forward, and the GT6's problem was that it had strong initial understeer which could easily be converted into something rather more alarming when the rear tyres let go.

The GT6 grew up rapidly in the late 1960s, giving birth to the re-skinned Mk III of 1970-1973.

The all-synchromesh gearbox (already blooded on competition Spitfires, and really the ancestor of the 1970s-style Dolomites, Spitfires and Morris Marina boxes) and the much more robust axle were fitted, the ratio being 3.27:1. Inside the car was a stylish facia with wooden paneling, a carpeted boot floor and many other luxurious touches.

The GT6 was quick – speeds of more than 100mph were easily reached – but there was no doubt that the handling was not liked in Britain. Although about 8000 GT6s would be produced in the first year (1966/67) the car could not be built for long without important changes being needed. In great haste, though not by ignoring the need for careful proving, a revised system was evolved for the rear suspension. It was rather expensive, but it was extremely effective.

The existing chassis and the same basic layout was retained, including the entire frame, the chassis-mounted differential and the transverse leaf spring. The drive-shafts, however, were no longer of fixed length (they had a rubber 'doughnut' part-way along their length, which absorbed both torque and plunge), and a complex but geometrically-correct reversed bottom wishbone now pivoted between the chassis frame and the wheel's hub-carrier. This 'lower wishbone' installation, as it was always known, completely cured the GT6 of its previous bad habits and turned the car into the 'mini E-Type' which it had always promised to become. The Mark 2 GT6 was also quicker due to a power boost helped along by the TR5's cylinder head and a more ambitious camshaft. From the autumn of 1968, and in spite of a price rise from £800 to £879 (basic), the car was a much better bargain.

The Mark 2, however, ran for only two years, as at the end of

From late 1970, all Spitfires and GT6s were built with a re-skinned body style, which included the sharply cut-off signature tail end.

accompanied by the first of the Vitesse 2-litre cars. This model (available, as usual, in saloon and convertible forms) used the GT6's engine, all-synchromesh gearbox and back axle, along with the wide road wheels and the bigger front disc brakes. The Vitesse 2-litre, predictably, suffered the same handling defects as did the original GT6, so when the GT6 was given its ingenious lower wishbone independent rear suspension, so was the Vitesse, which then became the 2-litre Mark 2. From autumn 1968, therefore, the Vitesse, complete with radial-ply tyres and a 104bhp engine, was a real little sports saloon and it behaved accordingly. Yet in the Triumph spectrum of new cars, which by 1968/69 was looking increasingly comprehensive and attractive, the Vitesse was overshadowed by more exotic cars like the fuel-injection TR5s and 2.5 PIs.

With the arrival of the Toledos and 1500s, and with the exciting prospect of the Dolomite ahead, the Vitesse was speedily run down. Although the GT6 would continue until 1973, and even the Herald until the autumn of 1971, the Vitesse was withdrawn in the summer of 1971.

Neither the GT6 nor the Vitesse can be judged an outright success in terms of cars sold or of profits generated, but they were both worthwhile extensions of the Herald and Spitfire themes that only Triumph's separate-chassis philosophy could accommodate. It is worth remembering that the Herald's layout was conceived in 1956/57 with ultimate versatility in mind, and in this it succeeded admirably.

1970 it was supplanted by the Mark 3, which included all the body engineering and style changes proposed for the Mark 4 Spitfire, such as the retooled bonnet and the cutback tail layout. In this form the GT6 continued to sell steadily, if not dramatically well, with production limited partly by the capacity of the single assembly track which had to accommodate Heralds, Vitesses and Spitfires. Its future, too, by the beginning of the 1970s, was tied closely to that of the Spitfire, and also to what imposts the North Americans proposed to heap on European car makers.

The Vitesse had also been more closely linked with the GT6 for some time. In its original 1596cc form, the saloons and convertibles were brisk, compact and profitable enough to keep in production. However, in 1963 there was stiff competition, particularly from Ford with its new Cortina GT, and it looked as if the Vitesse would need a boost in performance to keep it competitive.

When the cars were to have been used by the works competition department, it had been proposed that a triple-SU carburettor installation should be standardised for homologation purposes, but nothing came of this. Once the GT6 project got under way it made economic sense for the Vitesse to be brought into line with it as far as possible. There was no question of the chassis frame being altered (this had already been commonised, with important but minor changes, with the Herald frames), but the complete power train came in for careful attention.

When the GT6 was launched in October 1966 it was

As produced from 1970 to 1973, the GT6 Mk II was an attractive and extremely practical sporting hatchback.

'Sabrina' and a New TR

Finding a successor to the TR3 took a long time, much longer than it should have. Fortunately, however, Standard-Triumph started thinking about new models before the original TR had even reached maturity, which proved to be a very wise policy. The basic problem, of course, was that the TR2/TR3 was forging its own legend; whatever followed it would have to be at least as good, if not better, in all respects.

Perhaps if Alick Dick had not authorised special twin-cam engines to be built with an entry at Le Mans in mind, and perhaps if Harry Webster had not made sure that these engines could easily be 'productionised,' then the job could have been done much quicker. Even if the twin-cam engines had been physically no bulkier than the standard production unit, it would have helped. As it happened, two dimensions, 3¾in (the extra length of the twin-cam engine) and 6in (the extra length of wheelbase originally thought necessary to house it) caused no end of complication.

We must first backtrack to 1955/56, when the TR2/TR3 had at last established itself after a rather shaky start, the directors were beginning to look forward to what they hoped would be a rosy future for Standard-Triumph, and when the young members of the management team were beginning to think about more advanced cars for the 1960s.

There had been styling proposals for a new TR4 as early as the spring of 1956; this took the shape of a car quite a lot bulkier and more completely equipped than the existing two-seater cars, with four seats, Capri-style, and unheard-of luxuries such as wind-up glass windows. Still, no serious or acceptable work was done until Giovanni Michelotti was taken under contract in the summer of 1957.

As already recounted, Michelotti had met Harry Webster and Martin Tustin through his work for businessman Raymond Flower. Stunned by Flower's claim that he could get prototype bodies – painted, trimmed and decorated shells – in about two months, and complete cars in about three, they challenged him to organise the manufacture of a sporting 'dream car' on the Triumph chassis, subject to prior approval of styling drawings and sketches.

As Harry Webster said: "We still didn't know who Flower's genius was, but about ten days later he came back, laid out five or six sketches, and said, 'Which one would you like?' First of all we had to find out what it would cost, and when he quoted a price for the complete car, inside and outside, for around £3000, this knocked Tustin and I right back, not because it was expensive, but because by British standards it was very cheap, even for the 1950s.

"So we agreed to this, it was ready within three months, and it was only when we went to see the nearly completed vehicle in Italy that we discovered it was Michelotti. I was introduced to Michelotti when I went over there, and it didn't take me long to decide that we really ought to sign him up for our future work."

The 'dream car' – a very fashionable full-width creation, painted black and white, with such arresting features as a full-width grille and wind-up windows, not to mention the hooded headlamps and the pronounced tail-fins – was finished early in 1958 and was exhibited at the Geneva Motor Show in March of that year. Later it was brought to Coventry, given a British registration plate, and was used by members of the management to let them mull over its style and features.

Although there was never any serious intention to put this particular car into production, it served as an efficient sounding-board for the TR's future. In the form presented it had a shape which would certainly have dated too quickly, and it was altogether too luxurious for what Triumph thought it needed for its next new model. Further, it would have been an expensive body to tool-up for production. However, in the long-term it sparked off the idea that wind-up windows were quite practical for a TR if the styling suited them, and that this type of style in general would be acceptable. In the short-term, too, it provided the inspiration for the TR3A grille and nose, which was approved just before the end of 1956, for production during 1957.

Michelotti was therefore taken under contract, and apart from restyling work on the Standard Vanguard he shortly got involved in the Zobo (Triumph Herald) project. It would be some time before he could concentrate on a new TR, which was probably just as well. By then, the new racing engine had come on to the scene and was already beginning to cause problems.

It all stemmed from Triumph's successful showing at Le Mans in 1955 with the disc-braked TR2s. Although all three cars had finished, and finished well, they were not fast enough to challenge other cars in their 2-litre class, nor could they stop two complete teams of Porsches and Bristols from beating them in the team contest. Alick Dick was anxious for Triumph to make a better showing in future events, and demanded to know what could be done about it.

Ted Grinham, who knew nothing about competition cars, preferred to leave all this to Harry Webster, who knew quite a lot. Webster realised that Alick Dick's desire for Triumph to win that team contest could not be satisfied with the existing power unit (after all, it had been designed in 1945/46 and it had never been intended for racing), and therefore he proposed a new power unit. With the proviso that it should be as simple as possible, and with the far-sighted direction that it should be suitable for quantity-production if at all possible, Alick Dick agreed.

If all had gone well, Triumph could have been back at Le Mans in 1958, as the engine ran for the first time in 1957, but in the end the new cars would not be race-ready until 1959, despite being built in 1958. Work on the new engine, mainly done by Dick Astbury, took a long time to complete (if ever there was a production-car crisis, luxuries like competitions projects had to be put away for the time being).

The new unit, which Harry Webster reminded us was a high-performance test-bed for the latest die-casting techniques as much as it was a racing engine, was intended for the 2-litre category, because that was the racing class with which Triumph was familiar, and because it was a convenient production-car size if ever it had to be translated into quantity production. It was physically quite large, even though its cylinder dimensions – 90mm bore and 78mm stroke (1985cc) – were not far removed from the 83 x 92mm, 1991cc layout of the standard engine.

Because it had a five-bearing crankshaft, and because it was stressed with an eventual power output of 100bhp/litre in mind – in other words with a maximum output of 200bhp – the load-carrying castings were solid and rugged. The fact that it had a 'classic' twin-overhead-camshaft cylinder head, with the camshafts driven from the nose of the crank in the accepted manner, helped to make it a big and bulky engine; it was 3¾in longer than a TR3 pushrod engine, but at 438lb it was actually slighter lighter.

The construction was novel, in order to make the die-casting development simple. Harry Webster would have liked to make every major casting in light-alloy, but the pressure of development and the need to get it right first time meant that the crankcase/block was in cast iron. In general it was an intricate but extremely logical sandwich – made up of the sump, then lower crankcase, upper crankcase, block, water jacket and finally the cylinder head

– with through-bolts from the main-bearing caps to the cylinder head. The cylinder head layout was typical of its day, with two overhead camshafts, and valves operated by the popular method of coil springs and inverted 'bucket' tappets, the valves being opposed at an angle of 73 degrees. There were part-spherical combustion-chambers, single offset sparking plugs, and the inlet manifold stubs were cast in unit with the cylinder head. Carburation was by the rare twin-choke SU units (two chokes and two cylinders on a single twin-choke central casting), as being used on Coventry-Climax FPF racing engines of the period. For the most part, layout of the engine looked as if it might have been based on Climax, Jaguar, Ferrari or Maserati lines, but this, after all, was the accepted pattern for un-supercharged racing engines of the 1950s.

One visual detail made the 20X engine (for such was its code) stand out – literally – from its contemporaries. All the auxiliary drives were contained in the timing arrangements hidden behind the engine's front cover, and the sprockets at the nose of each camshaft had bulbous covers. Then, as now, most new projects attracted nicknames and the 20X engine was no exception. It just so happened that at the time one of the supporting characters in a popular Arthur Askey TV series was a girl with an extremely well-developed and attractive figure. It would be true to say that her bust was her most prominent asset, so it was hardly surprising that her stage name – Sabrina – was applied to the Triumph engine, and like all good pet names it stuck. Before long even the directors were using it.

Right from the start, Sabrina, though quite heavy, was also powerful, and it all looked very promising. For its first races the engine produced more than 150bhp at 6500rpm, at least 50 more than the output developed by the pushrod engines in the 1955 Le Mans cars, and probably 20 to 25 more than a super-tuned pushrod unit could manage while keeping its reliability.

But it was a physically big engine – too big, it was reasoned, for the existing chassis. But why were Triumph looking for a much more powerful TR when a more specialised sports racing car would have been better suited to Le Mans? The answer, very simply, was that the company always liked to link its racing efforts to the production-car programme – current or planned; an ultra-sleek prototype racing car, even in an event where such things were expected, would encourage the wrong image. This explains why, for instance, the 1955 Le Mans cars were virtually standard, and why the later Le Mans Spitfires would be recognisably based on the Spitfire road cars.

For the 20X's first Le Mans in 1959, it was agreed that the cars should look as much like TR3As as possible. However, to install the bulky Sabrina engine, the chassis frames needed to be lengthened (or so the engineers thought); new frames with many existing TR3A parts were laid-out on a 94in wheelbase, though with strengthened and deepened side-members. This was puzzling, as

Le Mans was always noted for its billiard-table surface, and the TR's big problem was that it was already heavy. No-one has ever given us a satisfactory explanation of the decision to build heavier frames when lightened units would have been perfectly adequate. On the Spitfires, a few years later, the lesson was learned, lighter frames were built, and no trouble was ever experienced.

The extra six inches on the wheelbase was accommodated in the region of the engine – effectively between the front suspension and the scuttle. A TR3A body-style was to be used (though with many glass-fibre panels and with specially swept windscreen and side-screens) and the body lines had to be altered slightly to suit – though as little as possible to preserve the 'standard-car' illusion.

Under the skin, the Sabrina engine was allied to a special heavy-duty back axle (which we now know used many Daimler SP250 parts – Salisbury being the supplier), specially cooled four-wheel Girling disc brakes, a front anti-roll bar and stiffer-than-usual suspension.

Their performance in the race was a disappointment, for three cars started and all three retired. One reason, in view of the lengthy build period, the use of glass-fibre bodies and the light-alloy components used freely in the engine, was that the race cars were very heavy. The lightest TR3S car weighed 2125lb; only four other cars in the race were heavier. Another feature impossible to justify was the use of fan blades on the engines (no car needs a fan when it spends nearly half the lap at or around its planned maximum speed), and in the race two cars retired because the blades fractured, puncturing the radiator shells, which swiftly cooked the engines.

Among the many proposals put up by Michelotti to produce a new-style TR for the 1960s, the Zoom prototypes of 1959/60 were extremely promising. Two such cars were built, with lengthened wheelbase versions of the TR3A chassis, both of them fitted with road-going versions of the Sabrina twin-cam engine at first. Shortly, however, they were abandoned in favour of the normal wheelbase Zest which was a visual restatement of this developing theme.

Because the aerodynamics were no better than the TR2s had been in 1955, the cars' maximum speed went up from about 120mph to 135mph, though faster acceleration helped the cars to complete laps in about 4 minutes and 45 seconds if pushed (Sanderson's car recorded 4 minutes, 46 seconds at 105.3mph). The team were desperately unlucky not to bring one car home in a very creditable position. After the two fan-blade failures had occurred, the third car (driven by Peter Jopp and Dickie Stoop) was called in to have them removed. It pressed on and was lying seventh behind two Aston Martins and four Ferraris when, after 22 of the 24 hours, the oil pump drive failed.

In the short term the 1959 Le Mans race was a public disaster for Triumph, though the good news for the engineers was that the 20X Sabrina unit had proved itself to be basically sound. The fan-blade failures had been caused by a combination of constant high speed, slight out-of-balance problems and ultimate fatigue, while the oil pump drive failure was a one-off problem, never repeated. If the engine was basically good enough to be raced for 24 hours, its prospects for road use looked good.

Meanwhile, the search for a TR4 – successor to the wildly-successful TR3A – was beginning to hot-up. Some of the members of the management were beginning to get very restless about the

time it was taking to agree on a new style. Way back in August 1957, with the TR3A trembling on the brink of quantity production, the directors had been considering a product plan for the next few years. Apart from approving an official start to the Zobo (Herald) project, they talked of a restyled notchback Standard Pennant (the 'Zeta'), and of a successor to the Standard Vanguard ('Zebu'); they also talked of a TR4 'Zest' for the very first time. At the time, this car might have had all-independent suspension and a completely new bodyshell, and could have been ready for production in 1959, but the massive investment in the Herald project put a stop to all this and the priority of the TR4 project slipped back for a time.

The Zest style however, soon took shape, and in the winter of 1957/58 Michelotti produced a hardtop two-seater sports car on the existing live-axle TR3A chassis, which used a borrowed Triumph Herald coupé roof, and in side view at least, it looked remarkably like the TR4 which would eventually mature. The Herald roof, incidentally, was a bolt-on item, and it was suggested that a soft top version of the car could easily be arranged.

At this time, Michelotti's little studio was extremely busy, as during 1958 he also found time to produce a smart fixed head coupé on the standard TR3A chassis, which was shown by Vignale on its coachbuilders' stand at the Turin show in November 1958. When first seen, this car had a drooping nose with faired-in headlamps and a radiator grille hidden under the front bumper, but the final version had a conventional nose and front wings, similar to those of Michelotti's later offerings to Triumph.

This car was actually put into production in Italy by Vignale as the Italia 2000 with a rolling chassis bought from Triumph in Great Britain. One car a day was built in 1959, with a coachbuilt steel body, but production slowed down and eventually ceased altogether in 1963 after about 300 examples (almost all of them with left-hand drive) had been built. Although the car did not influence Triumph's management, it certainly influenced what Michelotti himself would propose for a new TR4.

By the beginning of 1958, well before the first TR3S Le Mans car had been designed, the directors again returned to the subject of a TR4, and discussed a proposal that by mid-1959, or at the very least by the autumn, a car should be on sale. There would possibly be "a glass-fibre TR4 with the Sabrina engine, and ... a steel TR4 with the normal engine."

Nothing came of this, but during 1958, and into the winter of 1958/59, thoughts on a new car began to crystalise. A new project, 'Zoom' (Harry Webster's Z-prefix four-letter words were having a field day around this time), began to develop. Although its chassis

would be superficially similar to that of the production TR3A, there would be an extra six inches of wheelbase to accommodate the road version of Sabrina (this was before the engine had been publicly launched), the wheel track would be widened, and rack-and-pinion steering fitted.

In 1959, therefore, Michelotti delivered two prototype bodyshells to this brief, basically the same in concept but with different styling touches. Both his Zooms had conventional noses, with headlamps in the wings, while in side profile they looked much like his earlier Zest. One car had plain rocker-panels under the doors, while the other had more sculptured lines, which carried on to the tail behind the wheelarches. Both cars had twin-cam Sabrina engines installed for development purposes.

At this stage a decision was made about the future of the TR4. Although Zest was liked, Zoom was preferred, and by the beginning of 1960 it was decided to go ahead with that shape for production. The directors were also sure that they should (and could afford to) productionise the Sabrina engine, and were planning on 1000 such units for 1960/61, 2100 in 1961/62 and 2600 in 1962/63.

To reassure themselves of the public's reaction to the Zoom style, they concluded that four new Le Mans cars should be built for 1960. Two of the original TR3S bodies were scrapped, while one eventually found a home on a lengthened TR3A, with basically standard road-car equipment. After a very protracted, scruffy and controversial life, the remains of that car survived, yet it was still not restored as the 2010s approached the end.

The existing Le Mans chassis were modified (with wide tracks and rack-and-pinion steering) along with a spare frame unused in 1959, and four new bodies (glass-fibre in some sections, steel in others) were built using the simple-shaped derivative of Zoom as

All four of the TR5 race cars of 1960 and 1961 survive – and here were two of them, caught together, at the Roadster Factory in the USA in the 2000s.

When the Conrero was finally stripped out, preparatory to a rebuild, in the 2010s, its unique multi-tube chassis layout was exposed. This, it seemed, had originally been an Alfa Romeo project.

their pattern. Certainly these new cars were no less aerodynamic than the originals had been, but by the time they appeared in public their future usefulness was in doubt. Zoom, as a production shape, was about to be superseded.

The new Zoom-shaped Le Mans cars failed in 1960, though all three completed the 24 hours. None, however, qualified as an official finisher as they did not achieve the set target speeds, which were much higher than in 1959. Forgetting technicalities, however, the best of the three cars (crewed by Keith Ballisat and Marcel Becquart) should rightfully have been awarded fifteenth place, and actually averaged 89.56mph. Even when fit the cars were substantially slower than in 1959 (the regulations which insisted on taller windscreens cannot have helped) – the best lap being 4 minutes and 55.2 seconds at 102mph – and later in the race the valves stretched, all tappet clearance was lost, and power outputs suffered accordingly. The engines were running without fans and suffered no problems of any other nature. The weight, too, had crept up (the lightest weighed 2180lb), and the best recorded maximum speed was down to 128.6mph.

The breast-beating which followed the 1960 race can well be imagined. By now, Alick Dick had set his heart on that elusive Le Mans team prize, and even though he was having to impose cut after cut on departmental budgets during that awful financial period of 1960/61, the Le Mans programme was allowed to survive intact.

The result was a complete vindication of all his original hopes. In the 1961 race, three TR5 cars started and all three finished. In all major respects they were 'as 1960,' though the engines were marginally more powerful (about 155bhp). The best lap speed was cut by eight seconds (to 4 minutes 46.9 seconds, though this was no faster than the TR3S cars had achieved in 1959), and the best race average soared to 98.91mph, with a total distance covered of 2373 miles over the 24 hours. The cars finished ninth, eleventh and fifteenth (Keith Ballisat and Peter Bolton being in the leading car), and took that elusive team prize.

Following that successful outing, Leyland (who had been overseeing the project since the beginning of the year) closed down the department and the cars were sold-off to the United States, where some of them sometimes appeared at Triumph club meetings. Nothing, not even a spare engine, was retained by Triumph in Britain.

If only Standard-Triumph had continued being prosperous in 1960 and 1961, an even more ambitious Le Mans project was being planned for the future. In September 1960 the directors agreed that: "the Italian tuning expert, Conrero, is to build-up four new Le Mans cars for the 1961 race at an approximate cost of £25,000 ..." As it happens, the company's cash crisis caused the building of all but one of these cars to be cancelled, and the survivor was not completed until the Richardson-managed department had been closed down.

The 'Conrero' (as it was known at Triumph) combined all the TR5's normal Le Mans mechanicals in a multi-tubular chassis frame, topped by a lightweight light-alloy closed two-seater bodyshell, and had originally been produced by Conrero for Alfa Romeo, who had then cancelled its own Le Mans effort. The

If Standard-Triumph's finances had been in better shape, the factory had planned to enter three Conrero-designed, Sabrina-engined, coupés in the 1962 Le Mans 24 Hours race. In the end, only one car was completed, and never raced.

basic chassis design, with a much shorter wheelbase that the TR5, was styled by Michelotti, and the car was unique in that its Sabrina engine was fitted by Conrero with two twin-choke Weber carburettors, which were said to give it a real boost in performance. As front-engined competition cars go this one looked right, even when standing still, though it had certainly never been introduced to a wind-tunnel, and its potential could only be guessed-at. A real change in company policy would have been required for such an obvious prototype to be used in public with a Triumph badge on its nose, and that would probably have been an even greater stumbling block than any reliability problems likely to have been found on a new design.

Before the Zoom-shaped TR5 Le Mans car appeared at the French circuit in 1960, however, there were second thoughts about the future production TR4. With the company's business nose-diving into serious trouble it was decided to simply go for a new body-style on the existing TR mechanical layout, and to leave mechanical innovation for a more sunny future. Accordingly, plans to produce road-going versions of the Sabrina engine were frozen, and this automatically meant that the long-wheelbase chassis was not needed.

Michelotti was therefore asked to sort-out a finalised style which would use a TR3A chassis with the widened Zoom front and rear suspensions, and, of course, rack-and-pinion steering, but on the normal 88in wheelbase. In double-quick time he combined the best-liked of all the features offered so far, which meant using the scuttle, doors, centre-section and tail of the sculptured-variant Zoom, along with a widened and refined update of the original 1957/58 Zest nose. Such was the rush that the combined effort kept a Zest code (even though there was more Zoom in it), and the first proper prototype did not run until the first months of 1961, even though announcement was slated for September of that year.

In the meantime, and with all the indecision over TR4s going on, the company took another look at its long-running TR3A. By the spring of 1960 it was already clear that TR3As were being over-produced, and a steady but persistent cut-back of the build-rate began. Coincidentally, it also began to look as if the company could not then afford a new bodyshell for its sports car, so in a tearing hurry a mid-1960 proposal to build TR3Bs was concocted. These were to use a wide-track (ie TR4-type) chassis complete with rack-and-pinion steering, and the bodies were basically to be TR3A shells, but with restyled and rather more bulbous front and rear wings to provide adequate splash cover over the wheels, which had been pushed out by the increase in track.

Although the engineering department built two prototypes,

All the Michelotti TRs had their bodies pressed, assembled, painted and trimmed at the original Speke (Liverpool) factory between 1961 and 1976.

and although the directors gave approval for the cars to be built at their July 1960 meeting, the TR3B or 'Beta' never went ahead in this form. What did go ahead as a TR3B, in 1962, is closely related to the TR4 production start-up, and is described below.

By 1960, with the final restyle of the Zoom/Zest body going ahead, the TR4's introduction had been firmly set for the autumn of 1961. Whether or not the company could truly afford it, it realised that the TR3A was dying, and fast; by the end of 1961, it reasoned, it might as well be selling a new sports car instead of no sports cars at all.

The TR4 was to have the same basic chassis as that of the TR3A, altered in many details. The frame itself would only be altered at the front, where the suspension towers and details connected with them were spaced wider apart to accommodate the increased (49in) front track and support the rack-and-pinion steering. At the rear the increased track could simply be accommodated by lengthening the axle tubes and half-shafts, while retaining the existing semi-elliptic springs and mounting pads.

The standard engine was to be the 2138cc unit which had been optional on TR3As since 1959, though the 1991cc engine would continue as an option (although few TR4s would eventually be built with this engine). Behind the engine there was to be a newly-developed all-synchomesh four-speed gearbox using mainly TR3A mechanicals but with a completely new case. This extravagance would never have been justified for the TR4 on cost grounds if it had not also been intended for use in other future Triumph models.

The pressed-steel body, by Michelotti, was the car's most important feature. To be produced in its entirety by Standard-Triumph Liverpool (in the old Hall Engineering factory which the company had taken over at the beginning of 1960), it had a stylish full-width shape, and broke new ground for a sports Triumph with its wind-up door glasses and its novel hardtop. The hardtop was another of the inventive Michelotti's proposals, one which he had reputedly fashioned for a Vignale Ferrari a few years earlier, and made in two sections. At the rear a stout light-alloy casting doubled as the surround for the rear window and as a roll-over bar in case of accident. Bridging the gap between this casting and the screen rail was a pressed-steel roof-member which bolted into place. As an option there was a 'Surrey top' in place of the roof itself, which was a vinyl roof panel supported by a light frame. Who said that Porsche invented the targa top in 1966? Triumph had such a fitting in 1961, but didn't make as much fuss about it. Perhaps, on reflection, it should have done so.

The TR4 Zest was so completely different in layout and philosophy from what we now call the 'classic' or 'sidescreen' TRs that it was bound to cause controversy. When prototypes were shown to the North American Triumph importers their reaction was that the car had gone 'soft' rather too abruptly, and that there would be customer resistance to the new model, particularly at a higher price. As a fail-safe policy, and even though they knew that the TR3A was beginning to lose popularity in the United States, they elected to take a big allocation of TR4s for 1962 but asked if the company would mind carrying on building TR3As as well!

That wasn't easy, as the TR4 had taken over the production engineers' attention, but as the main items involved were chassis frames and bodyshells (much of the rest would be shared with the TR4), and as both suppliers – Sankey and Mulliners/Forward Radiator – confirmed that they could supply further sanctions, its request was agreed. The biggest single problem was over gearboxes, as the TR4 was going to use the all-synchromesh design which had attracted a great deal of investment capital.

As it happens, only 3331 of these new cars (retrospectively called TR3B by Triumph enthusiasts, even though such a name does not appear in company archives) were built, all in eight months during 1962. Even so, there were two quite distinct series. The first, or 'TSF' cars (to use their chassis-number prefixes), were

After producing variations on a theme, Michelotti finally produced this very smart body style for the TR4 (which was coded 'Zest' at the development stage) in 1961. (Courtesy D M Williams)

away at the costs. Even though the philosophy behind the design was one of increased sophistication, Leyland wanted to know if the wind-up windows could be replaced by canvas side-screens, and considered canceling the all-synchromesh gearbox.

Neither idea got very far – it was soon discovered that the wind-up windows were actually the cheapest method available for the new body, and the long-term advantages of having an all-synchromesh gearbox (with implications for future Triumphs) soon became obvious.

What is surprising is that there was never any doubt about the new two-piece hardtop design which, with its big alloy casting around the back window, was much more costly than it might have been. Another feature which survived, even though it would be a considerable advance on anything offered by the MG, Austin-Healey, and even Jaguar rivals, was the adjustable face-level ventilation.

Once the decision to make the TR4 had finally been taken, tooling was completed as soon as possible. The entire bodyshells were to be pressed and assembled (also painted and partly trimmed) at the Hall Engineering factory in Liverpool. Its previous connection with Triumph, before takeover, had been in the supply of Herald body components (notably bonnet assemblies), and this was to be the company's first major motor car assembly job. Press tools for the car were completed by Auto Body Dies of Dunstable, which was a subsidiary of Hall. Considering the group's deteriorating financial position while the TR4 was being developed it was brought into production remarkably quickly. The final body-style was not approved until the autumn of 1960, yet the press tools and assembly jigs were completed by the following summer. The first production car rolled out of the new Canley assembly hall in August, and the car was publicly released at the beginning of September 1961. It is worth noting that Zoom had been slated for production start-up in March 1961 when discussed by the directors

in every way like the obsolete TR3As, and were sold with crash-first-gear transmissions and the 1991cc engine as standard. There were 530 of those. The other 2801 cars, the 'TCF' series, were built to an altogether more interesting specification, complete with the 2138cc engine and the all-synchromesh TR4-type gearbox. Both cars, of course, used the original narrow-track TR3A type chassis.

Yet, in a way, this car was unnecessary. The Americans took to the TR4 in a big way, and virtually turned their backs on the good old TR3As and TR3Bs. Even though the TR3Bs with TR4 mechanicals were fine cars, lower in price at $2365, and have become prized collectors' items in recent years, it was not until the first months of 1963 that the last TR3B was sold in North America. Without the TR4, which after all looked very smooth and modern compared with the hairy-chested TR3A, perhaps the interim car would have been more popular.

Although Leyland put an immediate and short-lived freeze on all capital projects when it took over Standard-Triumph early in 1961, it was a matter of days before it agreed to go ahead at full speed with the TR4 Zest. Considering that Standard-Triumph was losing money at the rate of £600,000 a month at the turn of 1961, and that the total production tooling costs for the TR4 were now totting up to £933,000, this was a real declaration of faith in the new project. The Spitfire (Bomb) project, incidentally, was to be approved in July 1961 – two major new sports cars being committed to large-scale investment in the same year!

Not that this was Leyland's final word on the TR4. Although the company liked the basic concept it was still anxious to pare in April 1960, and that as late as July both Zoom and Zest were ongoing and parallel projects, provisionally to be named Vitesse and Dolomite, respectively! When Sir John Black had taken control of Triumph in 1945 he had also taken over the trademarks retained by the old independent concern. Both Dolomite and Vitesse would eventually be used on important quantity-production Triumphs, but other names such as Scorpion and Southern Cross were ignored. From 1973, the Scorpion name was used for one of the light-alloy armour-protected and (originally) Jaguar XK-engined tanks being manufactured by Alvis, another British Leyland subsidiary.

The Liverpool facility, therefore, was becoming increasingly important to the group, and it certainly made an efficient job of the Zest body supplies. Special 12-car transporters were acquired so that shells could be delivered in bulk by road. By the middle of 1962, when TR4 production was going ahead flat-out, one of these transporters would be leaving Liverpool for Coventry every hour of the working day.

Although the Herald 1200 was the first new Triumph model announced after the traumas of the Leyland takeover, the TR4 was the first really new shape the world saw in the following months. Leyland had had time to make various reassuring statements about the company's future, and there had been the encouraging display at Le Mans to add to the good name of Triumph's sports cars. The new TR4 car got a very friendly reception from the world's press, even if one wag noted it as 'Alick Dick's last Triumph' (the managing director had been removed from office, very suddenly, only the week before).

Apart from those who wanted a rugged TR to be replaced by another rugged TR (and their numbers would diminish rapidly in the ensuing months), most observers and dealers agreed that this new car was a fine effort. In one swift and effortless bound it moved the Triumph sports car firmly up the market, and with a hardtop fitted it brought saloon-car comfort to sports car motoring. Not only were there well-fitting doors and excellent vision (that back window was huge), but there was an excellent fresh-air heater as one of the many options.

Not only did the new body look smart and modern, but it was also practical. The boot was larger, there was more space – lengthwise and across – in the passenger compartment, and the windscreen was not only bigger, but well-curved and with laminated glass. The body was also rather lower than that of the TR3A, and the headlamps were nicely integrated into the full-width grille. The bonnet was also full-width – from wing crown to wing crown, side to side – hinged at the front instead of the scuttle/bulkhead, and so low that it had to include a streamlined power-bulge to give clearance for the dashpots of the twin SU carburettors. These did not come close to fouling the panel when the engine was at idle or running smoothly, but they would have made contact when the unit rocked hard on its mountings under acceleration.

It is worth recalling that there might also have been a six-cylinder version of the car (the same 1998cc 'six' developed for the Standard Vanguard – and the future – but in tuned form) if Triumph's late 1950s plans had come to fruition, and this engine would not have needed a bonnet bulge.

Predictably, there was no mention of the twin-cam 20X Sabrina engine as a high-cost option, as it would have been an expensive tooling proposition with little prospect of achieving substantial sales for the company. Its future had never looked rosy once Leyland took over, but its prospects could not have been helped by the public's reaction to, and MG's experiences with, the MGA Twin-Cam. This car had been announced in the summer of 1958, before the 20X had been publicly revealed as a racing unit, but it was withdrawn in the spring of 1960 due to all manner of service problems. Even though the Twin-Cam was an extensive conversion of an existing unit, MG only sold 2111 Twin-Cam cars; since the MG engines were built in Coventry the grapevine soon let Triumph know what the problems were all about.

There was also the engine installation problem, but this – to most people's surprise – turned out to be a massive red herring. Road-going

Although the TR4 of 1961 had a completely new body style, under the skin much of the running gear was developed from that of the TR3A.

6206 VC was originally a standard TR4 when built and registered in 1962, but was then used by the factory stylists for many tasks involving proposed face-lifts for future models.

versions of the 20X with different cylinder heads, milder camshaft profiles, twin single-choke SU carburettors and about 120bhp, had been fitted to the Zoom prototypes without problems, but these cars had been designed around the engine, and featured the longer 94in wheelbase. In the winter of 1961/62, however, with the TR4 already in production, it was decided to try to squeeze a 20X Sabrina engine into a production car. To most people's surprise (and delight) the engine shoe-horned itself comfortably into the existing space once the auxiliaries, cooling pipes and the chassis frame's detachable front suspension support tube had been reworked. So the extra long wheelbase had not been necessary after all!

Even so, and in spite of the fact that Martin Tustin, who had by then become President of Standard-Triumph Inc in North America, made brave 'could-be' statements about the 20X's future. This was no more than window-dressing, as the decision had already been made to abandon it.

Although the Laycock overdrive was to be continued as an option (it was very popular and the majority of cars were built with overdrive) the TR4, like the TR2/TR3, was never offered with automatic transmission. Prototypes had been built on both models, but in each case there were installation problems, as the Borg-Warner Type 35's torque converter was quite a lot bulkier than the normal clutch bellhousing, which would have necessitated a new type of gearbox cover, a repositioned handbrake, realigned pedals, and rather less space for feet and legs. The prototypes had been shipped over to the United States, where it was thought that most of the demand would occur, but the response from company staff was

not encouraging. At that time the Americans wanted their sports cars to have manual transmission, and left lazy motoring for the type of cars produced in Detroit. The automatic MGB, too, was a commercial failure. Later, in the 1970s, this attitude was to change, and a fair proportion of automatic TR7s were delivered to North American (and other) customers.

The introduction of the TR4 and, equally as important, its easy transition into full-scale production, made a dramatic difference to the TR's fortunes. Whereas the good old TR3A had virtually died as production and assembly was being switched to the new assembly hall, the TR4 came into it right from the start. Before the end of 1961 nearly 2500 TR4s had been delivered (only 10 of them to British customers), and in 1962 this jumped to nearly 15,000, with nearly 1000 released to the home market. It was not that more cars could not have been sold at home, but the lion's share was needed for export territories. Although the TR3A's frenetic 20,000-plus year of 1959 would not be surpassed until the TR7 came to maturity in 1976, the TR was back in favour with a vengeance. Almost everyone liked it, though on the one hand there were still those who complained that the TR had gone soft (they went out and bought TR3Bs instead), and on the other there were those who thought it was not soft enough. One recurring comment about the TR4, which would obviously need attention in time for the next major improvements, was that the ride was too hard and the roadholding not up to scratch. Once the smooth MGB had been announced in the autumn of 1962 the comparisons made were rarely in the TR4's favour. But there were few complaints about the lusty 2138cc engine, and almost everyone loved the new ventilation arrangements. The Surrey-top feature – the use of a vinyl panel in place of the removable hardtop one – never really caught the public's imagination. However, as Lyndon Mills said a few years ago, "most people never bothered to read their handbooks and discover that the hardtop's roof panel could be removed. If we'd reintroduced the feature as a novelty on the TR6 I bet we would really have had something to sell!"

Harry Webster and the team at Fletchamstead were already thinking about a successor to the TR4 (by the end of 1962 his fellow directors had started nagging him in formal meetings), but first of all they had an intriguing sideline to sort-out for themselves. Standard-Triumph, flying in the face of the general rule that it is always better to let a supplier do the job than tackle it yourself, had decided to design its own carburettor!

"It all started in the 1950s," Harry Webster told us, "when we were getting our TR supplies from SU in Birmingham. SU, as you know, was controlled by BMC, and although it had a jolly good production in that constant-vacuum device, it knew it and it didn't play fair. For a set of carbs for the TR3, for instance, I know that we were having to pay twice as much as MG was paying for the same things.

"So here we were, cutting costs wherever we could, and yet really we were wasting pounds on carburettors from SU. It really got my goat, so in the end I set my chaps to think up something new that we might use for ourselves."

'Something new' was the design of a carburettor, something not tackled by a major manufacturer for many years (and it would not happen again until Ford started building its own components in Northern Ireland in the 1970s), and it was a project riddled with potential problems. Webster knew that he preferred the constant-vacuum type of instrument (where the mass flow of air through the choke automatically thrusts a piston out of its way and helps itself to the correctly metered amount of fuel), but he knew that SU had certain patents which made it difficult for a competitor to evolve a similar design.

Nevertheless, this was done, mainly because Standard had gained a good deal of expertise in carburettor design and development through its wartime contacts with Claudel-Hobson (whose units were made in large quantities in Coventry). A design was worked-up which kept the best (non-patented) features of the SU design, and included details which allowed the rising piston and needle to be operated in a completely novel way. By the beginning of 1960 the new instrument was performing well in prototype form, but Standard-Triumph then had to decide whether it could afford to build it at all (capital investment was going to be considerable, and the times were increasingly hard for the firm), and even if there was anywhere within its empire where such a delicate job could be tackled.

For a time, the second problem was solved by handing over the project to Alford and Alder (whose Hemel Hempstead-based factories had been taken-over at the beginning of 1960), but even this company was not at all sure it could tackle the job correctly.

In the end Alick Dick, in one of the last major jobs he carried out before leaving Standard-Triumph, decided to indulge in a bit of power politics. On the one hand, he opened negotiations with the Amal carburettor company in Birmingham (it was controlled through Marston Radiator by the IMI combine), which was looking for work, while on the other hand he offered to hand over the design to Zenith on the condition that Standard-Triumph would be guaranteed the first supplies, and of course a good fee for the design rights.

As Alick Dick told us with an impish smile, "of course it was all great stuff because we knew we had a potential winner. Either company could have done the job. Amal was really looking round for new business – the British motorcycle industry was already running down. We could have taken over Amal – I'm sure IMI would have been willing to sell-out.

"So we told Douglas Richards, Zenith's chairman, that if he decided not to do the deal with us we would go ahead, buy-up Amal, and soon we'd be his competitors. And of course at that time we did a lot of business with Zenith (it made Solex carbs, too) for our other models.

"Zenith took over the design from us, prepared it for production, and that's how the Zenith-Stromberg carburettor was born!"

The name Stromberg, in this connection, had no mystic significance. It was a trademark taken over by Zenith some years earlier (there were Stromberg carburettors on many famous between-the-wars cars, including the Austin Sevens), and it was not, at the beginning of the 1960s, in current use. Later, the carburettor became generally known as the Zenith CD unit (CD = Constant Depression), and it gained a very good reputation, particularly where USA-specification anti-emission engines were concerned.

The irony of all this is that although it was Standard-Triumph who invented and partly developed the Zenith-Stromberg carburettor, the instrument was rarely found in its late 1970s line-up. As part of the British Leyland car conglomerate, of which the SU company was also one of the constituents, Triumph tended to use more and more SU installations (and even Lucas fuel-injection) in those years. One presumes that, as 'one of the family,' the prices charged were more reasonable.

Since the CD unit had been developed as an SU-replacement for Triumph's sports cars, it was reasonable to see it first used on a TR. Tested and approved on prototypes in 1961 and 1962, the first quantity-production Zenith-Strombergs were fitted to a batch of 100 TR4s built towards the end of 1962, and the SUs were completely banished during 1963. There was virtually no difference in performance between an SU-equipped and a Zenith-equipped TR4 engine (even though the Zenith had much more efficient-looking inlet manifolds) – factory testers could not pick out which engine they had without lifting the bonnet to take a peep.

The Zenith's attachment flange, incidentally, was the same as that of the SU, and Zenith had done this for a very good reason. Not only could the company's existing inlet manifolds be used if it should decide to abandon SU, but Zenith could offer its new-fangled carburettors as an after-sales accessory.

At a casual glance one might think that the TR4 soldiered on for more than three years without major change (though a walnut dash was added later for America) but this was not the case. The car, after all, had been put into production so rapidly that certain features planned for use were not ready in time. After

Late in the 1950s, Harry Webster sent Ray Bates and a small team of engineers to think about future Triumph sports cars. One of their earliest projects was to develop this cheap-and-cheerful independent rear suspension layout.

about 4000 cars had been built (in the early spring of 1962) the front-suspension geometry was changed, something denoted by the use of a smoothly-curved top wishbone, and at about the same time, the definitive TR4 braking system was fitted, with smaller and lighter Girling front brake calipers. Towards the end of 1962, too, the seating design was radically changed. Early cars had seats looking identical to those used in the TR3A, but the new design, with its flatter squabs and cushions, would then continue in basic form on non-federal TRs until the TR6 was withdrawn in 1976.

For all this, there had always been a feeling inside the company that the TR4 could only be considered as an interim model. If financial crisis had not intervened when it did, a car to replace the TR3A might have been more complex, technically more advanced and in general more exciting. Even though the TR4 sold well (more than 40,000 examples would be sold before it was superseded), management were actively looking for ways to improve it within months of its launch.

The road-testers, in Europe and in the United States, were almost unanimous. They liked the new style and they favoured the type of equipment. They were satisfied, if not overwhelmed, with the performance. But none of them liked the suspension; certainly sports car standards were improving rapidly.

The new steering, so precise and so light, showed up the rest of the suspension's lack of refinement, and it was cars like the new MGB and the latest Alfa Romeos which proved that sports cars didn't have to have hard springing to succeed. For the TR4, the problem was always at the rear, where the chassis frame ran under the back-axle, and effective axle and wheel movement was severely limited. 'Bump steer' was the phrase bandied about, a trait which is all very well if you like that sort of thing, but one rather shown-up by smoother-riding cars from the opposition.

It was not that Standard-Triumph was against independent rear suspension (it had, after all, been in production with such systems

In 1965, the TR4A succeeded the TR4, with a virtually unchanged style, though with more power, independent rear suspension on most versions, a new front grille, and chrome stripes along the side of the shell.

When the TR4A took over from the TR4 in 1965, no body pressings changes were made to the shell, but enthusiasts could immediately identify it by the new grille, the new turn/indicator lights, and the chrome embellishment along the flanks.

was vastly different from the car it was to replace. The TR4A was as different, in its own way, from the TR4, as that car had been from the TR3A. It was yet another step along the transitory path which was to convert the rugged little TR2 into the smooth and thoroughly modern TR6.

Webster's team was faced with one over-riding problem – although they had been asked to design an independently-sprung TR, they also had to make provision for the United States, where the cars would still be sold with a solid axle. No matter how much pressure was applied, the North American importers insisted that they could still sell TRs with live axles at the right price, that ultimate roadholding was not yet critical to sales over

since 1959, and the Spitfire also had IRS), but that up to then there had been the twin bogeys of extra cost and resistance from USA importers. Although independent rear suspension had first been mentioned on a TR project in 1955 (and a prototype was built in 1957), and it was a serious proposal for the TR4 at first (and not abandoned until 1960), the car still went ahead with the conventional layout.

By the end of 1962 Harry Webster had been instructed to devise independent suspension for the TR, though the North American import organisations were still saying that they could sell cars without it. The directors asked Webster what sort of scheme he would propose, and whether this could be adapted to a TR4, but Harry responded that an easy conversion would not be possible and that in any case he wanted to wait to see how the all-independent 'Barb' – the Triumph 2000 – settled down.

There was no way that such a radical redesign on the basis of the TR4 could be completed without the car changing its character, and therefore the TR4A project was automatically born. It was one of those cars which evolved steadily until the completed product

there, and that IRS was bound to be more costly. Accordingly it was agreed that the new chassis would make provision for both layouts, and that both versions would be available in the United States. It was not considered practical to retain the TR4's chassis for the live axle TR4A.

The new chassis frame had a radically different layout from its predecessors. The type of independent rear suspension chosen was the semi-trailing wishbone-plus-coil-spring design already tested and found to be satisfactory on the new big Triumph 2000 saloon. Car to car, parts were not interchangeable, but the philosophy was adopted intact. Purely for convenience of installation, the TR4A's damping would be by lever-arm units, whereas the higher 2000 saloon would be using long telescopic units. For the independently-sprung version a massive pressed-steel bridge-piece supported the differential casing and provided abutments for the coil springs. On live axle cars the bridge-piece was omitted, and long semi-elliptic leaf springs were used.

When the TR4A prototypes were ready for the road, one was loaned to managing director Stanley Markland, who pronounced the new chassis "safe for 120mph," after which he began to demand more power for the next model! On the TR4A, the lack of a dramatic power advance over the TR4 was a bit of a problem. Tradition, once again, coloured the decision to retain the ageing wet-liner 2138cc unit, though it has to be admitted that at this stage the alternative six-cylinder unit was neither powerful nor torquey enough for it to be viable. Experiments with six-cylinder TRs continued, but they would not mean anything for another couple of years.

At one stage it was proposed that the wet-liner 2138cc engine should be supplanted by a 93mm bore 2499cc dry-liner version (the change was not too expensive to contemplate), but although prototypes were built and tested, they never gave the increases in power and torque which had been hoped, and in spite of the fact that brave words were spoken about them being smoother than before, in some quarters it was alleged that there had been a considerable loss in refinement. With the end of the Healey 100/4 in 1956 the days of the thumping 'big four' had virtually ended, and Triumph reluctantly agreed with this. In its place the 2138cc engine received its final boost, to 140bhp at 4700rpm.

The TR4A was phased-in smoothly and without major dramas at the beginning of 1965. Body production at Liverpool was barely affected as changes were confined to a new grille, decoration and badging, along with new body-to-chassis mountings. On announcement the TR4A was well-received, not least because the technical press is always very happy to see its criticisms accepted, and because they always like to make discreet displays of 'we told you so' at the results. However, this was yet another 'first' for Triumph. Although all-independent suspension British sports cars were not sensationally new – apart from the Spitfire there was, of course, the Jaguar E-Type – it meant that the entire passenger-car range, from the Herald 1200 to the Triumph 2000, had four-wheel independent suspension. In 1965, and for some time to come, no other British company could match that.

In spite of the fact that it had unavoidably put on weight as it grew older (a TR4A weighed 2240lb compared with 2050lb for a TR3A), the TR continued to be a successful competition car.

After Leyland took control of the business in 1961 it allowed the Le Mans entry to go ahead, with great success, and then abruptly closed the competition department. Ken Richardson was dismissed, the mechanics were dispersed to other jobs, and the special racing TR5s languished in a storeroom. Along with the Conrero coupé, they would be sold-off to North America at the end of 1962.

Marketing pressure for competition, however, was intense, and a new department, this time directly under Harry Webster's control instead of being in conflict with him, opened in February 1962. The budget was tiny (nominally, it was a mere £12,000 in 1962), and the programme was restricted, but the intentions were serious. A team of powder-blue TR4s were prepared, and progressively modified to make them competitive in an increasingly fierce rallying scene which had seen the last works TR3As nearly outclassed in 1960.

In two seasons they had little luck, sometimes because of breakdowns and crashes, but usually because of two factors – the use of excessively rough roads on some events, and intense competition from Porsche and Austin-Healey. Even by the end of 1963, when in performance and specification they were as quick as a Richardson-prepared car could have been in 1958, they could not hope to challenge for outright wins.

Mechanically, much could be done to make the cars lighter, stronger and faster. Every skin panel could be light-alloy, the window 'glass' could be Perspex, trim and fittings could be removed and many details discarded. On the technical side, much could be – and was – done to make engines more powerful. The 2.2-litre's output was boosted from 100bhp to about 130bhp, first by using a gas-flowed cylinder head and free-flow tubular exhaust manifold, then by a high-lift camshaft (this had never been attempted in the Richardson era) and finally with the use of two twin-choke Weber carburettors. Gear ratios were altered, limited-slip differentials tested and standardised, sturdy under-chassis protection developed, and roadholding improved.

The cars' individual best performance was in the Alpine Rally of 1962, when Mike Sutcliffe's car took an unpenalised Coupe des Alpes, its class and fourth place overall. Both Jean-Jacques Thuner (Geneva Rally in 1962) and Vic Elford (Tulip and Alpine Rallies in 1963) put up fine individual shows only to be frustrated by mechanical breakdowns or driver error. Elford's performance on the Tulip, however – third fastest on scratch timing behind a 4.7-litre Ford Falcon and a 3-litre Austin-Healey – ranks as one of the best TR performances of all time, even though the handicap system weighed against the car's overall position.

Team prizes were gained in Europe – the RAC Rally in 1962 and the Tulip Rally in 1963 – and in Canada – the Shell 4000 Rally in 1964 – but the cars were beaten in the end by the rough roads which they were being asked to tackle. Only the Alpine remained of the old 'road races'; even the Liège, which now rushed between Spa and Bulgaria and back again, had degenerated into a high-speed rough-road event which low-slung sports cars hated most of all. For these a big strong saloon was ideal, and in 1964 the Triumph 2000 proved to be just the job for the factory's team.

In the United States, particularly with cars prepared under the direction of 'Kas' Kastner, the marque's fortunes were more successful. Apart from the very few international races like the 12 Hours of Sebring, where a production sports car stood little chance of success against the brutish racing cars from Ferrari and Porsche, most of the events were to SCCA regulations, where the classes and regulations were sorted to make the competition as tight and close as possible. Engine sizes, even price categories, meant little – the

SCCA committee was anxious to make it as easy for a TR driver as for a driver of a Cobra, Ferrari or even an older model to be competitive and win. If one type of car proved to be too good one year, for the next year it would be compulsorily moved up to the next, more powerful, class!

As with Brooklands, the trick was to find a competitive car, wring-out all its secrets, make sure that it was fast enough to beat its opposition, but not so fast as to be embarrassing, and have the very best driver who could excel in 'traffic' or in difficult conditions. In 1962, and for years to follow, the combination of a TR supported by the importers, preparation masterminded by Kastner (who was a positive wizard where engine tuning was concerned) and driving by Bob Tullius, was supreme.

Kastner had been an SCCA racing driver himself and he and his cars were so good at one stage that unofficially he was warned-off by the organisers. Like Mark Donohue, in later years and in a different car, he had the 'unfair advantage', and knew all the tricks. In California, backed by a prolific and talented motor-racing fraternity, he could prepare engines the likes of which the factory at Coventry could not match. It has to be said, in their defence, that engines for sprint events were never needed in Britain and Europe, whereas Kastner knew little about the type of units needed for day-after-day motoring. By the time he had finished with the wet-liner 2.2-litre engine it was capable of about 150bhp; if that sort of engine could have lasted an Alpine Rally it would have made the TR4s competitive for outright victory again!

Apart from the Kastner-Tullius partnership, there was also time for one entry to be made at Sebring, in 1963. Three cars started and two finished first and second in their 2½-litre GT class. It was as much as could ever have been hoped.

On the road, however, neither the TR4 nor the TR4A was as fast as some critics expected. A TR4A, in fact, was very little quicker than the TR3A, with its optional 2.2-litre engine, had been in 1959, and even by comparison with the TR2s of 1953 there had not been a dramatic improvement. The fuel consumption possibilities (not critical on a sports car, but significant for a car which was originally so frugal) had deteriorated. The TR4A, in short, was not as outstanding as the 'classical' TRs had once been. Triumph's sales department began to get reaction on this score from all round the world, not least from Europe, where great lengths of new motorways had made continuous high speeds possible (and such antics were neither economically crippling nor were they considered anti-social in the mid-1960s).

The designers and product-planners were therefore asked to consider yet another change to the TR formula, but this time they would have to achieve a quantum leap in performance. With the famous old engine at the end of its development life (and having been there since the end of the 1950s), something drastic would have to be done about this. With the Triumph 2000 in mind, and with the experience of competition behind him, Harry Webster set his team to do just that.

Leyland Takes Over

Standard-Triumph's first move to preserve its independence probably sealed its fate. This, at first sight contradictory, statement is borne by the facts. It was the takeover of Mulliners, the Birmingham bodybuilders, which brought on the crisis with Massey-Harris-Ferguson, and it was the selling-off of tractors in response to this which eventually hastened Standard-Triumph's cash crisis of 1960. Thereafter, Alick Dick and his directors had no choice; they had to find a partner or their company would rapidly be forced out of business.

During the 1950s Triumph had become the dominant marque in Canley, and in only five years Standard-Triumph found itself with a most exciting and gratifying sporting-car image. The Standard cars, on which John Black had based the company's vast expansion since the end of the 1920s, were completely overshadowed. That was the good news. The bad news was that profits from car manufacture were still hard to come by, and the situation was very worrying.

Alick Dick spent much of his time between 1954 and 1960 looking for a partner to secure Standard-Triumph's future, but he also encouraged a policy of expansion by acquisition. Not only would this make Standard-Triumph financially more attractive to a suitor in the long run, but it would also help to make it independent of major suppliers who were already being taken over by rivals.

Selling off the Ferguson tractor-manufacturing operation had been a good move in one sense, for it liberated a great deal of cash and offered prospects of a quiet corporate life, but it upset the company's balance for a time, and left it vulnerable to outside pressures. The money made available by shrugging off the Banner Lane operation was used as rapidly as possible to buy-up suppliers; it was a classic 'dash for growth,' which might have succeeded if the country's financial climate had been right.

In 1958 Alick Dick had told his directors that to remain competitive Standard-Triumph should be capable of making 261,000 vehicles (of which 100,000 should be tractors) by 1960/61. The big new assembly hall in Canley and the 'green field' site at Liverpool, close to Hall Engineering, were both needed to make that sort of figure practical. Even after the tractor business had been sold, the sales departments were talking about a selling potential of nearly 185,000 by 1960/61.

The euphoria lasted until the spring of 1960, when it was clear that things were starting to go wrong. Sales in Britain and in North America were not meeting expectations, and at the very time when Standard-Triumph's operations had been geared up for making more private cars it found that they were not needed after all. In Britain, for instance, the nation's economy was fast becoming 'overheated,' and a series of measures (including more expensive hire-purchase and credit) took the edge off the retail trade. More anti-inflationary measures, including increased taxation, would follow.

While capital was pouring out of Standard-Triumph in exchange for new buildings and facilities, the cash-flow situation began to worsen. Projects were either frozen, postponed or even cancelled. The replacement for the Standard Vanguard (which will be analysed later) was put off yet again, and the complicated TR3A replacement programme was drastically simplified. Nevertheless, this did not stop the company buying a £32,000 Cessna light aircraft for travel between the far-flung factories.

To replace the deferred Vanguard-replacement project, Alick Dick now started talking to the American Motors Corporation. It was interested in breaking into Europe with a much altered version of its Rambler American compact car. Very small by American standards, it was about the same size as a Vanguard (one inch longer, two inches wider and slightly shorter in the wheelbase), and fortunately it was due to be restyled for 1961. The original 1958 car had been depressingly dull, but the new car, if not exciting, was at least up to the minute in its concept.

The deal proposed to Standard-Triumph was that the Rambler American bodyshell and basic suspensions should be assembled in Coventry (this meaning that very little capital cost would be involved), and that the design should be altered to make provision for the new Vanguard six-cylinder engine and the entire choice of manual, overdrive and automatic transmissions. Fortunately for us, none of this ever matured, as it would have done nothing for Standard-Triumph's reputation. What Michelotti thought of this proposal is not known, but it can be imagined.

By November 1960 Standard-Triumph's position was desperate. Though profits for the year ending in the summer of 1960 were soon to be announced at £1.8 million (after tax), the company was already in the red and the situation was deteriorating daily. The fact that Alick Dick and Mike Whitfield had already lunched with Sir Henry Spurrier and Donald Stokes of Leyland Motors must have been encouraging. Ostensibly this meeting had been to discuss some amalgamation of interests in overseas territories, and conversation had been limited to these subjects, but under the surface there had been hints of a possible get-together on a massive and total scale.

Leyland Motors, in fact, was looking for ways to expand its operations. It was already a major influence in the commercial-vehicle industry, and it wanted to get back into private cars. Get back? Yes, for Sir Henry Spurrier had a long memory, and could recall not only when a handful of exquisite eight-cylinder Leyland cars had been built in the 1920s, but that Leyland had once controlled the destinies of Trojan.

By November, Leyland had decided to mount a takeover bid for Standard-Triumph, with or without Alick Dick's blessing. As soon as Dick came back from a visit to American Motors in Detroit, Spurrier travelled to Coventry to see him. With almost no small-talk at all he put Leyland's offer on the table – it would like to make an agreed takeover, offering one Leyland share for eight Standard shares.

To Alick Dick this must have seemed like a visit from a fairy godmother, but he hid those feelings for now. He wanted Standard's merchant bankers to get involved (which Sir Henry resisted), and he wanted a little time to consider the matter. In a meeting, he forecast an annual production of 120,000 in the short-term (a long way below theoretical capacity, but a lot more than looked likely in the immediate future), and he admitted to the possibilities of a loss in the current financial year.

This time, unlike the abortive talks with Rootes, Rover, Ferguson, and the other less likely suitors, matters were finalised cordially and quickly. On Monday December 5, 1960, the agreed merger was made public, with both Sir Henry Spurrier and Standard's retiring chairman Lord Tedder commending it to its shareholders. In the whirlwind days following Sir Henry's first approach, the terms altered slightly – two Leyland shares would be offered for every 15 Standard shares – which was slightly more in Standard's favour; the offer, at existing stock market valuations, was worth about £18 million, a figure which many thought to be well below the company's worth.

This might have been so, but at the time it also had to be taken into account that Standard-Triumph was losing money at a frightening rate. By the middle of January 1961, before the deal could be formalised, Leyland Motors was threatening to pull out

of the deal as it had discovered that Standard-Triumph was losing £600,000 every month, and had lost more than £3 million since the beginning of the financial year in September 1960. Estimates of sales had also been cut – to 100,000 – and the company was not expected to start making operating profits again until mid-1961.

All this begs the question that Leyland might have been too hasty in bidding for, and rushing into, Standard-Triumph. Alick Dick later cheerfully admitted that Leyland paid "far too much for the company, in fact it was a ridiculous price, everything considered. It could have beaten us down quite a bit, and we would still have been prepared to sell-out." This apart, both companies were alarmed to learn that Chrysler, from Detroit, was threatening to bid for both companies and swallow them up even before the marriage could be solemnised.

Leyland, therefore, dismissed its misgivings, went ahead with the formal offer to Standard shareholders, and announced that it had gained control in April 1961. The first Standard-Triumph board meeting held under Leyland control took place in May 1961, when Sir Henry Spurrier took the chair, and Donald Stokes, Stanley Markland and Sidney Baybutt all joined the board. Sir Henry effectively read the riot act, and suggested that much attention would have to be paid to economy of operation and to quality of the product.

For top management, the next few months were very unhappy, as it was found that Leyland methods and standards were not at all like those considered normal in the motor industry of the Midlands. There were staff redundancies, some demotions, and many executives lost the use of a company-owned car. One Leyland man commented: "we spent the whole time going round and turning off money taps. Money was just pouring out of the place." Leyland, in general, did not think that enough control was being exercised at this critical time, and was horrified to see that not only did Standard-Triumph not start making profits again in May 1961, as forecast, but that the year's losses would exceed £7 million.

Something would have to be done and, in characteristically ruthless North Country style, something was. The showdown came in August, as Harry Webster later told us so vividly:

"About 9.30 one morning, Sir Henry and Stanley Markland came into my office, looked around and asked 'Anything to show us? Anything interesting?' So I took them off to look at the Le Mans cars, which had just been stripped-out for examination. We then went back to the front offices, where they said, 'Do you mind if we use your office for an hour or two?' Well, I didn't know what was going on, but I left them to it, and I pottered off into engineering, where I could always find something to get involved with.

"Then, of course, directors started arriving one by one – Aspland, Whitfield, Weale, Dixon and Woodall – seeing Sir Henry and Stanley in my office, and disappearing looking grim. After about an hour-and-a-half I got back to my office and we set off to carry on with the tour. Next I took them into the styling studio to look at Barb proposals, and there, in a corner, behind another car, were all the directors, having a meeting. Now, I didn't know what had actually been going on, but there was an atmosphere, and – believe me – it was very embarrassing!"

What had happened was that the Leyland directors had suddenly lost all patience with the Standard board, and had decided that they would all have to go. Accordingly, they had asked for Alick Dick's resignation (after offering him the job of running the group's Australian business, which he thought of as a 'South Seas dumping ground'), and then dealt out the same treatment to the directors.

All this happened on Thursday, August 17, and on the following Monday Sir Henry Spurrier issued this statement to the press:

"Leyland Motors have decided that it must streamline and integrate the STI organisation into the parent company at an early date.

"Mr A S Dick is to resign from the company, and Mr S Markland is appointed managing director of Standard-Triumph International Ltd as from today.

"Further, they have asked Messrs K Aspland, E Brimelow, M T Tustin, H S Weale, M Whitfield and L A Woodall to retire from the board of STI, some of whom will be retained in an executive capacity."

It was almost a complete clear-out. Frank Dixon, ex-managing director of Hall Engineering, remained on the board (but would leave at the end of the year), and apart from him the entire direction of the company would be in the hands of Leyland personnel. It had taken weeks of persuasion for Stanley Markland to agree to take on this new and very daunting job. It was daunting for all the obvious reasons, plus the fact that he would continue to be in charge of Albion Motors in Glasgow, and to be deputy to Sir Henry Spurrier of Leyland Motors Ltd. Markland was a blunt, clear thinking, but just and kindly man who had been 'a Leyland man' all his working life. He had joined the company as a trade apprentice in 1920, and had become its chief design engineer in 1945. From 1953 he had been works director at Leyland, and he was the ideal man to bring order and tight control to the beleaguered Standard-Triumph premises throughout the country.

He and financial-man Sidney Baybutt decided that Standard's costs could immediately be cut by an annual £3 million. Some 800 people – almost all of them from the salaried staff – were sacked, 200 company cars were

withdrawn (and sold-off for precious cash), the capital programme was slashed, the unsuccessful Atlas Minor van was dropped, and the production lines were put on the drastically-cut rate of 2½ work days a week. But even then production of the new Herald 1200 had to be cut to 750 a week to balance build against sales. That most obvious status symbol of all – the Cessna aeroplane – was handed over for Leyland's corporate use.

It was the bottom of the trough, and after a thoroughly frightening few months the company's morale began to improve. A solid forward programme for new models is always an indication of confidence, and Leyland Motors had soon settled on its future intentions. At first, in the spring of 1961, it had contented itself with approval for the TR4 (Zest) and Spitfire projects. In the next few weeks it asked for all manner of crazy half-breeds to be built in engineering (would you believe a Herald-engined Vanguard, for instance?), and it wasn't long before it decided to cancel the Zero tractor completely. Leyland was already beginning to worry about a replacement for the Triumph Herald, but first it had to think about a replacement for the Vanguard.

The Vanguard, by 1961, was already dying on its feet. The six-cylinder engine transplant, even allied to a four-speed gearbox, had not helped. By the standards of the day, the car's styling had dated very rapidly, and the road behaviour was not up to much. In its time the Vanguard had done great things for Standard. The original car (1948 to 1953) had sold to the tune of nearly 185,000, and the Series 2 (1953 to 1955) had sold 88,000. The Series 3 cars, with bodies from Pressed Steel and styling by American Carl Otto, had not been as successful.

Work on replacing it, under the code-name Zebu, had been

This was the original 1958 version of the Zebu project, a separate-chassis, independent suspension transaxle design intended to replace the Standard Vanguard.

The original Standard-Triumph Zebu, complete with reverse-slope rear window, was an extremely elegant machine, but it never progressed past the prototype stage.

commissioned at a board meeting in August 1957. At that stage Zebu was to have been a 1500/2000cc car with two versions of the six-cylinder engine being developed; it would have four-wheel independent suspension (perhaps even with pneumatic springs), and a rear-mounted transmission. Styling was to be by Standard (not even Michelotti, as then conceived), and Pressed Steel would build the bodies. The first production cars were wanted for the spring of 1960. However, by the time serious work began on this project, Michelotti had become contracted to Standard-Triumph, and was asked to produce a suitable four-door style.

"Zebu was a fine-looking car, a really striking design," Harry Webster recalls, "and when we started designing it I insisted on better weight distribution than usual. So we put the gearbox and the back axle together (which gave us much more space in the front instead of a great big hulking hump between the foot-wells), and we went for MacPherson-strut front suspension and semi-trailing-link rear with double-jointed half-shafts and coil springs.

"But the most dramatic feature was the body. It had a notchback (reverse-slope) rear window, and we'd got

This was the startlingly original Michelotti style proposal for the Zebu project, as seen with its reverse-slope rear window feature in 1958.

This was an early example of the 2.5 PI, later fitted with accessory alloy road wheels.

rid of the B/C post between the doors. In fact on the first car we had a bar across the back of the seats holding two pressed-steel stalagmites together, but we were going to eliminate that in due course.

"The prototype was one of the best I have ever driven when it was 'green' and undeveloped. It ran as smooth as silk, apart from one vibration problem connected with propeller-shafts, which I knew we could have solved in time.

"Everything went well, and it was all beginning to look good, until one day Chris Jennings, who was then the editor of *Motor*, came in to have a privileged look at our prototype cars. He took one look at 'Zebu', turned to Alick Dick, and said, 'I think it's beautiful, but confidentially I must tell you that you'll be accused of copying because there is another British car coming which will beat you into production by quite a long way, and it has got a cut-back window just like yours.'"

That car, of course, was Ford's new Anglia, and what even Chris Jennings did not know was that it would similarly be followed by the bigger Classic, with an identical cut-back window feature. Reverse-slope rear windows had already been introduced in the United States, on Ford's 1958 Mercury range. Alick Dick, therefore, lost heart at the thought of this (though Jennings apparently never told him the new car was to be a Ford), and in its original form Zebu was scrapped. Harry Webster said: "it would have been very difficult just to restyle the rear – somehow it would have

unbalanced the whole car's lines, and in any case the tail was quite short and a conventional rear line would have meant lengthening it. So Alick asked us to consider a completely new style, on the lines of the new Herald, and I distinctly remember that for our first mock-up on the Zebu underframe (which had become a monocoque) we literally hot-cross-bunned a Herald saloon body, cut it into quarters, and offered that up for a first-thoughts viewing!"

Here, unfortunately, the programme began to lose direction. Somehow the new type of styling couldn't be made to work, and after the transmission had been moved forward to a conventional position behind the engine, the impetus of mechanical innovation was also lost. This, and the enforced move of the entire department from Banner Lane to Fletchamstead North, took months out of the schedule. By the spring of 1960 the car's introduction had tentatively been put back to the autumn of 1962, and in September, when the company's finances were in a parlous state, the project was cancelled altogether.

When the Vanguard Luxury Six was released in time for the 1960 Earls Court Motor Show, Standard-Triumph literally had nothing in mind to take its place in future years. Through that desperate winter of 1960/61 the situation did not change, and it was not until Leyland gave its approval to a new model programme that a larger car could be considered once again. Work then went ahead at a frantic, but not slipshod, rate. Working on the fail-safe

Michelotti's final Zebu proposal of 1960 was voted to be too bland, and the project was soon cancelled altogether.

principle, the company asked Michelotti in Turin, and Les Moore in Standard's own studio, to come up with styling proposals, which would be reviewed by the autumn of 1961. At its July 1961 board meeting, the directors were told that the new car, code-name Barb, could be ready for the 1963 Earls Court show if a good style evolved before too long.

It was an incredibly tight schedule, almost crippling by standards of the 1950s and certainly so by the more complex standards of today. In 1977, for instance, Chrysler made much of the speed with which it produced its new '424' Sunbeam (20 months), and it had the advantage of existing floorpan and door pressings, engines and suspensions. For the new Barb, with a 24-month cycle in prospect, Standard-Triumph would only be carrying over the engine and transmission units. Everything else, which included the entire bodyshell, would have to be tooled-up from scratch.

By November 1961, the job had been done, and Michelotti's styling proposal chosen. Pressed Steel was given the job of tooling for and then building the bodies, which would be conventional four-door monocoques. It was a symbol of Leyland's faith in Standard-Triumph's future.

To speed-up the proving process, the very first running Barb prototype was nothing more than a rolling chassis – which is to say that it was a structural underpan with all the mechanical components in place – but it had a splendidly crude and eye-catching angle-iron space-frame welded to the under-frame in order to ensure a modicum of torsional rigidity, and to provide some protection for the test drivers. Such a car could only be useful for endurance, and it became a familiar sight on the company's test routes in the Cotswolds. It was fortunate for the company's medical advisers that it was not ready for the road until the worst of the 1961/62 winter was over.

Barb, technically, was a rather different car from the Vanguard it was to replace. Although the engineering of the bodyshell was conventional, it featured a long nose and rather a stubby tail – both reflecting the heritage of the original Zebu layout – with the big bonnet panel hinged from the nose the same way already proved satisfactory on the TR4. Under the skin there were developed versions of the MacPherson-strut front suspension (allied to rack-and-pinion steering, but without an anti-roll bar) and semi-trailing-link independent rear suspension, both as conceived for Zebu way back in 1958.

"It was a lovely style which we all liked," Harry Webster said, "but I had long arguments with Michelotti about it. I thought it should have been two or three inches wider than it was, to give more passenger space, but he argued that this wasn't necessary, and anyway it would all add weight. He won, of course, but I still think he was wrong. I once had one built that bit wider, and I thought it was better ..."

While the engines (at that stage to have been in 1596cc and 1998cc form) and four-speed gearbox were basically as used in the Vanguard Six, the engine was more powerful (90bhp from the 2-litre with Zenith-Stromberg carbs instead of 80bhp with Solexes), and the gearbox was to have a TR4 type of remote-control linkage for the change-speed lever. There would be an overdrive option, or an automatic option (though the automatic would be several months late into production). The axle casing was entirely new (Standard-Triumph had not previously produced a large car with IRS) but the differential and details were the same as on the Vanguards.

As originally conceived, the semi-trailing wishbones were cast in light-alloy, with the intention of designing pressed-steel components for quantity production, and they were pivoted from the floorpan itself. Somehow or other the design team never got round to designing the pressed members and, more importantly, it was discovered that direct mounting set up unacceptable vibrations. With less than a year to go until the assembly of production cars would begin, and in an operation which actually delayed that start-up, the rear-end was designed to incorporate a subframe crossbeam, which solved the problem.

While Barb was being developed, Standard-Triumph's morale was improving rapidly. At the beginning of 1962 Stanley Markland arbitrarily decided to increase its production from March (the TR4 had also made a flying start, and public confidence in the much-improved Triumph Herald 1200 was obvious), and this gamble paid off within weeks when purchase tax was reduced on sales in Britain. The following November things got dramatically better when that tax was reduced yet again.

In March, a Herald 1200 saloon sold for £700, and a TR4 (if you could find one without waiting) for £1095. By December, after the two reductions, those prices had been slashed to £580 and £908, respectively. It was just the sort of business tonic which Standard-Triumph needed, and sales responded accordingly. Before long the production lines were back on full-time, and overtime was being worked in certain areas – a situation unheard-of over the past couple of years.

As if to signal its confidence in existing managers, Leyland also appointed three new directors: Harry Webster, George Turnbull and Les Woodall (the latter being re-appointed only months after that dreadful day in August 1961 when he, along with his colleagues, had been dismissed by Sir Henry Spurrier). The company's financial position was improving, and would continue to improve steadily. In 1961/62 Standard's losses were reduced to £1.5 million, by the end of 1962 it would be operating profitably, and in 1963/64 it would turn in a profit of £1.5 million.

But before the new big car was ready to be released, a fundamental decision had to be faced. It was not something which could be taken lightly, even though it was merely a model name which was involved. At BMC (or at General Motors in Detroit), badge engineering and juggling with names was normal practice, but at Standard-Triumph it was not. The problem, quite simply, was whether or not the new car should be a Standard or a Triumph?

There were several factors to be weighed in the balance. Perhaps the most important one was that in the previous ten years the Triumph name had come to mean a great deal in the world of motoring – a great deal more, indeed, than the name had ever meant when the Triumph company had been independent. Standard, on the other hand, was already a name in decline. Its high point, probably, had been in the 1930s and the 1940s (when first the Flying Standards and later the Vanguards

brought much good publicity to the company), but with the Standard 8/10/Pennant range replaced by new small Triumphs, and the Vanguard sliding towards obscurity, it was becoming irrelevant.

Another, and more significant, factor was that in recent years the word 'standard' had come to mean basic or cheap in some parts of the world. Whereas in the beginning Reginald Maudslay had wanted his new cars to set a high standard, and he let it be known that his cars were the standard to which other cars should strive to be equal, the language had been debased over the years.

By the 1960s a 'standard' product was far too often taken to mean the cheapest and the lowest possible specification of any range which a company was prepared to sell. It was a fact, by this time, that in some parts of the world a prospective customer would look at a Vanguard and say: "If this is the Standard, where are the De Luxe and the Super?"

The company therefore decided to bow to the pressures of modern fashion and advertising. Standard would be phased-out, and after the last of the Vanguard family had been built every car to come from Canley would be a Triumph. If Triumph's founder, Siegfried Bettmann, could have heard this decision from his resting place, he must surely have been delighted.

The last new Standard model, in fact, was the Ensign de Luxe,

The original 2000 of the early 1960s had this simple facia/instrument panel.

which was really an updated and austerity version of the good old four-cylinder Vanguard. It was announced in June 1962 as no more than a stop-gap model to provide a low price-base for the Vanguard range. Although it was a slow seller (the company, indeed, might have been greatly embarrassed if it had been otherwise) it fulfilled a valuable short-term need. Appropriately enough, therefore, an Ensign de Luxe was the very last Standard car to be made, rolling off the Canley assembly lines in May 1963.

At about the same time it was finally decided not to build the 1596cc version of the new 'Barb.' In some ways a 1600 might have made sense, but it had become clear that it could not have been sold much cheaper than the 1998cc version, and it would have been a great deal slower and more ponderous. The new car, therefore, was to be the Triumph 2000, and in the last few months before announcement its level of trim and furnishing was improved considerably.

The new Triumph 2000 was pushed up-market for a very good reason – that it was to face formidable competition from another new 2-litre saloon, the Rover 2000. This project, of course, had been well-known to Standard-Triumph for some years. Not only was the existence of Rover's P6 something of an open secret in the Midlands for some time, but it had also been revealed to Standard-Triumph in its last round of abortive talks with the Rover company in 1959. Even though the new Rover car had not been finalised by then, it was recognisably like the car which would be announced just a week ahead of the new Triumph.

The face-to-face competition was intriguing. The Rover had been developed in a typically leisurely manner, whereas the Triumph had progressed from mock-up to announcement in little more than two years. The Rover was brand new from stern to stern, and adventurous in its structural layout and suspension details, while the Triumph used mostly carry-over engine and transmission components. The Triumph, however, used a smooth-as-silk six-cylinder engine while the Rover used a four.

When the two cars were announced, the Rover got more than its share of attention in the press, mainly because a new model from Rover was quite a rarity, and because this particular car had many newsworthy features. However, it was noted that the Triumph was going to be considerably cheaper than the Rover (£905, basic, compared with £1046 when both cars became generally available at the beginning of 1964), and that there were overdrive and automatic transmission options which the Rover lacked.

It was a fascinating battle, won by the Rover in terms of favourable press comment and on performance figures, but decisively won by the new Triumph in terms of actual sales and profits. The Rover took an early but insignificant lead, as it was already in slow but steady production when announced on the eve of the Earls Court Motor Show because it simply had to be there; it would not, however, go on sale until the new year.

Standard-Triumph, in truth, was not quite ready to make the cars in quantity, so it made a virtue of necessity by announcing that 40 early cars would be assessed by a typical cross section of potential buyers. This was done, and comments were studied, but the minor changes made to the cars which went on sale early in January 1964 could not possibly have been a result of this test as the cars were being built while the driving was going on! Donald Stokes made much of the process, however, and managed a sly dig at his BMC competitors by saying: 'we have done our production testing on the potential customer and not, as so often happens, on the customer who has already paid his money.' BMC, in those days, was rather notorious for selling partly-developed cars which gave trouble at the early production stage. By the time the Triumph went on the market it was already being manufactured at the rate of 350 a week, and in the next couple of years this would steadily be pushed up to more than 800 a week.

Through and round all this, Triumph's whole future was being settled by Leyland. The big push for export sales in 1962 (every TR4 went abroad for a time, along with 60 per cent of all Heralds built) had been consolidated in 1963, and the company's sporting image was strengthened. Some schemes had misfired: the Herald 1200s, for instance, were far too slow for the Americans' taste (Kas Kastner once told us that he was almost too frightened to take a Herald on to a Los Angeles freeway, "unless I can find a steep down-sloping ramp to give me a flying start"), while the Vitesses, called Sports Sixes in North America, were rather strangled by the optional air-conditioning equipment which many customers demanded. Even so, the Spitfire was exactly what the world wanted, as the sales figures proved.

Even in mid-1961, as the tractor project was being discarded and the Spitfire and 2000 projects gained formal approval, Stanley Markland and Donald Stokes had started to talk about a successor to the Triumph Herald, and hoped that it would be ready for announcement in 1964. This car, they thought, would not have to be designed with overseas manufacture in mind (those subsidiaries which survived the takeovers and subsequent rationalisation would be happy to carry on building the Herald for a time), and had to be completely competitive with whatever Ford, BMC, Vauxhall and Rootes were planning to sell.

This programme, however, was to slip several times before a finalised style was agreed in May 1963, with announcement set for October 1965. For one very good reason – that the revamped Herald in 1147cc form was beginning to sell really well – the pressure eased for a time, and it also became clear that with the Spitfire, the 2000 and the TR4A all under development at Fletchamstead North, there simply was not enough capacity for the engineers to deal with it at the time.

By 1963, more management changes were brewing-up, too. Sir Henry Spurrier became seriously ill late in 1962 and this, complicated by a further Leyland merger (with Associated Commercial Vehicles, which made, among other things, all the famous London Transport buses), meant a reshuffle. Stanley Markland thought that he would take over from Spurrier, and was astonished to find that Sir William Black of ACV was preferred in his place. A consequence was that Markland resigned from all his posts in the corporation, and at the end of 1963 Donald Stokes became chairman of Standard-Triumph.

Markland's reign at Standard-Triumph lasted less than three years, but his influence was felt for much longer. As Harry Webster likes to remember him: "He was a big bluff north countryman, and he was actually the only Leyland import in those first months. He was a great engineer, and he came to us with a hell of a reputation. Everyone thought he would be a hatchet man – he had been one with other companies he had been asked to run – but he never did this with us at Triumph. It was Markland, more than anybody, who made us look again at the idea of building-in top-gear flexibility to our cars. He used to have this test of putting a car into top gear, slamming his foot hard down at 10mph, then holding the car there on the brake. It was a hell of a test, and if the carburation was wrong the engine would soon load-up and stall ... it was a great test of poor distribution, and it made us work harder to make our cars pass it. I just can't tell you how much we owed to Markland, both for his leadership and the encouragement we got from him."

One of Stanley Markland's last moves was to get involved in the complications that developed around the form of the new Herald replacement. From the beginning this car was coded 'Ajax,' and in its original guise it was to have been built in two-door or four-door form. In price, it should have been in every way a match for the Herald, and it was intended to replace it completely as far as British-made Triumphs were concerned.

Most of the controversy revolved around what the new car should look like. Its shape took ages to evolve for two major reasons: because it was to be a conventional monocoque once more (the Herald, of course, having had a separate chassis), and because of the mechanical components it had to hide.

"Effectively I was still my own product-planner in the early 1960s," Harry Webster explained, "and I'd had a good look round at what other people were doing, and which way the smaller motor cars appeared to be developing. Of course we – first Alick, then Stanley Markland, and myself – were much influenced by what Issigonis was up to at Longbridge. The Mini had worked well right from the start, and then, while we were scheming the Ajax, he produced the Morris 1100 as well."

Gradually, by that indefinable process of osmosis which occurs in all such cases, the idea of front-wheel drive for the new car began

Because front-wheel drive cars became popular during the 1960s, Triumph produced just such a layout for the 1300 saloon, which was announced in 1965.

to gain favour at Standard-Triumph. If properly done, such a layout would give packaging and potential handling advantages, and it was undoubtedly a fashionable sales feature at this time.

Shortly after the new car had been announced, early in 1966, Harry Webster was interviewed by Ronald Barker for a feature in *The Autocar*, and had some fascinating comments to make.

"Back in 1953 I did produce some drawings with my old colleague Albert Coaley ... it's amusing to recall that the engine in that case was the Triumph two-cylinder motorcycle engine placed across the chassis with the gearbox in the sump, front-wheel drive and rack-and-pinion steering ... We didn't enter into front-wheel drive lightly, and in fact we did a complete brochure of various types of engine-transmission layouts, including the across-the-chassis types ... We wanted fairly big wheels and tyres, combined with a really good steering lock, then we preferred to keep the transmission oil separate, and we wanted to preserve the possibility of combining engine variants with this transmission ..."

It was Webster himself who made all the original sketches (the lettering on the drawings we have seen confirms this), and who devised the ingenious layout for which the Ajax car was to be noted. Determined to use a fore-and-aft engine position, and to give the car a reasonably long-wheelbase while keeping its overall length right down, he reasoned that the engine would really have to be on top of its transmission. Unavoidably this would mean that the power pack would be quite tall (later this penalty was estimated to be about 1¾in), which would lead to extra difficulties for Michelotti at the styling stage.

Various layouts were studied: drive out of the back, and the gearbox under the engine; drive out of the front, and the gearbox under the sump; and finally drive out of the back, gearbox below and behind the engine, and final drive actually under the sump. The latter gave the most compact layout, the easiest layout for manufacturing purposes, and the unpublicised but rather obvious possibility (for later applications) of four-wheel drive. Further, it allowed Standard's existing final-drive machines to be used, and apart from a special crankshaft and sump casting, the Herald engine – bored-out to 1296cc – could be used intact. The eventual possibilities of optional overdrives and/or automatic transmission were not forgotten; both were proposed and part-developed, but neither actually saw the light of day.

It took Michelotti a good deal of time to reconcile his various directives for Ajax ("make it a Junior 2000" being one of the most restricting), but the final scheme was approved in 1963 and tooling went ahead at once. To get quick road experience of the new front-drive power-pack, one was hastily installed in a Morris 1100 bought in great secrecy from an unsuspecting BMC dealer many miles from Coventry, and in addition a 'birdcage' of the type invented for the Triumph 2000 was also constructed to check-out the under-frame and suspensions.

Mechanically, most of the story was contained in the front-wheel drive layout, as already discussed, but we should also point out that this was the first use of the 1296cc engine size, and that it also marked the arrival in quantity production of an eight-port cylinder head developed from those which had roared so lustily in the racing and rallying Spitfires of 1964/65. The power-pack was installed such that the drive-shafts took up a slight angle of trail to the driven front wheels; this helped to allow for a really tight steering lock, and made the universal joints work the whole time, even when the car was running straight ahead. Front suspension was a normal double-wishbone system, and at the rear, a simplified form of semi-trailing independent suspension was chosen.

The project, in the meantime, had inexorably pushed itself up the price range. On the one hand the Herald was continuing to sell very well (along with its Spitfire and Vitesse variants, to say nothing of the GT6 which was following it), while on the other it became clear that a marketing hole was developing above the Herald's price bracket. By the end of 1963, therefore, all pretence of a Herald replacement being developed had been dropped, and for the time being the idea of a two-door car was also abandoned. The Ajax, which might also have been called the LTl (LT standing for Leyland-Triumph), was soon named the Triumph 1300 and was to be given a really lavish set of trim and furnishings.

As a gesture of confidence in the future of the Standard-Triumph (Liverpool) project it had long ago been decided that the new car's bodies should be built up there, alongside the TR4/TR4A shells. Leyland wanted to encourage this move towards independence of outside bodybuilders; in fact the Triumph 2000, which might have been built in-house if it could have been developed at a more normal pace, was the last to be built by an outside supplier, and after 1968, when events leading to the formation of British Leyland had matured, even this didn't matter any more.

As with the 2000, the 1300 was announced in October, but was not available for sale in the showrooms until the following January (1966); in the interim period 30 of the first track-built machines were assessed by about 100 members of the public – which is to say that a large number of possible fleet customers, dealers and their more important clients were invited to try out the cars – and certain minor changes were made.

With its two obviously related saloons, the 1300 and the 2000, selling well and helping the Leyland-owned company's reputation to yet greater peaks, the future of Triumph looked secure. There was great buoyancy in all departments, and there was every inducement to think up new ways to spread the cars' appeal ever wider.

Surprisingly enough very little was done to the 1300 car in its first few years, at least not so far as the public were concerned. Two years after the original car had been announced a 1300TC, effectively the 1300 with the Spitfire Mark 3 engine, was announced, but that was all. In the meantime a new down-market version of the car, the appropriately-named 'Manx' (which had a shortened tail), was being developed, but nothing was to come of it. By 1968, however, a major change in design philosophy would occur, and the 1300/1300TC concept would be altered completely.

Most of the excitement and intrigue was concerned with the big Triumph 2000, and what management thought they should be doing to widen its appeal. In every way the saloon had been a success, with sales racing ahead of any achievement the Canley production lines could manage. The facia facelift of 1966 was certainly not needed to stimulate demand, but was part of the normal improvement process.

Even before the saloon was launched, there was heated discussion about the variants which should follow it. At one time or another in 1963 there was talk of an estate car, a fastback coupé, or even of a convertible. An estate was the most obvious addition to the range, but cost calculations showed that it might be too expensive to sell in quantity, and Pressed Steel estimates of an extra £400,000 for bodyshell tooling were received with horror. The convertible scheme was soon discredited when the sales staff said they could only sell 1000 such cars a year – in developed form this project would reappear as the Stag.

The estate car derivative of the 2000, with bodyshells completed by Carbodies of Coventry from partly-built shells by Pressed Steel, was a lasting success, available with one of several engine types. This is a Mk 2, of course, with the lengthened nose.

By 1967/68, the 2000 was available with saloon or five-door estate car bodywork. Although it had been launched immediately after the Standard Vanguard had died away, the Michelotti-styled 2000 looked dramatically more elegant and more modern.

For months there was a running battle, philosophically speaking, between a Triumph 2000 estate car and a 2000GT with fastback styling, both cars being shaped by the prolific and irrepressible Michelotti in Turin. Even though sales would finally agree that they might sell 2500 a year of a 2000 convertible, and thought that less estate cars might be sold, the estate began to gain favour. The problem, quite simply, was that management was not prepared to consider having the car expensively tooled-up by Pressed Steel in case it was a failure, and much time was spent looking for ways around this dilemma.

The factory competitions department, in the meantime, rallied a team of much-modified 2000 saloons with some success (they also managed to turn up one rough-road fault on their very first event, when all three cars retired close to each other with deranged rear suspension caused by subframe mountings tearing out of the bodyshell. This was rapidly solved on all future production cars, and the problem never recurred. Among other things, the department found to their delight that the 1998cc engine could be super-tuned to give 150bhp with great reliability, if horrifying fuel consumption. Thus the idea of an uprated 2000TS car was born, and the thought was that such an engine could give the fastback car a sparkling performance.

A solution to the dilemma followed in September 1964, when the thorny problem of body tooling was resolved. Instead of having to face a large tooling bill from Pressed Steel for the estate car body sections, it was decided that the conversion – literally a conversion of a partly-complete saloon shell – should be carried out for Triumph by the Carbodies Ltd coachbuilding concern in Coventry. Carbodies had a rather similar history to Mulliners in that it had evolved from a small-scale producer of special coachwork into a medium-scale supplier of bodies, in this case to firms like BMC and Daimler.

This tipped the balance in favour of the estate car, and left the single but very desirable 2000GT fastback high and dry. Used for several years as high-speed executive transport around the Coventry area, that was an intriguing might-have-been in Triumph's history. The sales forecast for estate car sales, incidentally, proved to be remarkably accurate. In its best year, and when being sold in two distinct varieties, nearly 2800 were sold; a more representative average sale was 2000 in a year.

About this time Standard-Triumph was tempted to become involved in the four-wheel drive cross-country vehicle business. The Triumph 1300's power-pack had always been laid-out with a four-wheel drive conversion in mind, and this eventually matured in the shape of a stubby and lightweight 'Pony' prototype. Pony was designed in 1963, and the first vehicle was built in 1964, but the decision to produce the machine in quantity was repeatedly deferred. Eventually, in 1966, and therefore nothing to do with the

merger with Rover, the entire design was shipped off to Autocars, in Israel (with whom Leyland then had links), where the vehicle was eventually produced.

By the mid-1960s, as will have become obvious, Triumph's Coventry factories were booming. Without exception, each new model announced since Leyland took control had been a success, the nation's (and the world's) economy had expanded confidently, and sales had rocketed accordingly. Total production (and this includes cars shipped in KD ('knocked down') form developed like this:

Financial year	Cars produced
1959/60	138,762
1960/61	78,735
1961/62	78,383
1962/63	100,764
1963/64	119,937
1964/65	121,405

There would be a slight dip in 1966 and 1967, due to the British Government's domestic policies, but production bounced up again in 1967/68 to a new record of 139,488. One should note that the figure for 1959/60, which would be unsurpassed until 1967/68, was when Standard-Triumph was really over-producing cars to boost its cash-flow as much as it possibly could. The big drop experienced in 1960/61 was as much due to this as it was to a genuine drop in demand for Triumph cars; dealers all over the world started 1960 with their showrooms and warehouses stuffed with stock.

During the 1960s the interest in performance cars increased tremendously. Cars like the BMC Mini-Cooper and the Ford Cortina-Lotus helped to provide sparkling performance at low cost. All over the world the motorway networks continued to spread – even Great Britain, which started later than almost any other country, had two major motorways in use by the early 1960s.

Triumph, like the other car makers, picked up this need for more performance and decided to act on it. One half-hearted attempt to keep up with the sporting homologation-race was proposed: the Vitesse should be marketed in a 90bhp version with three SU carburettors. This this was never carried through. The Vitesse, eventually, was up-engined to 2 litres, and the GT6 was introduced as a 2-litre car when 1.6 litres might originally have been chosen.

The need for more performance then began to affect Triumph's bigger and more expensive models. Even as it was being announced it was clear that the 2000 saloon was being outpaced in maximum speed by the rival Rover, if not in acceleration and flexibility. The

In 1964/65 Triumph's own stylists produced this simple, elegant, two-seater proposal of a 2-litre/6-cylinder-engined sports car coded 'Fury.' It might have become the TR5, but only one prototype was built, and it did not progress. It survives to this day.

TR4A, introduced in 1965, was really no quicker than the TR4 it replaced, and the MGB, 340cc smaller in engine size and £100 cheaper in basic price, was almost its match. From European markets, in particular, Triumph concessionaries were asking for much faster acceleration and much higher potential maximum speeds. It was not considered anti-social, nor against the public interest, to drive fast in those days.

Sooner rather than later, therefore, there would have to be a new, faster and obviously more powerful TR. At the same time it

was readily assumed that this would mean the end of the famous wet-liner four-cylinder engine. TR traditionalists, of course, would be against this, but as far as the factory was concerned there was no way it could be continued. In the heyday of the TR3As the engine had also found use in the Vanguards (private and commercial), and in the Ferguson tractors. By the 1960s, the only other user of the 2138cc engine was Morgan, and its order of (at best) five or six engines a week was not enough to make production viable.

In 1964 and 1965, too, Triumph engineers indulged themselves a little, designing yet another new sports car – one that was never to be put into production and for which, officially, there was never a requirement. 'Fury' was an important stepping-stone in the general updating of the sports car, even though only one prototype was built.

Fury was completely new whereas the TR4 and TR4A cars used many carry-over components. It was Triumph's first-ever open car with a monocoque body/chassis unit in pressed steel, and it was also its first attempt at a sporting car complete with a modern six-cylinder engine, MacPherson-strut front suspension and semi-trailing-link rear suspension. There was no inspiration from Stag (which nobody in Coventry had seen at the time), and no parts were common with the Triumph 2000 (though many were inspired or developed from this car). Fury, in fact, was one on its own. In style it looked uncannily like a grown-up Spitfire (complete with pop-up headlamps, a feature which Michelotti, who shaped the body, wanted on his cars at the time), and in size it fell between the Spitfire and the TR4A. Designed in 1964, prototype manufacture began in the winter of 1964/65, and the sole prototype was finished in 1965. It was a soft top two-seater whereas the TR4A was almost a 2+2 (some people must have thought so, for they ordered the optional occasional rear seat).

Although the car looked like a Spitfire, it had 2000-inspired suspensions and some transmission parts, and a developed version of the 1998cc six-cylinder engine. The gearbox and axle, in fact, were identical with TR4A items, which were themselves almost the same as those used in the big saloons.

Where would it have fitted in? Probably as a third Triumph sports car, slotting between the Spitfires and the TRs. It was dropped almost as soon as it had been built, not because it did not perform satisfactorily, and certainly not because the structure didn't measure up to the required standards (it fulfilled all requirements well), but because it was going to cost a fortune and take time to be tooled. On that basis it lost out to the new GT6, which was a much easier new model to produce.

But it proved that a six-cylinder engine could be fitted into a sports car without destroying its balance, or making it any less of a car for sportsmen. Triumph kept it (as it kept most prototypes), used it for various jobs until 1968, then sold it to a Triumph motor trader in the Midlands.

Even in 1964, therefore, before the TR4A had even been announced, the designers had decided that the Triumph 2000 engine, in tuned-up or modified form, would be fitted to the next TR. Although the six was longer than the four, installing it into the existing TR4A chassis frame was not very difficult. Only a minor reshuffle of auxiliaries and minor changes to brackets and the turret cross-brace were needed. A bonus would be that the six-cylinder engine was just a few pounds lighter than the four it replaced. The

existing transmission would be retained – the bellhousing face stayed in exactly the same place, and the scuttle/toe-board would not need alteration.

That much was straightforward, but the problem was in getting the right sort of power from the engine. The last of the TR4As produced 104bhp at 4700rpm, but even in its most powerful form (GT6 prototype) the six-cylinder engine only produced 95bhp at 5000rpm. Up to that time, tuning the six had been an unrewarding business, principally because of the very restricted breathing of the cylinder head design. Normal changes involving more ambitious camshaft profiles, better manifolding and other details found the power stuck stubbornly at around 110/115bhp, and the engine's flexibility suffered badly. Rally cars with three twin-choke Webers could dispose of 150bhp at 6000rpm, but this sort of treatment was quite impractical.

One answer was a new design of cylinder head, and the other, if possible, would be to increase the engine size. A Triumph 2000 (actually an ex-works rally car) was raced by Bill Bradley in 1966; fitted with the new cylinder head, with Lucas fuel-injection and the wildest possible camshaft profile, it had at least 175bhp. The breathing possibilities of the new head were well-proven.

But Triumph was wedded to the Markland/Webster philosophy of having flexible engines, and the new cars would not have to suffer in this respect. Therefore, to boost the torque it was necessary to look for an enlarged engine. Doing this by enlarging the cylinder-bore was not practical (the engine, after all, was descended from the original 803cc four of 1951/52 which had a 58mm bore, and now it was already up to 74.7mm), so the only alternative was to increase the stroke; Webster, of course, had considered this alternative in the late 1950s. Although this flew in the face of all accepted modern trends it worked surprisingly well, and provided a relatively simple way of enlarging the 1998cc unit to 2498cc. The same treatment, but not to such an extreme degree, allowed the small four to be enlarged to 1493cc for that engine's future requirements.

Even so, the power of this bigger six was still not up to requirements. By the time the unit had been tamed, maximum power was back to about 110bhp, which was still a long way down on the 125bhp minimum needed for the new TR.

It was about this time that salvation in the guise of Lucas fuel-injection came on to the scene, even though it was not at first intended for boosting the power. The catalyst, in fact, was the shock administered by the first wave of United States anti-emission regulations. The maximum level of pollutants specified may look laughably lax by today's standards, but at the time it caused panic in almost every engine laboratory in the world.

To control the fuel/air mixture really carefully it was thought that fuel-injection might be needed (the alternative was thought to be after-burners and catalysts which were even less known and trusted), but after it became clear that the Lucas system would need extra environmental controls, attention turned to really carefully set Zenith-Stromberg carburettors, which did the job beautifully. Harry Webster and John Lloyd then got their heads together, assessed all the experience they had on injection (plus the obvious power-producing potential exemplified by the racing 2000), and applied it to a new version of the 2498cc engine. The result was the TR5 power unit, lusty and flexible, if a little lumpy under heavy traffic conditions, which pushed out 150bhp (gross) at 5500rpm.

The new TR, coded 'Wasp' internally, might once have been called the TR4B, but it was eventually launched as the TR5, and went into production at the beginning of August 1967. Buyers in the United States, however, who made up the majority of TR buyers, had to make do with the detoxed engine and Zenith CD

carburettors, which was good for about 105bhp and gave the new car the same performance as the old TR4A. To distinguish it even further from the TR5 the 'federal' car was called TR250 and given special colour-striping across its nose. The live rear axle alternative from the TR4A, thankfully, was discontinued; the Americans, it seemed, had discovered roadholding after all.

The TR5/TR250 cars, however, were to be very short-lived – in production for only 17 months and just over 11,000 cars built because even before the car was released management had decided that the car would soon have to be restyled. The TR4/TR4A/TR5 style had, after all, been around since 1961, and customers were beginning to expect a new shape.

Michelotti was completely tied up with other work at that time (for Triumph and for Leyland itself, who were now using

It's what's up front that keeps you out front.

You've got 6 cylinders going for you in the new TR-250. 6 cylinders displacing 2½ litres. And that means power up front to keep you out front.
To back it up, you've got independent rear suspension, 4 forward synchromesh gears, rack-and-pinion steering, red-band radial ply tires, and disc brakes up front.
And as a finishing touch, reflective safety striping highlights the vinyl top.
If you've got the spirit, the new TR-250 is the car that can move you.

🔺TRIUMPH TR-250

Launched in the autumn of 1967, the TR5 was not only the first six-cylinder engined TR, but the first British series-production car to have fuel-injection.

When the first six-cylinder TR was put on sale at the end of 1967, the special North American car was known as the TR250. This derivative, complete with Zenith-Stromberg carburettors was not sold anywhere else in the world.

his services for commercial-vehicle styling), and Triumph had to look round for outside assistance. After surveying the European scene, a 'mission impossible' job was awarded to Karmann in West Germany (who was already noted for its work with VW, BMW and Porsche among others). Not only was it charged with evolving a significant face-lift for the TR4A/TR5 body which would retain the existing scuttle/doors/inner panels, but it also had to undertake the production of new tooling, for which the contract period was a mere 14 months! That Karmann achieved this is a credit to its speed of working, and to the fact that its first clay-model proposal was accepted in September 1967, just as the TR5 was being launched.

The first revised cars – called TR6 whether for North American or other world markets – were built in November 1968, and were released at the beginning of 1969. Times and fashions had changed, and of course Triumph also had the GT6 on offer in much-improved form by then, so the TR6 never looked like selling at the rate of the TR3A or even the TR4 in its first year, but it was undoubtedly a continuing success for Triumph in the 1970s. By 1971 or 1972 the company had much on its mind which would preclude further attention to the TR6 (the development of the British Leyland empire, and work on an entirely new TR, the TR7,

for instance), and after the end of 1974 the TR6 in any case was living on borrowed time. Nevertheless, it sold well until the very last car was built in July 1976 – nearly 95,000 had eventually been produced, either at Coventry or in KD form for assembly in other countries.

As far as British customers and those in the rest of the world outside America were concerned, a 1976 TR6 was much the same as a 1969 model, apart from various cosmetic changes and a reshuffle of gearbox/overdrive ratios to match the car with the Stag. In the United States, however, there were annual changes to keep the car abreast of the latest legislation developments. It is to Triumph's credit that in spite of the ever-tightening engine restrictions, it managed to keep the TR6's power output up to a nominal 106bhp at 4900rpm to the bitter end, and even though it had to put on some weight in terms of bigger and more complex bumpers and door inserts, it was still fun to drive.

But sports cars standards were changing fast, and whereas the chassis of a TR4A had been hailed as a great advance in 1965, that of a TR6 in the 1970s was described as "the last of the Dinosaurs, a real rugged monster." The spirit which had welcomed the TR2s and Austin Healeys in the 1950s had completely died, except among

Although much of the TR6's engineering was only lightly developed from that of the TR5/TR250, the style (influenced by Michelotti, and Karmann of Germany) was a great success. The TR6 would sell strongly from 1969 to 1976.

TRIUMPH

The Group 44 T.R.6 of
Bob Tullius arrives at London Airport

This photograph may
be reproduced without
charge.

NEGATIVE
NUMBER
224576

Right: Bob Tullius's amazingly successful TR6 race car was flown in to the UK for some high-speed demonstrations at Silverstone.

Bottom Left: By the mid-1970s, although the USA-market TR6 was still an elegant and effective sports car, its styling had been afflicted by the use of two vast rubber bumper over-riders, which allowed it to meet the latest crash-test regulations.

Bottom Right: As advertised for sale, this was the way that British Leyland showed off the facia/driving compartment of the TR6.

Eventually dubbed 'the last of the British hairy-chested sports cars,' the TR6 still looked attractive in this 1973 guise.

This was one of the very last separate-chassis TR6s to be sold in the USA, this one sporting the red-rimmed tyres, and the massive '5 mph' bumper over-riders of the period ...

the enthusiasts; modern sports car fans wanted smoothness, a soft ride and preferably not even the wind in their hair. The motoring scene for the 1970s was not the same as it had been, but fortunately Triumph was alive to see all this, and had great things in store.

Triumph Cars for the 1970s

By the middle of the 1960s Leyland control had put Standard-Triumph finances back into a thoroughly healthy position. Sales and production boomed and profits were growing. The model range was complete and modern, and all kinds of exciting new developments were on the way. The corporation, too, was expanding fast. Donald Stokes was determined to make Leyland the country's biggest and most important producer of vehicles.

To do this by natural growth, by expanding existing factories, looked like it was too long a way round to satisfy the thrusting Leyland management. It would have to be done by acquisition, by takeovers. In any case, the economic climate and all the trends in the 1960s made this desirable. It made a lot of sense for smaller groups to merge themselves into bigger ones, to take advantage of the efficiencies and economies of scale, to commonise designs and to establish rationalised sales-and-service networks.

Almost like the tiny snowball which eventually sets up an avalanche, the Leyland purchase of Standard-Triumph in 1960/61 triggered a wave of motor-industry mergers – one which climaxed with the foundation of British Leyland in 1968. While taking the risk of diverting the enthusiast's interest from Triumph cars, we must now analyse what happened, why it happened, and how it affected Triumph along the way.

Though the British motor industry indulged in an rush of rationalisation in 1960s, it left Ford, Vauxhall and the Rootes Group quite unaffected. The three concerns which gradually, but inevitably, came closer together were Leyland, the British Motor Corporation and Jaguar. Rover, from Solihull, which was about the same size as Standard-Triumph in 1960, and which was still proudly independent, would soon be sucked into this process.

The British Motor Corporation (BMC) had been formed in 1952, but by the beginning of the 1960s it was still a rather loose and uneasy alliance between the old Austin and Nuffield groups. Still, it was the single biggest producer of cars in Britain, and its chairman, Sir George Harriman, was continuing to look for growth. Sir William Lyons, who controlled Jaguar both functionally and financially, was also looking to expand.

Let us deal with Jaguar's moves first. At the end of the 1950s its prestige was high, but it was leaning against the limits of its productive capacity. To improve this, Sir William took over Daimler in 1960 (sold-off to him by BSA, which had controlled the famous motor company for many years). A year later he purchased Guy Motors (who made trucks and buses) from the receivers. In 1963 he concluded a very amicable takeover of Coventry Climax Engines from the personal control of Leonard Lee, and a year later he completed his collection by buying Henry Meadows Ltd (who built proprietary engines, and whose factory was very conveniently next to that of Guy in Wolverhampton).

BMC, on the other hand, was not looking for small captures, but was primarily interested in securing its future body supplies. It'd had Fisher and Ludlow since the 1950s (the design of the Herald and the sourcing of its bodies had much to do with that takeover), but Pressed Steel was still independent. Pressed Steel had been building bodies, and more recently complete monocoque structures, at Cowley since 1927, and the old Nuffield factories, which were literally across the road, relied heavily on Pressed Steel for their supplies.

The Cowley-based group also had important factories in Swindon, Wiltshire, and in Linwood, near Glasgow, and it supplied in bulk to Rootes (the Humber, Hillman, Sunbeam group), Rolls-Royce, Jaguar, Rover and Standard-Triumph. Therefore, when the news broke in July 1965 that a merger between Pressed Steel and BMC was proposed, it caused great consternation throughout the industry.

In Coventry, for instance, it immediately caused Standard-Triumph directors to re-focus their attention on the great tract of land on the outskirts of Liverpool, which was still largely undeveloped from the days when Alick Dick had authorised work to start. Leyland, in fact, was becoming so desperate for more productive space that it had already made an offer to take over the redundant Armstrong-Whitworth factory on the south-east corner of Coventry's Baginton airfield, but the A-W management had not thought the sum offered high enough, and negotiations broke down.

For Triumph, at least, there was the medium-term possibility of being able to secure its body supplies from Liverpool (and, of course, from Mulliners/Forward Radiator in Birmingham), and Rootes had similar plans of its own, but the future began to look very problematical for Rolls-Royce, Rover and Jaguar. It was not that Pressed Steel's new masters would be cutting-off body supplies – its merger press release specifically promised that it 'intended to maintain the existing goodwill and business relationships that Pressed Steel enjoy with its own customers' – but the implications of having its future styling and product plans known to a competitor were obvious.

Therefore, when BMC and the Jaguar group got together in July 1966, no-one was unduly surprised. At a stroke it secured Jaguar's future, gave them access to the massive resources of BMC, allowed Sir William Lyons to stop worrying about the successor he would have had to find when he decided to retire, and brought the Guy-Daimler truck group into contact with BMC's own large commercial-vehicle business.

As far as the formation of BMH (British Motor Holdings, the amalgamation of BMC with Jaguar) was concerned, it made Donald Stokes more determined to expand Leyland as quickly as possible. There was only one sizeable car-making firm left free now – Rover. Within weeks of the BMC-Jaguar deal being settled, Stokes was in contact with Rover's Sir George Farmer at Solihull. The overtures could not have come at a better time for Rover. Having bought Alvis in 1965, it was also looking forward to a period of expansion, with new large saloon cars, an exciting sports coupé, and a luxurious four-wheel drive car in mind. Its problem was that a great deal of capital would have to be found to fund it – and it was not at all sure where the bodies were to come from in the end.

The proposed Leyland-Triumph merger with Rover was made public at the end of 1966, was favourably received by both sides of the deal, and was formalised early in the new year of 1967.

All that now remained was for the British prime minister, Harold Wilson, to engineer and influence talks between Sir George Harriman and Sir Donald Stokes. These were going on for weeks, in a rather desultory fashion, but at the turn of the year they became more serious, and the news of the final monstrous merger which gave birth to the British Leyland complex broke on January 17, 1968.

Each and every one of these corporate moves affected Standard-Triumph, either directly or indirectly, and they certainly all had an effect on the cars the engineers were encouraged to develop while it was going on. However, right up to 1968 and the formation of British Leyland, there were no direct outside influences on product design. Even after the merger with Rover, when it immediately became clear that the new combine should not eventually be building two very similar 2-litre cars, and that it should not be supporting two V8 engines, nothing was done to develop a policy

of rationalisation. Nothing, that is, except for the cancellation of the mid-engined P6BS Rover sports coupé, partly because of new capital spending priorities and partly because Stokes and Harry Webster were opposed to it.

While all the manoeuvring of these corporate mammoths was going on, Triumph had been looking at its future engine-design policy. The first meetings, which featured Harry Webster and Lewis Dawtrey, were held in 1962/63, against a background assumption that all Standard-Triumph passenger cars would be using either the Herald/2000 four-cylinder or six-cylinder engines by 1967.

The famous old wet-liner Vanguard-TR-Ferguson-tractor engine range would not be used in the new Triumph 2000 car, and it would not last all that much longer in the TR sports cars. With a stretch to 1296cc for the little four-cylinder engine already under development for the new front-wheel drive car, and the last stretch of all – increased strokes – already proved feasible on paper if not yet in practice, the existing engine lines appeared to be near the end of their lives. This, in fact, was soon proved to be too pessimistic, as both power boosts and additional usage for the engines were found in future years, while the combination of Lucas fuel-injection to tame a wild camshaft profile was most effective in the 2498cc PI and TR5/TR6 engines. In four-cylinder form, of course, the engines which had originally been designed in 1951/52 were still in production in 1980 in Coventry (for Spitfire and Dolomite 1300/1500 models) when all car production at Canley was terminated.

Harry Webster's instruction to Dawtrey was that he should survey the contemporary engines scene throughout the world. He should take into account the company's machining and assembly capabilities. He should consider the cars already being made, those under development, and even those merely being talked about. He should then stir in a goodly pinch of crystal-gazing and inspiration, and recommend a range of new engines which should be laid down for production to start by the end of the 1960s, and should be capable of lasting throughout the 1970s.

For Dawtrey, who had been connected with Standard since the 1920s, it must have been an enthralling, if rather terrifying assignment. He was not asked to discard anything – which meant that he could consider gas-turbines, Wankels, or any other unlikely layouts if he thought they had possibilities. One constraint he had to acknowledge was that the new engines might need to be slotted into existing Triumph cars, and that they should also be compatible with a front-wheel drive system, which had already been schemed-out for the Triumph 1300 model.

The Wankel and gas-turbine possibilities were speedily put aside (this obviously saved the company many years, many millions of pounds and severe development and service problems), and the survey then ranged over the layout of piston engines. Any engine layout which could be very wide (a flat-four or a flat-six, for example) was also discounted because Triumph was firmly wedded to providing compact turning circles, which could only be achieved by arranging for spectacular wheel-lock angles.

In the end, Dawtrey's choice had to be made between an all-new family of straight-fours and sixes, or a family of fours and related V8s. There was a third alternative – V4s and V6s – but this was never seriously considered, even though it was known that BMC was designing on that basis (the engines were eventually cancelled before they saw the light of day), and that Ford was also proposing to produce such a range.

The choice, effectively, was between a straight-six or a V8 for the larger version in the family, and the V8 layout got Dawtrey's vote because it was that much more compact and potentially lighter in terms of lb/bhp. Triumph already had a good reputation with its six, but it was thought to be too long for the future generation of cars then being considered.

Dawtrey's submission, made in 1963, was accepted without modification, and it looked like providing an ideal base from which Harry Webster and his product-planning colleagues could begin to plan their Triumphs for the 1970s. It was at this point that strange coincidences brought the company into contact with another company – Saab.

The Swedish concern, famous up to that point only for making cars with two-stroke engines, had begun to plan for a completely new type of car. Saab called this the Project Gudmund (Gudmund day is April 2 in Sweden, the day when the Saab 99 project was officially launched), and began to work closely with Ricardo Engineering on a new engine design once it had assessed the Lancia Fulvia power train. Saab had no four-stroke experience of its own, so a link with a distinguished consulting concern like Ricardo was logical.

Ricardo and Saab got as far as designing and building prototype engines in 1300cc (55bhp) and 1500cc (68bhp) guise which showed promise, but Saab was always worried about having to set-up its own production lines for an all-new design. Consequently, it was very intrigued to learn from Ricardo that there was a British car firm which was also proposing to build a new range of engines which looked astonishingly similar to those already in use in Saab 99 prototypes, and that it thought some sort of collaboration could be arranged. Thus it was that Saab's Tryggve Holm approached Standard-Triumph at the end of 1963, well before the first engine had even been built and tested!

There is no question that Triumph's new family of engines was designed by Ricardo – that would be doing a great injustice both to Lewis Dawtrey and to Harry Webster's team – and it's true that Ricardo had a general engine-development contract with Triumph and was usually kept informed of anything new which was being planned.

This was the first slant-four engine of the late 1960s, which was used by Saab for three years before Triumph was ready to use it in the Dolomite 1850.

Saab's interest in the new engines was confined to the four, which would be canted over towards the nearside of the Triumph car, at 45 degrees, to idealise cylinder block machining arrangements of a four and a related V8. Nevertheless, in Dawtrey's original skeleton the V8 was the basis of a common design, from which a slant-four could conveniently be made. Although he looked at extremes of 1000cc to 2000cc for each bank of cylinders (which meant that the equivalent V8 could be either a 2-litre or a 4-litre, with anything else in between as well), it was thought that the more practical limits were 1200cc for the four to three litres for a V8. As any student of engine design will know, once space has been allowed in the basic block for such variables, the permutations can easily be accommodated.

Saab, it seemed, was committed to using front-wheel drive for its new car, and as Triumph was also looking at (and beyond) the front-wheel drive Ajax model, this gave the two sides even more common ground. Saab wanted a simple but efficient engine producing about 80bhp, and thought it should be between 1.5 and 1.7 litres. This all sounded ideal to Triumph, so much so that Tryggve Holm was invited to visit the plant in January 1964 to view schemes and plans for the new engines. He was impressed by the single overhead camshaft layout that he saw, and told them he would need between 30,000 and 40,000 engines a year by 1968.

Since Triumph was not planning on having cars ready for its

own engine before then, it pushed hard for the Saab business, even though it would have to grant Saab its exclusive use (in four-cylinder form) for a time. Like all major commercial links – especially those in which there was no question of the companies themselves moving closer together – it all took time to arrange. However, by March 1965, when the first engines were just beginning to prove themselves on the test beds in Coventry, the deal was done and a public announcement was made. At that time Saab was talking publicly of 'engines up to 1500cc,' and was quoting quantities to be supplied from Coventry to Sweden at the rate of 50,000 every year. It is worth noting that Saab's requirements – power, torque and related figures – were all met from a very early stage, and it was the Saab 99's unstoppable increase in weight over the years, not a lack in engine power, which caused the engines to be modified and enlarged so often before the early 1970s.

All this was for the future, for the late 1960s, if not the 1970s. The slant-four engine, soon almost universally called the Saab engine inside and outside the works, would be ready first, and a V8 derivative would follow it. Although the engines should have come on-stream in the same order at Triumph, Saab's demands were such that it would be the V8 which first found its way into a Triumph car.

In the meantime, there were three important new model developments to be settled, one mainly new (the Stag), and two being important revisions (the 2000 and 1300). Along with extensive work planned for the Spitfire and TR sports cars, this was going to keep Standard-Triumph occupied for the next three or four years without a break.

The 2+2 Stag evolved almost by accident, though the company became interested in it at a very early stage. In 1964 Giovanni Michelotti, having produced a very satisfactory style for the Triumph 2000, was anxious to create a sporting version of the car, more obviously special than the fastback saloon he had already built. Accordingly, an old prototype was delivered to him by road (in fact, straight from the Le Mans race where the Spitfires had made their impressive racing debut, and where it had been used for general transport), and Michelotti began a transformation.

No-one at Triumph really knew what the little Italian had in mind (it was not an officially sponsored effort), so one can imagine Harry Webster's surprise when, on a routine visit to Turin at the beginning of 1966, he was confronted with a sleek new coupé using Triumph parts.

"Michelotti wanted to use it for a piece of advertising for his own skills," Harry Webster recalled, "he was proposing to put it in a motor show. I instantly made my own decision on behalf of the company, and told Michelotti that I couldn't let him use it in a show now that he had finished it, but that I wanted to keep it! In fact, we then got it back to Coventry and kept it on ice for some time. It was the usual problem of priorities, and money to tool it."

The new car looked so good that Webster thought there must be a market for it all over the world. He reported to his fellow directors in February, pointing out that he thought it to be more promising than the TR4A face-lift then being studied. For a few short weeks, the new car was called a TR6, which was most confusing. By the summer, the product-planning staff had surveyed world markets, decided that a suitably modified car would sell well, and formally proposed that it should be adopted. They estimated that 12,000 cars a year could be sold, that tooling costs would be about £2.3 million, and that the car could be launched in 1968, initially with a 2498cc six-cylinder engine and later with the new V8.

The project got under way, with the code-name Stag. This, incidentally, was an out-of-the-blue choice, for the usual security reasons,

Only one prototype Stag fastback was built, but it was never put into production. When it came to committing capital for tooling, the 2000/2.5 PI saloon face-lift won the battle.

but was liked so much from the directors right down to the people who would have to sell it that the name stuck. It is the only case we know of a Triumph code-name being carried through to the production cars.

During the winter of 1966/67 complications set in due to the implications of the Leyland merger with Rover. One major talking point was that the combined companies found themselves with two new V8 engine projects. Rover's ex-Buick unit was ready to go into quantity production in the summer of 1967, and Triumph's own engine was planned for 1968/69 (though even this ambitious date began to look problematical as testing and tooling proceeded – it was always a desperately tight schedule). There was no immediate directive to look for rationalisation, and it does not seem as

To provide much-needed stiffness to the body structure, the Stag was provided with a permanently-fixed T-bar structure above the seats. This stayed in place even if the optional hardtop was later added.

This was Michelotti's very first prototype Stag of 1966/67, which was based on the platform and much of the running gear of a Triumph 2000. At this time it was proposed that the headlamps should live behind sliding shutters, and the stiffening T-bar (above the seating area) had not been developed.

Originally built as a 2.5-litre power unit, but ultimately as a 3.0-litre, the Stag V8 engine produced 145bhp. Original plans to make it available on developed version of the 2000/2.5-litre saloons and in a sports car were both abandoned.

if there was ever a serious threat to cancel one of the designs (that cancellation, incidentally, would have fallen on the Triumph V8, as Rover had already spent a good deal of money on its engine, rights for which had been acquired in 1965), but there were attempts to mate the Stag body with a Rover engine. These failed because the Rover engine was physically too large (or so the unenthusiastic workshop fitters insisted – but this was what we might call 'special pleading'). Even so, if it had been essential the two units could have been made to fit each other, as later private conversions have proved.

The original intention to release the car in 1968 was soon rendered impractical, due to the combined effect of design-and-development changes, production priorities and the onset of North American safety legislation. As conceived by Michelotti, the Stag used a shortened Triumph 2000 underframe, had headlamps concealed behind slide-away sections of the grille, and a conventional convertible style. The general lines were not changed between prototype and production car, but detail alterations could be counted in their thousands.

As Triumph's John Lloyd once told us: "we thought we could get away with modified 2000 tooling parts, but by the time we'd had to chop off a bit here, add on a bit there, and particularly to provide roll-over protection, there was precious little left of the original pressings. Our body-design people then pointed out that all-new tooling would be as cheap as modified tooling, especially if we did most of it ourselves. Stag as produced doesn't have a single panel in common with the 2000 saloon, even though it may look like it."

The biggest holdup of all, however, was due to a major upheaval in new-model priorities. Whereas the Stag was originally due to go into production in 1968, and nothing was immediately planned for the big saloons, by 1967 it became clear that the saloons would shortly need a boost in sales appeal, which could only be achieved

with a major face-lift. Michelotti, therefore, was asked to do one of his miraculously quick jobs, responded superbly, and came up with a much-changed saloon body which – in front, rear, and facia styling – looked remarkably similar to the new Stag!

There was a two-fold improvement plan for the 2000. First, and before any restyling could be prepared, it was decided to introduce a really high-performance version. The prototype 2000TS cars had not proved to be fast or sparkling enough, so they were discarded. In their place, when the TR5 was under development, prototypes were built with fuel-injected 2498cc units. Two cars were prepared to compete in the 1967 RAC Rally – one to be driven by world champion F1 racing driver Denny Hulme, and one by Roy Fidler – but this event was cancelled at the last minute and the cars' potential could not be assessed.

The new car, called the 2.5 PI, was introduced in the autumn of 1968. With few external or even interior trim changes, and with a slightly tamed TR5 engine (132bhp was claimed instead of the TR5's 150bhp), it was a splendid 'Q-ship' with exhilarating performance. An estate-car version was phased-in from March 1969, and nearly 7000 cars were built in the first 12 months.

The restyle, coded 'Innsbruck' for no good reason, was scheduled for 1969, at first for the Geneva Motor Show in March, which meant that the original fuel-injected cars would be rare beasts. While retaining the existing passenger cabin and the general lines, Michelotti had transformed the car's looks by extending the nose and tail sections. Apart from the use of a wider rear track, the car's chassis and mechanical components were barely changed. The nose had lost its distinctive roll-over panel ahead of the bonnet, and now had a more integrated sweep which included the quadruple headlamps, while the tail, though longer, had a sharp cut-off and more distinctive features. The boot was much larger – a very good selling point. The ensemble was quite remarkably like that of the Stag, though the general public was not to know of this in 1969.

Exterior changes were pleasing enough, but the real advance was in the facia layout, where the jumbly layout of the original Triumph 2000 was ditched in favour of a smoothly swept panel with clear instruments and logically-placed controls.

Approval for this revised saloon car came in October 1967, actually in the same week that the second Stag prototype was being finished, and the

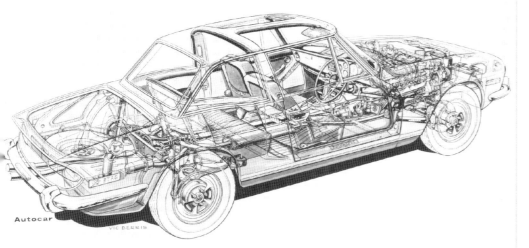

Autocar

VIC BERRIS

This masterly cutaway, produced by Vic Berris in 1970, shows all the elements of the Stag – this particular version having the optional hardtop and Borg Warner automatic transmission. Production, in this form, spanned from 1970 to 1977.

Long nose, long tail, smart wheel covers: this one of the 1974 range of Mk 2 2000s which continued to give Triumph market leadership.

With a short-wheelbase derivate of the 2000/2.5 PI 'chassis' platform, the Stag was a well-proportioned four-seater, available in fold-back soft top or removable hardtop versions.

directors learned that while Pressed Steel could not complete the new press-tools in time for a 1969 launch, Karmann (which had just secured the TR6 retooling deal) would be delighted to oblige.

Thus it was that the revised Mark 2 Triumph 2000/2.5 cars came to be rushed through, and the Stag was pushed aside for a time to take its place in the queue for facilities. It also helps to explain the general misunderstanding about the sequence of events for these cars. Although the Stag was announced last it was conceived first, and is the true progenitor of the Mark 2 saloons. By the end of the 1960s, too, a smart and distinctive family resemblance was developing across the range of Triumph cars. Large and small saloons, large and small sporting cars, were all getting the same distinctive cut-off tails, and even the noses had a lot in common.

While the Mark 2 saloons were being rushed through, work continued on the Stag. North American safety regulations were read and re-read, and as a result the Stag's distinctive T-brace roll-over bar was adopted, while the headlamps came permanently out into the open. The slide-away covers had, in any case, given trouble at an early stage: they relied on electric motors and tracks for their operation, and when thick ice was deposited on the tracks the strain on the mechanism often caused the motors to burn out.

The biggest problems, however, were in the time schedule and in the power trains. Even by the autumn of 1967 it was clear that the Stag could not be ready before 1969, and its marketing success appeared to hinge on the performance of its fuel-injected 2½-litre V8 engine; the idea of selling it, at first, with a TR5 engine had already been dropped. In the spring of 1968, just as Harry Webster was moving out (to become technical chief of Leyland's newly-purchased Austin-Morris car division of BMC) and Spen King was moving in, it was agreed that this engine's low-speed torque was not satisfactory, and it was agreed that the engine should be enlarged to a full 3-litre.

Such a power boost (whether from a carburettor or Bosch-injected engine – both were proposed) necessitated changes to the rest of the chassis. Spen King therefore authorised a stronger gearbox, a more robust back-axle, bigger brakes and, because of the latter, bigger 14in road wheels. By then the Stag was completely different from its 2000 origins, and it was only a later rationalisation of chassis and transmission components which brought it someway back into the fold.

Tooling for the Stag brought the Liverpool factories into even greater prominence. The body tools were concentrated at the original (ex-Hall) Liverpool factory, but the shells were assembled, painted and completely trimmed at the brand-new No 2 factory, a real mammoth building for which Alick Dick had bulldozed the first sod off the green-field site in 1960. Final assembly was, and always would be, at the Canley plant in Coventry. The car, after a protracted and complicated birth, was eventually launched in June 1970, but it was some months before supplies really began to get to their customers.

In the meantime, Standard-Triumph had become involved, quite unwittingly, in the biggest motor-industry merger Britain had ever seen; for the implications and the complications of this giant marriage were to affect the company for years to come. Leyland Motors had followed up its purchases of Standard-Triumph (1961) and ACV (1962) by taking over the Rover-Alvis group at the beginning of 1967. This, on its own, would have been enough to give Triumph and Rover planners a lengthy dose of corporate indigestion, but at the beginning of 1968 their task was complicated even further when, with the British Government's encouragement, Leyland merged with British Motor Holdings (of which BMC was the dominant part).

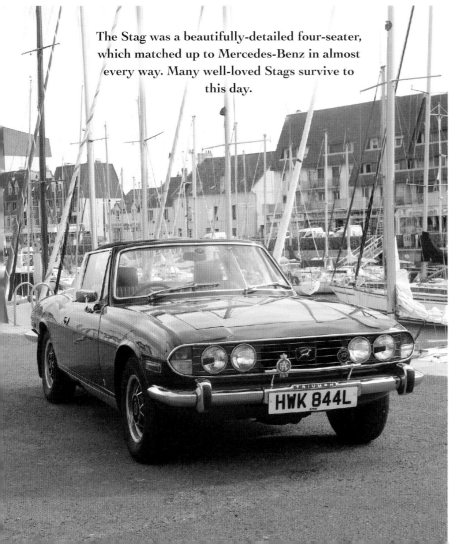

The Stag was a beautifully-detailed four-seater, which matched up to Mercedes-Benz in almost every way. Many well-loved Stags survive to this day.

Here seen in standard soft-top form, the Stag was a popular and versatile four-seater tourer. Many owners also owned the optional detachable hardtop, but kept it for use in the winter months.

This is how British Leyland originally advertised the Stag when it appeared in 1970.

Henceforth this was going to mean that Austin-Morris, MG, Jaguar-Daimler, Coventry Climax and many other subsidiaries would all have to co-exist with Standard-Triumph and Rover. Eventually, no doubt, rationalisation would have to be considered. Whatever Triumph might have wanted to do in the 1970s, even if in harness with Rover, would have to be looked at in the light of the new and final merger. The sports cars, after all, would have to take MG and Jaguar into consideration, while the saloon cars would have to advance alongside the Austin-Morris and Rover vehicles. How Triumph's resources were to be used in the 1970s would now depend on corporate policy, if and when it became clear.

For Triumph, the central problem, because they were the fastest selling of all the company's products, was the future of the front-wheel drive 1300/1300TC family. Any new variants, and even any new models, would have to take account not only of Triumph's experience since production had begun in 1965, but of future corporate policy. Not only would the cars' own worth have to be considered, but that of the BMC 1100/1300 and any front-drive or conventional successors which may be in the works at Longbridge.

Even before the merger was announced, Triumph was having grave doubts about its front-wheel drive installation. The fact was that it had not worked out as well as had been hoped, neither in terms of roadholding and handling, nor in terms of first costs, or of service-and-guarantee experience. Before long it became clear that if two new and desirable models were ever to be made available – a down-market cheap version, and a car with automatic transmission – then a massive change would have to be considered. 'Manx', the original short tail Triumph 1300, had eventually been cancelled when it became clear that it would never be cheap enough. Something more drastic would be needed.

By the end of 1967 (that year, in retrospect, counts as one of the most significant in Triumph's modern design sequences), Harry Webster had talked at great length with the sales, finance and planning staff. Even though they realised that some sections of the press (and no doubt their rivals in the industry) would make a great deal of fuss about a change, they prepared to abandon front-wheel drive, at least on some of the models. In coding terms, Ajax was to be split into two new projects – 'Manx II' and 'Ajax III.'

Put simply, and this was not a simple process as it evolved,

the 1300 would be up-engined, substantially restyled, and sold for a higher price. That car was Ajax III. On the other hand a cheap car would be evolved by scrapping front-wheel drive, completely reworking the floor-pan and major structure to allow for a conventional drive line with a live rear axle, allowing for two-door and four-door versions and fitting more simple equipment. That car was Manx II. Michelotti would get the unenviable job of reworking what had been a single basic style into two separate styles.

Allowing for two-door or four-door shells was quite straightforward, as this had been in his original Ajax brief in 1961. The front-wheel drive shell, while basically unchanged, had both tail and nose sheet-metal lengthened, thus increasing the boot stowage space (and ensuring the Triumph family tail could be added) and giving scope for a new front-end style. The rear-wheel drive shell, only made and announced in two-door form at first (though a four-door car followed in a year or so), used the original 1300 tail pressings, and yet another different nose with rectangular headlamps. This gave the Liverpool factories something to think about; previously they had no permutations, but from 1970 they would have to build two distinct models, two-door or four-door shells, and a host of sub-divisions depending on the export markets to be served.

Structural changes were less comprehensive than might have been feared. A new floorpan, from toe-board to back-axle, made provision for manual or automatic gearboxes, and for a propeller-shaft, along with pick-up points for either the live rear axle (cheap car) or the beam dead axle (up-engined front-drive car). The suspension was reverted back to non-independent rear suspension as it was found that the original independent suspension gave neither the roadholding nor the ride advantages that had originally been hoped.

Up front, it was easy to arrange a front suspension geometrically similar to the front-drive layout, but without the complications, and the Michelotti restyle allowed for the larger Saab engine to be installed in the engine bay if necessary. Incredibly, even though the Saab engine was being designed before the original Triumph 1300 layout was frozen, it became embarrassingly clear that one could not be fitted into the other at first!

Incidentally, it is not generally realised that a conversion from front-drive to rear-drive also made a four-wheel drive car a distinct and feasible possibility. By juggling bodies and transmissions, and by borrowing components from the 'Pony' project, a four-wheel drive special (actually a rally cross competition car) was prepared for Brian Culcheth to use in a televised event at Lydden Hill, in Kent, but after only one successful appearance the car was crashed, withdrawn, and subsequently broken-up.

Approval of this complex new programme was given in the spring of 1968. The front-drive car got the long-stroke 1493cc

In Triumph's reshuffled saloon car range for the 1970s, the Toledo was the 'entry-level' model to the smaller-car range, this being the two-door: there was also a four-door version. Note the apt background location!

engine which Harry Webster had proved to be possible way back in 1959, while the conventional car stayed with its 1296cc unit, although certain export territories received their machines with the 1493cc engine; most confusing. The front-drive car, logically enough, became the 1500, while the rear-drive car became the Toledo. Bodies for all versions would be pressed and assembled at the original Liverpool factory. The big new No 2 plant was now ready for use, however, so it was decided that the Toledo models would be completed there, while final assembly of front-drive 1500s would continue to be carried out in Coventry.

For the Liverpool project, therefore, it was the culmination of ten years of growth. From

As lined up in 1974, (left to right) the 1500TC, the Stag and the Toledo.

pressing and assembling Triumph Herald bonnets, to building bare bodies for the TR4, to building completely painted and trimmed Stag shells, and now building an entire model, it had been a logical progression. But, as will become clear in the next chapter, even more exciting things were in store for the new Liverpool factory. Not that this plant would have an illustrious future. A crippling strike in 1977 and 1978, coupled with British Leyland's financial problems, caused the operation to be closed down completely, and the assembly to be moved to Coventry.

Of the three ranges of Triumphs which were involved in the future model programme approved in 1968, and which appeared in a variety of specifications during the next few years, the Stag was to prove the least successful, though it was made in the same basically unchanged form until June 1977. In those seven years nearly 26,000 cars were built, 5446 in the best year, which was 1973.

There were engine troubles, particularly in regard to main-bearing life, cylinder head warping (often caused by overheating due to a blown cylinder head gasket) and other problems, all of which unerringly became known to the sort of clientele which might buy the car. The Stag's biggest failing was that it did not take any export market by storm – of the 25,877 Stags built, only 6780 were sold abroad, whereas the sales departments had hoped for at least a 50/50 split in sales.

Even though the Stag was quick enough (115/120mph in overdrive top gear) and nicely presented with features like power-assisted steering, optional hardtop, optional automatic transmission (which a majority of customers chose) and other details, somehow it was not quite exclusive enough to seriously dent the Mercedes/Lancia/Alfa Romeo market in export territories. It was more expensive than it might have been because the V8 engine was never shared with any other Triumph model. Without the Rover merger it is likely that a Stag-engined Triumph 2000 saloon/estate would have been marketed. The fact that the V8 engine fitted a Stag's engine bay meant that it slotted straight into that of a saloon. One car was built, and was pronounced gorgeous by the more romantic of Triumph's engineering staff, but it was not offered as it would have been a direct competitor to Rover's V8-engined 3500.

In 1970, the works competitions department at Abingdon built four very special 2.5 PIs to contest the *Daily Mirror* World Cup Rally from London to Mexico. Brian Culcheth, driving a sister to this machine, finished a remarkable second overall.

By 1977, too, British Leyland was happy to drop the Stag engine, not only because of the high guarantee claims it'd had to suffer, but because it was proving to be an embarrassment where flow-production of four-cylinder Dolomite/Dolomite Sprint engines was concerned. Both cylinder block and cylinder head tooling was partly commonised, and it has often been said that in terms of engines built per shift, three four-cylinder blocks could be made for every single V8 block. With four-cylinder engines in great demand (even though Saab had set up its own production facilities in Sweden by 1972) the implications were obvious.

Even so, much of what was tried and produced first on the Stag, later found a home on other models – the transmission, the power-assisted steering, the brakes and the cast-alloy wheels all being good examples. The last, and most cruel blow to the Stag's future was that it had to be withdrawn from sale in the United States. Three-quarters of all Stags sent to the United States had suffered valve gear problems.

The Innsbruck saloons, more properly known as Triumph 2000 Mark 2s (and their derivatives) were always successful, and the 2.5 PIs made their mark in no uncertain manner in 1970 when Brian Culcheth and Paddy Hopkirk took two cars into second and fourth places in the 16,000 mile London-to-Mexico World Cup Rally. Although they were rather more special than British Leyland claimed at the time (the bodyshells, for instance, received

all manner of loving care, modification and strengthening at the hands of Pressed Steel before they were delivered to Abingdon for assembly), they proved to be admirably rugged and suitable for this event.

Mark 2 cars were in production from the autumn of 1969 to the summer of 1977, after which they were phased-out in favour of the new corporate design of Rover 2300s and 2600s (which, incidentally, used Triumph-designed engines and transmissions). A poignant photograph was published in Leyland's own employees' magazine showing the last bodyshell of all dropping off the assembly line in Swindon; nearly a quarter of a million had been built. In those eight years there were no significant body or styling improvements, and no changes of any nature to the sheet metal.

Triumph's biggest disappointment with these otherwise successful cars was that the Lucas fuel-injection used on 2.5 PI models continued to give trouble throughout the period of its use. This type of injection had always been an expensive (but effective) method of extracting and taming the ultimate power from the engine, but somehow the installation never settled down to give a reputation of serene reliability.

There was even, at one time, a known history of engine-compartment fires, a malady later cured. It was never easy for minor adjustments to be made, and trouble in the high-pressure metering unit always meant complete replacement; service complaints were higher than expected. Therefore, although the 2.5 PI served as a valuable and exciting flagship to the range, in saloon or estate car form, it eventually fell from favour.

Phasing-out the PI model was really a two-stage process. In the summer of 1974 the 2500TC model was introduced, which was really the 2.5 PI engine without fuel-injection and with rather milder cam timing. The maximum power output was a long way down (99bhp instead of the PI's final figure of 120bhp – both being measured to the strict DIN standards) and performance was also down, but the new car was quite a lot livelier than the basic 2000 model.

Finally, in June 1975, the PI model was discontinued in favour of a new 2500S version, which used a boosted (106bhp) engine with carburettors, 14in Stag road wheels, overdrive as standard and a front anti-roll bar for the first time ever on a Barb/Innsbruck car. The 2500TC, likewise, received the boosted 2498cc engine, while even the good old 2000 (now renamed the 2000TC) got an extra 7bhp, and all shared the new stiffer front suspension.

In 1970 and 1971, before British Leyland's rationalisation plans had been finalised, and before it had been decided to make one operating company out of Triumph and Rover, there were thoughts about a new big Triumph saloon, the engine for which later found a home in the Rover 2300/2600, but this, like other fine ideas that made little sense in the face of 1970s economics, was soon abandoned.

At the end of the 1960s and early in the 1970s, however, a great deal of effort was being put behind the development of the Toledo/1500 cars. In no time at all, after the establishment of British Leyland, the idea of gradually turning Triumph into the builders of sports and sporting saloon cars began to take shape. Without prejudice to the future of such fast-selling cars as the Toledo and 2000, it gradually became known that in the long-term, Rover would be building the large cars in this sub-group, while Triumph would be building the medium cars. Small cars (or, rather, cheaper cars) would be the responsibility of the Austin-Morris division. It was a logical policy decision, but its implementation was going to take time. First, therefore, Triumph decided to boost the appeal of the Toledo/1500 range. Even in the autumn of 1968, well before the

The 2500S-engined derivative of the Mk 2 range was not only smart and fast, but was beautifully and carefully trimmed and furnished, too.

The final derivation of the Triumph slant-four engine made by Saab was to turbocharge it in the mid-1970s. Such a development was never copied by British Leyland.

The original Dolomite 1300 of 1976 was effectively an updated, re-badged version of the four-door Toledo. More than 32,000 would be sold in the next four years.

The 1300 of 1965, and the 1500 of 1970 which followed, were both small, well-equipped, and successful front-wheel drive saloons. The Dolomite of 1972 would evolve from that basic design.

The slant-four engine fitted snugly into the engine bay of the Dolomite 1850 – while the 16-valve version which followed was an even tighter fit!

rear-wheel drive Toledo had been committed to full production, MG's Abingdon competitions department had been asked to look at every corporate possibility in the search for an ideal competition car to underpin their future. Peter Browning, the department's manager, asked for a Marina (to be launched by Austin-Morris in 1971) fitted with a twin-cam version of the Saab engine, the special engine to be designed and built in small quantities by Coventry Climax. This request was refused by Lord Stokes, and a modified request for a twin-cam engine to be fitted to a Toledo also received the thumbs down.

In hindsight, this was a ghastly mistake, for it relegated Leyland to the category of also-ran in the fast-developing saloon car racing and rallying business of the 1970s, just as Ford's formidable Escort RS1600s came to maturity.

There was never any doubt, however, that the existing single-cam Saab engine would be fitted to the Ajax/Manx bodyshell. One of the objects of the 1500's longer nose had been to make space for the bulkier single-camshaft engine, though it was not intended to make a front-wheel drive car of this. Even though Saab itself was going into production with a front-wheel drive 99, this was not at all related to that used in Triumph's 1300s and 1500s: the installations were completely different. In the Saab, the engine was turned 180 degrees, so that its flywheel and clutch were at the front of the car, and the engine leaned over to the right-hand side of the car, while the actual transmission was Saab's own design.

By the beginning of 1971, soon after the new-shape cars had been launched, the existence of a high-performance Dolomite became something of an open secret in the world of motoring. First it was due to be released in the summer, then in November, and finally it made it to the showrooms at the beginning of 1972. The problem was not with the car itself, but with the labour-relations situation in British Leyland, by then approaching anarchy in some factories. Production cars had been built and stored by summer 1971, but would not be delivered until 1972.

The Dolomite was yet another permutation on the Toledo/1500 theme. It used the long nose/long tail 1500 body, but the Toledo's rear-drive transmission layout, and was the first Triumph car in which the new slant-four engine was made available. Even then the engine was not the same as that supplied to Saab. While Saab's unit had a single carburettor and 88bhp, Triumph's had twin Zenith-Strombergs and 91bhp. (Within a year Saab would be building its own engines, which would be fully 2 litres, of greatly modified

The overhead cam-engined Dolomite of 1972 was that family's first 100mph car, and had a stylish and well-equipped instrument layout to match.

design and with an option of petrol-injection.) Both, by then, had been enlarged to 1854cc, an engine size which was still used in Triumphs until 1980. The Dolomite's transmission showed signs of rationalisation with that in other British Leyland models – it shared its axle with that of the Morris Marina, and the basis of its manual gearbox, but the very close-ratio gears were those already well-known and liked in the GT6.

Once launched the Dolomite was a great success in Britain and abroad. It was perhaps going too far to compare it with the smaller BMWs (Triumph never made this claim, but the motoring press were quick to draw the parallels), but there is no doubt that the Dolomite was a great advance on most other British compact cars. Even without the optional overdrive it could reach 100mph, and the stiffened-up suspension made it a delight to drive.

But this was not Triumph's last word on the subject. Peter Browning's request, back in 1968, had not been on purely theoretical grounds. Having got its single-overhead-cam engine into production, Triumph was now proposing to improve it even further. It might not be willing to complicate matters with a twin-cam cylinder head, but it was prepared to improve the breathing by other means. Spen King, in cahoots with corporate advisers from Coventry Climax and Jaguar, was proposing to build a 16-valve version!

At the end of the 1960s, when this remarkable engine conversion was first proposed, engines with four valves per cylinder had become familiar, but they were simply not being sold to the general public. The Cosworth FVA unit, a much-modified Ford engine, was winning Formula 2 races, and in 1969 another much-modified Ford, the BDA, had been announced. Although

Ford threatened to sell a limited number of these engines in its new 2+2 Capri coupés, this never came to anything, and the first-ever BDA-engined road car to be sold to the public was the Escort RS1600 of 1970.

Triumph's own 16-valve cylinder head was an ingenious layout. While its four valves per cylinder were arranged in the classic manner – two inlet and two exhaust side-by-side and opposed to each other at an included angle of 35 degrees – there was still only a single overhead camshaft. This was placed above the line of the inlet valves, operating them directly through inverted bucket-type tappets, and it operated the exhaust valves via long rockers. That much was ingenious enough, but the production engineer's dream was that both inlet and exhaust valves were operated by the same camshaft profile. There are, therefore, only eight cam profiles (instead of 16) on what would otherwise have been an incredibly complicated shaft. At the same time as the engine was being developed, and to bring it closely in line with a sporting class limit, the cylinder bore was increased from 87mm to 90.3mm, which resulted in a capacity of 1998cc. It must be pointed out here that the Saab-built engine had a 90mm bore, a 1985cc capacity, and was a completely different engine by that time, after some years of separate development. Further, when Saab decided to build a 16-valve cylinder head for its very special rally cars of the mid-1970s, it chose a twin-cam layout which had nothing in common with the Triumph layout. Triumph's own head, while inspired by Spen King, Walter Hassan and Harry Mundy, was detailed in the first place by Lewis Dawtrey, and was the final project which can be credited to his excellent reputation at Standard-Triumph.

With careful attention to the porting and breathing (twin SU carburettors were chosen to look after induction arrangements), the new engine – PE114 to the engineers, Dolomite Sprint to the publicists – produced a lusty 127bhp at 5700rpm. Even in this un-tuned form (and as Spen King once said: 'I went away on holiday, and when I came back I found that someone, was already running a development engine at 150bhp'), it was going to be too much for the existing transmission. The Sprint, therefore, was given a Triumph 2.5/TR6/Stag gearbox, and a new live rear axle with the TR6 crown-wheel-and-pinion. The suspension was redeveloped, and the car equipped with GKN cast-alloy wheels with 5½in rims.

When it was released, the Dolomite Sprint caused a sensation. Even though it was basically an eight-year-old body-style, the new car was an obvious BMW-beater, and the advertising agencies went to great lengths to emphasise this. A Triumph so small which could exceed 115mph, sprint to 100mph in less than half-a-minute from rest, and still return average fuel economy figures of 26-28mpg was

Even before the Dolomite Sprint was officially launched, Brian Culcheth drove this works prototype in British rallies.

a remarkable bargain. Whereas the 1500 sold for £1010 (basic) and the Dolomite 1850 for £1210, the Sprint retailed for £1460, and was worth every penny.

A revitalised British Leyland competitions department soon started racing and rallying the Dolomite Sprint in earnest (Brian Culcheth, in fact, had used a prototype Sprint in several rallies – where the regulations allowed this – though not with any great success). To get the car homologated into FIA Group 2 meant that 1000 cars had to be built. The company applied for approval so soon after announcement that the governing body was suspicious and demanded an inspection. When shown an assembly hall at Coventry which was brimming with 16-valve cars, the inspectors were astonished. 'Never before, never,' the inspector said, 'have we actually seen 16-valve cars in mass-production like this. Your competitors merely offer kits, and not many of them at that!'

It was time, now, to make sense of the rest of the range, where the 1500 with front-wheel drive was beginning to look uncomfortably out of place. In the autumn of 1973, just a few months after the Dolomite Sprint had been released, this situation was remedied. By a judicious reshuffle, the 1500 became the 1500TC; the new car used the existing 1500 body and decoration, but with a Dolomite/Toledo floorpan and rear-drive transmission line, allied to a boosted 1493cc engine. At long last an automatic-transmission option could be made available, something about which the sales force had been nagging since 1966.

For more than four years the family was built in two separate locations – the Toledo being entirely assembled, from pressing the body to the complete car rolling out to its delivery transporter, at the big Liverpool No 2 factory, while all other models were finished-off and their power trains installed at the Coventry factory. In the late autumn of 1974, the Toledo was moved out of Liverpool to make way for the new TR7 sports car (described fully in the next chapter), and was henceforth finished in Coventry. Coincident with the move, the two-door option on the Toledo (latterly it had been £46 cheaper in basic price than the four-door) was dropped.

One other rationalisation remained to be enacted, after which the anomalies of the early 1970s could be forgotten, and this was publicly announced in March 1976. The short nose/short tail Toledo body was dropped, and all existing mechanical permutations were concentrated on the long nose/long tail shell, all being named as Dolomites.

From that time on, the entire Dolomite range – 1300, 1500, 1850 and Sprint – was based on the style of the original Michelotti-shaped 1300 car. Bodies were pressed and assembled at the old Hall Engineering (No 1) factory in Liverpool, for a time shipped up the road to the No 2 factory for painting and protection, then shipped to Coventry for final assembly. After No 2 was closed, bare shells were sent straight to Coventry for completion.

After a further re-jig of model types and duties, the Toledo was discontinued, and became the Dolomite 1500. This was the Dolomite SE version, a very late model which was discontinued in 1980.

Dolomite 1500 SEs of the late 1970s used a 71bhp/1493cc version of the famous SC engine, which had started life in 1953.

Meanwhile, soon after pilot production of the TR7 had begun, and while production of Toledos was being moved to Coventry, British Leyland ran into a massive cash crisis, and for a few days it looked possible that this giant corporation could be forced out of business. A combination of Britain's soaring cost inflation, and the impact of the Yom Kippur war-inspired oil price increases had hit the corporation when it was not equipped to shrug it off.

As a consequence, and in a matter of weeks, British Leyland had to be rescued by the British Government. By the spring of 1975 the corporation was more than 90 per cent owned by the British nation. Lord Stokes was eased out of his job as chairman and became the honorary President, while John Barber (who had been Leyland's managing director before the financial crash) was forced out completely.

The Government asked Lord Ryder, as head of its newly-established National Enterprise Board, to prepare a plan for the corporation's future. This, published in April 1975, took a ludicrously optimistic view of British Leyland's future prospects, and proposed a massive and regular injection of public money to finance an investment scheme. As far as Triumph was concerned, it was only immediately involved by becoming a part of the Leyland Cars group, instead of merely Rover-Triumph.

Soon it began to become clear what the future might hold for Triumph. Leaked information – the news was never spelt out in the form of public announcements – suggested that the Innsbruck range (the 2000/2500 cars) would soon give way to a new big-car range then being developed by Rover. Later, the group publicly announced that it intended to complete all Triumph final assembly in the huge new assembly hall at Solihull (the home of Rover, where the new Rover saloons were to be assembled), except, of course, for the TR7 family, which it planned to continue building at Liverpool. The big Canley assembly hall, new in 1960/61, was to be converted into a production building for components for Rover, Triumph and other Leyland Cars plants. The Dolomites, it was said, would move

No matter what level of the Dolomite range, all the cars had a neat, and well-equipped facia/instrument display – this being the Dolomite 1500SE.

This was how the nationalised Leyland Cars concern advertised the entire Dolomite range in the late 1970s.

to Solihull in 1978, and the long-running Spitfire sports car range would be allowed to fade gracefully away.

That was all well and good, except that two very important factors – the company's financial problems in the winter of 1977/78 and the ruinous strike which paralysed the big TR7 factory in Liverpool for 14 weeks during the same period, along with strong union objections among the Coventry work force – caused the Government-dominated management team to think again.

For many disheartening weeks the situation was utterly confused, but under a new boss (Michael Edwardes, who was soon to be knighted for his work in leading the company), a new purpose emerged and most of the decisions taken during the Ryder era in 1975 and 1976 were speedily abandoned.

The Canley assembly facility was reprieved, with the Dolomites and the Spitfires continuing to be built there until they were both discontinued in the autumn of 1980. To help fill up the production lines, all TR7 final assembly was moved down to Canley from Liverpool in the aftermath of the closure of the Merseyside plant.

However, with British Leyland being renamed BL, various loosely merged businesses being hived off once again to find their own feet (Jaguar, Land Rover and Unipart all benefited from this), and the company almost 100 per cent owned by the British Government (whose vote-catching decisions often took precedence over commercial good sense), this situation was not likely to persist for long.

The Triumph marque, in any case, was already in turmoil. The Dolomite range was getting old and was overdue for replacement, and a Rover-Triumph project, SD2, had been under way for some time. SD2 was, in effect, meant to be a smaller relation of the very successful SD1 series of Rover 2300/2600/3500 hatchbacks, and it shared many suspension and running gear components with the TR7. Several prototypes had already been built before the project was cancelled in 1976/77. BL Cars, which was beginning to work on similarly-sized Austin models, did not have the resources to invest in both types.

According to British Leyland's mid-1970s master plan, the car known as the SD2 family car should have replaced the Dolomite range, and would have used much of the same engine, transmission, chassis and running gear components as the TR7. Unhappily, it was cancelled as the corporation's finances worsened – though this prototype survives.

By mid-1979, and in spite of Sir Michael's oft-repeated talk of a 'product-led' recovery programme, BL's finances were in deep trouble. As he writes in his fascinating book *Back from the Brink* (published by Collins in 1983):

"In manpower terms, a further 25,000 jobs would have to go, to reduce manning levels and production capacity to a tolerable level. Triumph car assembly in Canley would have to cease. The MG models produced in Abingdon, near Oxford, would have to be discontinued ..."

And so it came about. In what had become a beleaguered business, BL found itself with far too many assembly facilities for the 1980s. Not only Canley and Abingdon, but Vanden Plas in Kingsbury and even Rover cars (but not Land Rover/Range Rover types) at Solihull also had to be sacrificed, all future car assembly therefore being concentrated on the Longbridge and Cowley plants.

In the end, the TR7 was only to be built in Canley for two years; the last Spitfire was produced in August 1980 and the final Dolomites were built in November 1980. The massive assembly hall, which had been brand-new only 20 years earlier, then fell silent, and it was some time before a corporate reshuffle made it part of the Unipart concern.

In the middle of all this financial and industrial turmoil, Triumph persevered with the development of a new sports car, and the TR7 was launched in 1975. Wherever it went, and no matter who was talking about it, the TR7 and all its derivatives attracted controversy. The story of its birth and evolution deserves a complete chapter to itself.

TR7 and TR8

In December 1967, Triumph and MG were deadly rivals, and proud of it. By the spring of 1968, however reluctantly, they had become allies, or at least commercial partners. This was just one of the illogical situations resulting from the Leyland-BMH merger of January 1968.

For better or worse – and in many ways it was certainly for the worse – the foundation of British Leyland upset a lot of long-term plans. What Triumph and MG had in mind for the 1970s was not at all what was actually carried out. At Abingdon, MG effectively stagnated until being closed down in 1980. The later Triumphs were not at all the same machines that Harry Webster and John Lloyd had been scheming in 1967.

When British Leyland formally came into existence there was no shortage of financial pundits willing to talk glibly about the 'economies of scale,' the possible rationalisations, and the other heartless benefits which might result from this biggest of all mergers, though none of them seemed to worry about the human miseries and hardship which could so easily have followed from a wholesale and immediate upheaval of the firms affected.

What actually happened was less dramatic. Although Lord Stokes set up several study groups immediately after the merger was announced, and soon told the world that the new group had settled on a ten-year product plan after little discussion, the individual companies carried on very much as before. The future of the corporation's sports cars, which mainly concerns us at this juncture, was not tackled at all until 1969 or 1970, and even then not in a decisive manner.

British Leyland had a good line-up of sporting cars, current or in development. Already on sale were the Spitfire and Sprite/Midget, TR5, MGB, MGC and Jaguar E-Type. A restyled body for the TR5, which would make it the TR6, was already being tooled-up. Triumph's Stag and Jaguar's V12 E-Type were also going ahead, but neither were much more than gleams in their sponsors' eyes. The venerable old Austin-Healey 3000 had just been withdrawn, and the luscious mid-engined P6BS Rover coupé had been cancelled in the face of opposition from Triumph and Jaguar.

Almost everyone – from Lord Stokes downwards – realised that there were far too many separate designs to be supported by a sensibly slimmed-down concern, and almost everyone had their own ideas of what should ideally be done. The obvious choice was to have one small sports car (Spitfire or Midget?), one medium-sized sports car (TR5/6 or MGB?) and one large sporting car (Stag or E-Type?).

Nothing of this nature was ever authorised. There was, for instance, ample time for the entire Stag project to have been cancelled – body tooling was not sufficiently advanced to cost a fortune in cancellation charges, and Canley's production experts would have been delighted to know that they did not have to arrange the slant-four Saab engine line to cater for a V8 as well; the potential aggravation due to frequent changes and adjustments had already become clear.

One major problem of drastic rationalisation would have been the sudden vacation of production lines as cars were withdrawn. Canley might have been able to survive the loss of one range, but if either the Sprite/Midget or the MGB/MGC had been dropped in Abingdon the position would be serious. There was also the very ticklish subject, with the dealer chain, of franchise rationalisation to be considered – particularly in important export territories like the United States, where Triumph and MG dealers were in high-volume competition.

For a time, according to the new corporation's public announcements, all was sweetness and light at British Leyland, and no clue was given as to what the product-planners had in mind. Even so, there never seems to have been any doubt that Donald Stokes saw Triumph as the dominant sports car in the British Leyland of the future; what happened in Leyland's first ten years bore this out, for since the mid-1960s MG development had all but halted. The MGB appeared in 1962, got its five-bearing engine in 1964 and its GT body in 1965. The Midget was given a 1275cc engine in 1966. After that, the only major technical changes were to launch the short-lived big-engined MGs – the 3-litre MGC of 1967/69 and the MGB V8 of 1973/76 – and the adoption of a Triumph Spitfire engine in the Midget from the autumn of 1974.

This last change, incidentally, was enough to send traditional MG enthusiasts into tearful decline.

Abingdon, where all the Austin-Healeys and MG sports cars were assembled, was 'closed' so often by the pundits that its workforce must have got used to threats. The fact is, however, that although Abingdon was an efficient little plant in terms of cars produced per man, by the end of the 1970s it was a loss-maker, like Canley.

After the Ryder Report of 1975 was published and partly implemented, it looked for a time as if Abingdon might survive, but as Britain's pound soared against the American dollar, Michael Edwardes' management team had other ideas. As he wrote in his book:

"We calculated that in the summer of 1979 we were losing something like £900 on every MG we sold in the United States ... the age and uniqueness of the MG range offered us no alternative but to cease production."

The major re-engineering which followed Michelotti's styling efforts for the Spitfire Mark 4 has already been described, and visually the little car was destined not to be changed again after that.

Triumph's problem with the Spitfire was that every year it seemed to be getting slower, rather than quicker. In the United States the exhaust-emission limitations became more severe each year, while Europe's law-makers were making a start on the same process. The Mark 4, rated in Europe at 6lbhp (DIN), was no quicker than the original Mark 1 of 1962 had been, while in the United States it suffered even further. By 1972 a 'federal' Spitfire had only 48bhp (DIN) and a single-carburettor engine for its owners to boast about. The fact that rival cars – like the Sprite or Midget, for example – were also in trouble was little consolation.

'Big brother,' the GT6, was having similar problems, but as it had started from a high point of 104bhp the losses were not quite so obvious. Time, and other safety legislation, however, were catching-up with the GT6. Sales in the United States were not all that high, and the cost of incorporating things like beams in the doors to ward off side impact intrusion, massive '5mph' bumpers at front and rear, and catalytic converters and similar fittings to the already strangled engine, began to look unjustified.

Even so, for the 1973 selling season, there were Spitfire and GT6 changes. The GT6 lost its unique wishbone IRS and inherited the Spitfire's cheaper swing-spring transverse-leaf layout. Purists had hoped that rationalisation would have been in the other direction. Experience shows that the lower-wishbone layout was rather more effective than the swing-spring installation, though either is vastly more predictable than the original swing axle suspension.

At the same time, the wheel tracks were increased and rationalised – that of the GT6 going up by one inch, and that of the Spitfire by two inches. The GT6 also got a stouter front anti-roll bar, which shifted the handling balance towards understeer in all normal motoring manoeuvres.

To back this, there were minor cosmetic changes, including the fitting of fire-retardant seat-trim materials, a smaller steering wheel, revised instruments and reclining seats on the Spitfire model (they were already specified for the GT6). As a final touch the Spitfire was given a wood-veneer instrument panel to bring it into line with the TR6 and GT6 models.

This was enough to keep the Spitfire selling really well, but nothing could save the GT6. After only a further 4218 cars had been built, the last car came off the production lines in Canley at the end of 1973, and the model became just another of the interesting machines killed off by North America's myopic lawmakers.

A minor change for 1974 Spitfires was a glass fibre air dam under the front bumper, said to do wonders for high-speed stability, and just a little for high-speed fuel consumption, but much more important changes were due for 1975 models.

Although the federal Spitfires had been fitted with a 1493cc engine for some time – to regain some of the torque and power lost to the emission-strangled 1296cc unit – it had not spread to other versions of the car. For 1975, the car being officially launched in December 1974, it would be standardised for all markets. But in October, something far more earth-shattering had occurred (at least as far as MG enthusiasts were concerned) – the same 1493cc Triumph engine was standardised for the Abingdon-assembled MG Midget!

Strangers to the British motoring scene can have little idea of the agonies this brought to Abingdon-lovers, nor would they understand the broad grins worn by Spitfire owners for the next few weeks. It was as though one's lover had suddenly and brazenly been unfaithful. Worse, having done so, she was cheerful and none the worse for her experience.

The reasoning was very simple. It was high time that the two small Leyland sports cars came closer together wherever possible (the Austin-Healey Sprite version, incidentally, had been demoted to become an Austin at the beginning of 1971, and disappeared altogether in July of that year). The Midget's 1275cc 'A' Series engine was no longer able to cope with stricter and stricter emission limits without losing most of its power, and could not be enlarged any further. Substituting the Triumph engine, which was a well-proven unit, was both logical and straight-forward.

An added bonus, which had not escaped the planners of British Leyland, was that North America's EPA was usually ready to compromise on compulsory long-distance testing if two cars had similar engines. This move was going to save time and money for the engineers in future years.

Abingdon fans can take heart from the fact that the Midget 1500 went into production first; Triumph's records show that the first unit was built at Tile Hill at the end of August 1974.

When the equivalent Spitfire was released it also broke the sequence of 'Mark' numbers. Logically it should have been the Spitfire Mark 5, but instead it was called – and stylishly badged – the Spitfire 1500. For the North American market, the single-carburettor engine used in 1974 would be standardised on Spitfires and Midgets. For the rest of the world, carburation was by twin SUs, and the claimed power output became 71bhp (DIN) at 5500rpm. More important was that the torque was boosted from 68 to 82lb/ft at 3000rpm, which made the car much easier and lustier to drive.

The performance gains (in non-USA trim) were substantial. The maximum speed, aided by higher overall gearing, was increased by nearly 10mph, and a healthy Spitfire 1500 could therefore nudge 100mph on a still day. At least eight seconds were carved off the time needed to sprint to 80mph from rest, and overall fuel consumption had slipped back by as little as two or three miles per gallon.

Apart from minor installation details (and exhaust-pipe runs) Spitfire and Midget engines were identical and quoted power outputs were the same. Both cars used the corporation's single-rail Marina/Toledo type of gearbox (which was itself descended from the first all-synchromesh GT6 unit). The Spitfire had always been higher-geared than the Midget, but on the other hand the Midget was rather lighter as it did not have a separate chassis frame.

Since the end of 1974, the Spitfire's design was changed only slightly, usually to keep abreast of the latest United States safety legislation. In the spring of 1977 minor styling improvements were phased-in without any attention being given to the chassis, and in the end the car was allowed to run comfortably on to retirement in the summer of 1980.

The situation regarding final assembly of cars at Coventry, already mentioned in the previous chapter, was only resolved in 1979. According to the much-maligned Ryder plans (not all of which were ever made public, for admirable commercial reasons), the old Innsbruck saloons would be withdrawn in favour of large Rovers to be built at Solihull, and Dolomite assembly would also be moved to Solihull. This would have made the Spitfire the very last Triumph car to be finished-off in the Canley assembly halls, which were to have been converted to fulfil a massive new component-machining function.

After the corporation's second major crisis, in the autumn of 1977, all these plans changed again. Whereas the Spitfire would have been built in Canley until it died off, squeezed-out by machinery, it continued until 1980, as did the Dolomite, which was built on parallel assembly lines. Not only that, but the TR7 assembly lines went into operation in Canley from the autumn of 1978. All this, however, is getting ahead of the major Triumph story of the decade, which concerned Triumph sports cars for the present and future.

The development of new Triumph TRs under British Leyland rule was a fascinating saga of choice and counter-choice, inspiration and commercial pragmatics, common sense and folly. It was a long-running and somehow tragic story.

Even as the Leyland-BMH merger took place in 1968, preparations were in hand for the launch of the TR6, which duly made its public bow in January 1969. Thereafter it was certain that the original 'classic' strain of TRs had reached the end of their useful development career, and that an entirely new breed of TR would have to follow them.

In the meantime, too, Harry Webster had moved on to even

Spen King took over from Harry Webster as Triumph's technical chief in 1968.

higher things with Austin-Morris at Longbridge, and Rover's Spencer King had moved across to direct Triumph's engineering efforts. His first and most urgent task, as we have seen, was to finalise both the Stag and 2000/2.5 Mark 2 projects, then to get the much-changed Manx II/Ajax III cars ready, and only then to turn his attention to new sports cars.

Even within a year of the merger, when there was much talk about rationalising Leyland's sports car plans, there was precious little action. The rather cumbersome MGC was allowed to die in the face of poor demand, the Stag was modified yet again and urged on to a 1970 launch, and the V12 E-Type began to take precedence over twelve-cylinder saloons at Jaguar.

It was then decided that some basic rethinking was needed on the volume-selling sports cars. At one and the same time – in effect this developed into an unofficial design competition – MG was asked to look at the possibilities for a new mid-engined car, while Triumph was invited to consider a new front-engined TR. One might ask why the requests were planted in that particular way, but the corporate reasons are obvious. MG had a long association with its masters at Longbridge, who had transverse engines like the 1800's 'B' series, the Maxi's 1750 and the 2200's E6 all in quantity production.

Even without this brief from the ivory towers in Berkeley Square, Triumph would probably have gone along the front-engined route in any case. Its experiences with integral engines and gearboxes (in the 1300/1500 saloon cars) told them that the cost and complication were rarely worth the better packaging. It also knew that it was very difficult to give a mid-engined design any versatility (as Porsche was then finding out) and – more important – it wanted to design not one car but two!

Even with the long-term possibilities of overhead-cam six-cylinder engines to be taken into account, Triumph did not see much future with such a unit in its sports cars. The TR6's petrol-injection, shared with the 2.5 PI saloon, was troublesome enough for a decision to be made to drop it in 1975, the basic design was quite old, and for another thing it was rather greedy of space. In any case, it was a carry-over from the old design, and Triumph wanted none of that.

In 1969 and 1970, therefore, work started on the layout of two new cars – an open two-seater (which rapidly became a two-seater coupé as a result of proposed USA rollover regulations) and a fastback 2+2 car with a longer wheelbase. 'Bullet' and 'Lynx,' as they were then coded, were soon styled in quarter-scale fashion, and photographed together on the Canley sports field, where they carried distinctive number plates which suggested that the 2+2 car could be launched in 1972 and the two-seater a year later. The two cars were to be mechanically similar, were intended to share aspects of engineering and some of the pressed-steel inner body panels, but would look rather different.

In 1969, certainly, the factory's first priority was given to the larger Lynx. In the space of a few months no less than six prototypes were commissioned, but before planning could get much further advanced, British Leyland's overall policy began to change and the project was abruptly cancelled.

Bullet, on the other hand, continued to prosper, and came in for much attention from stylists and engineers. Its 'chassis' (the term we have to give for mechanical components even though the project always included a monocoque body/chassis structure in pressed steel) had a lot in common with the Dolomite saloon range, and with advance thoughts for a car which would eventually replace the Dolomites and related cars after the next sports cars had been launched.

This, therefore, meant a complete change for the TR's image. It was thought at Coventry that TR engineering and specifications had

This Michelotti-style design of a proposed 'Bullet' came along in 1969/70, but was rejected by British Leyland.

gradually and undesirably become more complex. A new design would give every opportunity for reversing the process, and in a way it would be closer to the ideals of the first TR2s.

There would be space in the new shell for several different engine installations (these are mentioned in more detail later in the chapter), but at first work was concentrated round the PE104S engine, the slant-four that was already being supplied to Saab, and was to be fitted to the Dolomite, originally planned for introduction in 1971. This could be in eight-valve or 16-valve form. For the first time on a production TR there was to be an automatic transmission option, and right from the start it was decided to offer either the commonised l500TC/Toledo/Marina Dolomite/Spitfire four-speed gearbox, or the brand-new 77mm five-speed gearbox. There would be a rigid rear axle layout (Spen King was no believer in independent rear suspension unless it was really sophisticated, and that of the TR6 was most certainly not), the axle being either the Toledo/Dolomite/Marina unit, or the new medium-duty unit being designed for Rover's new SD1 saloon car.

While the general mechanical layout came together sweetly enough, the styling was a long-running problem. For one thing there was the constraint of USA rollover regulations, fuel-tank protection laws, crash rules relating to frontal and side impact, and the need for stylish 5mph bumpers, all of which effectively pointed the way to a closed car. For another, there was the vexing fact that no matter who tried to do the job, it never seemed to come out quite right; it was neither modern enough nor dramatic enough.

In 1971 Spen King had been masterminding the latest efforts (Spen was an excellent 'amateur' stylist himself – see the general proportions of the Range Rover and the one-off P6BS mid-engined Rover coupé of 1967, both of which were to his credit),

The original TR7 of 1975 was sold purely in the North American market, and it was not until mid-1976 that this 'Rest of the World' derivative was put on sale, complete with SU carburettors.

This was Harris Mann's original artwork, proposing a new style for the Triumph Bullet, which did so much to convince the British Leyland board that his scheme was superior to that being suggested by Michelotti.

which were looking pleasant enough, but still not outstanding. At this point, Harry Webster, who kept a paternal eye on all things Triumph from his headquarters position at Longbridge, mentioned the problem to Harris Mann, who was in charge of styling at the Austin-Morris division.

Mann, at that time, was greatly impressed by the sheer glamour of mid-engined 'show specials' like Bertone's Carabo, and the original non-running Stratos, and was already thinking in terms of wedges for the next Austin-Morris saloon (this became the 18-22 series Princess). His own personal quick effort was a simple sketch of a new wedge-shaped TR coupé.

Even though Triumph's own designs had become mildly wedge-shaped, this new proposal electrified Leyland's management, who then asked Longbridge, not Coventry, to build a full size clay model for assessment. What happened then is still a cause for regret at high level. One typical comment was: "Whenever we altered anything to suit the production engineers, or to get the costs down, or to meet more legislation, the car seemed to lose a bit more of its style. We couldn't reverse that process somehow."

There's no doubt that the finished job, fashionable or not, caused a great deal of controversy among customers, dealers and press alike. Even though a large number of the cars were sold (more, indeed, than all other models in the long-running TR family), there were cohorts of hardened press men and rival enthusiasts prepared to swear that the car was ugly, yet there were many loyal company men who thought it astonishingly attractive.

Once the style had been approved, by the end of 1971, the tug-of-war regarding production facilities got under way. Where would the bodyshell be built? Where would final assembly take place? When would it be ready for production? How many versions should there be? Would it be badge engineered? In the good old days, as long-term Triumph enthusiasts were quick to point out, there would have been none of this horse-trading, but under British Leyland rule, with maximisation of facilities all-important, it was not at all simple.

It was perhaps with this in mind that the TR7 was first planned to have its bodies pressed and assembled at Pressed Steel Fisher at Cowley, near Oxford, with some shells then going to Abingdon and some to Liverpool for completion. Next, it was thought that MG versions could be assembled at Liverpool alongside the Triumphs, but finally the whole idea of having badge engineered MGs was abandoned. At this point, in April 1972, it was finally and firmly decided that the TR7 should be built in its entirety at Liverpool.

The Stag, of course, had its bodies pressed and assembled at Liverpool, but final assembly was at Coventry. The ageing TR6,

Compared with the outgoing TR6, the chassis of the TR7, new for 1975, was at once simpler, more modern, yet capable of further development. Many of these components were originally intended, too, for use in the still born SD2 saloon project of the late 1970s.

From 1974 to 1978, the TR7 was manufactured at Speke, close to Liverpool – this shot showing the way that the pressed-steel bodyshell came together before being sent off for painting and, finally, for assembly.

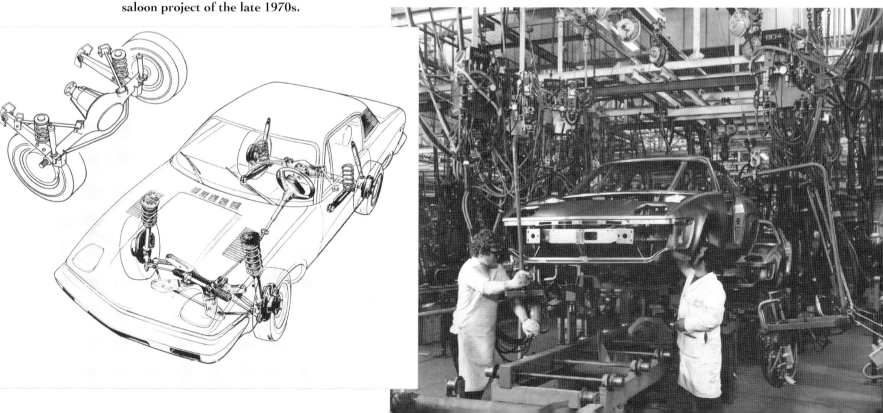

which would not immediately be replaced by the TR7 but run alongside it, had its bodies built in the cramped surroundings of Triumph's original Liverpool factory, just a mile away from the new complex, and these bodies, too, were ferried to Coventry for completion.

Pilot-build of off-tools shells was brought to fruition at the beginning of 1974, and the first true production cars followed in the autumn of that year. By doing this, British Leyland set several precedents; the TR7 was to be the first sports car completely assembled in Merseyside by any major manufacturer, and for the time being it would be the only complete car in Liverpool's care.

The big new plant, of course, had been building Toledos since 1970, but these were moved out (to Coventry) in 1974 to make way for the new TR7. TR7 sheet-metal pressings, therefore, would be produced in the ex-Hall Engineering No 1 factory. They would then be shipped across to the No 2 plant, welded-up, painted and trimmed, and completely assembled with engines and transmissions from Coventry or (in the case of the five-speed gearbox) from BL's plant in South Wales.

In truth, and British Leyland have never made any secret of this, the Liverpool factory was far too big to be profitable when making only one model – unless, that is, that one model could sell in numbers quite out of the reach of previous TRs. The fact that the Stag died quietly in the summer of 1977, and was never replaced, was an unfortunate factor in later developments; the delayed introduction of new variants was another, and the persistent failure of the TR7 to sell in the way its sponsors had hoped was another.

It really was very sad indeed that the troubled No 2, or Speke, plant finally closed its doors in May 1978, and was eventually sold-off for other industrial uses. It is also, of course, merely one result of the very complex financial situation in which state-controlled British Leyland found itself in 1977/78, but for posterity we should now summarise the various developments in the story.

At the core of the dramatic developments which took place over the winter of 1977/1978 was the fact that Leyland Cars continued to be a very substantial financial loss-maker. Abrupt and politically sordid changes in the top management resulted in the appointment of the dynamic Michael Edwardes, with virtually a free hand from the British Government, who now recognised, belatedly, that profitability was a more desirable long-term goal than merely providing work for people in depressed areas.

Two things then happened. On the one hand Edwardes cast a very practical eye over future capital spending programmes (related to potential profitability and volume sales), while on the other hand the misguided and stubbornly-led Merseyside workforce went on strike over a manning dispute – and this in an area where unemployment was already very high!

The Liverpool factory, which was never profitable with only one model in production, therefore became a principal focus of attention for the company accountants, and as the dispute dragged on (with the workforce apparently unable to see that they were jeopardising their own future, and with management determined not to give in to what they considered ill-advised shop-floor muscle) it became increasingly clear that the factory might be discarded altogether.

There is no point in hiding the imminent 'might-have-beens,' as the British press has had a field day in describing them. The Speke strike, which was not finally settled (if, in fact, it was ever 'finally' resolved at all) until the spring of 1978, immobilised pilot production of the 1978 model range of TR7s, which would undoubtedly have been radically more attractive to buyers, particularly in the United States.

During the autumn of 1977 there had already been a seven-week stoppage of work, through no fault of the Liverpool workforce, but due to strikes in other parts of the British Leyland empire (one problem, for instance, being the halt of axle production at the Radford component factory), and on November 1 the workers, just back from this lay-off, were called out in the manning dispute. Already in build, and ready for quantity production (so that the shipping pipeline to North America could fill up before the beginning of 1978) were a V8-engined (Rover 3528cc) version of the TR7, and – perhaps even more important for sunny North America – a convertible version of the TR7 which could accept the four-cylinder engines at first, and no doubt the V8 engine later. Not only this, but the 16-valve (Dolomite Sprint) engine, already homologated by Abingdon for sporting purposes, was also working its way onto the production line.

Michael Edwardes was in no mood to be pushed around by a recalcitrant workforce, and he made it clear that it was their attitude (along with that of other groups of workers in Leyland) which led him to cancel another important new model – coded 'Lynx' – which had been planned to replace the Stag and would have given Liverpool an important second model to build alongside the TR7.

No doubt the very existence of the Lynx would still be denied by company spokesmen if Edwardes had not leaked his decision to the financial press at the beginning of 1978, and no great detail of this car was ever been made known to the public. However, newspaper stories, sneak pictures and unofficial information all confirmed that the Lynx was effectively a long-wheelbase (about 12 inches longer) TR7 chassis, to be fitted exclusively with the V8 engine, but to have a 2+2 seating layout and a fastback coupé body style somewhat reminiscent of the latest Lotus Eclat model. The nose and screen were common with the TR7, and the basic chassis engineering was unchanged. The Rover-derived five-speed gearbox and the medium-duty axle would have been standardised. The pictures we have seen (and official leaking of the car itself in later together with appeals to MPs, trades unions and other pressure groups. It was all to no avail; in due course it was announced that the TR7 final assembly facilities would be moved down to Coventry (where, arguably, they should have been the whole time) and that the Liverpool factory would close at the end of May 1978. Redundancy terms were offered to the workforce on the understanding that work was resumed in the meantime and that there would be no opposition to the eventual move – otherwise, the company threatened, the factory would be closed immediately and the TR7 project cancelled altogether.

By March everything was being resolved in a very unhappy manner. The factory re-opened, TR7s were actually built again for some weeks and the bickering became mainly about severance terms. The reformed company then got wind of rumours that a factory-occupation plan was still afoot among the hot-heads and the doors were locked abruptly in the middle of May, several days ahead of the publicly announced closure date.

In later life, many TR7s were beautifully and sympathetically restored to their original glory.

life) confirmed that the Lynx was a beautiful project, which would have matched anything then being sold by deadly rivals like Toyota, Datsun or Lancia, and if it had not been for the high tooling and production costs to be incurred by building it at Liverpool we have no doubt that it could have been a winner.

Like all the best Greek tragedies, however, this took a long time to unfold. Mr Edwardes' leaks, at the very beginning of 1978, suggested that he was quite prepared to close down the larger of the two Liverpool factories altogether, and move production of the TR7 to another location. All that was supposedly 'off the record,' but it was printed anyway, and an embarrassed Leyland press office then spent weeks denying anything of the sort. On February 15, however, the closure decision was confirmed, amid howls of anger from the workforce, who were still on strike, nearly four months later.

What followed were the classic actions of aggrieved workers whose bluff had been called. There were angry threats of sit-ins, of occupation, of blacking of work-transfer to other factories,

The TR7 and the exciting new derivatives were withdrawn from production until such time as the production lines could be re-opened in Coventry, and this was not to be until it was time to announce the 1979 model-year cars. A whole year, therefore, was effectively lost, and with it a massive amount of customer confidence in North America, where the sports car competition was very intense.

Figures released after the closure of the factory (the old No 1 factory, by the way, was unaffected, and carried on making Dolomite bodies and TR7 pressings) show that TR7 sales in 1977 had been targeted at 43,000 (higher than ever before for a TR, but still not as many cars as were being made on the MGB lines at Abingdon), that the building's capacity was for no less than 100,000 cars a year, but that no more than 27,657 had been delivered in the last full year of production – 1976. Only if another car (which ought to have been Lynx) was phased-in, could Liverpool ever become at all viable.

The saga of the TR7 – even with more than 76,000 built before close-down in May 1978 – was an unhappy one, and even though the car was eventually relaunched, with more derivatives and a better productivity record, this was not enough to rebuild its reputation as a modern sports car.

In the meantime, however, there was other news from Triumph, which emphasises how the Fletchamstead North engineering division's role had changed in recent years. The projected merger of Triumph with Rover, announced in 1972, and already discussed in an earlier chapter, was the public acknowledgement of something which had looked likely ever since Rover had been drawn into the Leyland group in 1967. Although Rover got responsibility for designing larger cars, and Triumph for sports and sporting cars (including the stillborn SD2 five-door machine which might have replaced the Dolomites if company policy had not killed it off at an advanced stage), Triumph would also bear the brunt of a great deal of work on a new family of 'building block' components for cars of the 1970s and 1980s.

This policy became clear in 1976 and 1977 as the brand-new Rover SD1 family – in 2300, 2600 and 3500 forms – was revealed. Not only were the new axle and the five-speed gearbox designed in Coventry, but so was the new, technically-interesting overhead-camshaft six-cylinder engine. All, with the possible exception of the engine itself, had multiple potential applications to other Rover and Triumph models, and need brief analysis to show the way that Triumph's future was being shaped.

There is nothing exciting about an axle, or even a gearbox, except to an engineer, so we will merely point out that the axle had already found a home on the Rover saloons and the TR7, and that the '77mm' gearbox (so called because that is the distance between the centre lines of the main shaft and the layshaft) could be built in either five-speed or four-speed (Rover 2300 guise) form. The gearbox had already been adopted for certain Jaguar saloons, and no doubt would be useful for other new Leyland products in future years. It was a worthy successor to the solid all-synchro unit first used in the TR4 of 1961, and standardised on the big saloons and the Stag for the next 16 years.

The story of the engine is altogether more interesting, and shows how one good idea might lead to another, and how the final form of any engineering assembly may not be the same as that originally considered at the outset.

The engine project first took shape in 1970 when Mike Loasby (later to be technical director of Aston Martin, but then working under Jim Parkinson's instructions) was asked to put together proposals for an overhead-camshaft conversion on the existing 1998/2498cc Triumph Six, so that the newly-announced Mark 2 cars could eventually be updated, or new models prepared. This, of course, was in early British Leyland days when traditionally rival firms were still able to push on with new designs, even though it made little economic sense in corporate terms.

The engine that finally appeared in 1977 was radically and completely different from the simple conversion started in 1970, yet it all happened in logical steps. The first 'paper' engine of 1970 was a comprehensive conversion on the existing bottom-end, with in-line valves and a cogged belt camshaft drive, but retaining the familiar four-bearing crankshaft layout.

By the beginning of 1972, however, with the Triumph-Rover merger about to be announced, it was clear that Triumph could not have its own new car, so the 'Puma' and 'Bobcat' projects were cancelled. The new engine, therefore, had to be tailored to fit the existing 2000/2.5 shell and the new SD1 car. At this point, the original design was abandoned and a more ambitious scheme, with opposed valves in part-spherical combustion chambers and a simplified version of the Dolomite Sprint (Dawtrey-designed) valve gear, took shape. Cylinder centres were also shuffled round within the confines of the existing cylinder block, and the larger bore of 81mm allowed a new 2350cc size to be planned.

By the end of 1972, however, complications and compromise had set in to affect the design of the first Mark 1 engines. The Mark 2 of 1973 had a shallower cylinder block, a longer stroke (84mm) than the original 76mm, and therefore a different engine size of 2597cc. At this stage, with the cylinder block design being shuffled yet again, an 86mm cylinder bore was even considered, which would have given a maximum possible size of 2928cc, but this was later sidelined for possible future consideration.

Commercial pressures now became intense. Leyland decided to drop the existing large Triumphs as soon as the six-cylinder version of the new Rover could be made ready for production, and while it was originally thought this could be done by the winter of 1976/77, it was not until the autumn of 1977 that the changeover was actually announced, and the 2300 version of the car was not actually to reach the showrooms until May 1978.

The final engine redesign took place in 1973, just before the layout of production tooling had to be finalised for installation at Coventry. The long-suffering cylinder block layout was changed once again, and all links with the old engine were finally lost, as it was lengthened by 20mm (0.79in), so that water could be allowed to circulate round the repositioned cylinder-bores. By this stage, too, the distributor drive had taken up its final position in the cylinder head and was driven by the camshaft; previously it had been in the old position, driven from the jackshaft remains of the original camshaft.

The new units produced impressive amounts of power – Spen King and John Lloyd claim to have spent more time trying to get the power down and the fuel economy up than in trying to get acceptable power figures. A 2300 was good for 123 bhp at 5500rpm and a 2600 for 136 bhp at 5000rpm, but 150 bhp was easily possible from the 2600 with little change.

A study of the new design showed that a good deal of development potential was locked away inside the basic unit, and if BL's financial problems had improved in the next few years several more exciting versions might have been developed. The new cylinder block was enormously strong, and there was talk not only of a diesel version, but of a 24-valve 3-litre derivative also being produced.

This, unfortunately, never happened. The SD1 range ran into trouble because of doubtful build quality and durability, and even though it was face-lifted in 1982 (and final assembly was moved from Solihull to Cowley), no significant changes were ever made to the six-cylinder engines. For a diesel engine, the company turned to VM of Italy, while the most powerful SD1s continued to be powered by V8 engines. As it transpired, the straight-six was not used in any other BL product, and the last SD1s were built before the end of 1986.

With this fascinating new engine, Triumph's engineering story brings us back up to when Michael Edwardes became BL's chief executive. From that moment, the marque's corporate future became securely locked into that of BL Cars, as part of the Jaguar-Rover-Triumph Division, and it was always to be subject to the fortunes and misfortunes of other branches of the tree. The cancellation of the Lynx and SD2 projects showed that Triumph's place in the directors' list of priorities (which had been so marked in the early 1970s) had slipped. Even so, the expertise of the engineers was not lost, and ever more corporate work from other areas of BL found its way to Coventry in the months and years which followed.

From the autumn of 1978, the TR7 sports car was relaunched in five-speed gearbox form, with Pressed Steel Fisher now responsible for building the bodyshells, and with final assembly in Canley, which was still by no means bursting with activity. While the general public never found out the full story, the entire expansion programme for the TR7 had been changed.

Although the BL competitions department, based at Abingdon, somehow convinced the authorities that a V8-engined TR7 was a

production car in 1978 (and began rallying it in that year), it was not actually put on sale until the beginning of 1980, while the 16-valve Dolomite Sprint-engined TR7 (which was also homologated for use in motorsport) was never put on sale at all, though 25 pre-production cars called 'TR7 Sprints' were completed.

The convertible version of the TR7, so much smarter and more nicely detailed than the coupé had ever been, went on sale in the USA in mid-1979,

The Spider was one of several successfully marketed limited editions of the TR7, carefully cosmetically enhanced in many details.

By the late 1970s, the works TR7 V8 (not, please not, known as the TR8) was a formidable rally car, especially on sealed surfaces.

By the end of its works career, the TR7 V8 – aka TR8 – was a formidable rally car, particular on tarmac-surfaced stages. This was Tony Pond, on his way to winning the Manx International Trophy event of 1980.

and was introduced to the UK market in early 1980. The V8-engined car, called the TR8, which was officially sold only in the USA, was finally launched at the beginning of 1980, just as Americans were turning away from V8 cars in the aftermath of the second energy crisis.

There was further so-called rationalisation in 1980, when the Canley assembly facility was progressively closed down. First the Spitfire, then the Dolomite, went out of production, while assembly of the TR7 and TR8 models was transferred yet again, this time to the modern Rover factory, a few miles away in Solihull. Development work was already well advanced on a 'Mk II' TR7, with smoothed-out body flanks, which was to use the Longbridge-designed overhead-camshaft BL O-Series engine to replace the expensive Triumph Four, and work had also begun on a further version, coded 'Broadside,' which would have had a lengthened wheelbase, and the above mechanical modifications.

By this time, the TR7/TR8 range, which relied so heavily on sales in North America, was struggling very hard indeed against a soaring British currency. A new Conservative government had been swept to power in 1979 and value of the pound had risen sharply from a rate of $1.80 to $2.40 to the Pound sterling by mid-1980.

By mid-1981 the BL board was facing huge losses yet again; every TR7 built was losing money for the company (for if the USA list price had been raised, the car would have been unsaleable) – and so it was decided that the assembly side of the Solihull plant would have to be closed down.

Suddenly, it became clear there was no future for the TR7 and the TR8. The UK introduction of the TR8, once forecast for spring 1981, was cancelled, as was the O-Series engine transplant, and the last of these unlucky sports cars was produced in October 1981. Was this really the end for Triumph?

One of the many attempts to upgrade the TR7, in particular to amend its controversial styling, was the Broadside project, which featured a longer wheelbase than the TR7, modified styling along the sides and at the rear, and would have been powered by a British Leyland O-Series engine.

Scheduled at one time for fitment to the 1982 TR7 and its successor, this 2-litre O-Series would have replaced the existing slant-four power unit.

Acclaim and a Sad End

17

Let us be quite adamant about this. The so-called Triumph Acclaim of 1981-1984 was a slightly-altered Japanese Honda, built in Britain, but with many Japanese-made components, and it was only meant to be a stopgap model. It had no links with any previous Triumph car, and none with any other current, or planned, British Leyland production.

To the Triumph purist, neither the car nor the chapter which describes it has any place in a book about Triumph products. As motoring enthusiasts ourselves, the authors sympathise, but if this book is to be a complete history of the Triumph marque, then the Acclaim was badged as such, and deserves space.

Events which led to the birth of the Triumph Acclaim began to unfold in 1977, and intensified in 1978. The basic problem, as seen by the Ryder-led management, and as confirmed by Michael Edwardes' team, was that BL needed to develop a number of new models to survive, but that this could not all be done 'in-house' with the existing staff.

The new small-car project (which eventually matured in October 1980 as the Austin Metro) was already well under way, but it looked as if the next new volume car (the medium-sized hatchback which would be named the Austin Maestro) could not be ready before 1983. Another new car was needed for launch in 1981 or thereabouts, but there were no people, facilities or money available to tackle this. Yet if the 'product-led recovery' strategy was to work at all, something would have to be done.

The only way to break out of this impasse, it seemed, was to do what several other companies had already done – either co-operate or merge with another company. Peugeot and Citroën had already got together, Fiat now owned Lancia, Vauxhall and Opel were no longer separate entities, while Peugeot, Renault and Volvo were all collaborating on common engine programmes.

Even before Michael Edwardes became BL's chief executive in November 1977, his predecessors in the Ryder management team had begun discussions with Renault. In the next year, not only did Edwardes continue talking to Renault, he also had discussions with Vauxhall and Chrysler-Europe.

At that point BL began to look outside, at motor companies all around the world, and after a comprehensive search the spotlight fell on Honda of Japan. Discreet and delicate contacts were made in August 1978, and the first face-to-face meeting between Honda and BL directors took place in October.

From that moment events moved swiftly and a strategy of

The Honda Ballade-based Acclaim was utterly different from any previous Triumph, and was powered by a Japanese 4-cylinder engine.

This was the neat engine bay of the Honda-based Triumph Acclaim, and was on sale from 1981 to 1984.

The facia/driving compartment of the Triumph Acclaim was utilitarian, not at all sporty.

"BL will manufacture a new passenger car designed by Honda which will have a high technical specification and will be a Triumph. BL will have exclusive rights to sell it in the EEC and in Britain."

At that time, however, although the choice of car was settled, it was not at all clear where it would be assembled. At first it was to have been built in Canley, then Solihull was considered, but finally the new 'Triumph' found a home at Cowley, where it was built alongside cars like the Austin Princess/Ambassador and the Morris Ital.

So it was, then, that the last of the real Triumphs, the TR7/TR8 range of sports cars, was produced at Solihull in October 1981, just as assembly of the car already nicknamed 'Triumph Honda' was getting into its stride at Cowley. BL boldly launched it under an advertising slogan which claimed that it was 'Totally Equipped to Triumph,' and put three cosmetically different versions on sale at UK prices varying from £4688 to £5575 (total).

Triumph enthusiasts hated the car – and MG enthusiasts were delighted that it had not been foisted on them – and one could see their point. Although BL claimed that it had 70 per cent local content (this effectively meant that the bodyshell was manufactured in the UK, along with all the trim, and that it was all screwed together at Cowley), the general public still looked upon it as a Japanese car built in Britain.

In all major respects, it was a conventional, state-of-the-art, front-wheel drive car, with MacPherson-strut suspension all round, and a choice of 'end-on' mounted transmissions – five-speed manual or three-speed semi-automatic Hondamatic. The 1335cc engine had overhead-camshaft valve gear and churned out 70bhp, but the larger and more powerful 1488cc/80bhp unit fitted to Honda Ballades was never made available in the Acclaim.

Although the Acclaim was not outstanding in any respect – it had a 92mph top speed, usually recorded upwards of 30mpg, and behaved similarly to the latter-day Triumph Dolomite 1500 in many ways – it was at least reliable and offered good value. Like so many Japanese cars, however, it seemed to be totally without character, and we doubt if any real Triumph enthusiast actually fell in love with one.

The Acclaim, in fact, was built at Cowley for less than three years before the company introduced its replacement. The next-generation Honda Ballade had been launched in Japan in autumn 1983, with a new bodyshell and a different, larger and more powerful engine, so from mid-1984 it was inevitable that the Austin-Rover Group (as the car-producing company had become known) would follow suit.

collaboration developed rapidly. BL had decided that it needed a small-medium family car, larger than the LC8 (Metro), but smaller than the projected LC10 (Maestro) model. Having gained Honda's confidence, a BL team visited Tokyo in January 1979, and was delighted to find just what they needed – a new Honda, still only at the styling model stage, which was to be launched in late 1980. It was a saloon car derivative of the Civic hatchback, and was to be called the Ballade. Like all modern BL products, the Ballade had a transversely-mounted engine with front-wheel drive.

News of a BL link with Honda broke in the press in April 1979, and in May the company announced:

The Triumph Acclaim was a conventional (by Japanese standards!) four-door, four-seater family saloon.

It was something of a relief to Triumph enthusiasts that there had been yet another change of strategy; from that point the 'Triumph' name was judged to be surplus to requirements, and the Acclaim's replacement was entitled the Rover 200. In those last three years, however, the Acclaim had been a measurable marketing success for ARG, as no fewer than 133,626 examples had been built.

Requiem

Looking back, it is easy to see that the Triumph marque suffered a long, slow and painful decline before finally being dropped in 1984.

Under pre-nationalisation British Leyland management its prospects were bright, for not only was the TR7/TR8 family being developed, but the Dolomite-replacement, project SD2, was due to follow in the late 1970s.

The Ryder regime, so devoid of its own ideas that it picked up the Stokes-Barber strategy of 1974 and embraced it as its own, confirmed Triumph's future in 1975, but as the group's market share declined and financial losses mounted it was forced to retrench. The SD2 project was cancelled, nothing was schemed up to take its place, and the extension of the TR7 range was put on hold because of poor sales.

Michael Edwardes and his 'new broom' management team, which took over in the winter of 1977/78, had no sentiment for marque names, only for healthy balance sheets, and soon decided to let existing Triumph models die a natural death and to introduce no new ones. When the Dolomite family disappeared in 1980, we looked forward only to an honourable and lengthy career for the TR7 and TR8. For all those interested in Triumph as an identifiable marque, it would have been best if the name had died when the TR7 and TR8 were dropped. Instead, the use of the name 'Triumph' on the Japanese-sourced Acclaim was an insult and an irrelevance.

Later, it seemed, the corporation which once owned so many famous marque names had progressively decided to drop all except

What did the Triumph Acclaim, based as it was on the Honda Ballade, have to offer? Nothing more – or less – than modest styling, four-seater economy and enviously high Japanese build quality.

Rover and MG. From that point the Triumph story was seen as complete, and the marque was therefore abandoned. What a pity – and what a waste. We can all, however, be glad that so many fine Triumph cars were produced in the years which really mattered and that so many of them survive in good hands. When the Rover Group, ARG, BL Cars, British Leyland and all the other names which flitted so precariously across the headlines in the 1970s and 1980s have been forgotten, the glories of Triumph, especially its sports cars, will remain.

RIP

Triumph Derivations

1932-36 Vale Special

This low-slung, aggressive-looking sports car was the prewar antecedent to many independently-built cars using Triumph components. About 100 Vales were made, marketed by the Vale Engineering Company (Vale Motor Company from 1935), at Portsdown Road, Maida Vale (hence the name), London.

In its early form the car provided a sporting alternative to the upright Super Eight. It appeared a year before the Glorias, using the Eight's 832cc engine, four-wheel hydraulic drum brakes, clutch, gearbox and worm-drive rear axle. Despite these extensive Triumph bits, significant modifications were made. There was a higher final-drive ratio – 5.75:1 – plus an optional 5.25:1 ratio for higher road speeds without stressing the three-bearing Super Eight engine. The Vale's frame bore no resemblance to the Triumph's, being underslung and extremely rigid in construction. Live axles were employed front and rear – the former of tubular construction and mounted above the frame which was therefore dead straight from axle to axle. The wheelbase was 94 inches, the track 46 and 43¼ inches front and rear respectively. Overall the car measured 132 inches long and only 31 inches high with the hood down.

Sporting alterations to the engine included a lightened flywheel and 6:1 compression ratio, plus a downdraught SU carburettor with an internally machined induction-pipe to permit a more free flow of gases. The tail-mounted fuel-tank held 11 gallons and delivered its contents via an SU Petrolift pump. Vale steering was unusual; the steering-box was located at the end of the column, over the dumb irons, where a drop-arm connected to a transverse drag-link ahead of the axle. This put it in compression, and Vale claimed it enabled the driver to 'lead' the car instead of 'push' it!

With a Maserati-like radiator grille, the aluminium two-seat body featured cut-down doors, folding windscreen, lots of passenger space and room for oddments behind the one-piece seatback. The bonnet extended back a long way, exposing the gearbox, clutch and starting motor as well as the engine when open. Cycle wings, which turned with the front wheels, were fitted and the spare tyre was carried at the end of the rounded tail. Two colours were offered, the completed car selling for £192 10s, in which form 70mph was claimed. If so, it provided good performance for the money.

In September 1934 new management took over, changed the firm's name and switched to the 10hp Gloria engine, sold with a Brooklands certificate assuring 85mph. A Gloria Six of 1476cc was also offered. For £150 the firm would even convert older 832cc Vales to the new specification – stripping and re-cellulosing the body, rebuilding the engine, fitting new tyres and guaranteeing the result for one year.

In May 1935 Vale produced a special 1.5-litre four-cylinder Special with belt-driven centric supercharger. The engine, especially built for the exercise by Coventry Climax, gave a 6.7:1 compression and was equipped with a close-ratio four-speed gearbox. Mounted on a shorter 84-inch wheelbase with a wider track, it was timed at 100mph at Brooklands. Vale was prepared, *The Autocar* noted, "to repeat the order at £625."

A few Vales have survived and are cherished today, and evidence that they were well-regarded in the 1930s is abundant. As *Motorsport* put it then, "the Vale possesses the attributes of a hand-made car in that it is responsive and sensitive to the driver's touch ... Discerning motorists will like it."

1950-68 Morgan Plus 4

Certainly the most respected and successful Triumph-powered car, the Plus 4 actually preceded the TR2 in its use of the wet-liner Vanguard 2088cc 'four' – but the old Malvern firm had a relationship with Standard predating even 1950. Morgan began fitting Standard engines to its 4/4 line in 1939, 1267cc overhead-valve units adapted from the Standard Ten but never used in a Standard car in this form. Desiring a quicker car, Morgan contracted to purchase the Vanguard engine in stock form from Sir John Black, hooked it to a separately-mounted proprietary Moss gearbox and fielded the Plus 4 – an instant success. It was this car, as mentioned in the main text, which prompted Sir John to approach H F S Morgan with a take-over in mind. Though Standard's offer was politely refused, it didn't seem to adversely affect the supply of Vanguard engines.

Morgan quickly adopted the TR2 version as soon as it was available, though it had earlier experimented with its own tuned versions of the Vanguard – notably at Le Mans in 1952, where the Plus 4 retired due to valve gear troubles. TR-engined Plus 4s started coming off the lines in 1954, and production never faltered until the model was replaced by the Rover-engined Plus 8 in 1968. Also in 1954, the traditional flat radiator grille and free-standing headlamps were dropped in favour of a more streamlined grille and faired-in headlamps, Lucas having put the old lamps out of production.

The Morgan Plus 4 used a wet-liner TR engine for many years.

Plus 4s were initially offered in two models: the basic two-seater roadster at £652 ($1852) and the striking drophead coupé at £722 ($2028). Later a four-seater tourer was added. Between 1963 and 1966 Morgan also built 26 TR-powered fibreglass coupés named Plus 4 Plus, which sold sparingly at £1275. Specifications usually duplicated those of the concurrent TR, though Morgan developed its own Lawrence-tuned Super Sports with twin-choke Weber carbs, racier cam, four-branch exhaust manifold and gas-flowed cylinder head. In such guise a Morgan won the 2-litre GT class at Le Mans in 1962, averaging 93.96mph. In all, Morgan built 4510 Plus 4s, of which 772 were Vanguard-engined and the rest TR-powered, plus the 26 Plus 4 Plus models.

1954 – 1955 Swallow Doretti

Although the Swallow Doretti was developed with the approval of Standard-Triumph, and was both attractive and fast, it was too costly for many enthusiasts, and was only on sale in 1954 and 1955.

The Doretti of 1954/55 was an extremely smart two-seater, which used TR2 engine, transmission and many chassis items.

Sir John Black never liked the TR-powered Doretti, and he had cause: it was in one of these cars that he suffered the accident which gave the board 'official' reason to explain his resignation. The car looked like a serious rival to the TR when first introduced (many wondered why Standard had sold its engine for this application) but a stiff £1102 price tag and less lively performance made it less of a threat.

The builders were the Swallow Coachbuilding Co Ltd (1935), of Walsall Airport, Staffordshire – removed, by several generations and company realignments, from William Lyons' old Swallow Coachbuilding concern. Doretti's then-parent firm, Tube Investments, supplied the tubular chassis frame, while the very strong steel-panelled body with aluminium skins was built by Swallow. Lack of solid engineering experience showed. Though nicely styled, the Doretti was short on legroom, luggage space and seat size, even though the car was five inches longer than a TR and had a 95in wheelbase. The engine was set back too far in the chassis, and the instrumentation – with rev-counter in front of the passenger – impractical. Off the line, a Doretti was about 1.5 seconds slower to 60mph than a TR, with commensurately greater fuel consumption. The sleek, smooth bodywork was a positive shock to Triumph dealers when they saw it, but they needn't have worried – the TR's place was secure.

(For the record, Lyons sold SS to Messrs Mills-Fulford, who sold-out to Grindlays of Coventry. Grindlays registered the 'Doretti' title in 1935, then sold-out to Helliwells, who sold the firm to Tube Investments. TI ended-up at Walsall Airport and was the firm which negotiated with Standard for the TR engine.)

1957-60 Peerless GT

A manifestation of the nation's craving for a home-grown gran turismo in the 2-litre category, Bernie Rodger's Peerless GT was an enthusiastic if naive effort to fill an important market gap. Announced in August 1957 by Rodger's new company in Slough, Buckinghamshire, the GT used a tubular space frame of extremely light weight, wishbone IFS with coil springs and Armstrong dampers, de Dion rear suspension and a 16-gauge aluminium-panelled body with plastic mouldings for the floor, bulkhead, rear seat pan and luggage locker. Powered by the standard TR3 engine, it weighed less than 2000lb. Its UK price of £1498 7s included leather upholstery, heater and purchase tax. Options were Dunlop centre-lock wire wheels and Laycock de Normanville overdrive operating on the upper three gears. By June 1958 all-fibreglass bodies were being used, manufactured by James Whitson and Co Ltd, in West Drayton, Middlesex.

Most of those who drove it excused its squeaks and rattles and praised the car's roadholding and high level of performance. The British liked it because, as one chap put it, there was now a replacement for the much-lamented ZB Magnette, and other models of that ilk by then out of production. The Americans liked it for the civility it provided compared to the TR3. At $3800 in the USA the GT was most affordable; *Road & Track* said it was worth the money. The magazine achieved 110mph flat-out and scored

The Peerless: own chassis, GRP body, but mainly Triumph TR running gear.

up to 32mpg (US). Of particular interest was its performance compared to that of the TR: "The Peerless is nearly as good to 70mph, slightly better over the standing quarter-mile and definitely faster to 90 ... Thus it appears that the coupé body gives about 7% less drag. Despite a test weight that is 70 pounds higher, once the Peerless gets over 70mph its streamlining is enough to offset the disadvantage of its 3.7 axle ratio and it will equal the performance of the TR3 with the 4.10 axle ratio." Curiously, the testers said nothing about handling, but it was generally conceded that the Peerless tended to cling better than the TR by virtue of its more sophisticated rear suspension.

Unfortunately, 'cling' was all the Peerless Company ever did in the business world. It was reorganised in 1959 and predicted 25 cars a week by 1960, but such output never materialised. The cars were continually criticised for sloppy assembly, excess engine and road noise and poor finish inside and out. Such things were inexcusable in a car costing this much, even if one favoured the underdog effort of this fledgling concern. By February 1960 Peerless filed for bankruptcy, owing £13,700 in unpaid purchase tax and about £50,000 to a host of creditors.

1960-62 Warwick GT

Where Peerless failed, Warwick would succeed – or so Bernie Rodger thought. After the affairs of Peerless were settled, a new firm was set up at Colnbrook, Buckinghamshire, with Rowland Ham as managing director and Rodger held over as technical director. Bodies, still supplied by James Whitson, were greatly improved.

Extensive sound-proofing was applied and fit and finish were given careful attention. The Warwick was 80 pounds lighter than the Peerless, its body much stronger. The improvements cost money, of course, and the GT was priced at £1620 with tax and now-standard overdrive. The only option was Dunlop wire wheels.

Five cars a week were planned, but the firm ran into cash-flow problems early on, and Rodger bought it out in December 1960. Still at Colnbrook, it was now known as Bernard Rodger Developments Ltd, with Mr Ham as board chairman. *The Autocar* said a Warwick rode harder than a Peerless, but Rowland Ham responded that their criticism was the fault of the individual test car, and the Peerless' well-known stability was retained. Overall, the Warwick has to be rated a significant improvement on the Peerless, but sales weren't any better and the small firm soon perished. Its principals went on to experiment with a Buick V8-engined Warwick for the American market, and eventually designed the V8 Gordon Keeble, another worthy but undercapitalised project.

1961-68 Amphicar

Amphicar stories are like Irish/Polish jokes – there are untold legions of them. The writers' favourite is the one about the road-tester, seaborne, attempting to slow while approaching a sturdy cypress pier. He put his foot on the brake and smashed head-on. It was quite a catastrophe – almost the disaster the Amphicar project was. The company never made money with it.

Even so, the German-built Amphi was a brilliant idea and it lasted quite a while. Perhaps the most successful civilian amphibian, it was the product of Hans Trippel, a clever engineer with a lifetime's fascination for road-and-water vehicles. Trippel tried to interest the Wehrmacht in his ideas during the 1939- 45 war, and kept peddling the basic notion afterwards, but it wasn't until 1961 that Deutsche Industrie-Werke was organised to build the production car at Lubeck-Schlutup. Ungainly-looking, in or out

The Amphicar was not a very good car, and not a good boat either, but it coped well with both environments.

of the water, the Amphicar was a chassisless convertible, sporting fashionable tail fins and twin propellers which surprised following traffic over the road. Triumph's contribution was the 1147cc Herald engine, which was rear-mounted and provided both land and sea propulsion. The Amphi could achieve close to 70mph on the road and 6.5 knots in the water; one of them actually crossed the English Channel in 1962, though the voyage was perilous. Theoretically, door seals were supposed to squeeze into position when entering the water; steering was rather clumsily provided by the normal method, the front wheels acting as rudders. A bilge pump was provided by the thoughtful Germans for any 'emergencies.'

Amphicars, believed the only private passenger-carrying amphibians ever built, were quite popular in coastal sections of the United States. A memorable advertisement shows one storming at breakneck speed down a long boat ramp and plunging into the smiling Chesapeake Bay. Presumably the door seals were already locked in and the bilge pump was at the ready. Lack of sales finally ended the company in 1968, but many Amphis have survived the inevitable corrosion and weak door seals. A small but active enthusiasts club now operates in America. Their motto: 'United We Float.' Divided, of course, they sink.

1962 Fairthorpe

This small Buckinghamshire firm was founded in 1954 by Air Vice-Marshal D C T Bennett, its earliest cars being glass-fibre saloons with rear-mounted BSA motorcycle engines. It was reorganised at Gerrards Cross in 1961, and in Denham in 1964, by which time it was already using 1147cc Herald engines in the tiny Electron EM III. With some pretensions toward sportiness, the Electron was plastic-bodied, with a tubular ladder frame and IFS. In 1968 it was transformed into the EM IV with the 1296cc Spitfire engine, and performance was enhanced. An even more interesting variation on the same theme was the 1962-65 Rockette, using the 1.6-litre Vitesse six-cylinder engine.

Developed from the Rockette, the closed coupé TX GT Fairthorpe on a longer wheelbase used the 2-litre version of the Vitesse engine. The size and weight of the cars promoted very high-performance. An EM Mark IV with the 1296cc, 75hp engine could reach 108mph, for example, while the 112hp 2-litre TX-S would record 115. Ultimate development was the 1969 TX-SS, a sleek-looking coupé with the engine tuned for 140bhp at 6000rpm. It was capable of 130mph.

1963-71 Bond Equipe

Bond Cars Ltd in Preston, Lancashire, manufacturers of three-wheelers, expanded to four-wheel vehicles in the early 1960s. Tom Gratrix, former managing director, said: "I decided that we'd had a great deal of experience in glass-fibre work and knew about laminating from industrial work, and it seemed fairly logical to do something about four-wheel motor cars. The difficulty was marketing ... I decided that the trick was to do a link-up with one of the major manufacturers. I had a rather reasonable entrée to Standard-Triumph, went over to see Stanley Markland and found him very receptive. He took the view of, well, there was nothing to lose.

"My initial proposition was that if Standard-Triumph would agree to sell us the Herald – then Vitesse and Spitfire – running gear, we would clothe it in what we thought was a suitable reinforced-plastic body. But I also wanted a distribution arrangement whereby it would distribute the car ... a dozen of its distributors who we knew were interested in specialist cars. This was agreed. It had never happened before to my knowledge – a small specialist manufacturer selling through somebody else's dealers."

Gratrix didn't bother approaching any other manufacturer: "Triumph was the only company producing a car with a chassis; everything else was monocoque. This ... did limit our design to some extent – wheelbase, door shape, etc. We couldn't greatly modify because after intensive discussions I got Triumph to agree to offer its warranty on the car, exclusive of non-Triumph parts. This was very important to us because we could advertise the car with the Triumph warranty ... while it made its warranty costs by becoming the source of parts. It was extremely important."

The first Bond Equipe was a sharply raked fastback with a simple, clean front end, selling for £822 with purchase tax and the 1147cc Herald engine. It would do about 83mph and return 35-39mpg of premium fuel. Its designer, interestingly, was a man called Lawrence Bond. He had earlier designed the Bond three-wheelers and also some motorcycles. In mid-1965 the original Equipe was

supplemented (and ultimately replaced) by the GT 4S, a somewhat more ungainly looking model with livable passenger space in the rear seat, priced at £829. Though fitted with the 67bhp Spitfire Mark 2 engine, the GT 4S was about 100 pounds heavier than the first Equipe, and was actually slower in the indirects, though it offered a 92mph top speed.

Undoubtedly the most appealing Bond-Triumph was the 1968-71 2-litre GT designed by Peter Jackson of Specialised Models in Preston, with detail assistance from Gratrix's own staff. Initially offered in four-seat coupé form, it was powered by the 95hp Vitesse/2000/GT6 engine, married to an all-synchro Triumph four-speed gearbox with the usual Triumph chassis underneath. Though still based on Herald bodywork, this fact was cleverly disguised, and the GT was a rather neat-looking affair. Bond included, as standard, hinged rear quarter-lights, walnut-veneered facia, built-in radio antenna, heater and demister, wheel trims (wire wheels optional), main-beam flasher, boot light, reversing light and a padded leather steering wheel. As with previous models, the seats were specially made for Bond, deep buckets with good side support.

The GT sold for £1095 13s 6d in the United Kingdom, alongside the GT 4S at first, but by itself from 1968. It was capable of 0-60mph in 11.5 seconds, 20-60mph in 9.1 seconds, and had a top speed of over 100mph. For 1969 the 104hp engine improved performance in the GT Mark 2, which was offered in drophead form as well as the sleek coupé.

Gratrix's main business was with three-wheelers (although he had approached production of 4000 Equipes per year at the height of success), and in this field he was out-gunned by Reliant, who

The 1962 Bond Equipe, as well as using Herald/Spitfire chassis and mechanicals, also featured many Herald body panels too.

The Bond Equipe 2-litre GT was the third clothing of a Triumph chassis by the Preston-based company, this time with a six-cylinder GT6 engine.

held the lion's share of the market. He sold-out to Reliant in 1969, who closed the Preston plant in 1970 and discontinued all previous Bond models. The Bond Bug, a Reliant-built mini-car, was the only survivor in the 1970s.

1963-64 Dove GTR4

In 1963 a British Triumph distributor, Dove's of Wimbledon, thought it had detected a small market for GT models of popular sports cars. The Harrington firm of Hove, Sussex had successfully grafted an attractive glass-fibre GT top to the Sunbeam Alpine, and Dove asked them to perform like-wise for the TR4. Harrington sheared-off the TR's rear bodywork between the wings, and replaced it with a many-cornered, rather clumsy-looking fastback, starting from the original TR4 windscreen and capping the side windows. The backlight was hinged for luggage loading, and a new 15-gallon petrol tank was mounted in the original roadster's boot pressing. The extra luggage space thus gained was considerable, though rear-seat passengers (theoretically provided for by Dove's upholsterers) were not meant to travel for long distances. What headroom they had was given by the high roofline, but this gave the car a peculiar look from the outside. Some suggested that the TR4's styling just wasn't conducive to a fastback variation; certainly the Dove was poor by comparison to the svelte MGB GT, which not only looked good but sold well, and at £1250, compared to £949 for the TR4 with Surrey top, the GTR4 wasn't even popular in Wimbledon. Dove's exercise seems to suggest that such modifications, if made at all, ought to be by qualified factory stylists. Still, it's hard to imagine the angular TR lending itself well to any fastback – which by definition is a much smoother-looking affair.

The TR4 Dove was an interesting GT product, produced privately by the Triumph distributor L F Dove Ltd. This particular, created by TR Register chairman Paul Hogan, actually started life as a TR250, but took on all the Dove body work, retained independent rear suspension – and the registration number is now appropriate.

1969-76 Saab 99

Using Triumph's new slant-four overhead-cam engine, Saab immediately became the largest customer ever for a Triumph power plant – in fact, it was even ahead of Triumph, who was not ready to use the engine in 1969. To provide adequate power for the new, heavy 99, the engine shipped from Coventry to Sweden displaced 1709cc (83.5 x 78mm) and produced 80bhp (net) at 5200rpm. Compression was 8.8:1 and a single Zenith-Stromberg carburettor was fitted. Saab experimented considerably with the engine, only the second four-stroke unit it'd ever used (the first was Ford-Cologne's V4 for the Saab 96, but that was shipped and installed intact). It is known, for example, that Saab engineers found assembly tolerances extraordinary and were appalled by the amount of oil the engine burned in normal operation. They also wanted more power, and in 1971 asked for increased displacement to 1854cc, achieving 88bhp at 5000rpm.

From 1972 Saab built its own completely redesigned 2-litre version of the engine: 1985cc, 80 x 78mm, 95bhp at 5200rpm. It also used the 88bhp engine in the basic 99 two-door saloon. A special 2-litre was used in the 99EA4 automatic-transmission version, which with Bosch fuel-injection developed 110bhp (net) at 5500rpm. Saab never adopted the Triumph dual-carburettor arrangement, preferring to use either a single carb for de-tuned engines or the Bosch injection system. The Saab-built engine, of course, was later turbocharged.

Saab used Triumph slant-four engines in its front-wheel drive Saab 99 range for years, initially of 1709cc, later of 1854cc. From 1972 Saab then developed its own version of this engine, and used that until well into the 1980s.

1970-71 Marcos Mantis

The last passenger-carrying Marcos of the 1970s, and the car that is alleged to have sunk the original company, the four-seater Grand Touring car, was originally styled by Dennis Adams, but changed a lot before public announcement. Initially planned as a GT-estate, the car ended up with fastback styling, using a wedge shape glass-fibre body with permanently raised headlamps upsetting the smoothness of the bonnet. The chassis was multi-tubular and semi-space frame, and the engine was originally supposed to have been Ford's 3-litre V6. The latter developed problems when hooked to electric overdrive, however, and Marcos thought the fuel-injected Triumph 2.5 would be a better alternative. The Triumph engine was duly fitted to the 32 Mantis production cars, providing a top speed of 120mph and 0-60mph acceleration in the eight-second range.

Despite its high speeds and capable handling, the Mantis was extremely comfortable. The 102-inch wheelbase chassis had unequal length wishbones and anti-roll bar up front, while the live rear axle was carefully positioned with trailing links and liberal rubber bushes, combined with adjustable shock-absorbers and oversize coil springs. Inside, the car was comprehensively equipped with reclining front seats, electric window-lifts and extensive padding. Unfortunately, the company expired shortly after it appeared, and as a result the Mantis is often blamed for its demise. Not so, said Peter J Filby in his book, *Specialist Sports Cars*: "The real reason was a big loss on Volvo-powered Marcos models stranded in the US, where they'd failed to pass Federal regulations. At the same time,' Filby noted, 'the company also incurred heavy costs by moving to a new factory, and a general sales decline sealed its fate."

1970 TVR 2500 & 2500M

Both TR6 and Spitfire engines powered this range of stubby, short-chassis TVR coupés, beginning with the 2.5-litre 2500 for 1970. Based on the V6 and V8 Tuscan series, the 1970 2500 used a federal TR6 engine to qualify the car for American importation, and two-thirds of the cars produced wound up in the United States. In late 1971 the Blackpool firm introduced a new multi-tubular chassis with a longer body, the 2500M series, sold in kit or component form with a variety of engines. Fifteen 2500Ms were powered by the 1300cc Spitfire engine; more popular was the larger Triumph-powered version, as well as the Cortina 1600 and Ford V6 models. The Spitfire-engined cars were underpowered, and the TR6 in federal guise didn't provide very exhilarating performance, either, but it was – as in the TR6 itself – strong and smooth, and it kept TVR in America for some years.

1971-73 Trident Tycoon

During one of TVR's periodic financial upsets, this TVR design was sold to William J Last of Woodbridge, Suffolk, a TVR agent. The Trident was originally designed for TVR by stylist Trevor Fiore, and was a really striking modernisation of the short coupé motif which

The 1970 Marcos Mantis came complete with a TR6 fuel-injected engine and gearbox, plus overdrive. Triumph was not responsible for the controversial styling.

The TVR2500 was one of a range of sporting coupés built by the Blackpool-based company. The majority of the 2500 models were sold to the United States, and were powered by the 'federal' version of the TR6 engine.

was enthusiastically received at Geneva in 1964. When Martin Lilley resuscitated TVR in 1966 he wanted it back, but Trident had already exhibited the car and planned to build three a week, powered by a 4.7-litre Ford V8 engine. The Triumph-powered Tycoon was announced in 1971.

Tridents used coil-spring IFS and a live rear axle with semi-elliptics on an Austin-Healey 3000 cruciform-based, boxed-platform chassis, later replaced by a TR6 chassis. Open and closed models were offered with four seats, the rears strictly 'occasional.' They were fast, good-looking, comprehensively equipped cars, well-respected by testers. A small export programme got under way with the Ford-powered cars (Trident Clippers), and might have continued when the TR engine was added. But by 1971 US regulations were greatly affecting bodywork as well as exhaust emissions. Thus the Tycoon was sold with the petrol-injection system only, and confined to Europe. Financial woes caused liquidation of the now Ipswich-based firm in 1972, but Tridents were kept available for a time by Viking Performance Ltd, an affiliate company.

1975-77 Panther Rio

Robert Jankel's specialist house of Panther-Westwinds, located in Byfleet, Surrey, near the old Brooklands Track, began issuing customised Dolomite Sprints in late 1975, though sales were hardly of the boom category. Using straight-Sprint components under the skin, Rio's exterior was completely reworked by Panther craftsmen, and finished to Rolls-Royce standards of perfection. The chunky, dated Michelotti styling was relieved by hand-rolled and beaten aluminium panels, pin-striped and knife-edged. The roofline was lowered and the front end cleaned up with an upright radiator grille and oblong quartz-halogen headlamps. Inside, Panther fitted selected burr walnut on the instrument panel and door fillets, thick woollen carpets and a headliner. Connolly Leather door panels and seats were provided, along with extensive sound-proofing. Electric windows, radio and heated rear window were standard. Upmarket was the Rio 'Especial,' with alloy wheels, overdrive and tinted glass. The option list included automatic transmission, laminated glass, headrests, electric sunroof, air-conditioning, leather headlining and even television! Rios sold for £7500 and up, and as a result few were moved out, though the price was later a lot more comparable to the Triumph-built Sprint than it had been originally. The cars did provide a high level of performance (115mph, 0-60mph in 8.5 seconds) together with simply unprecedented quality of finish on any Triumph motor car. But the competition in this price bracket was sophisticated and exotic – too much for the Rio.

In the mid-1970, Panther produced his completely re-skinned and refurnished Dolomite Sprint, christening it the Rio. It was too expensive, and therefore not a success.

The 1971 Trident Tycoon, which had originally been a TVR design, featured a TR6 engine and a Borg Warner automatic transmission.

Production Factories 1923 to 1984

Priory Street, Coventry – 1923 to 1940
Triumph's famous motorcycle production factory, acquired in 1895, was a former silk-spinning mill. With seven levels, it was unsuited to assembling cars. Many Triumph car mechanical components (including engines and transmissions) were produced here. Sold-off with all motorcycle assets and trademarks in 1936, but a section leased for service and spare-parts stock departments. Destroyed by bombing in November 1940. No longer in existence as the postwar Coventry city centre was completely replanned and rebuilt.

Clay Lane, Stoke, Coventry – 1923 to 1946
The original Triumph car assembly factory, bought from the Dawson Car Co in 1921 and later extended to give a frontage on Briton Road. Final assembly and mechanical design/development moved out in 1935 (to the new Gloria Works), but design, development and coachbuilding of bodies stayed. Let to the Armstrong-Whitworth Aircraft Co during the Second World War, but badly damaged by bombing in November 1940. Sold-off to the B O Morris Group in 1946.

Gloria Works, Holbrooks Lane, Coventry – 1935 to 1939
Bought from White & Poppe (who had made proprietary engines there until 1934), brought into service in 1935 and used for final assembly of cars, and for mechanical machining operations. Sold-off by the receiver to the government in 1939, for use by Claudel-Hobson to make aero-engine carburettors. Later became part of the Dunlop Rim and Wheel complex (along with the neighbouring one-time SS-Jaguar buildings).

Canley/Fletchamstead complex, Coventry – 1945 to 1984
Owned by Standard Motor Co Ltd since 1916, and was its principal assembly facility between the wars. First Standard-owned Triumphs assembled there in 1946, and assembly continued until the last true Triumphs (Dolomite saloons) were phased out in 1980. A big new assembly hall (nicknamed the 'Rocket Range') was completed in 1960/61. Under British Leyland control, intended to become a large-scale component manufacture plant for other factories, but

this idea was abandoned. All complete car assembly ended in 1980. In early and mid-1980s, the site was completely rejigged and split – part to be operated by Unipart (then the Parts Division of Austin-Rover), and part to be used as the Rover Group's (was Austin-Rover Group) administrative, design and styling HQ. Finally completely demolished in 1995, and replaced by light industry units.

Banner Lane, Coventry – 1945 to 1959
One of the 'phase two' motor industry 'shadow factories,' operated by Standard from 1940, and throughout the Second World War. Converted for Ferguson tractor manufacture in 1945/1946, supplied components for Triumph cars in Canley, and housed design/development departments until 1959. Sold by Standard-Triumph in 1959 to Massey-Harris-Ferguson (along with tractor interests), and used for that purpose until the end of the 20th century. Later demolished, and replaced almost entirely by new housing.

Kirkby, Liverpool – 1951 to 1953
Stillborn project to expand into Merseyside area, caused by necessary expansion following start-up of production of Rolls-Royce Avon gas-turbine aero-engines in Coventry. Would have housed spares, spares production and engine reconditioning plants. Sold to Kraft Foods.

Beans Industries, Tipton, Staffordshire – 1956 to 1984
An existing business, producers of heavy castings and components (had also built George Eyston's Thunderbolt land-speed-record car in the 1930s) and already important suppliers to Standard for Ferguson tractor castings.

Radford factory, Coventry – 1957 to 1986
Originally part of the 'phase one' Daimler shadow factory close to the existing Daimler assembly buildings. Lease taken over by Standard-Triumph in 1957. Retained by BL, later ARG, into the 1980s, building axles and other transmission parts for Triumph, Rover and other cars. Manufactured MG Metro 6R4 V6 engines in 1985. Later demolished, replaced by private housing.

Mulliners Ltd/Forward Radiator Company, Bordesley Green, Birmingham – 1958 to 1981

Famous old coachbuilding concern, dating back to the 18th century. Had been building bodies for Standard since the 1930s, Triumph since 1946, and concentrated purely on Standard-Triumph requirements from 1954. Financially taken over by Standard-Triumph in 1958. Made, among other things, TR2/TR3 bodies, Spitfire and GT6 bodies, plus Herald sections and other details.

Note that this company never had any connection, financial or otherwise, with the H J Mulliner concern of London, who concentrated on exclusive hand-built coachwork for Rolls-Royce and similar chassis.

Tile Hill, Coventry – 1958/1959 to early 1980s

Built specially by Fisher & Ludlow Ltd in 1938 to manufacture Standard Flying Eight bodies. Also built Standard 8/10 bodies from 1953 to 1958. Taken over by Standard-Triumph, originally for some Herald and other body preparation. (There was once to have been a three-mile conveyor alongside the railway line to Canley/Fletchamstead to convey the bodies!

Alforder Newton Ltd (Alford and Alder), Hemel Hempstead – 1959 to 1981

Originally a supplier of proprietary suspension and steering components to several UK companies, including Standard-Triumph. Taken-over by Standard-Triumph at end of 1959.

Liverpool No 1 factory – 1960 to 1981

Originally Hall Engineering, who made office furniture and light pressings. Supplier of Herald body sections in 1959, then taken over by Standard-Triumph at the beginning of 1960. Later greatly expanded, produced TR4/TR4A/TR5/TR6 bodies throughout their lives, and the 1300/1500/Dolomite range of bodies, plus pressings for TR7 and the Stag.

Liverpool No 2 factory – 1969 to 1978

Site originally acquired by Standard-Triumph in 1960, about one mile from No 1 factory, but building not started until 1966/67.

Production of complete Toledo cars began in 1969/70, along with assembly of Stag bodies. Toledo was moved out to Coventry at the end of 1974 and replaced by TR7 family and derivatives. A serious 14-week strike in 1977/1978, allied to the poor productivity of this factory, brought permanent closure in 1978. The buildings were subsequently sold-off.

Solihull factory (near Birmingham) – 1980 to 1981

The Solihull site was originally a WW2 shadow factory operated by Rover, became Rover UK and car assembly plant from 1945. New assembly hall for Rover SD1 executive car production completed in 1976. This hall once earmarked for all late 1970s Triumph assembly (see Canley/Fletchamstead, above), but eventually only TR7 and TR8 sports cars assembled there, in 1980 and 1981.

All private car assembly ceased in 1982, but Land Rover assembly increased considerably. Production then continued, under BMW, then Ford, then Tata ownership, until today.

Cowley factory (near Oxford) – 1981 to 1984

William Morris chose Cowley to build his cars from 1913 onwards. From late 1920s Pressed Steel built a body manufacturing factory close by. From 1965, Pressed Steel and Morris were both part of the BMC group, and from 1968 were both in British Leyland (later BL, later ARG) with rationalisation and modernisation.

The Honda-designed Triumph Acclaim was assembled at Cowley throughout its life, with bodies from Pressed Steel and engines from Japan. Entire site (except the ex-Pressed Steel area) was later demolished, and replaced by private housing.

Honda factories, Japan – 1981 to 1984

Honda business began building motorcycles after WW2, with the first cars built in 1962. Under co-operative agreement with BL (later ARG), Triumph Acclaim was a badge-engineered Honda Ballade. All UK-built Acclaims had engine/transmission units manufactured in Japan, then trans-shipped to Britain.

10/20 (produced 1923 to 1926)

Engine: Four-cylinder, 63.5 x 110mm, 1393cc, Zenith carb, 23bhp at 3000rpm.
Transmission: Four-speed, axle ratio 4.75:1. Overall gear ratios 4.75, 6.80, 10.30, 15.80, reverse 20.40:1.
Suspension and brakes: Beam axles with two longitudinal semi-elliptic leaf springs front and rear; no dampers. Worm-and-roller steering. Expanding-shoe rear-wheel brakes operating in drums on hubs. 3.50-21in tyres on detachable steel wheels.
Dimensions: Wheelbase 102in; track 46in front and rear. Length 140in. Unladen weight 1908lb.
Basic price: £430 for two-seat tourer and four-seat tourer, £460 for Weymann-type saloon.

10/20 Sports (produced 1923 to 1926)

Specification as for 10/20 except for:
Transmission: Axle ratio 4.18:1. Overall gear ratios 4.18, 6.00, 9.00, 14.00, reverse 19.00:1.
Suspension and brakes: Hartford dampers on all four wheels. Tyres mounted on detachable wire wheels.
Dimensions: Unladen weight 1568lb.
Basic price: £425 for aluminium-bodied duck-back tourer.

13/35 (produced 1924 to 1926)

Engine: Four-cylinder, 72 x 115mm, 1873cc, Zenith carb, 35bhp at 3000rpm.
Transmission: Three-speed, axle ratio 5.25:1. Overall gear ratios 5.25, 8.50, 17.75, reverse 21.91:1.
Suspension and brakes: Semi-elliptic leaf springs front and rear; lever-arm dampers. Worm-and-roller steering. Lockheed hydraulic four-wheel brakes with contracting bands. 4.95-19in tyres on detachable steel wheels.
Dimensions: Wheelbase 108in; track 56in front and rear. Length 151in. Unladen weight 2128lb.
Basic price: £495 for saloon; five-seat tourer also offered.

15 (produced 1926 to 1930)

Specification as for 13/35 except for:
Engine: 77.5 x 115mm, 2169cc, 40bhp (est.) at 3000rpm.
Transmission: Axle ratio 5.20:1. Overall gear ratios 5.20, 8.40, 17.60:1, reverse 21.70:1. 18.3mph/1000rpm (est.) in top gear. 5.25-21in tyres.
Dimensions: Wheelbase 112in; track 56.75in front and rear. Length 161in. Unladen weight 2576lb.

Super Seven (produced 1927 to 1932)

Engine: Four-cylinder, 56.5 x 83mm, 832cc, CR 5.0:1; Zenith, B&B and Solex carbs, 21bhp at 4000rpm. Maximum torque 35lb/ft at 2000rpm. Tuned engine 23.1bhp at 4000rpm. Cozette supercharged engine, power output not stated.
Transmission: Three-speed, axle ratio 5.25:1. Overall gear ratios: Tourers 5.75, 10.46, 18.70, reverse 24.90:1; Saloons 6.25, 11.40, 20.30, reverse 24.90:1. Four-speed on 1932 Pillarless Saloon (see Super Eight). 13.6mph/1000rpm in top gear.
Suspension and brakes: Beam axles with semi-elliptic leaf springs at front and quarter-elliptics at rear (semi-elliptics in 1932); friction-type dampers. Worm-and-wheel steering. Lockheed hydraulic brakes all around. 4.40-19in tyres on detachable steel-spoke or wire wheels.
Dimensions: Wheelbase 81in; track 42in front and rear. Length 118in (de Luxe Tourer 124in). Width 51in. Height 62-65in. Unladen weight 1064lb, saloon 1288lb.
Basic price: £149 10s-£200 in 1928, rising to £162 10s-£198 in 1930, dropping to £140-£157 10s in 1932.

Super Eight (produced 1933 to 1934)

Specification as for Super Seven except for:
Engine: 21.5bhp at 4400rpm. Maximum torque 31.3lb/ft at 2500rpm.
Transmission: Same as Super Seven in 1933. In 1934, four-speed with free-wheel, axle ratio 5.75:1. Overall gear ratios 5.75, 8.81, 13.67, 22.42, reverse 30.36:1. 13.62mph/1000rpm in top gear.
Suspension and brakes: Semi-elliptic leaf springs front and rear,

hydraulic dampers at front. 4.00-19in tyres on wire wheels.
Dimensions: Track 43.5in front and rear. Length 128-132in. Width 53in. Height 64in. Unladen weight 1600-1800lb.
Basic price: £155 in 1933, rising to £175 in 1934.

Scorpion (produced 1931 to 1932)
Engine: Six-cylinder, 56.5 x 80mm, 1203cc, Solex carb, 25bhp (est.).
Transmission: Three-speed, axle ratio 6.25:1. Overall gear ratios 6.25, 11.1, 21.8, reverse 27.2:1. On 1932 de Luxe, four-speed, axle ratio 5.75:1.
Suspension and brakes: Beam-axles with semi-elliptic leaf springs at front and quarter-elliptics at rear; in 1932 semi-elliptics all round; friction-type dampers; in 1932 hydraulic dampers. Worm-and-wheel steering. Lockheed hydraulic brakes all round. 4.00-19in tyres on wire wheels.
Dimensions: Wheelbase 86¾in, in 1933 92½in; track 42½in front and rear, in 1932 43½in front and rear. Length 137in, 146in in 1932. Width 53in, 53½in in 1932. Height 61in on open cars, 65½in on saloons. Unladen weight (chassis only) 1120lb.
Basic price: £230-£237 10s in 1931, dropping to £179-£210 in 1932.

Twelve-Six (produced 1932 to 1933)
Specification as for 1932 Scorpion except for:
Dimensions: Wheelbase 92¼in; track 42in front and rear. Length 143in. Width 53½in. Height 65½in.
Basic price: £198 for Coachbuilt Saloon, £214 for de Luxe.

Super Nine (produced 1932 to 1933)
Engine: Four-cylinder, 60 x 90mm, 1018cc, Solex carb.
Transmission: Four-speed, axle ratio 5.25:1. Overall gear ratios 5.25, 8.05, 12.47, 20.42, reverse 23.50:1. 15.25mph/1000rpm in top gear.
Suspension and brakes: Beam-axles with semi-elliptic leaf springs front and rear; hydraulic dampers all round. Worm-and-wheel steering. Lockheed hydraulic brakes all around. 4.40-19in tyres on wire-spoke wheels.
Dimensions: Wheelbase 86¾in, in 1933 92¼in; track 42¼in front and rear, in 1933 45in. Length 137in, in 1933 147in. Width 53¼in, in 1933 55in. Height 65in, in 1933 67in. Unladen weight 2112lb (1933 saloon).
Basic price: £179-£197 10s in 1932, rising to £198 upwards in 1933.

Southern Cross 8.9hp (produced 1932)
Specification as for Super Nine except for:
Dimensions: Wheelbase 92¼in; track 45in front and rear. Length 152in. Width 48in. Height 60in. Unladen weight 1850lb (est.).
Basic price: £225.

Southern Cross 9.8hp (produced 1933 to 1934)
Engine: Four-cylinder, 63 x 90mm, 1122cc, in 1934 62 x 90mm, 1087cc. CR 5.75:1, Solex carb, 35bhp at 4500rpm. Maximum torque 52lb/ft at 2500rpm.
Transmission: Four-speed, axle ratio 4.8:1. Overall gear ratios 4.80, 7.15, 11.41, 18.52, reverse 25.34:1. 13mph/1000rpm in top gear. Free-wheel optional.
Suspension and brakes: Beam-axles with semi-elliptic leaf springs front and rear; Luvax hydraulic dampers. Screw-and-nut steering. Lockheed hydraulic brakes all round. 4.50-19in tyres mounted on wire wheels.
Dimensions: 1933-34 Tourer: wheelbase 92½in; track 45in front and rear. Length 149in. Width 48in. Height 60in. Unladen weight 1904lb. 1934 Sports Saloon: wheelbase 96in; track 45in front and rear. Length 152in. Width 55in. Height 61in. Unladen weight 2027lb.
Basic price: £225 in 1933, dropping to £215 in 1934 for Tourer. Sports Saloon £225, offered 1934 only.

Ten (produced 1933 to 1934)
Specification as for Southern Cross 9.8hp except for:
Engine: 33.5bhp at 4300rpm. Maximum torque 51lb/ft at 2500rpm.
Transmission: Axle ratio 5.25:1. Overall gear ratios 5.25, 8.05, 12.47, 20.42, reverse 23.50:1. 13.3mph/1000rpm. Free-wheel standard.
Dimensions: Wheelbase 96in; track 45in front and rear. Tourer and Coachbuilt Saloon – Length 158in, Width 58in, Height 65in, Unladen weight 2252lb. 2/4-seater – Length 152in, Width 58in, Height 60in, Unladen weight 1904lb. Popular Saloon – Length 150in, Width 55in, Height 65in, Unladen weight 2224lb.
Basic price: £225, dropping to £198 for Popular Saloon in 1934.

Gloria '9.5' Four (produced 1934 to 1936)
Engine: Four-cylinder, 62 x 90mm, 1087cc, CR 6.4:1, Solex carb (twin Solexes on Special). 40bhp at 4500rpm (46bhp at 4600rpm on Special). Maximum torque 54lb/ft at 2500rpm (56.5lb/ft on Special).
Transmission: Four-speed, free-wheel. Axle ratio 5.22:1. Overall gear ratios 5.22, 7.99, 12.42, 20.36, reverse 27.56:1. 15.1mph/1000rpm in top gear.
Suspension and brakes: Beam-axles with longitudinal semi-elliptic leaf springs front and rear; hydraulic dampers. Screw-and-nut steering. 12in hydraulic brakes all round, handbrake operating on rear drums. 4.75-18in tyres on wire wheels, in 1935/36 5.00-17in.
Dimensions: Wheelbase 108in; track 48in front and rear. Length 165in. Width 60in. Height 61in. Unladen weight 2576lb.
Basic price: £285, rising to £295 in 1936; 1934 Special £300.

Gloria Monte Carlo (produced 1934 and 1935)

Specification as for Gloria '9.5' Four except for:
Engine: Four-cylinder, 66 x 90mm, 1232cc, CR 6.8:1 (est.), two Zenith carbs. 48bhp at 4750rpm.
Transmission: No free-wheel.
Suspension and brakes: Hartford, later Andre, adjustable dampers. Handbrake operating on transmission.
Dimensions: Length 154in. Height 60in. Unladen weight 2000lb.
Basic price: £325.

Gloria Six (produced 1934)

Specifications as for Gloria '9.5' Four except for:
Engine: Six-cylinder, 59 x 90mm, 1476cc, CR 5.85:1 (6.3:1 on Special), two Solex carbs. 44.7bhp at 4000rpm (52bhp at 4600rpm on Special). Maximum torque 67lb/ft at 2500rpm (70lb/ft on Special).
Transmission: 15.5mph/1000rpm in top gear.
Dimensions: Wheelbase 116in. Length 173in. Unladen weight 2688lb.
Basic price: £325.

Gloria '10.8' Four (produced 1935 to 1937) (and on 1934 Monte Carlo)

Specification as for Gloria Monte Carlo except for:
Engine: CR 6.4:1, two Solex carbs. 46bhp at 4600rpm. Maximum torque 56.5lb/ft at 2500rpm.
Transmission: Four-speed, free-wheel. 15.1mph/1000rpm in top gear.
Suspension and brakes: Hydraulic dampers all round, handbrake operating on rear drums. 5.00-17in tyres in 1935, 5.75-16in from 1936.
Dimensions: Wheelbase 108in, 96in on Southern Cross and 1935 short-chassis coupé; track 50in front and rear. Length 165½in. Width 62in. Height 61in. Unladen weight 2744lb.
Basic price: £288, dropping to £268 by 1937.

Gloria-Vitesse Four (produced 1935 to 1936)

Specification as for Gloria '10.8' Four except for:
Engine: CR higher, 50bhp at 5000rpm.
Transmission: Four-speed, free-wheel, synchronised gears offered in 1936. 15.5mph/1000rpm in top gear.
Suspension and brakes: 5.00-17in tyres in 1935, 5.75-16in in 1936 except Southern Cross.
Dimensions: Height 60in (saloon).
Basic price: £275-£382 in 1935, £295-£365 in 1936.

Gloria Six (produced 1935 to 1936)

Engine: Six-cylinder, 65 x 100mm, 1991cc, CR 6.3:1, two Solex carbs, 55bhp at 4500rpm. Maximum torque not stated.
Transmission: Four-speed, free-wheel, synchronised gears offered in 1936. Axle ratio 4.75:1. Overall gear ratios 4.75, 7.28, 11.30, 18.50, reverse 27.56:1. 16mph/1000rpm (est.) in top gear.
Suspension and brakes: Beam-axles with longitudinal semi-elliptic leaf springs front and rear; hydraulic dampers. Screw-and-nut steering. 12in hydraulic brakes all round, handbrake operating on rear drums. 5.25-17in tyres on wire wheels, 6.00-16in in 1936.
Dimensions: Wheelbase 116in; track 50in front and rear. Length 180in. Width 62in. Height 60in. Unladen weight 3024lb.
Basic price: £340-£415 in 1935, £395-£415 in 1936.

Gloria-Vitesse Six (produced 1935 to 1936)

Specification as for Gloria Six except for:
Engine: CR higher, two Solex carbs, later two SU carbs. 65bhp at 4750rpm.
Dimensions: Height 59in.
Basic price: £335-£445 in 1935, £390-£445 in 1936.

Dolomite Straight-eight (produced 1934 to 1935)

Engine: Eight-cylinder, 60 x 88mm, 1990cc, CR 6.1:1, Zenith carb (later SU), Roots-type supercharger with 10psi boost operating at 1.5 times engine speed. 120bhp at 5500rpm. Maximum torque not stated.
Transmission: Four-speed Wilson-type preselector. Axle ratio 4.0:1 or 4.5:1. Overall gear ratios with 4.0:1 rear axle, 4.00, 4.92, 7.40, 12.40:1. 20mph/1000rpm in top gear.
Suspension and brakes: Beam-axles with semi-elliptic longitudinal leaf springs front and rear, front radius-rods, Hartford adjustable dampers. Screw-and-nut steering. 16in or 12in Lockheed hydraulics all round. 5.25-19in tyres on wire wheels.
Dimensions: Wheelbase 104in. Unladen weight 2128lb, bare chassis 1568lb.
Basic price: £1225 complete, £1050 for chassis. (Two complete cars, three chassis and six engines built.)

Gloria 1½-litre (produced 1937)

Engine: Four-cylinder, 69 x 100mm, 1496cc, CR 7.0:1, SU horizontal carb. Brake horsepower and torque not stated.
Transmission: Four-speed, synchromesh. Axle ratio 5.00:1. Overall gear ratios 5.00, 6.89, 10.81, 16.60, reverse 20.50:1.
Suspension and brakes: Beam-axles with longitudinal semi-elliptic leaf springs front and rear; hydraulic dampers. Screw-and-nut steering. 12in hydraulic brakes all round, cable handbrake. 5.00-17in tyres on wire wheels.
Dimensions: Wheelbase 108in; track 50in front and rear. Length 163in. Width 62in. Height 61in. Unladen weight 2800lb.
Basic price: £285, six-light Saloon £298.

Gloria Fourteen (produced 1938)

Specification as for Gloria 1½-litre except for:
Engine: 75 x 100mm, 1767cc, CR 6.6:1, one or two SU horizontal carbs.
Transmission: Axle ratio 4.75:1. Overall gear ratios 4.75, 6.54, 10.27, 15.77, reverse 19.47:1.
Dimensions: Length 164in. Height 63in. Unladen weight 2850lb.
Basic price: £288.

Vitesse 14/60 (produced 1937 to 1938)

Engine: Four-cylinder, 75 x 100mm, 1767cc, CR 6.6:1, two SU horizontal carbs, 62bhp at 4500rpm. Torque not stated.
Transmission: Four-speed, synchromesh. Axle ratio 4.75:1. Overall gear ratios 4.75, 6.54, 10.27, 15.77, reverse 19.47: 1.
Suspension and brakes: Beam-axles with longitudinal semi-elliptic leaf springs front and rear; hydraulic dampers. Screw-and-nut steering. 12in hydraulic brakes all round, cable handbrake. 5.00-17in tyres (5.75-16in on six-light Saloon) on wire wheels.
Dimensions: Wheelbase 108in; track 50.5in front and rear. Length 163.5in. Width 62in. Height 59in. Unladen weight 2700lb.
Basic price: £318 for Saloon in 1937, dropping to £298 in 1938.

Vitesse 2-Litre (produced 1937 to 1938)

Engine: Six-cylinder, 65 x 100mm, 1991cc, CR 6.8:1, two SU horizontal carbs, 72bhp at 4500rpm. Torque not stated.
Transmission: Four-speed, synchromesh. Axle ratio 4.50:1. Overall gear ratios 4.50, 6.20, 9.73, 14.90:1.
Suspension and brakes: Beam-axles with longitudinal semi-elliptic leaf springs front and rear; hydraulic dampers. Screw-and-nut steering. 12in hydraulic brakes all round, cable handbrake. 5.25-17in tyres on wire wheels.
Dimensions: Wheelbase 116in; track 52.5in front and rear. Length 167.5in. Width 62in. Height 59in. Unladen weight 2968lb.
Basic price: £348 for Saloon in 1937, dropping to £338 in 1938.

Dolomite 14/60 (produced 1937 to 1939)

Specification as for Vitesse 14/60 except for:
Dimensions: Wheelbase 110in; track 52.5in front and rear. Length 175.5in. Width 65in. Unladen weight 2940lb.
Basic price: £348.

Dolomite 14/65 (produced 1939)

Specification as for Vitesse 14/60 except for:
Engine: 65bhp at 4500rpm. Torque not stated.
Dimensions: Track 52.5in front, 50.5in rear. Unladen weight 2800lb.
Basic price: Roadster-Coupé model only, £395.

Dolomite 2-litre (produced 1937 to 1939)

Specification as for Vitesse 2-litre except for:
Engine: On Roadster-Coupé only, with two and later three SU horizontal carbs, 75bhp at 4500rpm.
Transmission: Axle ratio 5.00:1. Overall gear ratios 5.00, 6.89, 10.89, 16.6, reverse 20.50:1.
Suspension and brakes: 5.50-17in tyres.
Dimensions: Track 52.5in front and rear. Length 181.5in. Width 65in. Height 63.5in. Unladen weight 3304lb.
Basic price: £368 in 1937, rising to £425 in 1939.

Continental 2-litre (produced 1937)

Specification as for Dolomite 2-litre except for:
Transmission: Axle ratio 4.50:1. Overall gear ratios 4.50, 6.20, 9.73, 14.90, reverse 18.45:1.
Dimensions: Unladen weight (est) 2950lb.
Basic price: £368.

Dolomite 1½-litre (produced 1938 to 1939)

Engine: Four-cylinder, 69 x 100mm, 1496cc, CR 7.0:1, SU horizontal carb. Optional 1938, standard 1939: 75 x 100mm, 1767cc, CR 6.6:1, one or two SU horizontal carbs.
Transmission: 1496cc models as for Gloria 1½-litre, 1767cc models as for Gloria Fourteen.
Suspension and brakes: As for Gloria 1½-litre.
Dimensions: Wheelbase 108in; track 50in front and 52.5in rear. Length 116in. Width 65in. Height 61in. Unladen weight (est.) 2900lb.
Basic price: £328 in 1938, rising to £332 18s in 1939.

Twelve (produced 1939)

Specification as for Gloria 1½-litre except for:
Dimensions: Track 52.5in front and rear. Length 168in. Width 65in. Unladen weight (est.) 2800lb.
Basic price: £285.

1800 'Town and Country' Saloon (produced 1946 to 1949)

Engine: Four-cylinder, 73 x 106mm, 1776cc, CR 6.7:1, Solex carb, 63bhp (net) at 4500rpm. Maximum torque 92lb/ft at 2000rpm.
Transmission: Axle ratio 4.86:1. Overall gear ratios 4.86, 7.06, 11.8, 19.18, reverse 19.18:1. 16.1mph/1000rpm in top gear.
Suspension and brakes: IFS, transverse leaf-spring, upper wishbones, lever-arm dampers: live rear axle, semi-elliptic leaf springs, anti-roll bar, lever-arm dampers. Cam-and-roller steering. 10 x 1.5in drum brakes all round. 5.75-16in tyres on 3.5in rims.
Dimensions: Wheelbase 108in; front track 50.5in; rear track 54.75in. Length 175in. Width 63.5in Height 63in. Unladen weight 2828lb.
Basic price: £650 in March 1946, rising to £775 by end of 1948.

1800 Roadster (produced 1946 to 1948)

Specification as for 1800 Saloon except for:
Transmission: Axle ratio 4.56:1. Overall gear ratios 4.56, 5.69, 9.51, 15.44, reverse 15.44:1. 17.1mph/1000rpm in top gear.
Dimensions: Wheelbase 100in. Length 168.5in. Width 64in. Height 56in. Unladen weight 2541lb.
Basic price: £625 in March 1946, rising to £775 by 1948.

2000 Saloon (produced 1949)

Specification as for 1800 Saloon except for:
Engine: 85 x 92mm, 2088cc, 68bhp at 4200rpm, maximum torque 108lb/ft at 2000rpm.
Transmission: Axle ratio 4.625:1. Overall gear ratios 4.625, 7.71, 16.73, reverse 18.99:1. 16.9mph/1000rpm in top gear.

2000 Renown Saloon (produced 1949 to 1951)

Specification as for 1800 saloon except for:
Engine: 85 x 92mm, 2088cc, 68bhp at 4200rpm, maximum torque 108lb ft at 2000rpm.
Transmission: Axle ratio 4.625:1. Overall gear ratios 4.625, 7.71, 16.73, reverse 18.99:1. 16.9mph/1000rpm in top gear. From June 1950, overdrive was optionally available, giving 3.89:1 (later 3.6:1) overall ratio. 20.1 (later 21.7) mph/1000rpm in overdrive top gear.
Suspension and brakes: IFS, coil springs, wishbones, anti-roll bar, lever-arm dampers. 9 x 1.75in brakes all round.
Dimensions: Rear track 54in.
Basic price: £775, rising to £825 by 1951.

2000 Limousine – known as 'Triumph Limousine' (produced 1951 to 1952)

Specification as for Renown except for:
Dimensions: Wheelbase 111in. Length 181in. Unladen weight 3024lb.
Basic price: £895, rising to £925 in 1952.

2000 Renown Saloon (produced 1952 to 1954)

Specification as for early Renown except for:
Dimensions: Wheelbase 111in. Length 181in. Unladen weight 2835lb.
Basic price: £825, rising to £925 by end of 1952, then £775 from June 1953.

2000 Roadster (produced 1948 to 1949)

Specification as for 1949 2000 Saloon, except for Roadster dimensions and weight.
Basic price: £775.

Mayflower Saloon (produced 1949 to 1953)

Engine: Four-cylinder, side-valve, 63 x 100mm, 1247cc, CR 6.7:1, Solex carb, 38bhp at 4200rpm. Maximum torque 58lb/ft at 2000rpm.
Transmission: Axle ratio 5.125:1. Overall gear ratios 5.125, 8.56, 18.14, reverse 21.04:1. 14:4mph/1000rpm in top gear.
Suspension and brakes: IFS, coil springs, wishbones and telescopic dampers; live rear axle, semi-elliptic leaf springs, telescopic dampers. Cam-and-lever steering. 8 x 1.5in drum brakes all round. 5.00-15in tyres (5.50 section for export) on 4.0in rims.
Dimensions: Wheelbase 84in; front track 45in, rear track 48in. Length 154in. Width 62in. Height 62in. Unladen weight 2016lb.
Basic price: £370, rising to £450 by 1953.

Mayflower Convertible (produced 1950)

Specification as for Mayflower Saloon except for:
Dimensions: Unladen weight 2100lb.
Basic price: £450.

'New Roadster' TRX prototype (produced in 1950)

Engine: Four-cylinder, 85 x 92mm, 2088cc, CR 7.0:1, two SU crabs, 71bhp at 4200rpm. Maximum torque 108lb/ft at 2000rpm.
Transmission: Axle ratio 4.375:1. Overall ratios 3.58 (overdrive). 4.375, 7.32, 15.5, reverse 17.96:1. 21.4mph/1000rpm in overdrive top gear.
Suspension and brakes: IFS, coil springs, wishbones, anti-roll bar, lever-arm dampers; live rear axle, semi-elliptic leaf springs, anti-roll bar, lever-arm dampers. Cam-and-roller steering. 11 x 2¼in drum brakes all round. 5.50-16in tyres on 4.0in rims.
Dimensions: Wheelbase 94in; front track 50.5in, rear track 54in. Length 166in. Width 70in. Height 55in. Unladen weight 2716lb.
Basic price: £975 – but no cars ever delivered.

TR2 (produced 1953 to 1955)

Engine: Four-cylinder, 83 x 92mm, 1991cc, CR 8.5:1, two SU carbs. 90bhp (gross) at 4800rpm. Maximum torque 117lb/ft at 3000rpm.
Transmission: Axle ratio 3.7:1. Overall gear ratios 3.7, 4.90, 7.43, 12.51, reverse 16.09:1. Optional overdrive, ratio 3.03:1. 20mph/1000rpm in direct top gear, 24.5mph/1000rpm in overdrive.
Suspension and brakes: IFS, coil springs, wishbones and telescopic dampers; live rear axle, semi-elliptic leaf springs, lever-arm dampers. Cam-and-lever steering. 10 x 2¼in front brakes, 9 x 1¾in rear brakes (from autumn 1954 10 x 2¼in brakes all round). 5.50-15in tyres on 4.0in rims (later 4.5in rims).
Dimensions: Wheelbase 88in; front track 45in; rear track 45.5in. Length 151in. Width 55.5in. Height (hood up) 50in. Unladen weight 1848lb.
Basic price: £555 at first, £595 from January 1954, £625 from October 1954.

TR3 (produced 1955 to 1957)
Specification as for TR2 except for:
Engine: 95bhp at 4800rpm, later 100bhp at 5000rpm.
Suspension and brakes: (from Chassis No TS13046, October 1956) 11in front discs, 10 x 2¼in rear drums.
Dimensions: Unladen weight 1988lb.
Basic price: £650 at first, £680 from May 1956.

TR3A (produced 1957 to 1961)
Specification as for disc-braked TR3 except for:
Suspension and brakes: Rear drum brakes (from Chassis No TS56377, autumn 1959): 9 x 1¾in.
Dimensions: Unladen weight 2050lb.
Basic price: £699 – unaltered for four years.
Note: From 1959, there was an optional engine: 86 x 92mm, 2138cc, CR 9.1:1. No official power or torque figures were ever released.

TR3B (produced 1962, USA market only)
There were two series. Cars with Commission Numbers in the TSF series were effectively identical to later TR3A models. Cars with Commission Numbers in the TCF series were as TR3As except for:
Engine: 86 x 92mm, 2138cc, CR 9.0:1; 100bhp (net) at 4600rpm; maximum torque 127lb/ft at 3350rpm.
Transmission: Overall gear ratios 3.7, 4.90, 7.43, 11.61, reverse 11.92:1; synchromesh on all forward gears. Optional overdrive, 20mph/1000rpm in direct top gear, 24.4mph/1000rpm in overdrive.
Basic price: These cars were never sold in Great Britain.

TR10 Saloon (produced 1957 to 1960)
Engine: Four-cylinder, 63 x 76mm, 948cc, CR 8.0:1, Solex carb, 40bhp at 5000rpm. Maximum torque 50lb/ft at 2700rpm.
Transmission: Axle ratio 4.55:1. Overall gear ratios 4.55, 6.60, 11.19, 19.43:1. 13.2mph/1000rpm in top gear.
Suspension and brakes: IFS, coil springs, wishbones and telescopic dampers; live rear axle with semi-elliptic leaf springs. Worm-and-nut steering. 8 x 1½in front and 7 x 1½in rear drum brakes. 5.60-13in tyres on 3.5in rims.
Dimensions: Wheelbase 84in; front and rear track 48.5in. Length 144in. Width 60in. Height 59in. Unladen weight 1760lb.
Basic price: $1699 for saloon, $1899 for estate, USA sale only.

Herald (948cc) Saloon (produced 1959 to 1961)
Engine: Four-cylinder, 63 x 76mm, 948cc, CR 8.0:1, Solex carb, 35bhp at 4500rpm. Maximum torque 51lb/ft at 2750rpm.
Transmission: Axle ratio 4.875:1. Overall gear ratios 4.875, 7.09, 11.99, 20.82, reverse 20.82:1. 13.5mph/1000rpm in top gear.
Suspension and brakes: IFS, coil springs, wishbones, anti-roll bar and telescopic dampers; IRS, transverse leaf spring, swing axles,
radius arms and telescopic dampers. Rack-and-pinion steering. 8 x 1¼in front drum brakes, 7 x 1¼in rear drum brakes. 5.20-13in tyres on 3.5in rims.
Dimensions: Wheelbase 91.5in; front track 48in, rear track 48in. Length 153in. Width 60in. Height 52in. Unladen weight 1764lb.
Basic price: £495.

Herald (948cc) Coupé (produced 1959 to 1961)
Specification as for Saloon except for:
Engine: CR 8.5:1, two SU carbs, 45bhp at 6000rpm. Maximum torque 51lb/ft at 4200rpm.
Transmission: Axle ratio 4.55:1. Overall gear ratios 4.55, 6.62, 11.2, 19.45, reverse 19.45:1. 14.0mph/1000rpm in top gear.
Dimensions: Height 51.25in. Unladen weight 1750lb.
Basic price: £515.
Note: Through special order, the saloon could be supplied with the coupé engine tune.

Herald (948cc) Convertible (produced 1960 and 1961)
Specification as for Saloon except for:
Coupé mechanical specification.
Dimensions: Unladen weight 1750lb.
Basic price: £540.

Herald 1200 Saloon, Coupe, Convertible (produced 1961 to 1970)
Specification as for 948cc car except for:
Engine: 69.3 x 76mm, 1147cc, 39bhp at 4500rpm. Maximum torque 61lb/ft at 2250rpm.
Transmission: Axle ratio 4.11:1. Overall gear ratios 4.11, 5.74, 8.88, 15.42, reverse 15.42:1. 15.7mph/1000rpm in top gear. Optional 9.0in front disc brakes from autumn 1961.
Dimensions: Unladen weight (Saloon) 1791lb, (Coupé) 1764lb, (Convertible) 1736lb.
Basic price: Saloon, £499, down to £479 at end of 1961, then finally to £544 by 1970; Coupé, £519, down to £499 at end of 1961; Convertible, £544, down to £531 at end of 1961, finally to £561 by autumn 1967.

Herald 1200 Estate (produced 1961 to 1967)
Specification as for 1200 Saloon except for:
Transmission: 16.3mph/1000rpm in top gear.
Suspension and brakes: 5.60-13in tyres on 4.5in rims.
Dimensions: Unladen weight 1918lb.
Basic price: £562, down to £548 at end of 1961, finally to £578 in 1967.

Herald 12/50 Saloon – produced 1963 to 1967

Specification as for 1200 Saloon except for:

Engine: CR 8.5:1. 51bhp at 5200rpm. Maximum torque 63lb/ft at 2600rpm.

Suspension and brakes: Disc front brakes standardised. Unladen weight 1855lb.

Basic price: £525, rising to £550 by 1967.

Herald 13/60 Saloon, Convertible and Estate (produced 1967 to 1971)

Specification as for 948cc cars except for:

Engine: 73.7 x 76mm, 1296cc, CR 8.5:1, Zenith-Stromberg carb, 61bhp at 5000rpm. Maximum torque 73lb/ft at 3000rpm.

Transmission: Axle ratio 4.11:1. Overall gear ratios 4.11, 5.74, 8.88, 15.42, reverse 15.42:1. 15.7mph/1000rpm (Estate 16.3) in top gear.

Suspension and brakes: 9.0in front disc brakes. 5.60-13in and 4.5in rims on Estate.

Dimensions: Front track 49in. Unladen weight (saloon) 1876lb, (convertible) 1820lb, (estate) 1988lb.

Basic price: Saloon, £568, rising to £648 by 1970; Convertible, £613, rising to £695 by 1971; Estate, £628, rising to £717 by 1971.

TR4 (produced 1961 to 1965)

Engine: Four-cylinder, 86 x 92mm, 2138cc, CR 9.0:1, two SU carbs (or two Stromberg carbs). 100bhp (net) at 4600rpm. Maximum torque 127lb/ft at 3350rpm. Optional 2-litre TR3A engine.

Transmission: Axle ratio 3.7:1. Overall gear ratios 3.7, 4.90, 7.43, 11.61, reverse 11.92:1. Synchromesh on all forward gears. Optional overdrive 3.32:1 (with 4.1:1 axle ratio). 20mph/1000rpm in direct top gear, 22.2mph/1000rpm in overdrive.

Suspension and brakes: IFS, coil springs, wishbones and telescopic dampers; live rear axle, semi-elliptic leaf springs, lever-arm dampers. Rack-and-pinion steering. 11in diameter front disc brakes, 9 x 1¾in rear drums. 5.90-15in tyres.

Dimensions: Wheelbase 88in; front track 49in; rear track 48in. Length 153.6in. Width 57.5in. Height (hood up) 50in. Unladen weight 2128lb.

Basic price: £750.

TR4A (produced 1965 to 1967)

Specification as for later TR4 model except for:

Engine: 104bhp (net) at 4700rpm. Maximum torque 132lb/ft at 3000rpm. No 2-litre engine option.

Suspension and brakes: IRS, coil springs, semi-trailing arms, lever-arm dampers. Optional (USA market only) live axle, semi-elliptic leaf springs and lever-arm dampers. 6.95-15in tyres.

Dimensions: Rear track 48.5in. Unladen weight 2240lb.

Basic price: £800.

TR5 (produced 1967 and 1968)

Engine: Six-cylinder, 74.7 x 95mm, 2498cc, CR 9.5:1, Lucas indirect fuel-injection. 150bhp (net) at 5500rpm. Maximum torque 164lb/ft at 3500rpm.

Transmission: Axle ratio 3.45:1. Overall gear ratios 3.45, 4.59, 6.92, 10.80, reverse 11.11:1. Optional overdrive 2.82:1. 21.2mph/1000rpm in direct top gear, 25.9mph/1000rpm in overdrive.

Suspension and brakes: IFS, coil springs, wishbones and telescopic dampers; IRS, coil springs, semi-trailing arms, lever-arm dampers. Rack-and-pinion steering. 10.9in front disc brakes, 9 x 1¾in rear drums, and vacuum-servo assistance. 165-15in radial-ply tyres on 5.0in rims.

Dimensions: Wheelbase 88in; front track 49.25in; rear track 48.75in. Length 153.6in. Width 58in. Height 50in. Unladen weight 2268lb.

Basic price: £985.

TR250 (produced 1967 and 1968, USA market only)

Specification as for TR5 except for:

Engine: CR 8.5:1, two Stromberg carburettors. 104bhp (net) at 4500rpm. Maximum torque 143lb/ft at 3,000rpm.

Transmission: Axle ratio 3.7:1. Overall gear ratios 3.7, 4.90, 7.43, 11.61, reverse 11.92:1. Optional A-Type overdrive, 3.03:1. 20.75mph/1000rpm in direct top gear, 25.3mph/1000rpm in overdrive.

Suspension and brakes: 185SR-15in radial-ply tyres.

TR6 – Non-USA versions (produced 1969 to 1975)

Basic specification as for TR5 except for:

Engine: 1969-72 models had TR5 engine specification. From start of CR-series Commission Numbers engine power was reduced and recalibrated to 124bhp (DIN) at 5000rpm. Maximum torque became 143lb/ft at 3500rpm.

Transmission: TR5 ratios until mid-1971. From gear gearbox numbers CD51163/CC89817, revised internal ratios gave overall gearing of 3.45, 4.78, 7.25, 10.33, reverse 11.62:1. From 1973 model (Commission Number CR567 onward) J-Type overdrive replaced A-Type overdrive. Overall ratio 2.75:1. 26.6mph/1000rpm in overdrive.

Suspension and brakes: Anti-roll bar added to front suspension and 5.5in wheel rims in place of 5.0in rims.

Dimensions: Length 159in. Width 58in. Unladen weight 2473lb.

Basic price: £1020 on 1969 announcement, £1045 in January 1970, £1111 in January 1971, £1220 in January 1972, £1340 in January 1973, then raised by leaps and bounds to £2022 when the TR7 was announced in January 1975, and finally to £2335 when discontinued officially in the autumn of 1975.

TR6 – USA 'federal' version (produced 1969 to 1976)

Basic specification as for TR5, except for:

Engine: 1969-71 – CR 8.5:1, two Stromberg carburettors, 104bhp (net) at 4500rpm, maximum torque 143lb/ft at 3000rpm. 1972-73 – CR 7.75:1, two Stromberg carburettors, 106bhp (net) at 4900rpm, maximum torque 133lb/ft at 3000rpm. 1974-76 – CR 7.5:1, two Stromberg carburettors, 106bhp (net) at 4900rpm, maximum torque 133lb/ft at 3000rpm.

Transmission: Axle ratio 3.7:1. Overall gear ratios 3.7, 4.90, 7.43, 11.61, reverse 11.92:1. Optional overdrive 3.03:1. 20.75mph/1000rpm in direct top gear, 25.3mph/1000rpm in overdrive. From gearbox numbers CD51163/CC89817 (introduced mid-1971) revised internal gear ratios gave overall gearing of 3.7, 5.14, 7.77, 11.06, reverse 12.47:1. From 1973 model (Commission Numbers CF1 onwards and CR567 onwards) J-Type overdrive replaced A-Type overdrive. Overall ratio 2.95:1. 26.1mph/1000rpm in overdrive.

Suspension and brakes: Anti-roll bar added to front suspension and 5.5in wheel rims in place of 5.0in rims.

Dimensions: Length 159in (1969-72), 162.1in (1973-74), 163.6in (1975-76). Unladen weight 2390lb (1969-74), 2438lb (1975-76).

Basic price: These cars were never sold in Great Britain.

Vitesse 1600 Saloon and Convertible (produced 1962 to 1966)

Engine: Six-cylinder, 66.75 x 76mm, 1596cc, CR 8.75:1, two Solex carbs, 70bhp (gross) at 5000rpm. Maximum torque 92lb/ft at 2800rpm.

Transmission: Axle ratio 4.11:1. Overall gear ratios 4.11, 5.16, 7.31, 12.06, reverse 12.06:1. Optional overdrive, 3.30:1. 16.4mph/1000rpm in direct top gear, 20.5mph/1000rpm in overdrive.

Suspension and brakes: IFS, coil springs, wishbones, anti-roll bar, telescopic dampers; IRS, transverse leaf spring, swing axles, radius arms, telescopic dampers. Rack-and-pinion steering. 9.0in front disc brakes, 8 x 1¼in rear drums. 5.60-13in tyres on 3.5in rims.

Dimensions: Wheelbase 89in; front track 49in, rear track 48in. Length 153in. Width 60in. Height 52.5in. Unladen weight 2004lb.

Basic price: Saloon, £608, rising to £626 by 1966; Convertible, £649, rising to £667 by 1966.

Vitesse 2-litre Saloon and Convertible (produced 1966 to 1968)

Engine: Six-cylinder, 74.7 x 76mm, 1998cc, CR 9.5:1, two Zenith-Stromberg carbs, 95bhp at 5000bhp. Maximum torque 117lb/ft at 3000rpm.

Transmission: Axle ratio 3.89:1. Overall gear ratios 3.89, 4.86, 6.92, 10.31, reverse 12.05:1. Optional overdrive, 3.11:1. 17.3mph/1000rpm in direct top, 21.6/1000rpm in overdrive.

Suspension and brakes: As for Vitesse 1600 except for 9.7in front disc brakes. 4.5in wheel rims.

Dimensions: Unladen weight 2100lb.

Basic price: Saloon, £681; Convertible, £717.

Vitesse 2-litre Mark 2 Saloon and Convertible (produced 1968 to 1971)

Specification as for Vitesse 2-litre except for:

Engine: CR 9.25:1. 104bhp at 5300rpm. Maximum torque 117lb/ft at 3000rpm.

Suspension and brakes: IRS, transverse leaf spring, lower wishbones, radius arms, lever-arm dampers. Tyres 155-13in.

Dimensions: Rear track 48.5in. Unladen weight 2044lb.

Basic price: Saloon, £743, rising to £827 by 1970; Convertible, £780, rising to £865 by 1970.

Spitfire Mark 1 (produced 1962 to 1965)

Engine: Four-cylinder, 69.3 x 76mm, 1147cc, CR 9.0:1, two SU carbs, 63bhp at 5750rpm. Maximum torque 67lb/ft at 3500rpm.

Transmission: Axle ratio 4.11:1. Overall gear ratios 4.11, 5.74, 8.88, 15.42, reverse 15.42:1. Optional overdrive from autumn 1963, 3.37:1. 15.7mph/1000rpm in direct top, 19.1mph/1000rpm in overdrive.

Suspension and brakes: IFS, coil springs, wishbones, anti-roll bar and telescopic dampers; IRS, transverse leaf spring, swing axles, radius arms and telescopic dampers. Rack-and-pinion steering. 9.0in front disc brakes, 7 x 1¼in rear drums. 5.20-13in tyres on 3.5in rims.

Dimensions: Wheelbase 83in; front track 49in, rear track 48in. Length 145in. Width 57in. Height 47.5in. Unladen weight 1568lb.

Basic price: £530.

Spitfire Mark 2 (produced 1965 to 1967)

Specification as for Spitfire Mark 1 except for:

Engine: 67bhp at 6000rpm. Maximum torque 67lb/ft at 3750rpm.

Basic price: £550.

Spitfire Mark 3 (produced 1967 to 1970)

Specification as for Spitfire Mark 1 except for:

Engine: 73.7 x 76mm, 1296cc. 75bhp at 6000rpm. Maximum torque 75lb/ft at 4000rpm.

Basic price: £582, rising to £669 by 1970.

Spitfire Mark 3 – USA versions

These differ from other Mark 3s as follows:

1969 model: 68bhp at 5500rpm, maximum torque 73lb/ft at 3000rpm. CR 8.5:1. Unladen weight 1652lb.

1970 model: 68bhp at 5500rpm, maximum torque 73lb/ft at 3000rpm. One Zenith-Stromberg carburettor. Unladen weight 1652lb.

Spitfire Mark 4 – aka Mk IV (produced 1970 to 1974)

Specification as for Spitfire Mark 1 except for:

Engine: 73.7 x 76mm, 1296cc, 63bhp (DIN) at 6000rpm. Maximum torque 69lb/ft at 3500rpm.

Transmission: Axle ratio 3.89:1. Overall gear ratios (all synchromesh) 3.89 (optional overdrive 3.12), 5.41, 8.41, 13.65, reverse 15.0:1. 16.7mph/1000rpm in direct top gear, 20.8mph/1000rpm in overdrive.

Suspension and brakes: Tyres 145-13in on 4.5in rims.

Dimensions: Rear track (from 1973 model on) 50in. Length 149in. Width 58.5in. Unladen weight 1717lb.

Basic price: £735, rising to £1163 by autumn 1974.

Spitfire Mark 4 – USA versions

These differ from other Mark 4s as follows:

1971 model: 58bhp at 5200rpm. Maximum torque 72lb/ft at 3000rpm. Zenith-Stromberg carburettor. 5.20S-13in tyres.

1972 model: 48bhp at 5500rpm. Maximum torque 61lb/ft at 2900rpm. CR 8.0:1. Zenith-Stromberg carburettor. Axle ratio 4.11:1. Overall gear ratios 4.11, 5.71, 8.87, 14.4, reverse 16.39:1. 15.9mph/1000rpm in top gear. 5.20S-13in tyres.

1973 model: 73.7 x 87.5mm, 1493cc. CR 7.5:1. 57bhp at 5000rpm. Maximum torque 74lb/ft at 3000rpm. Zenith-Stromberg carburettor. 5.20S-13in tyres.

1974 model: 155SR-13in tyres, engine as 1973 'federal' 1493cc unit.

Spitfire 1500 (produced from 1975 to 1980)

Specification as for Spitfire Mark 1 except for:

Engine: 73.7 x 87.5mm, 1493cc, CR 9.0:1, 2 SU carbs, 71 bhp (DIN) at 5500rpm. Maximum torque 82lb/ft at 3000rpm.

Transmission: Axle ratio 3.63:1. Overall gear ratios (all synchromesh) 3.63 (optional overdrive 2.89), 5.05, 7.84, 12.70, reverse 13.99:1. 18.0mph/1000rpm in top gear, 22.6mph/1000rpm in overdrive.

Suspension and brakes: Tyres 155-13in on 4.5in rims.

Dimensions: Length 149in. Width 58.5in. Unladen weight 1750lb.

Basic price: £1,290, rising to £4,524 (Total) by late 1980.

Spitfire 1500 – USA versions

These differ from other Spitfire 1500s as follows:

Engine: CR 7.5:1. 57bhp at 5000rpm. Maximum torque 74lb/ft at 3000rpm. Zenith-Stromberg carburettor.

Transmission: Axle ratio 3.89:1. Overall gear ratios 3.89 (optional overdrive 3.20), 5.41, 8.41, 13.65, reverse 15.0:1. 16.7mph/1000rpm in top gear; 21.2mph/1000rpm in overdrive.

Dimensions: Length 156.3in. Unladen weight 1814lb.

Triumph 2000 Mark 1 Saloon and Estate (produced 1963 to 1969)

Engine: Six-cylinder, 74.7 x 76mm, 1998cc, CR 8.5:1, two Zenith-Stromberg carbs, 90bhp (net) at 5000rpm. Maximum torque 117lb/ft at 2900rpm.

Transmission: Axle ratio 4.1:1. Overall gear ratios 4.1 (optional overdrive 3.28), 5.68, 8.61, 13.45, reverse 13.8:1. Optional automatic (from summer 1964) with 3.7 axle ratio. Overall ratios 3.7, 5.36, 8.84, reverse 7.73:1. 16.9mph/1000rpm (direct top), 20.6mph/1000rpm (overdrive), 18.7mph/1000rpm (automatic).

Suspension and brakes: IFS, coil springs, MacPherson struts; IRS, coil springs, semi-trailing wishbones, telescopic dampers. Rack-and-pinion steering. 9.75in front disc brakes and 9 x 1¼in rear drums, with vacuum-servo. 6.50-13in tyres (Saloon), or 175-13in tyres (Estate, from autumn 1965), on 4.5in wheel rims.

Dimensions: Wheelbase 106in; front track 52in, rear track 50.4in. Length 173.75in. Width 65in. Height 56in. Unladen weight (Saloon) 2576lb, (Estate) 2688lb.

Basic price: Saloon, £905, rising to £993 by 1968. Estate, £1135in 1965, rising to £1203 by 1968.

Triumph 2.5 PI Mark 1 (produced 1968 and 1969)

Specifications as for 2000 Mark 1 except for:

Engine: 74.7 x 95mm, 2498cc, CR 9.5:1, Lucas fuel-injection, 132bhp (net) at 5500rpm. Maximum torque 153lb/ft at 2000rpm.

Transmission: Axle ratio 3.45:1. Overall ratios 3.45 (optional overdrive 2.75), 4.78, 7.24, 11.32, reverse 11.62:1. Optional automatic 3.45, 5.00, 8.25, reverse 7.21:1. 20.2mph/1000rpm (direct top), 24.6mph/1000rpm (overdrive), 20.2mph/1000rpm (automatic).

Suspension and brakes: 185-13in tyres.

Dimensions: Unladen weight 2632lb.

Basic price: £1133.

Triumph 2000 Mark 2 Saloon and Estate (produced 1969 to 1977)

Specification as for 2000 Mark 1 except for:

Engine: (1969 to 1973) CR 9.25:1, (1973 to 1975) CR 8.8:1, 84bhp (DIN) at 5000rpm. Maximum torque 100lb/ft at 2900rpm. 2000TC (1975 to 1977) CR 8.8:1, two SU carbs, 91bhp at 4750rpm. Maximum torque 110lb/ft at 3300rpm.

Transmission: (1975 to 1977) Axle ratio 3.7:1. Overall gear ratios 3.7 (optional overdrive 2.96), 5.14, 7.77, 12.14, reverse 12.47:1. 18.6mph/1000rpm (direct top and automatic), 23.2mph/1000rpm (overdrive).

Suspension and brakes: (1975 to 1977) Front anti-roll bar.

Dimensions: Front track 52.5in, rear track 52.9in. Length (Saloon) 182.3in, (Estate) 177.25in. 5in wheel rims. (1973 to 1977) 175-13in tyres on Saloon. Unladen weight (Saloon) 2620lb, (Estate) 2750lb.

Basic price: Saloon, £1080, rising to £2284 by 1975. 2000TC Saloon, £2319 in 1975, rising to £3812 in 1977. Estate, £1290, rising to £2690 when dropped in 1975.

Triumph 2.5 PI Mark 2 Saloon and Estate (produced 1969 to 1975)

Specification as for 2.5 Mark 1 except for:
Dimensions: Front track 52.5in, rear track 52.9in. Length (Saloon) 182.3in, (Estate) 177.25in. 5in rims. Unladen weight (Saloon) 2760lb, (Estate) 2873lb.
Basic price: Saloon, £1220, rising to £2611 by 1975. Estate £1430, rising to £1999 by 1974 when dropped.

Triumph 2500TC Saloon and Estate (produced 1974 to 1977)

Specification as for 2000 Mark 1 with 2000 Mark 2 chassis dimensions except for:
Engine: 74.7 x 76mm, 2498cc, two SU carbs. (1974 to 1975) 99bhp (DIN) at 4700rpm. Maximum torque 133lb/ft at 3000rpm. (1975 to 1977) 106bhp (DIN) at 4700rpm. Maximum torque 139lb/ft at 3000rpm.
Transmission: Axle ratio 3.45:1. Overall gear ratios 3.45 (optional overdrive 2.75, standardised from 1975), 4.78, 7.24, 11.32, reverse 11.62: 1. Optional automatic with overall ratios 3.45, 5.00, 8.25, reverse 7.20:1. 19.9mph/1000rpm (direct top and automatic), 25.0mph/1000rpm (overdrive).
Suspension and brakes: (1975 to 1977) Front anti-roll bar. 185-13in tyres.
Dimensions: Unladen weight (Saloon) 2681lb, (Estate) 2801lb.
Basic price: Saloon, £1851, rising to £4285 by autumn 1977. Estate, £2283, rising to £2891 by spring 1975 when dropped.

Triumph 2500S Saloon and Estate (produced 1975 to 1977)

Specification as for 1975-77 2500TC except for:
Suspension and brakes: 175-14in tyres
Dimensions: Unladen weight (Saloon) 2696lb, (Estate) 2842lb.
Basic price: Saloon, £2796, rising to £4602 by autumn 1977 when dropped. Estate, £3199, rising to £5294 by autumn 1977 when dropped.

Triumph 1300 Saloon (produced 1965 to 1970)

Engine: Four-cylinder, 73.7 x 76mm, 1296cc, CR 8.5:1, Zenith-Stromberg carb, 61bhp at 5000rpm. Maximum torque 73lb/ft at 3000rpm.
Transmission: Front-wheel drive. Axle ratio 4.11:1. Overall gear ratios 4.37, 5.96, 8.87, 13.97, reverse 16.4:1. 15.4mph/1000rpm in top gear.

Suspension and brakes: IFS, coil springs, wishbones, telescopic dampers; IRS, coil springs, semi-trailing wishbones, telescopic dampers. Rack-and-pinion steering. 8.75in front disc brakes, 8 x 1¼in rear drums. 5.60-13in tyres on 4.0in rims.
Dimensions: Wheelbase 96.6in; front track 53in, rear track 54in. Length 155in. Width 61.75in. Height 54in. Unladen weight 2016lb.
Basic Price: £658, rising to £760 by summer 1970.

1300TC Saloon (produced 1967 to 1970)

Specification as for 1300 except for:
Engine: CR 9.0:1, two SU carbs, 75bhp at 6000rpm. Maximum torque 75lb/ft at 4000rpm.
Suspension and brakes: Servo-assisted brakes.
Basic price: £710, rising to £793 by summer 1970.

1500 Saloon (produced 1970 to 1973)

Engine: 73.7 x 87.5mm, 1493cc, CR 8.5:1, SU carb. (Up to October 1971) 61bhp at 5000rpm. Maximum torque 81lb/ft at 2700rpm. (From October 1971) CR 9.0:1, 65bhp at 5000rpm. Maximum torque 80lb/ft at 3000rpm.
Transmission: Front-wheel drive. Axle ratio 4.55:1. Overall gear ratios 4.04, 5.86, 8.73, 13.72, reverse 16.38:1. 16.7mph/1000rpm in top gear.
Suspension and brakes: IFS, coil springs, wishbones and telescopic dampers; rear dead axle, radius arms, coil springs, anti-roll bar, telescopic dampers. Rack-and-pinion steering. Servo-assisted 8.75in front disc brakes, 8 x 1½in rear drums. 5.60-13in tyres on 4.0in rims.
Dimensions: Wheelbase 96.6in; front track 53.5in, rear track 50.5in. Length 162in. Width 61.7in. Height 54in. Unladen weight 2128lb.
Basic price: £851, rising to £1010 by autumn 1973.

Toledo Saloon (produced 1970 to 1976)

Engine: Four-cylinder, 73.7 x 76mm, 1296cc, CR 8.5:1, SU carb, 58bhp at 5300rpm. Maximum torque 70lb/ft at 3000rpm.
Transmission: Rear-wheel drive. Axle ratio 4.11:1. Overall gear ratios 4.11, 5.73, 8.86, 14.4, reverse 16.4:1. 15.9mph/1000rpm in top gear.
Suspension and brakes: IFS, coil springs, wishbones and telescopic dampers; rear live axle, coil springs, radius arms, telescopic dampers. Rack-and-pinion steering. 9 x 1¾in front drum brakes, 8 x 1¼in rear drums. 5.20-13in tyres on 4.0in rims. (5.60-13in tyres on four-door version from August 1971).
Dimensions: Wheelbase 96.6in; front track 53in, rear track 50in. Length 156.7in. Width 61.75in. Height 54in. Unladen weight 1905lb.
Basic price: £697, rising to £1769 by spring 1976.
Note: From October 1972 servo-assisted 8.75in front disc brakes

were standardised. From March 1975 the two-door version was dropped, and later in the year 155-13in radial-ply tyres were standardised on the four-door car.

Dolomite 1300 (produced 1976 to 1980)
Specification as for Toledo except for:
Dimensions: Front track 53in, rear track 50.5in. Length 162in. 4.5in wheel rims. Unladen weight 2079lb.
Basic price: £1769, rising to £2524 by May 1978.

1500TC Saloon (produced 1973 to beginning 1976, then renamed Dolomite 1500, produced 1976 to 1980)
Engine: Four-cylinder, 73.7 x 87.5mm, 1493cc, CR 8.5:1, 2 SU carbs. (1973 to spring 1975) 64bhp (DIN) at 5000rpm. Maximum torque 78lb/ft at 3000rpm. (Spring 1975 onwards) 71 bhp (DIN) at 5500rpm. Maximum torque 84lb/ft at 3000rpm.
Transmission: Rear-wheel drive. Axle ratio 3.89:1. Overall gear ratios 3.89, 5.42, 8.39, 13.63, reverse 15.51:1. Optional automatic transmission, overall ratios 3.89, 5.64, 9.31, reverse 8.14:1. 16.9mph/1000rpm in top gear.
Suspension and brakes: IFS, coil springs, wishbones, telescopic dampers; rear live axle, coil springs, radius arms, telescopic dampers. Rack-and-pinion steering. Servo-assisted 8.75in front disc brakes, 8 x 1½in rear drums. 155-13in tyres on 4.5in rims.
Dimensions: Wheelbase 96.6in; front track 53.5in, rear track 50.5in. Length 162in. Width 61.75in. Height 54in. Unladen weight (1500TC) 2061lb, (Dolomite 1500) 2097lb, (Dolomite 1500HL) 2108lb.
Basic price: 1500TC: £1087, rising to £2004 by spring 1976. Dolomite 1500: £1885 rising to £2716 by May 1978. Dolomite 1500 HL: £2086, rising to £3079 by May 1978.

Dolomite (named 1850HL from spring 1976) (produced 1972 to 1980)
Engine: four-cylinder, single overhead camshaft, 87 x 78mm, 1854cc, CR 9.0:1. Two Zenith Stromberg carbs (from autumn 1973, two SU carbs), 91bhp (DIN) at 5200rpm. Maximum torque 105lb/ft at 3500 rpm.
Transmission: Rear-wheel drive. Axle ratio 3.63:1. Overall gear ratios 3.63 (optional overdrive 2.91), 4.56, 6.47, 9.65, reverse 10.95:1. Optional automatic with 3.27 axle ratio. Overall gear ratios 3.27, 4.74, 7.82, reverse 6.93:1. 18.0mph/1000rpm (direct top), 20.0mph/1000rpm (automatic), 22.5mph/1000rpm (overdrive).
Suspension and brakes: IFS, coil springs, wishbones, anti-roll bar, telescopic dampers; rear live axle, coil springs, radius arms, telescopic dampers. Rack-and-pinion steering. Servo-assisted 8.75in front disc brakes, 8 x 1¼in rear drums. 155-13in tyres on 4.5in rims.

Dimensions: Wheelbase 96.6in; front track 53.5in, rear track 50.5in. Length 162in. Width 61.75in. Height 54in. Unladen weight 2127lb.
Basic price: £1118, rising to £3434 by May 1978.
Note: Overdrive was optional from March 1973.

Dolomite Sprint Saloon (produced 1973 to 1980)
Specification as for Dolomite 1850HL except for:
Engine: 90.3 x 78mm, 1998cc, CR 9.5:1, two SU carbs, 127bhp (DIN) at 5700rpm. Maximum torque 124lb/ft at 4500rpm.
Transmission: Axle ratio 3.45:1. Overall gear ratios 3.45 (optional overdrive 2.75), 4.80, 7.25, 10.31, reverse 11.62:1. Optional automatic, overall gear ratios 3.45, 5.00, 8.25, reverse 7.20:1. 18.9mph/1000rpm (direct top and automatic), 23.7mph/1000rpm (overdrive). Overdrive standardised from May 1975.
Suspension and brakes: Rear suspension has anti-roll bar. 9 x 1¾in rear drum brakes. 175-13in tyres on 5.5in rims.
Dimensions: Unladen weight 2214lb (2295lb with overdrive).
Basic price: £1460, rising to £4186 by May 1978.

GT6 Mark 1 (produced 1966 to 1968)
Engine: Six-cylinder, OHV, 74.7 x 76mm, 1998cc, CR 9.5:1, two Zenith-Stromberg carbs, 95bhp at 5000rpm. Maximum torque 117lb/ft at 3000rpm.
Transmission: Axle ratio 3.27:1. Overall gear ratios 3.27, 4.11, 5.82, 8.66, reverse 10.13:1. Optional overdrive (with 3.89 axle ratio) 3.11. 20.1mph/1000rpm (direct top), 21.2mph/1000rpm (overdrive).
Suspension and brakes: IFS, coil springs, wishbones, anti-roll bar, telescopic dampers; IRS, transverse leaf spring, swing axles, radius arms, telescopic dampers. Rack-and-pinion steering. 9.7in front disc brakes and 8 x 1¼in rear drums. 155-13in tyres on 4.5in rims.
Dimensions: Wheelbase 83in; front track 49in, rear track 48in. Length 145in. Width 57in. Height 47in. Unladen weight 1904lb.
Basic price: £800.

GT6 Mark 2 (produced 1968 to 1970)
Specification as for GT6 Mark 1 except for:
Engine: CR 9.25:1, 104bhp at 5300rpm. Maximum torque 117lb/ft at 3000rpm.
Transmission: Some cars sold with optional overdrive and 3.27 axle ratio. 25.2mph/1000rpm in overdrive.
Suspension and brakes: Rear suspension by transverse leaf spring, lower wishbones, radius arms and telescopic dampers.
Dimensions: Rear track 49in.
Basic price: £879, rising to £925 by 1970.

GT6 Plus – USA versions of GT6 Mark 2 (produced 1968 to 1970)

These differs from other Mark 2s as follows:
1969 and 1970 models: 95bhp at 4700rpm. Maximum torque 117lb/ft at 3400rpm.

GT6 Mark 3 (produced 1970 to end of 1973)

Specification as for GT6 Mark 1 except for:
Engine: CR 9.25:1, 104bhp at 5300rpm. Maximum torque 117lb/ft at 3000rpm.
Suspension and brakes: Rear suspension (1970 to end of 1972) by transverse leaf spring, lower wishbones, radius arms and telescopic dampers. 1973 model as Mark 1 with pivoting leaf spring.
Dimensions: Rear track (1970 to end of 1972) 49in, (1973 model) 50in. Length 149in. Unladen weight 2030lb.
Basic price: £970, rising to £1285 by end of 1973.

GT6 Mark 3 – USA versions

These differs from other Mark 3s as follows:
1971 model: 90bhp at 4700rpm. Maximum torque 116lb/ft at 3400rpm.
1972 and 1973 models: 79bhp at 4900rpm. Maximum torque 97lb/ft at 2900rpm. CR 8.0:1.

Stag Convertible and Coupé (produced 1970 to 1977)

Engine: V8-cylinder, single overhead camshaft, 86 x 64.5mm, 2997cc, CR 8.8:1, two Zenith-Stromberg carbs, 145bhp (DIN) at 5500rpm. Maximum torque 170lb/ft at 3500rpm.
Transmission: Axle ratio 3.7:1. Overall gear ratios 3.7, (optional overdrive, 3.03, standard from October 1972; 2.95:1 from beginning of 1973), 5.13, 7.77, .11.08, reverse 12.46:1. Optional Borg-Warner automatic, overall ratios 3.7, 5.36, 8.84, reverse 7.73:1. 19.0mph/1000rpm in direct top and automatic, 23.1mph (later 23.7mph)/1000rpm in overdrive.
Suspension and brakes: IFS, coil springs, MacPherson struts, anti-roll bar; IRS, coil springs, semi-trailing wishbones, telescopic dampers. Power-assisted rack-and-pinion steering. Servo-assisted 10.6in front disc brakes, 9 x 2¼in rear drums. 185-14in tyres on 5.5in rims.
Dimensions: Wheelbase 100in; front track 52.5in, rear track 52.9in. Length 173.8in. Width 63.5in. Height 49.5in. Unladen weight 2807lb.
Basic price: Convertible, £1527, rising to £5904 by autumn 1977. Coupé, £1562, rising to £6180 by autumn 1977.

Stag – USA versions (produced 1970 to 1973)

These differ from other Stags as follows:
1972 model: 127bhp at 6000rpm. Maximum torque 142lb/ft at 3200rpm. CR 8.0:1.
1973 model: 127bhp at 5500rpm. Maximum torque 148lb/ft at 3500rpm. CR 7.75:1.

TR7 – USA 'federal' version (produced 1975 to 1981)

Engine: Four-cylinder, single overhead camshaft, 90.3 x 78mm, 1998cc, CR 8.0:1, two Stromberg carbs (except California in 1980, all USA states in 1981), Bosch L-Jetronic fuel-injection. Approximately 92bhp (DIN) at 5000rpm. Maximum torque approximately 115lb/ft at 3500rpm.
Transmission: Axle ratio 3.63:1. Overall gear ratios 3.63, 4.56, 6.47, 9.65, reverse 10.95:1. Overdrive not available. 17.9mph/1000rpm in top gear. Optional Borg-Warner Type 65 automatic transmission. Axle ratio 3.27:1. Overall ratios 3.27, 4.74, 7.82, reverse 6.83:1. 19.9mph/1000rpm in direct drive. Optional (1976-77) 5-speed manual gearbox. Axle ratio 3.9:1. Overall gear ratios 3.25, 3.90, 5.44, 8.14, 12.95, reverse 13.37:1. 20.8mph/1000rpm in fifth gear. Standard thereafter.
Suspension and brakes: IFS, coil springs, MacPherson struts, anti-roll bar; rear live axle, coil springs, radius arms, anti-roll bar and telescopic dampers. Rack-and-pinion steering. 9.7in front discs, 8 x 1.5in rear drums and vacuum-servo assistance. 9 x 1.75in rear brakes with 5-speed gearbox. 185/70-13in or 175-13in radial-ply tyres.
Dimensions: Wheelbase 85in; front track 55.5in; rear track 55.3in. Length 164.5in. Width 66.2in. Height 49.9in. Unladen weight 2241lb, with 5-speed gearbox equipment 2355lb.
Basic price: Not available in Great Britain.

TR7 – Non-USA version (produced 1976 to 1981)

Basic specification as for USA 'federal' version of TR7 except for:
Engine: CR 9.25:1; two SU carbs. 105bhp (DIN) at 5500rpm. Maximum torque 119lb/ft at 3500rpm.
Dimensions: Length 160.1in. Unladen weight 2205lb; with 5-speed gearbox equipment 2311lb.
Basic price: £2564 when introduced in May 1976, £2850 in January 1977, £2881 in May 1977.

TR8 – sold only in USA (produced 1980 to 1981)

Basic specification as for later TR7 model except for:
1980 models:
Engine: V8-cylinder, overhead valve (Rover manufacture) 88.9 x 71.1mm, 3528cc, CR 8.1:1, two Stromberg carbs (Lucas fuel-injection for sale in California). 133bhp (DIN) on carbs, 137bhp (DIN) on injection, at 5000rpm. Maximum torque (carbs) 174lb/ft at 3000rpm, (injection) 168lb/ft at 3250rpm.
Transmission: Axle ratio 3.08:1. Overall gear ratios 2.56, 3.08, 4.31, 6.44, 10.23, reverse 10.56:1. 26.1mph/1000rpm in fifth gear.

Optional Borg-Warner Type 65 automatic transmission. Overall gear ratios 3.08, 4.47, 7.36:1, reverse 6.44:1. 21.9mph/1000rpm in top gear.

Suspension and brakes: 9 x 1.75in rear drums standard. 185/70-13in tyres. Power-assisted steering.

Dimensions: Unladen weight 2565lb.

Basic price: Not available in Great Britain.

Note: For 1981 model year, Lucas fuel-injection was standardised on all cars, and manual fifth gear was raised to 2.44:1, giving 27.6mph/1000rpm in fifth gear.

Triumph Acclaim (produced 1981 to 1984)

Engine: four-cylinder Honda, single overhead camshaft, 72 x 82mm, 1335cc, CR 8.41:1, two Keihin carbs. 70bhp (DIN) at 5750rpm. Maximum torque 74lb/ft at 3500rpm.

Transmission: Front-wheel drive. Final drive ratio 4.642:1. Overall gear ratios 3.305, 3.927, 5.482, 8.188, 13.536, reverse 13.536:1. 19.8mph/1000rpm in top gear. Optional Honda automatic transmission. Final drive ratio 3.105:1. Overall ratios 3.204, 4.254, 6.356, reverse 6.067:1. 20.4mph/1000rpm in top gear.

Suspension and brakes: IFS, coil springs, MacPherson struts, anti-roll bar; IRS, coil springs, MacPherson struts, trailing arms. Rack-and-pinion steering. 8.47in front discs, 7.1 x 1.0in rear drums, with vacuum-servo assistance. 155-SR13in or (depending on model) 165/70-SR13in radial-ply tyres.

Dimensions: Wheelbase 91.3in; front track 53.5in; rear track 54.3in. Length 161.2in. Width 63in. Height 52.7in. Unladen weight from 1784lb.

Basic price: From £3763 when introduced in October 1981.

Triumph and Standard Body Sources 1945 to 1984

Triumph	Standard	Bodies from
	Flying Eight	Fisher & Ludlow, Birmingham
	Flying Twelve	Pressed Steel, Cowley, Oxford
1800/2000 Roadster		Standard-made in Coventry factory
1800/2000 Renown		Mulliners, Birmingham
	Vanguard I and 1A	Fisher & Ludlow, Birmingham
	Vanguard I/1A Estate	Mulliners (conversion from saloon)
Mayflower Saloon		Fisher & Ludlow, Birmingham
Mayflower DHC		Mulliners (conversion)
	Vanguard II	Fisher & Ludlow, Birmingham
	Vanguard II Estate	Mulliners (conversion)
TR2/TR3/TR3A		Mulliners
TR3B		Forward Radiator (subsidiary of Mulliners)
	8/10 (TR10)	Fisher & Ludlow, Tile Hill, Coventry
	8/10 Estate	Mulliners (conversion)
	Vanguard III/ Ensign	Pressed Steel, Cowley, Oxford

Triumph	Standard	Bodies from
	Vanguard III/ Estate	Mulliners (conversion)
	Pennant	Fisher & Ludlow, Tile Hill, Coventry
Herald and Vitesse		Triumph Coventry, from Mulliners, Hall Engineering, Auto Body Dies, and Pressed Steel, in sections
TR4/TR4A/TR5/ TR250/TR6		Triumph Liverpool No 1 (ex-Hall Engineering)
Spitfire, GT6		Forward Radiator
2000/2500 2.5 PI Saloon		Pressed Steel, Swindon
2000/2500/2.5/PI Estate		Carbodies, Coventry (conversion)
1300/1500/ Toledo		Triumph Liverpool No 1
Dolomite/Sprint		Triumph Liverpool No 1
Stag		Triumph Liverpool No 2
TR7		Triumph Liverpool No 2 (1974-78), Pressed Steel Fisher, Swindon (1978-81)
TR8		Pressed Steel Fisher, Swindon
Acclaim		Pressed Steel Fisher, Cowley, Oxford

Triumph Production Totals 1923 to 1984

Because the original company had all its written records destroyed in the bombing of Coventry in 1940, it has never been possible to provide accurate production figures for all the Triumph cars built up until 1939.

The 1923 to 1939 figures quoted below are based on painstaking work, research and analysis, by members of the Pre-1940 Triumph Owners Club. Originally carried out by Chris Watson, and in more recent times by Graham Shipman, these figures have been sifted, calculated and delineated by a study of all the cars which have passed through the records of this amazingly active little club.

This, therefore, is believed to be the most accurate estimate of the activities of the independent Triumph concern.

Total production, 1923 to 1939 (which includes a number of unidentified cars once known to the club) was approximately 34,963.

Years	Model	Cars built
1923-24	'Experimental'	5
1923-26	10/20	300
1924	13/35	1
1926-30	Fifteen	460
1927-32	Super Seven	14,850
1933-34	Super Eight	2,400
1931-33	Scorpion/Twelve-Six/ Southern Cross Twelve	1,600
1932-33	Super Nine/Southern Cross 'Nine'	3,500
1933-34	Southern Cross 10hp	200
1933-34	Ten range	1850
1934	Dolomite Straight-eight	2
1933-38	Gloria family	6,529
1935-39	Vitesse/Continental/Dolomite	3206
1939	Twelve	65

Post-1945 cars, built originally by Standard-Triumph, under Leyland control since 1961.

Years	Model	Cars built
1946-48	1800 Roadster	2501
1946-49	1800 Saloon	4000
1948-49	2000 Roadster	2000
1949	2000 Saloon (tubular chassis)	2000
1949-52	Renown I (108in wheelbase)	6501
1951-52	Renown Limousine	190
1952-54	Renown II (111in wheelbase)	2800
1950-53	Mayflower Saloon	34,990
1950	Mayflower Drophead Coupé	10
1953-55	TR2	8628
1955-57	TR3	13,377
1957-61	TR3A (includes Italian chassis)	58,236
1962	TR3B	3331
1957-59	10 (Standard Ten rebadged)	9907
1957-60	Estate Wagon (Standard Companion rebadged)	7351
1958-59	Pennant (Standard Pennant rebadged)	335
1959-62	Herald 948 Saloon and S	76,860
1959-61	Herald 948 Coupé	15,153
1960-61	Herald 948 Convertible	8262
1961-70	Herald 1200 Saloon	201,142
1961-64	Herald 1200 Coupé	5319
1961-68	Herald 1200 Convertible	43,295
1961-68	Herald 1200 Estate	39,819
1962-67	Herald 12/50 Saloon	53,267

Years	Model	Cars built
1966-71	Herald 13/60 Saloon	38,886
1966-71	Herald 13/60 'Sunroof' Saloon	1547
1966-71	Herald 13/60 Estate	15,467
1966-71	Herald 13/60 Convertible – plus CKD 13/60s	14,978
1962-66	Vitesse 1600 Saloon	22,814
1962-66	Vitesse 1600 Convertible	8447
1961-65	TR4	40,253
1965-67	TR4A	28,465
1962-65	Spitfire Mk 1	45,753
1965-67	Spitfire Mk 2	37,409
1967-70	Spitfire Mk 3	65,320
1963-69	2000 Saloon Mk 1	113,157
1965-69	2000 Estate Mk 1	8658
1969	2.5 PI Mk 1 Estate	371
1967-70	1300TC	113,008
1966-68	GT6 Mk 1	15,818
1968-70	GT6 Mk 2 (including GT6 plus)	12,066
1970-73	GT6 Mk 3	13,042
1970-74	Spitfire Mk 4	70,021
1966-71	Vitesse 2-litre (Mk 1 and Mk 2) Saloon	12,977
1966-71	Vitesse 2-litre (Mk 1 and Mk 2) Convertible	6974

Years	Model	Cars built
1967-68	TR5 PI	2947
1967-68	TR250 (USA market)	8484
1968-76	TR6 (all types)	94,619
1969-77	2000 Mk 2 Saloon	92,053
1969-75	2000 Mk 2 Estate	7118
1969-75	2.5 PI Mk 2	43,353
1969-74	2.5 PI Mk 2 Estate	4102
1974-77	2500TC & S Saloon	37,752
1974-77	2500TC & S Estate	2601
1970-77	Stag	25,877
1970-76	Toledo 1300	113,294
1970-76	Toledo 1500	5888
1970-73	1500 (front-wheel drive)	66,353
1972-80	Dolomite 1850	79,010
1973-80	Dolomite Sprint	22,941
1973-76	1500TC (rear-wheel drive)	25,549
1976-80	Dolomite 1300	32,031
1976-80	Dolomite 1500	43,235
1974-80	Spitfire 1500	95,829
1975-81	TR7	112,368
1980-81	TR8	2722
1981-84	Acclaim	133,626

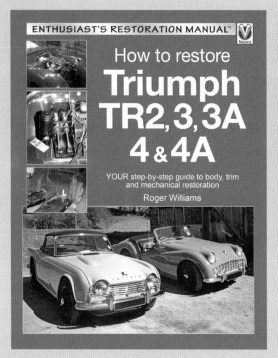
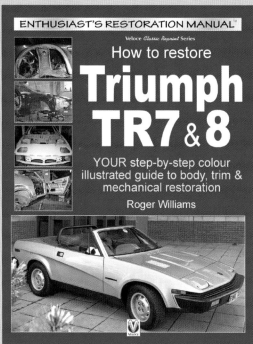

ISBN: 978-1-845842-70-3
Paperback • 19.5x13.9cm • 64
pages • 102 colour pictures

ISBN: 978-1-845843-16-8
Paperback • 19.5x13.9cm • 64
pages • 108 colour pictures

A small investment in an Essential Buyer's Guide could save you a fortune ... With the aid of the step-by-step expert guidance in these books, you'll discover all you need to know about the car you want to buy. They contain detailed and illustrated examination of sample cars, and are written by experts with the sole aim of helping you make an informed choice. Don't buy a Triumph without one of these books!

For more information and price details,
visit our website at www.veloce.co.uk
email: info@veloce.co.uk
Tel: +44(0)1305 260068

ISBN: 978-1-787112-72-8
Paperback • 19.5x13.9cm • 64 pages
• 98 pictures

ISBN: 978-1-845840-26-6
Paperback • 19.5x13.9cm • 64 pages
• 101 colour pictures

INDEX

ABC 40
AC 89
Ace wheel discs 76
ACV trucks and buses 182, 199
Adams, Dennis 231
Albion Motors 176
Alderson, Arthur 13
Alfa Romeo 57-59, 63, 65, 84, 163, 202
Alfin brake drums 132
Alford and Alder Ltd 145, 169, 234
Allan, Margaret 45, 46
Allen, T A W 67
Alpine Rally/Trial 122, 126, 128, 131, 133, 134, 153, 155, 156, 172, 173
Alpine-Renault 155
Alvis 15, 30, 41, 80, 81, 86, 95, 137, 167, 193
Amal carburettors 25
American Motors 174, 175
Amphicar 228
Andre shock absorbers 44, 237
Andrews, William 8
Antweiller, Louis 95, 104, 110
Arbuthnot, Robert 65, 66
Ariel motorcycles 55
Armstrong, P W 26
Armstrong shock absorbers 227
Armstrong-Siddeley 28, 30, 60, 83, 86
Armstrong-Siddeley gearbox 31, 60
Armstrong-Whitworth aircraft 90, 233
Ashby steering wheels 43
Aspland, K 176
Astbury, Dick 160
Aston Martin 218
Austin 6, 7, 17-20, 22, 23, 65, 69, 70, 82, 86, 88, 92, 115, 137, 138, 140, 145, 169, 191, 192, 209, 211, 222, 223
Austin, Sir Herbert 18
Austin-Healey 121, 123, 130, 133, 150, 152, 155, 166, 172, 210, 211, 232
Australian RAC Trial 25
Auto Body Dies 145, 166
Auto-Union 84
Autocar 7, 10-12, 14-16, 21, 23, 24, 30, 33, 36-38, 41, 45,

49, 51, 61-64, 72-74, 104, 113, 182, 225, 228
Autocars, Israel 185
Automobile Engineer, The 58
Automotive Industries 13, 20
Autovac fuel tank 14, 33
Avon bodies 76

B&B carburettors 20, 235
Ballard, Arthur 96, 97, 111
Ballisat, Keith 7, 133, 163
Band, Charles 86, 90, 91, 135, 136
Barber, John 208
Barker, Ronald 182
Barnett, Bernard 91
Baybutt, Sidney 175, 176
Beans Industries 140, 141, 233
Beardmore & Co, William 67
Beck, J 45
Becquart, Marcel 163
Beeston Humber motorcycle 10
Belgrove, Walter 19, 29, 34, 40, 49, 52, 55, 60, 61, 67, 70, 71, 73, 76, 78-81, 83, 84, 97, 99, 104-107, 110, 118, 120-122, 131, 136-138
Bennet, D C T 228
Bentley 39, 51, 56, 61, 66, 82, 91, 98, 136
Bentley, W O 91
Bertone Carabo 215
Bettmann, Mayer 8
Bettmann, Siegfried 8-11, 16, 28, 30, 38, 40, 47, 54, 55, 67, 80, 83, 113, 181
Biesolt & Lock 8
Biflex headlamps 37, 43
Birabongse, Prince 64
Birkin, Sir Henry 57
Birmabright metals 42, 77
Black, Capt Sir John 82, 83, 86-95, 97, 98, 100-102, 104, 106, 107-110, 112, 114, 116-119, 121, 123, 126, 135-137, 140, 167, 174, 225, 226
Black, Sir William 182
Bleakley, Pet 130
Blight, Anthony 57
BMW 7, 189, 234
Boddy, William 25
Bolton, Peter 163
Bond 6, 229, 230
Bond, Lawrence 229

Borg & Beck clutches 48, 112
Borg-Warner transmissions 168, 246, 247
Bosch fuel injection 99, 231, 246
Bowden, Ben 84
Boyd Carpenter 22
Bradley, Bill 156, 187
Briggs Bodies 132
Brighton Rally 25, 40
Brimelow, E 176
Bristol 88
British Leyland 7, 75, 87, 140, 152, 167, 169, 183, 189, 190, 192, 193, 200, 202, 203, 205-216, 218, 221, 222, 224, 233, 234
British Motor Corporation (BMC) 75, 86, 110, 137, 140, 146, 150, 169, 180, 181, 183, 185, 192-194, 199, 200, 234
British Motor Holdings 193, 199
BRM 65, 121, 130
Brooke, Leslie 131
Brooklands 15, 16, 24, 25, 36, 40, 43, 49, 56, 57, 62, 78, 84, 173, 225, 232
Brooklands Motor Course, The History of 25
Brown, Sir David 93
Brown, Michael 113
Browning, Peter 7, 84, 205, 206
BSA 18, 30, 192, 228
Buckle, W G 25
Buick 31, 40, 228
Burman-Douglas steering 42

C & E Motors 52
Cadillac 13, 31
Callaby, Frank 6, 7, 95, 97, 99, 114
Camm, F J 30
Campbell, Sir Malcolm 12
Darracq 32
Datsun 217
Davy, John 10
Dawson 11, 12, 14, 83, 233
Carbodies 7, 184, 185
Carrozzeria Touring 107
Caton, Henry 42
Centric supercharger 39, 225
Charlesworth Bodies 61
Charteris, Leslie 66
Chenard-Walcker 46
Chevrolet 18, 115
Chiron, Louis 45
Chrysler 31, 51, 57, 70, 113,

128, 137, 175, 179
Chula, Prince 64
Citroën 24, 102, 128, 222
Classic Car Club of America 39
Claudel-Hobson carburettors 88, 169, 233
Clement-Brooks, R C 45
Coaley, Albert 182
Cobra 173
Cocke, Dudley 52
Cohen, David 65
Colley, Harry 98
Connolly Leather 232
Conrero 163, 164, 172
Consten, Bernard 133
Continental engines 102
Cooper, Peter 130
Corsica bodies 65, 66
Cosworth engines 206
Coventry Bicycles 38
Coventry Climax engines 68, 192
Coventry Radiator & Press-work 42
Cozette, René 24
Cozette superchargers 24, 25, 235
Cripps, Sir Stafford 93, 109
Crosley 128
Cross, Colin 52
Cross, H 52
Cross & Ellis bodies 48, 51-54, 68, 76, 81
Culcheth, Brian 200, 202, 206, 207
Currie, Bob 53

Daimler 31, 83, 86, 88, 95, 98, 104, 137, 141, 161, 185, 192, 233
Dalton, Sir Hugh 91
Darracq 32
Datsun 217
Davy, John 10
Dawson 11, 12, 14, 83, 233
Dawson, A J 12
Dawtrey, Lewis 110, 135, 193, 194, 206
de Dion suspension 227
de Forest, Simone 39
De Havilland Aircraft 94
Delage 67
Dennis Brothers 53
Deutsche Industrie-Werke 228
Dick, Alick 7, 87, 90, 91, 108,

110, 118, 119, 126, 129, 135-142, 144-147, 150, 159, 160, 163, 167, 169, 174-176, 178, 192, 199
Dickson, Bobbie 130
Dietrich, Ray 17
Distillers Company 93
Dixon, Frank 145, 176
Donington circuit 63
Donohue, Mark 173
Dove, L F 230
du Cros, Harvey 9
Dugdale, John 7
Dunlop 9, 53
  brakes 128, 132
  tyres 21, 43
  wheels 31, 45, 227, 228, 233
DWS jacks 43

Earls Court Motor Show 103, 128, 138, 152, 178, 181
Edge, Stanley 6, 18, 19, 22
Edwardes, Michael 209, 211, 216, 219, 222, 224
Edwards, Joe 140
Elford, Vic 149, 172
Elliott, Jack 63
Ellis, A J 52
Ellis, Byron 13
Ellis, R A 52
England, Gordon 22, 27
ENV gearboxes 42, 50
ERA 17, 22, 27, 49, 60, 63, 64, 71, 80, 84, 89, 102, 172, 209
Evening Standard 74

Fafnir 10
Fairthorpe 228
Farmer, Sir George 193
Farmers Club 93
Fergus Motors 115, 118
Ferguson, Harry 93, 101, 113, 118, 135, 137
Ferguson, Joe 113
Ferguson tractor 93, 102, 141, 233
Ferodo brake linings 58
Ferrari 160, 165, 172, 173
Festival of Britain 112, 113
Fiat 39, 40, 222
Fidler, Roy 197
Filby, Peter J 231
Fiore, Trevor 232
Fisher & Ludlow 103, 111, 115, 118, 137, 138, 140, 142, 234

Flajole, Bill 115
Flower, Raymond 139, 159
Flynn, Oliver M 38
Ford 18, 62, 63, 86, 93, 115, 131, 145-147, 158, 169, 172, 178, 181, 185, 192, 194, 205, 206, 231, 232, 234
Ford, Henry 18
Fortune 8, 11, 83, 109, 113, 187, 210, 253
Forward Radiator Co 42, 141, 142, 150, 151, 165, 193, 234, 248
Fraser, Colin 93
Frazer Nash 24
Friedlander, Alfred 9
Frisky 11, 139

Gatsonides, Maurice 7, 130, 131, 133
General Motors 86, 180
Geneva Motor Show 122, 139, 159, 197
Geneva Rally 156, 172
Georgano, G N 7
Gibson & Ashford 80
Girling brakes 128
GKN wheels 206
Gloria Cycle Company 10
Good, Alan 91
Gordon Keeble 228
Graham, Howe 38, 52, 67, 80-82
Gratrix, Tom 6, 229
Griffiths, George 34
Griffiths, John 9
Grosvenor House 53, 54
Guy Motors 192

Haddock, Bert 34
Hadley, Bert 132
Hall Engineering 145, 165, 166, 174, 176, 207, 234
Ham, Rowland 227, 228
Hardy-Spicer joints 48, 112
Harriman, Sir George 192, 193
Harrington bodies 230
Harrison, Bert 19
Hartford shock absorbers 58, 235, 237
Hassan, Walter 206
Hastings, Morgan 22, 23
Healey 6, 25, 34, 40, 41, 44-46, 49, 51, 52, 56-60, 62, 63, 65-68, 71, 72, 75-86, 121, 172
Healey, Donald 6, 25, 34, 40, 44-46, 49, 56-60, 62, 63, 65-68, 71, 75-78, 80-84, 86
Healeys and Austin-Healeys 84
Heathcote, Kit 133
Helliwells 106, 227
Henderson, Ray 156
High Duty Alloys 58

High Speed Motors 64
Hildebrand & Wolfmuller 10
Hillman 12, 19, 20, 30, 34, 67, 86, 87, 116, 140, 192
Hillman, William 140
Hobbs, Jack 45
Hobourn-Eaton pumps 112
Hobson, H M 83
Holbrook, Col Sir Arthur 10
Holbrook, Col Sir Claude 11, 16, 28, 30, 34, 38, 39-41, 44, 45, 47, 53-55, 57, 62, 80, 81, 84
Holm, Tryggve 194
Hooley, E Terah 9
Hopkirk, Paddy 7, 202
Horsman, Victor 25
Hotchkiss 14, 17, 46
Hotchkiss drive 14, 17
Howe, Earl 57
Hudson 70-72, 115
Hulme, Denny 197
Humber 10, 12, 18, 30, 67, 84, 86, 192
Hunter, Terry 155

Ireland 84, 130, 133, 169
Irving, Capt. J X 20

Jackson, Peter 229
Jaguar 65, 73, 87, 94, 103, 105, 109, 117, 118, 128, 160, 166, 167, 172, 192, 193, 200, 206, 209, 210, 213, 218
Jankel, Robert 232
Jano, Signor 57
JAP engines 10
JCC 200-mile race 63, 64
Jeep 137
Jennings, Christopher 118
Jensen 76, 86, 128
Jensen, Alan 76
Jensen-Healey 86
Jones, Glyn 48, 51, 76
Jopp, Peter 161
Jordan 41

Kaiser-Frazer 115
Karmann bodies 189, 198
Kastner, Kas 181
King, Spen 7, 152, 199, 206, 212, 214, 215, 219
Knox, Trevor 93

Lagonda 56, 66, 91
Lahaye 39
Lampinen, Simo 156
Lanchester 86, 95, 137
Lancia 39, 194, 202, 217, 222
Land Rover 209, 234
Land's End Trial 40
Last, William J 232
Lawrence tune 226

Laycock overdrive 104, 119, 120, 168
Le Mans 57, 126-128, 130, 132, 133, 152-157, 159-164, 167, 172, 175, 195, 226
Lea, Alan 14
Lea, R H 13
Lea-Francis 13, 30, 34, 40, 73, 80, 81
Lee, Leonard 192
Leigh, Lord 28, 38, 67
Leinster race track 63
Lewis, Hon. Brian 57
Lewis, Tiny 134
Leyland Motors 146, 147, 150, 151, 175, 176, 199
Liège-Rome-Liège Rally 133
Light Car, The 12, 21, 39, 113, 115
Lilley, Martin 232
Lincoln 25, 70, 113
Lindsay, Hon. Patrick
Lloyd, John 7, 118, 188, 197, 210, 219
Lord, Sir Leonard 86, 93, 137
Lotus 128, 217
Louis, Harry 53
Lucas electrics 14, 41, 67, 75, 79, 82, 169, 187, 188, 193, 203, 226, 241, 243, 246, 247
Luvax hydraulics 49, 79, 236
Lydden Hill circuit 200
Lyons , Sir William 94, 192, 193

Mabbs, Geoff 134
MacPherson suspension 177, 179, 187, 223, 243, 246, 247
Majzub, Claudia 65
Majzub, Faud 65
Manley, George 26
Mann, Harris 7, 214, 215
Marcos 231
Margulies, Dan 65
Markland, Stanley 171, 175, 176, 180-182, 229
Marston radiators 169
Maserati 63, 84, 160
Mason, George 107, 114
Massey-Harris 135, 137, 140
Maudslay, Reginald 10, 180
Mays, Raymond 89
McCahill, Tom 108, 113
Meadows, Henry 192
Mechanix Illustrated 113
Meeson, W P 67
Mercedes-Benz 65, 71, 105, 199
Mercury 48, 178
Meredith, A H 76
Merrick, Tony 65
MG 24, 27, 39, 44, 56, 75, 97, 104, 109, 110, 117, 118, 121,

123, 126, 128, 149, 152, 157, 166, 167, 169, 200, 205, 209-211, 213, 215, 223, 224, 233
Michelotti, Giovanni 130, 139, 159, 195
Middleton, Stanley 71
Mille Miglia 126, 130, 131, 133
Mills, Lyndon 7, 168
Mills-Fulford 227
Minerva engine 10
MIRA test track 122, 123
Mitchell, Nancy 133
Montague-Johnston, Maj. 45
Monte Carlo Rally 25, 39, 44-50, 54, 58, 60-63, 131, 149, 237
Montlhéry, 1000kms race 155
Moore, Leslie 52, 98, 99, 111
Morgan 6, 22, 23, 63, 83, 86, 89, 110, 111, 115, 117, 118, 121, 131, 187, 225, 226
Morgan, H F S 86, 225
Morgan, Peter 6, 117
Morris 12, 14, 16, 18, 19, 57, 91, 138, 145, 147, 152, 157, 182, 183, 206, 223, 233, 234
Morris, B O 91
Morris, William 12, 18, 57, 234
Morris-Goodall, M 132
Moss gearbox 225
Moss, Stirling 138, 156
Motor 7, 51, 56, 69, 74, 118, 121, 128, 178
Motor Sport 35
Motor Trend 113
Mulliner, Arthur 95
Mulliner, H J 95, 234
Mulliners of Birmingham 90, 95, 98, 110, 137
Mundy, Harry 53

Nader, Ralph 110
Nash 24, 107, 115
National Automotive History Collection 6
National Enterprise Board 208
National Motor Museum 7
New Avon Company 22
Newnham, Maurice 45-47, 67, 71, 72, 77, 80-82, 84
Newsome, S 52
Nuffield, Lord 75, 81, 82, 86, 93
Nuffield Organisation 75, 86

Oblinger, Richard 113
Olympia motor show 16, 27, 31, 62
Ormerod, R E 71
Otto, Carl 105, 136, 137, 177
Owen, Sir Alfred 121
Owen, J H 83

Owen, Rubery 42

Panther 232
Parnell, F Gordon 19
Patrick Motors 35
Pearce, A Lew 40, 77, 83
Peerless 227, 228
Perkins diesel engines 143, 144
Petrolift fuel pumps 35, 225
Peugeot 39, 222
Philco radios 76
Pininfarina bodies 106
Pirie, Valerie 156
Plymouth 25, 113, 115
Pomeroy, Laurence 83, 84
Pomeroy, Laurence (Junior) 115
Porsche 165, 172, 189, 213
Practical Motorist, The 30
Pre-1940 Triumph Owners Club 249
Pressed Steel Co 52, 88, 95, 99, 119, 133, 137, 140, 142, 145, 147, 150, 177, 179, 183-185, 187, 192, 193, 198, 203, 213, 215, 219, 234
Price, A A 28

Quatresous 39

R & S Holdings 140
RAC Rally 77, 126, 130, 133, 138, 144, 172, 197
Radford 141, 216, 233
Rambler 115, 174
Ramponi, Giulio 64
Range Rover 209, 215
Ratcliffe 22, 35
Rawlings, Ken 119
Ray, Jimmy 131, 138
Regent Carriage Co 14
Reincke, H A 67, 84
Reliant 230
Renault 39, 115, 118, 137, 222
Ricardo, Sir Harry 11
Richards, Douglas 169
Richardson 7, 46, 121-124, 130-134, 136, 144, 172
Richardson, Ken 7, 121-124, 130-132, 136, 144, 172
Richmond, Miss Joan 46
Ridley, Charles 40, 41, 67
Ridley, Charles Jnr 40
Ridley, Jack 39, 40, 44-46, 62
Riley 30, 39-41, 44, 45, 56, 60, 63, 75, 80-82, 86
Riley, Victor 75
Road & Track 227
Robotham 59
Rodger, Bernard 228
Roesch Talbots 57
Rolls-Royce 57, 59, 73, 82, 88,

105, 192, 193, 232-234

Rolt, Maj. Tony 63, 64

Rootes, Geoffrey 140

Rootes Group 20, 84, 86, 95, 140, 192

Rootes, Sir William 140

Roots supercharger 24, 60, 57, 237

Rose, Flt Lt Tommy 49

Rotherham, John 10

Rothschild, Mike 133

Rover 7, 18, 30, 34, 40, 81, 82, 86-88, 105, 140, 145, 146, 175, 181, 185, 186, 192, 193, 196, 197, 199, 200, 202, 203, 208-210, 213-216, 218, 220, 224, 233, 234, 246

Roxby, Len 65

Roy, Basil 22

Ryder, Lord 208

Saab 194, 195, 200, 202, 205, 206, 210, 214, 230, 231

Saint, The 66

Salmons & Sons 79

Salmson 39

Sampietro, A C 84

Sanderson, Ninian 132, 161

Sangers 46

Sangster 55

Sankey frames 65

Sawyer, George 8, 9

Schloss, Philip 9

Schulte, Mauritz 10

Scott-Moncrieff Motors 64

Sebring, 12 Hours of 133, 155, 172, 173

Seigle-Morris, David 134

Sessions jacks 44

Shell 4000 Rally 172

Siddeley, Hon. Cyril 62

Siko, Odette 39

Silverstone circuit 190

Simca 39

Simpson. Mrs Gordon 46

Singer 9, 13, 23, 30, 44, 51

Slotemaker, Rob 155

Soisbault, Annie 133

Solex carburettors 20, 32, 35, 169, 235-240, 242

Sopwith Aviation Co 40

Spa circuit 63, 172

Specialised Models 229

Specialist Sports Cars 231

Spurrier, Sir Henry 175, 176, 180, 182

SS-Jaguar 70, 73, 81, 86, 87, 90, 94, 98, 102, 233

Standard 6, 7, 10, 14, 15, 17,

19, 21-25, 27-30, 32, 33, 35, 37, 38, 42, 44, 48, 51, 52, 61, 63, 72-76, 79, 81-107, 109-122, 124, 126, 128, 130, 132-147, 149, 150, 153, 155, 159, 160, 162, 164, 166-169, 174-177, 179-181, 183, 184, 193, 199, 203, 225-227, 229, 232-234, 236, 238, 246-248, 254

Standard Register 6, 10, 114

Stevenson jacks 38

Stokes, Lord 7, 205, 208, 210

Stoop, Dickie 161

Studebaker 31, 115

SU carburettors 106, 122, 167, 168, 185, 206, 214

Sunbeam 82, 86, 124, 179, 192, 230

Sunbeam-Talbot 105

Sunday Observer 74

Sutcliffe, Mike 172

Swallow Doretti 7, 136, 166, 226

Swetnam, George 57

Swift 30, 81, 82, 167

Sydney Motor Club 25

Sykes, Arthur A 14, 20

Symons, Humfrey 39

Tak 131

Talbot 82, 86

Taylor's 61

Tedder, Marshal of the RAF Lord 126, 136, 175

Thacker, Roger 39

Thomas, Sir Miles 80, 97

Thomson and Taylor 84

Thornton, Bill 34, 38, 40, 73

Thuner, Jean-Jacques 156, 172

Tickford bodies 22, 27, 28, 35

The Times 56, 169

Tomson, Alderman A S 9, 10

Tour de France 155

Tourist Trophy races 25, 126, 130, 133

Toyota 217

Trident 232

Trippel, Hans 228

Triumph, prewar
10/20 12-18, 235, 249
13/35 16, 17, 19, 31, 235, 249
15/50 (Light 15) 17-19, 21, 27, 31, 235
Continental 44, 49, 56, 57, 61, 70, 72-74, 102, 122, 238
Dolomite 6, 42, 43, 56-63, 65-79, 81, 84, 96, 97, 236,

238
Dolomite, straight-eight 7, 56-66, 68, 237
Flow-free 48, 49, 51, 52, 54
Gloria 10, 38-55, 60, 68, 69, 72-76, 80-84, 225, 233, 236-238
Monte Carlo 44-50, 54
Scorpion 28, 31-35, 37, 167, 236
Southern Cross 29, 31, 35-38, 40, 42, 45, 46, 49-51, 54, 63, 68, 75, 77, 167, 236, 237
Super Eight 25, 28-31, 34, 36, 225, 235
Super Nine 29, 31, 33-37, 42, 236
Super Seven 6, 18-29, 31-34, 36, 37, 40, 80, 235
Ten 9, 26, 29, 31, 33, 35-38, 42, 45, 74, 76, 89, 101, 109-119, 121, 124, 126, 127, 133, 137, 144, 147, 159, 180, 210, 225, 236
Twelve 35, 78-80, 95, 98-100, 102, 103, 142, 236, 238
Twelve-Six 33-36, 236, 249
Vitesse 48, 50, 51, 54, 55, 61, 68-70, 72-76, 238
Triumph, postwar
1300/1500 148, 182, 183, 185, 193, 195, 200, 201, 203-205, 207, 212, 213, 223, 234, 243-245, 248, 250
1800/2000 42, 85, 95, 96, 98, 101, 102, 104, 110, 213, 238, 239, 248, 249
2000/2.5 182, 195, 196, 198, 213, 218
Acclaim 222-224, 234, 247
Dolomite 7, 158, 167, 193, 194, 202, 204-209, 212, 214, 216-218, 220, 223, 224, 232-234, 238, 245
GT6 7, 34, 141, 147, 153-155, 157, 158, 183, 185, 187, 189, 206, 211, 212, 229, 234, 245, 246
Herald 7, 88, 116, 134, 135, 138, 139, 141-151, 157-159, 162, 166, 167, 172, 176, 178, 180-183, 192, 193, 202, 228, 229, 234, 240, 241
Mayflower 6, 89, 95, 98, 104, 107-119, 136-138, 239
Spitfire 7, 141, 146, 147, 150-158, 160, 166, 171,

172, 176, 181-183, 187, 193, 195, 209-212, 214, 220, 228, 229, 231, 234, 242, 243
Stag 7, 152, 185, 187, 189, 195-203, 206, 210, 213, 216, 218, 234, 246
Toledo 7, 148, 152, 201, 203, 205, 207, 212, 214, 234, 244, 245
TR2-TR3A 7, 48, 66, 93, 105, 107, 108, 110, 116-119, 122-135, 137, 139, 144, 159-174, 186, 189, 225-227, 234, 239-241, 248, 249
TR4-TR6, TR5, TR250 130, 132, 134, 146, 147, 149, 151, 153, 157, 159, 161-173, 176, 179-181, 183, 186-191, 193, 195, 197-199, 202, 206, 210-216, 218, 230-232, 234, 241, 242, 251
TR7-TR8 6, 7, 23, 138, 152, 168, 189, 207-210, 212, 214-221, 223, 224, 234, 241, 246, 251, 152
TR10 116, 135, 137, 240
TRX 105-108, 118-121, 239
Vitesse 34, 147-150, 153, 157, 158, 167, 183, 185, 228, 229, 242
Triumph cycles 12
Triumph motorcycles 10, 53
Triumph Motorcycles, The Story of 53
Triumph Sports Cars, The Story of 6, 16, 40
Tube Investments 227
Tulip Rally 133, 134, 172
Tullius, Bob 173, 190
Turin motor show 162
Turnbull, George 7, 119, 180
Turnbull, John 119, 121, 122
Turner, Edward 55
Turner, Jonathan 64
Turner, Ray 94, 96, 98, 100
Tustin, Martin 138, 139, 159, 168
TVR 231, 232
Twist, Brian 62

Ulster Tourist Trophy 25

Vale 225
Van Damm, Sheila 124
Vanwall 65
Vauxhall 52, 86, 146, 181, 192,

222
Vignale bodywork 139, 140, 162, 163, 166
Viking Performance 232
Volkswagen 84, 115
Volvo 222

Waddington, John 133
Wadsworth, Edgar 130
Wallwork, Johnny 130
Walton, Reg 76
Wankel engine 193
Ward, Ashley 82, 83
Ward, John 107
Ward & Co, Thomas 80
Warner, Frank 19, 34, 40-42
Warren gear control 54
Warwick 25, 86, 123, 227, 228
Watt, James 84
Weale, H S 176
Weber carburettors 134, 153, 164, 172
Webster, Harry 7, 94, 101, 102, 104, 110, 112, 118, 119, 121, 122, 126, 135, 138, 139, 141, 146, 149, 150, 152, 153, 157, 159, 160, 162, 168, 170-173, 175, 177-180, 182, 188, 193-195, 199-201, 210, 212, 213, 215
Weslake, Harry 87
Westcott, S 24
Weymann bodies 12, 22, 235
Whalley, J W 62
White, Col 104
White & Poppe 53, 233
White Sewing Machine Co 8, 9
Whitfield, Mike 121, 175
Whitson & Co, James 227, 228
Whitworth, Tim 64
Wignall, Jim 99
Wilks, Spencer 81, 82, 86, 140
Willys 115, 137
Wilson gearboxes 65
Wilson, Sir Harold 193
Wisdom, Tommy 45, 47, 57
Wolseley 31, 52, 80
Woodall, Les 176, 180
Woods, Mr &Mrs G A 25
World Cup Rally 202

Yale locks 51, 76

Zenith (and Stromberg) carburettors 14, 17, 20, 44, 45, 58, 169, 179, 188, 230, 235, 237, 241-246

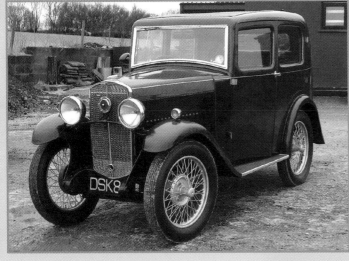

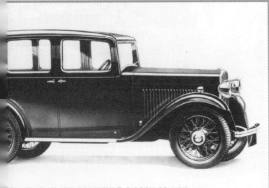

...MPH "TWELVE SIX" COACHBUILT SALOON DE LUXE, 1933.